Frommer's

Belize

1st Edition

by Eliot Greenspan

Here's what the critics say about Frommer's:

"Amazingly easy to use. Very portable, very complete."
—*Booklist*

"Detailed, accurate, and easy-to-read information for all price ranges."
—*Glamour Magazine*

"Hotel information is close to encyclopedic."
—*Des Moines Sunday Register*

"Frommer's Guides have a way of giving you a real feel for a place."
—*Knight Ridder Newspapers*

WILEY
Wiley Publishing, Inc.

Published by:

Wiley Publishing, Inc.

111 River St.
Hoboken, NJ 07030-5774

ISBN 0-7645-5817-X

Editor: Myka Carroll Del Barrio
Production Editor: Suzanna R. Thompson
Cartographer: Elizabeth Puhl
Photo Editor: Richard Fox
Production by Wiley Indianapolis Composition Services
Appendix C illustrations by Kelly Emkow and Joni Burns

Front cover photo: A bungalow in paradise
Back cover photo: A keel-billed toucan

For information on our other products and services or to obtain technical support,
please contact our Customer Care Department within the U.S. at 800/762-2974,
outside the U.S. at 317/572-3993 or fax 317/572-4002.

Wiley also publishes its books in a variety of electronic formats. Some content that
appears in print may not be available in electronic formats.

Manufactured in the United States of America

5   4   3

Contents

List of Maps

About the Author

Eliot Greenspan is a poet, journalist, and travel writer who took his backpack and type-writer the length of Mesoamerica before settling in Costa Rica in 1992. Since then, he has worked steadily as a travel writer, freelance journalist, and translator, and has continued his travels in the region. He is the author of *The Tico Times Restaurant Guide to Costa Rica* and *Frommer's Costa Rica*, as well as the chapter on Venezuela in *Frommer's South America*, and is co-author of *Frommer's Cuba*.

Acknowledgments

I'd like to tip my hat and extend my thanks to Myka Carroll Del Barrio. I'd also like to thank Emilie Walker for her dedicated and diligent help and her overall delightful demeanor, and Erin Z. Weaver for her assistance with the wildlife guide.

An Invitation to the Reader

In researching this book, we discovered many wonderful places—hotels, restaurants, shops, and more. We're sure you'll find others. Please tell us about them, so we can share the information with your fellow travelers in upcoming editions. If you were disappointed with a recommendation, we'd love to know that, too. Please write to:

Frommer's Belize, 1st Edition
Wiley Publishing, Inc. • 111 River St. • Hoboken, NJ 07030-5774

An Additional Note

Please be advised that travel information is subject to change at any time—and this is especially true of prices. We therefore suggest that you write or call ahead for confirmation when making your travel plans. The authors, editors, and publisher cannot be held responsible for the experiences of readers while traveling. Your safety is important to us, however, so we encourage you to stay alert and be aware of your surroundings. Keep a close eye on cameras, purses, and wallets, all favorite targets of thieves and pickpockets.

Frommer's Star Ratings, Icons & Abbreviations

Every hotel, restaurant, and attraction listing in this guide has been ranked for quality, value, service, amenities, and special features using a **star-rating system.** In country, state, and regional guides, we also rate towns and regions to help you narrow down your choices and budget your time accordingly. Hotels and restaurants are rated on a scale of zero (recommended) to three stars (exceptional). Attractions, shopping, nightlife, towns, and regions are rated according to the following scale: zero stars (recommended), one star (highly recommended), two stars (very highly recommended), and three stars (must-see).

In addition to the star-rating system, we also use **seven feature icons** that point you to the great deals, in-the-know advice, and unique experiences that separate travelers from tourists. Throughout the book, look for:

Finds	Special finds—those places only insiders know about
Fun Fact	Fun facts—details that make travelers more informed and their trips more fun
Kids	Best bets for kids, and advice for the whole family
Moments	Special moments—those experiences that memories are made of
Overrated	Places or experiences not worth your time or money
Tips	Insider tips—great ways to save time and money
Value	Great values—where to get the best deals

The following **abbreviations** are used for credit cards:

AE	American Express	DISC	Discover	V	Visa
DC	Diners Club	MC	MasterCard		

Frommers.com

Now that you have the guidebook to a great trip, visit our website at **www.frommers.com** for travel information on more than 3,000 destinations. With features updated regularly, we give you instant access to the most current trip-planning information available. At Frommers.com, you'll also find the best prices on airfares, accommodations, and car rentals—and you can even book travel online through our travel booking partners. At Frommers.com, you'll also find the following:

- Online updates to our most popular guidebooks
- Vacation sweepstakes and contest giveaways
- Newsletter highlighting the hottest travel trends
- Online travel message boards with featured travel discussions

The Best of Belize

Belize proves the cliché that big things come in small packages. This tiny Central American country has the longest continuous barrier reef in the Western Hemisphere; the largest known classic Mayan city, Caracol; and the highest concentration per square mile of the largest New World cat, the jaguar. It also has one of the most extensive and easily accessible cave systems for amateur and experienced spelunkers alike, as well as a nearly endless supply of some of the world's best snorkeling and scuba-diving opportunities. Depending on your personal preferences, you can choose to stay in an intimate and luxurious hotel, an isolated nature lodge in the heart of the Mundo Maya, or a tent on your own desert island. Or you can sample all three. The best part about all these world-class places and experiences is that Belize's compact size makes it easy to sample a wide range of them in a short period of time. The lists below should help you zero in on a few personal bests of your own.

1 The Best Purely Belizean Experiences

- **Spending the Night in a Mayan Ceremonial City:** An intimate and rather luxurious nature lodge, **Chan Chich Lodge** (© 800/343-8009 in the U.S., or 223-4419 in Belize; www.chanchich.com) is built right on the site of a minor Mayan ceremonial city. The hills just outside your private cabin are unexcavated residences and pyramids. There are ruins and basic excavations all around the grounds, and the surrounding rainforests are rich in bird and animal life. See p. 115.

- **Drinking a Cool Seaweed Shake:** Made from dried natural seaweed, blended with both condensed and evaporated milk, cinnamon, nutmeg, vanilla, and some ice, this drink is surprisingly refreshing and tasty. You can get these at several beach destinations around Belize, but Placencia seems to be the home of the seaweed shake. See "Placencia" in chapter 7.

- **Betting on a Chicken Drop:** A chicken drop is a sort of poor man's version of roulette, and much more fun. Numbers are painted on a grid and bets are placed. Then, a chicken is set loose on a wire mesh screen suspended over the grid. The winner is chosen by the chicken's first "drop." In addition to any monetary winnings, the "winner" often must clean the grid. One of the best and original chicken drops is held at Kitty's Place in Placencia, although there are also a couple held on Ambergris Caye. See "Placencia" in chapter 7.

- **Staying with a Mayan or Garífuna Family:** It certainly isn't going to be like a night at the Four Seasons, but if you're looking for a real cultural exchange experience, you should consider actually staying with a traditional Mayan or Garífuna Family. The **Toledo Ecotourism Association** (© 722-2096; ttea@btl.net) can organize this for you. See "Punta Gorda & the Toledo District" in chapter 7.

The Best of Belize

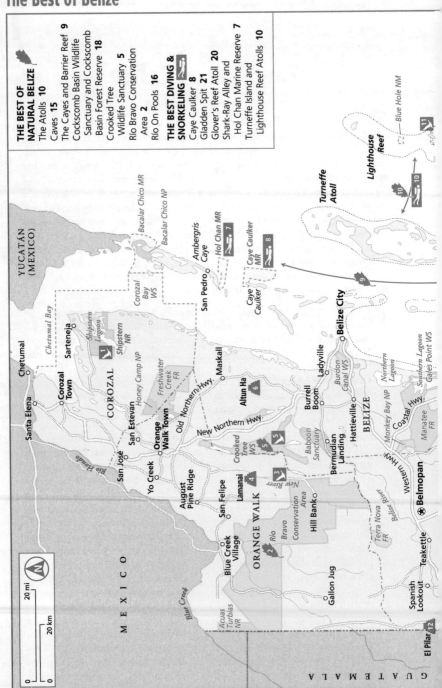

THE BEST OF NATURAL BELIZE
The Atolls **10**
Caves **15**
The Cayes and Barrier Reef **9**
Cockscomb Basin Wildlife Sanctuary and Cockscomb Basin Forest Reserve **18**
Crooked Tree Wildlife Sanctuary **5**
Rio Bravo Conservation Area **2**
Rio On Pools **16**

THE BEST DIVING & SNORKELING
Caye Caulker **8**
Gladden Spit **21**
Glover's Reef Atoll **20**
Shark-Ray Alley and Hol Chan Marine Reserve **7**
Turneffe Island and Lighthouse Reef Atolls **10**

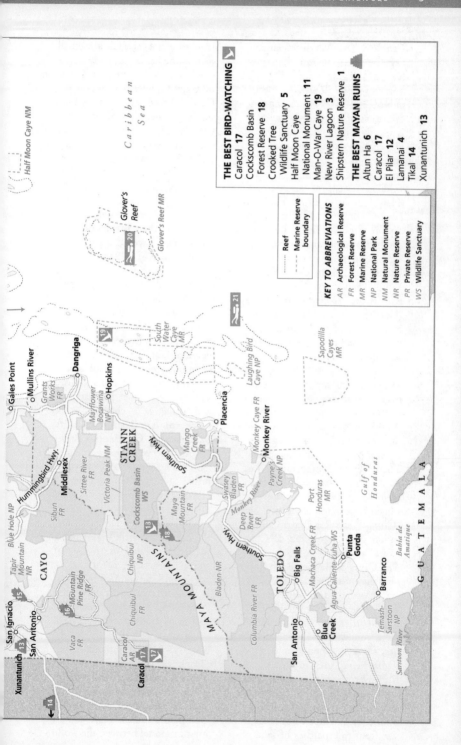

THE BEST BIRD-WATCHING
Caracol **17**
Cockscomb Basin
Forest Reserve **18**
Crooked Tree
Wildlife Sanctuary **5**
Half Moon Caye
National Monument **11**
Man-O-War Caye **19**
New River Lagoon **3**
Shipstern Nature Reserve **1**

THE BEST MAYAN RUINS
Altun Ha **6**
Caracol **17**
El Pilar **12**
Lamanai **4**
Tikal **14**
Xunantunich **13**

Reef
Marine Reserve
boundary

KEY TO ABBREVIATIONS
AR   Archaeological Reserve
FR   Forest Reserve
MR   Marine Reserve
NP   National Park
NM   Natural Monument
NR   Nature Reserve
PR   Private Reserve
WS   Wildlife Sanctuary

Caribbean Sea

Half Moon Caye NM

Glover's Reef

Glover's Reef MR

South Water Caye MR

Laughing Bird Caye NP

Sapodilla Cayes MR

Gales Point
Mullins River
Dangriga
Grants Works FR
Mayflower Bocawina NP
Hopkins
Placencia
Monkey Caye FR
Monkey River
Mango Creek FR

STANN CREEK

Hummingbird Hwy.
Middlesex
Sibun FR
Blue Hole NP
Sittee River FR
Victoria Peak NM
Cockscomb Basin WS
Maya Mountain FR

Swasey Bladen FR
Deep River FR
Bladen NR

Payne's Creek NP

Port Honduras MR

Gulf of Honduras

Bahia de Amatique

Southern Hwy.

TOLEDO
Big Falls
Punta Gorda
Machaca Creek FR
Agua Caliente Luha WS
Barranco
San Antonio
Blue Creek
Temash-Sarstoon NP
Sarstoon River

CAYO
Tapir Mountain NR
San Ignacio
San Antonio
Mountain Pine Ridge FR
Chiquibul NP
Chiquibul FR
Vaca FR
Columbia River FR
Caracol AR
Caracol

MAYA MOUNTAINS

Xunantunich

G U A T E M A L A

2 The Best of Natural Belize

- **Crooked Tree Wildlife Sanctuary** (Northern Belize): This preserve is a swampy lowland that is home to over 250 resident species of birds and serves as a resting spot for scores of migratory species. It is also the principal nesting site of the endangered jabiru stork, the largest bird in the Americas. It is an excellent place to spot other wildlife as well, including crocodiles, iguanas, coatimundi, and howler monkeys. The best way to explore Crooked Tree is by being paddled around the network of lagoons in a dugout canoe. See "En Route North: Crooked Tree Wildlife Sanctuary" in chapter 5.

- **Río Bravo Conservation Area** (Northern Belize): This massive mixed tract of virgin forest, sustainable-yield managed forest, and recovering reforestation areas is home to nearly 400 bird species and over 200 species of tropical trees. It also supports a healthy population of most of the New World cat species, and is one of the best areas in the Americas to try your luck in spotting a jaguar. The Río Bravo Conservation Area is also home to La Milpa, an ongoing excavation of a major Mayan ceremonial city. See "Going West: Río Bravo Conservation Area, La Milpa & Chan Chich" in chapter 5.

- **The Cayes & Barrier Reef:** Running the entire length of the country's coastline, the Belize Barrier Reef is the second longest continuous barrier reef in the world. Here you will find some of the best snorkeling opportunities and scuba-diving sites in the world. Moreover, the barrier reef is lined with hundreds and hundreds of small islands, or cayes. Most are uninhabited. These cayes range in size from tiny patches of sand or mangrove smaller than a football field to the larger and more developed vacation destination islands of Caye Caulker and Ambergris Caye. Whether you want the hustle and bustle of the latter, or the deserted isle feel of a smaller or even private caye—or something in between—your choices are many and uniformly inviting. See chapters 6 and 7.

- **The Atolls:** Belize's three mid-ocean atolls are arguably more spectacular than the barrier reef and its many cayes. Unique formations of small islands and reef surrounding a mid-ocean saltwater lagoon, atolls are unique, isolated, and stunning phenomena. Belize has three of them: Turneffe Island, Lighthouse Reef, and Glover's Reef. These atolls are very sparsely developed, and any visit here will be imbued with a sense of adventure, isolation, and romance. See "The Outer Atolls" in chapter 6 and "Dangriga" in chapter 7.

- **Cockscomb Basin Wildlife Sanctuary & Cockscomb Basin Forest Reserve** (Southern Belize): This is a huge protected area comprised of rugged forested mountains. The sanctuary was designed to protect and help researchers study the largest New World cat, the jaguar. The park is also home to Belize's other four wildcat species, as well as Baird's tapirs, coatimundis, tayra, kinkajous, deer, peccaries, anteaters, and armadillos, as well as some 300 species of birds. Inside the park you'll also find Victoria Peak, the country's highest mountain. See "Dangriga" in chapter 7.

- **Caves** (Cayo District and Western Belize): Belize has an extensive network of caves, which were considered by the ancient Maya to be a mystical portal between the world of the living and the underworld of spirits and the dead. They called this mystical realm Xibalba. In almost every explored cave in Belize, some evidence of use by the Mayans has been uncovered. Fire pits, campsites, burial mounds, and ritual altars have all been found. Numerous pieces of pottery and abundant skeletons, bones, and artifacts have also been encountered. These caves are relatively easily accessible and you should not leave Belize without at least one foray into Xibalba. See chapter 8.

• **Río On Pools** (Cayo District and Western Belize): This series of flowing falls and pools flowing is somewhat reminiscent of Ocho Rios in Jamaica. While the views and swimming are fine at the base of the falls, it's worth the hike upstream to even better views and numerous pools flowing between big rocks, which are perfect for sunbathing. This place can get crowded on weekends, when locals come for family picnics and getaways. See "Mountain Pine Ridge & Caracol" in chapter 8.

3 The Best Diving & Snorkeling

Belize is rightly considered one of the top scuba diving and snorkeling destinations on the planet. The Belize Barrier Reef, second only to Australia's Great Barrier Reef, runs the length of its coastline, and the country has three open-ocean atolls. Diving and snorkeling are superb all along the barrier reef; the following are just a few of the truly standout sites and dives.

• **Shark-Ray Alley & Hol Chan Marine Reserve** (Northern Cayes and Atolls): These two very popular snorkeling sites are threatened with overcrowding but still live up to their billing. Shark-Ray Alley guarantees a very close encounter with schools of large stingrays and nurse sharks. The experience provides a substantial adrenaline rush for all but the most nonchalant and veteran divers. Hol Chan Marine Reserve is an excellent snorkeling destination comprised of a narrow channel cutting through a rich and well-maintained shallow coral reef. See "Ambergris Caye" in chapter 6.

• **Caye Caulker** (Northern Cayes and Atolls): If you're looking for a relaxed vacation spot to serve as a base for some good snorkeling, you can't do much better than Caye Caulker, which has some excellent and easily accessible snorkeling sites. It's also much less developed and less crowded than its more popular neighbor, Ambergris Caye. Many of the dive sites are a very short boat ride from shore. Since the distance to the dive sites is so short, Caye Caulker is also a good place to hook up with a local sailboat captain with whom to go out to the sites. See "Caye Caulker" in chapter 6.

• **Turneffe Island & Lighthouse Reef Atolls** (Northern Cayes and Atolls): For many divers coming to Belize, these spots are the Holy Grail, and justifiably so. Both of these mid-ocean atoll formations feature nearly endless opportunities for world-class wall, drift, and coral garden diving. As a cherry to top this cake, this is also where you'll find the Blue Hole. A host of dive operators all across Belize offer day trips to dive these sites, although these usually involve a 2- to 3-hour ride each way. Alternatively, you can stay at one of the very few lodges out here, or take a vacation on a live-aboard dive boat. See "The Outer Atolls" in chapter 6.

- **Glover's Reef Atoll** (Southern Belize): Glover's Reef is the third of Belize's mid-ocean atolls. The diving here is spectacular and under-exploited. Unlike the Turneffe Island and Lighthouse Reef atolls, far fewer day-trippers visit the dive sites around Glover's Reef Atoll. The best way to really take advantage of the diving and snorkeling is to stay out here, and for this, **Glover's Atoll Resort** (② **520-5016** or 614-7177; www.glovers.com.bz) is your best option. See "Dangriga" in chapter 7.
- **Gladden Spit** (Southern Belize): More or less due east of Placencia, Gladden Spit is a world-renowned spot to dive with massive whale sharks. This mid-ocean site is the natural spawning ground for a variety of marine species. Whale sharks come regularly to feed on the energetically rich and very plentiful reproductive effluence. Whale-shark sightings are fairly common here in March, April, and May, and to a lesser extent from August to October and December and January. Since they tend to feed and cruise close to the surface, snorkelers and divers alike can enjoy the spectacle. See "Placencia" in chapter 7.

4 The Best Non-Diving Adventures

- **Chartering a Sailboat for Some Isolated Island Explorations:** The protected waters, steady gentle trade winds, and hundreds of isolated islands and anchorages make Belize an ideal place for bareboat charters. Given the shallow draft, increased interior space, and reduced drag, a multihull is your best bet. Both the **Moorings** (② **888/952-8401** in the U.S. and Canada, or 523-3351; www.moorings.com) and **TMM** (② **800/633-0155** in the U.S., or 226-3026; www.sailtmm.com) are two large-scale charter companies with operations on Ambergris Caye and in Placencia. See "Ambergris Caye" in chapter 6 and "Placencia" in chapter 7.
- **Fly-Fishing for Bonefish, Permit & Tarpon on the Outer Atoll Flats:** Belize is a world-class fishing destination, and while offshore fishing for bigger game is possible, the real draw here is fly-fishing for feisty and world-record size bonefish, permit, and tarpon (actually, the tarpon get as big as most deep-sea game). **Turneffe Flats** (② **800/815-1304** or 605/578-1304 in the U.S.; www.tflats.com) is an excellent dedicated fishing operation located on Turneffe Island Atoll. See "The Outer Atolls" in chapter 6.
- **Kayaking & Camping around Glover's Reef Atoll:** The relatively calm protected waters of the atoll and manageable distances between islands make this a perfect place to explore under your own power, paddling a one- or two-person sea kayak. Both **Island Expeditions** (② **800/667-1630,** or 604/452-3212 in the United States; www.islandexpeditions.com) and **Slickrock Adventures** (② **800/390-5715** or 435/259-4225 in the U.S.; www.slickrock.com) run various adventurous multiday kayak tours to small camps and lodges on private isolated cayes of Glover's Reef Atoll. See "Dangriga" in chapter 7.
- **Riding an Inner Tube through the Caves Branch River Cave System** (Cayo District and Western Belize): This is certainly the most popular and probably the easiest way to explore Belize's vast network of caves. You strap on a battery-powered headlamp, climb into the center of an inflated car

inner tube, and gently float through a series of limestone caves, your headlamp illuminating the stalactites and the occasional bat. The entire sensation is eerie and slightly claustrophobic, but fun nonetheless. Especially if you go with a small group on a day when the caves are not crowded. See "Belmopan" in chapter 8.

- **Canoeing, Kayaking, or Inner-Tubing on the Macal or Mopan Rivers** (Western Belize): These two rivers converge around the city of San Ignacio, in the Cayo District. Upstream from town on either river are ample opportunities for paddling or floating. Depending on the water level and the section you choose, this can range from a lazy canoe or inner tube paddle to a Class III kayak trip over rushing rapids. Any of the hotels in the Cayo District can help you organize one of these adventures. See "San Ignacio" in chapter 8.

- **Horseback Riding through the Cayo District** (Western Belize): The Cayo District is a perfect area to explore on horseback. Rides can be combined with visits to jungle waterfalls and swimming holes, as well as nearby Mayan ruins. **Mountain Equestrian Trails** (⌀ 820-4041; www.met belize.com) have one of the better stables and horse riding operations in the Cayo District. See "San Ignacio" and "Mountain Pine Ridge & Caracol" in chapter 8.

5 The Best Day Hikes & Nature Walks

- **Cockscomb Basin Forest Reserve** (Southern Belize): This large forest reserve has an excellent network of well-maintained trails. The Cockscomb Basin Forest Reserve—in addition to being the only dedicated reserve designed to protect the endangered jaguar—is also home to an amazing array of tropical flora and fauna. Truly adventurous hikers can arrange to climb Belize's tallest mountain, Victoria Peak, which is found inside this reserve. See "Dangriga" in chapter 7.

- **Guanacaste Park** (Cayo District and Western Belize): This small national park is located right on the side of the Western Highway, about 2 miles (3km) north of Belmopan. The gentle trails and easy accessibility here make this an excellent choice for an introduction to tropical forests. There are nearly 2 miles (3km) of well-marked and well-maintained trails in the park, with several benches for sitting and observing wildlife.

The park is bordered on the west by Roaring Creek and on the north by the Belize River. See "Belmopan" in chapter 8.

- **Blue Hole National Park** (Cayo District and Western Belize): This hike combines a pleasant 1.5-mile (2.4km) hike through dense primary and secondary tropical forest, with the chance to further hike inside the large and long St. Herman's Cave, while also stopping for a refreshing dip in the park's beautiful namesake swimming hole, or *cenote*, here. If you hire a guide, you can actually hike for several miles more inside the stunning **Crystalline Cave**. See "Belmopan" in chapter 8.

- **Tikal National Park** (Tikal, Guatemala): In addition to being one of the best excavated and preserved ancient Mayan cities, the extensive trail network running through the Tikal ruins happen to be dense tropical rainforest. Howler and spider monkeys clamor overhead and parrots squawk through the canopy. You can see a wealth of tropical fauna here, as you slowly wander from plaza to plaza and pyramid to pyramid. See "Tikal" in chapter 9.

6 The Best Bird-Watching

Belize is home to over 500 species of resident and migratory birds. With varied ecosystems, ranging from coastal mangroves and swamps, to isolated barrier reef cayes, to dense tropical rainforest and clear open savannahs, Belize is a wonderful destination for avid bird-watchers and amateurs alike.

- **Crooked Tree Wildlife Sanctuary** (Northern Belize): This rich wetlands is perhaps the top bird-watching site in Belize. Home to hundreds of resident and migrant species, it is one of the best spots to see the giant and rare jabiru stork, especially during the dry season. You can spot various heron and kingfisher species here, as well as the yellow-lored parrot and Yucatán jay. See "En Route North: Crooked Tree Wildlife Sanctuary" in chapter 5.
- **New River Lagoon** (Northern Belize): This wide open lagoon is reached via the winding and narrow New River, and branches off into a network of narrow canals, streams, and marshlands, the perfect and preferred habitat for a wide range of bird species. Common species here include the black-collared hawk, northern jacana, and purple gallinule. You can combine a bird-watching trip here with a visit to the Lamanai Mayan ruins, which also has wonderful opportunities for bird-watching all along its trails and from the peaks of its pyramids. See "The Submerged Crocodile: Lamanai" in chapter 5.
- **Shipstern Nature Reserve** (Northern Belize): Covering some 22,000 acres (8,800ha), including several distinct ecosystems, Shipstern Nature Reserve is home to over 250 bird species. You can explore the area on foot, as well as in little dugout canoes and flat-bottomed boats. See "Corozal Town" in chapter 5.
- **Half Moon Caye National Monument** (Northern Cayes and Atolls): This isolated wildlife and marine reserve is a major nesting site for the red-footed booby. Thousands of these birds can be spotted on the island at any one time, an amazing sight. In addition, you can also spot a wide range of resident and migratory sea birds here. See "The Outer Atolls" in chapter 6.
- **Man-O-War Caye** (Southern Belize): This small caye is a government-monitored bird sanctuary and major nesting site for the magnificent frigate, or "man-o-war." Circling the island in a small boat, you will see hundreds of these large sea birds roosting on and hovering above the tiny caye. In addition to the frigates, the island also is home to a large community of brown boobies. See "Dangriga" in chapter 7.
- **Cockscomb Basin Forest Reserve** (Southern Belize): In addition to its jaguar reserve, the Cockscomb Basin Forest Reserve is home to a large number of tropical forest–dwelling bird species. This is one of the best sites in Belize to spot the large and loud scarlet macaw, as well as several toucan species, and the imposing king vulture. See "Dangriga" in chapter 7.
- **Caracol** (Cayo District and Western Belize): Also a major Mayan ruin, Caracol and its surrounding forest is a prime bird-watching

destination. Here you can encounter numerous tropical forest species, including such stellar beauties as the keel-billed motmot and violaceous trogon, as well as such large species as the oscillated turkey, crested guan, and great curassow. There have even been isolated reported sightings of the harpy eagle here. See "Mountain Pine Ridge & Caracol" in chapter 8.

7 The Best Mayan Ruins

- **Altun Ha** (Northern Belize): One of the most easily accessible Mayan ruins from Belize City, Altun Ha is a small yet well-preserved site featuring two large central plazas surrounded by mid-sized pyramids and mounds. Only a few of the most imposing temples, tombs, and pyramids have been uncovered and rebuilt; hundreds more lie under the jungle foliage. Many jade, pearl, and obsidian artifacts have been discovered here, including the unique jade-head sculpture of **Kinich Ahau** (the Mayan sun god), the largest carved jade piece from the Mayan era. See "Along the Old Northern Highway" in chapter 5.

- **Lamanai:** One of the more interesting and picturesque Mayan ruins in Belize, Lamanai features three large pyramids, a couple of residential areas, various restored stelae, and open plazas, as well as a small and unique ball court. Moreover, nearby are the ruins of two 16th-century Spanish churches. The site is set on the banks of the New River Lagoon. Since it was still occupied by the Maya when the Spanish arrived, Lamanai is one of the few sites in Belize to retain its traditional name. See "The Submerged Crocodile: Lamanai" in chapter 5.

- **Xunantunich** (Cayo District and Western Belize): Xunantunich is an impressive, well-excavated, and easily accessible Mayan site, close to San Ignacio. Xunantunich was a thriving Mayan city during the Classic Period, from about A.D. 600 to 900. You'll find carved stelae and one very tall main pyramid here. To reach the ruins, you must cross the Mopan River aboard a tiny hand-cranked car-ferry in the village of San José Succotz. See "San Ignacio" in chapter 8.

- **El Pilar** (Cayo District and Western Belize): El Pilar just may be the most underappreciated major Mayan city in Mesoamerica. The site is huge, with over 25 known plazas, covering some 100 acres (40ha) that straddle the Belize and Guatemala border. Excavation and exploration here are in their early stages, and I don't think it will be long before El Pilar joins the ranks of Caracol and Tikal as one of the major Classic Mayan sites of this region. See "San Ignacio" in chapter 8.

- **Caracol** (Cayo District and Western Belize): Caracol (www.caracol.org) is the largest known Mayan archaeological site in Belize, and one of the great Mayan city-states of the Classic era. Located deep within the Chiquibil Forest Reserve, the ruins are not nearly as well excavated as Tikal or Xunantunich or any number of other sites. However, this is part of Caracol's charm. The main pyramid here, **Caana** or "Sky Palace," stands some 136 feet (41m) high; it is the tallest Mayan building in Belize and still the tallest manmade structure in the country. See "Mountain Pine Ridge & Caracol" in chapter 8.

- **Tikal:** Just over the Belizean border in neighboring Guatemala, **Tikal** is the grandest of the surviving classic Mayan cities. Tikal is far more extensively excavated than any ruins in Belize. The pyramids here are some of the most perfect examples of ceremonial architecture in the Mayan world. The peaks of several temples poke through the dense rainforest canopy. Toucans and parrots fly about, and the loudest noise you'll hear is the guttural call of howler monkeys. In its heyday, the city probably covered as much as 25 square miles (65 sq. km) and supported a population of over 100,000. See "Tikal" in chapter 9.

8 The Best Views

- The main pyramid at Xunantunich, **El Castillo,** rises to 127 feet (38m). It's a steep climb, but the view from the top is worth it. On a clear day, you'll be able to make out the twin border towns of Benque Viejo, Belize, and Melchor de Menchos, Guatemala. See chapter 8.
- Try watching the **sun rise over the New River Lagoon** from a hammock strung on the front porch of your veranda at the **Lamanai Outpost Lodge** (© 800/733-7864 in the U.S. or 322-2199 in Belize; fax 727/864-4062 in the U.S.; www.lamanai.com). It is a view you'll always treasure. The view is lovely throughout the day, but it's worth waking up early for. See chapter 5.
- The **Blue Hole** is probably best experienced and viewed from above. A perfectly round sinkhole measuring some 1,000 feet (300m) across in the middle of the Lighthouse Reef Atoll lagoon, the Blue Hole appears as a deep dark blue circle in a sea of shimmering turquoise. The best way to take advantage of this view is to stay at the **Lighthouse Reef Resort** (Big Northern Caye, Lighthouse Reef Atoll; © 800/423-3114 or 863/439-6600 in the U.S.; www.scuba-dive-belize.com) since they have their own airstrip, and a charter flight in and out of the resort is included in every stay. See chapter 6 for more details.
- Although the **main temple at Cerros** is a just a diminutive 70 feet (21m) tall, it offers excellent views across Corozal Bay. Moreover, this is an easy climb for most, and far easier than the climbs to the tops of most other major Mayan ceremonial pyramids. See chapter 5.
- Poking their heads over the dense rainforest canopy, the **pyramids of Tikal** offer some of the best views to be found in all of Central America. Temple IV is the tallest, and the preferred platform for enjoying this view, but Temple II just off the Great Plaza is really just as good. Get here early, or stay late, to enjoy the views without the hustle and bustle of busloads of tourists. See chapter 9.

9 The Best Destinations for Families

- **Belize Zoo** (near Belize City): The Belize Zoo (© 220-8004; www.belizezoo.org) houses over 125 animals, all of native Belizean species. It is considered a national treasure and a model for the possibilities of a conservation-based zoo. The zoo itself is wonderfully laid out, on meandering trails with large and well-maintained enclosures for the animals. See "What to See & Do" in chapter 4.

- **Ambergris Caye** (Northern Cayes and Atolls): Ambergris Caye is the most developed of Belize's beach and diving destinations. As such, it has the greatest selection of hotels and activities, many of them either geared towards or just plain great for kids. From snorkeling to paragliding to touring the island on golf carts, there's plenty to keep families and kids of all ages occupied here. **Xanadu Island Resort** (© 226-2814; www.xanaduresort-belize.com) and **Captain Morgan's Retreat** (© 888/653-9090 or 307/587-8914 in the U.S., or 226-2207 in Belize; www.belizevacation.com) are two good choices for families. See "Ambergris Caye" in chapter 6.
- **Jaguar Reef Lodge** (Hopkins Village, Southern Belize; © 800/289-5756 in the U.S., or 520-7040 in Belize; www.jaguar reef.com): This intimate beachfront resort has a range of amenities and activities that will make parents happy and keep kids occupied. In addition to the pool, beach, sea kayaks, and mountain bikes, these folks have a "day lodge" on the Sittee River, as well as a private caye, which can be visited for a day of snorkeling and diving or on an overnight adventure. See p. 182.
- **The Inn at Robert's Grove** (Placencia, Southern Belize; © 800/565-9757 in the U.S., or 523-3565 in Belize; www.roberts grove.com): This is another small beach resort that is well suited for families. As at Jaguar Reef, there's a wide enough range of activities available here to keep families active and interested for a full vacation. To slightly trump Jaguar Reef, these folks even have two swimming pools and two private cayes. See p. 192.
- **Cayo District** (Western Belize): The Cayo District is the heart of Belize's Mayan world, as well as its prime ecotourism destination. Between a full plate of active adventure activities and a steady diet of Mayan ruins and ancient burial caves, families will find this a great place to spend time in Belize. **Chaa Creek** (© 824-2037; www.chaacreek.com) is not only extremely comfortable for families, but they also have their own butterfly breeding project and natural history museum on-site. And if parents need a little pampering, they also have an excellent spa. See chapter 8.
- **Caves Branch** (Cayo District and Western Belize): You'll be heroes in your kids' eyes after you take them inner tubing through the dark and spooky network of limestone caves traversed by the slow-moving Caves Branch River. Families looking for some creature comfort would be wise to choose **Jaguar Paw** (© 888/775-8645 in the U.S., or 820-2023; www. jaguarpaw.com), while those with a real hankering for adventure should head to **Ian Anderson's Caves Branch** (© 822-2800; www.cavesbranch.com). See "Belmopan" in chapter 8.

10 The Best Luxury Hotels & Resorts

- **Radisson Fort George Hotel & Marina** (Belize City; © 800/333-3333 in the U.S. or 223-3333 in Belize; www.radisson. com): This is hands-down the top business-class and luxury hotel in Belize City. This oceanfront hotel is located in the quiet Fort George neighborhood, out by the lighthouse, just a block from the cruise ship tourist village. The hotel has a great swimming pool, a well-equipped gym, several restaurants and bars, and easy access to the best Belize City has to offer. See p. 87.

- **Maruba Resort Jungle Spa** (off the Old Northern Hwy.; **800/627-8227** in the U.S. or 322-2199 in Belize; www.maruba-spa.com): This small resort and spa is set in a patch of lush forest and flowering gardens. The whole operation is an eclectic orgy designed to please the eyes and all other senses. The individual villas here are spectacular. A wide range of spa treatments is available, and excellently and professionally done. Don't miss out on their signature Mood Mud Massage, perhaps one of the few massage experiences for which you'll want to bring a camera. See p. 105.

- **Captain Morgan's Retreat** (Ambergris Caye; ℂ **888/653-9090** or 307/587-8914 in the U.S., or 226-2207; www.belizevacation.com): This is probably the best of the full-scale resort hotels on Ambergris Caye. The accommodations are a mix of individual bungalows and one- or two-bedroom suites. All are quite close to a long and beautiful stretch of beach. The hotel has two swimming pools and a beach volleyball court; it also offers a whole host of activities, tours, and adventures. See p. 142.

- **Victoria House** (Ambergris Caye; ℂ **800/247-5159** or 713/344-2340 in the U.S., or 226-2067; www.victoria-house.com): Casual elegance and attentive service await you at this Ambergris Caye resort. A varied collection of rooms, suites, and villas are spread around an expansive piece of land planted with lush tropical gardens. The hotel also has one of the best

restaurants in the country, as well as a wonderful patch of soft white sand beach. See p. 141.

- **Cayo Espanto** (just off the coast of Ambergris Caye; ℂ **888/666-4282** in the U.S. and Canada; www.aprivateisland.com): What could be more decadent and luxurious than staying in a private villa, with a private swimming pool, a private dock, and a personal butler, on an almost private island? (There are five villas here, although you can rent out the whole island if you like.) This place pulls out all the stops, providing all the modern conveniences and pampering possible on a desert island getaway. See p. 143.

- **Turtle Inn** (Placencia; ℂ **800/746-3743** in the U.S., or 523-3244; www.turtleinn.com): Building on the experience gained from his Blancaneaux Lodge, and building upon the ruins of a hotel destroyed by Hurricane Iris, director Francis Ford Coppola has upped the ante on high-end hotels in Belize. The individual villas here are the most beautiful and luxurious in Belize. The hotel is set right on an excellent stretch of beach, and the service and dining here are top-notch. See p. 193.

- **Jaguar Paw** (near Belmopan; ℂ **888/775-8645** in the U.S., or 820-2023; www.jaguarpaw.com): Set in a section of dense tropical forest on the edge of and entrance to one of Belize's most spectacular cave systems, this hotel is one of the most unique nature lodges in Belize. The rooms themselves are all distinct and feature bold architectural and decorative touches. The food is excellent, and this is the best place in the country to combine comfort with intensive spelunking and cave explorations. See p. 217.

- **Chaa Creek** (off the road to Benque Viejo, Cayo District; © 824-2037; www.chaacreek. com): A pioneer nature lodge in Belize, this collection of individual and duplex cottages was also a pioneer in the whole concept of rustic luxury. Cool terra-cotta tile floors, varnished wood, thatched roofs, and beautiful Guatemalan textiles and handicrafts are elegantly yet simply combined. The property is set on a steep hillside over the lovely Macal River. Service here is very friendly and personable, and the lodge provides easy access to a wealth of natural adventures and ancient Mayan wonders. See p. 231.

- **Blancaneaux Lodge** (Mountain Pine Ridge Reserve, Cayo District; © 800/746-3743 in the U.S., or 824-3878; www.blancaneaux.com): Francis Ford Coppola's first Belizean mountain retreat remains one of the most elegant and luxurious nature lodges in the country. The hotel is set on a steep pine-forested hillside, overlooking the Privassion River and a series of gentle falls. The individual cabañas are all spacious, are beautifully decorated, and feature a private balcony or deck designed to take in the excellent views. The hotel recently added a wonderful riverside spa facility. See p. 239.

11 The Best Moderately Priced Hotels

- **San Pedro Holiday Hotel** (Ambergris Caye; © 226-2014; www.sanpedroholiday.com): This brilliantly white three-building complex with painted purple and pink trim sits in the center of San Pedro town and the center of the action. This was the first hotel on Ambergris Caye when Celi McCorkle opened it over 35 years ago, and it's still one of the best. Grab a room with an oceanview balcony and you'll be in tropical vacation heaven. See p. 139.

- **Tides Beach Resort** (Ambergris Caye; © 226-2283; www.amber griscaye.com/tides): Every room comes with either a private or shared balcony or veranda overlooking the Caribbean Sea. The hotel and its in-house dive shop are run by the very friendly and highly respected local couple of Patojo and Sabrina Paz. See p. 140.

- **Lazy Iguana Bed & Breakfast** (Caye Caulker; © 226-0350; www.lazyiguana.net): You can't beat the views from the fourth floor open-air thatched terrace of this intimate bed-and-breakfast. The rooms are spacious and well appointed, and your hosts are a wealth of knowledge about the island. See p. 158.

- **Hopkins Inn** (Hopkins Village; © 523-7013; www.hopkinsinn. com): These clean and comfortable individual cabins are located in the heart of a small traditional Garífuna fishing village. The cabins are just steps from the ocean on a beautiful patch of beach. See p. 183.

- **Blue Crab Resort** (Seine Bight Village; © 523-3544; www.blue crabbeach.com): Simple, comfortable, and cool rooms located on a beautiful and isolated patch of beach make this a wonderful option. Throw in an excellent restaurant serving eclectic international fare, and you've got the makings of a perfect getaway. This place is located just a little bit north of the traditional Garífuna village of Seine Bight. See p. 194.

- **Cahal Pech Village Resort** (San Ignacio, Cayo District; © 824-3740; www.cahalpech.com): With a commanding hillside perch, this collection of individual cabins and hotel rooms is an excellent option in the San Ignacio area. The resort is located just beyond the entrance to the Cahal Pech Mayan ruins, and a whole host of tours and activities can be arranged here. See p. 227.

12 The Best Budget Hotels

- **Belcove Hotel** (Belize City; © 227-3054; www.belcove.com): This budget hotel is set on the banks of Haulover Creek, just a block from the Swing Bridge and the heart of downtown Belize City. The riverview balconies are one of my favorite spots in all of Belize to sit and read a book, or watch the sporadic action on the river and streets below. See p. 88.
- **Hok'ol K'in Guesthouse** (Corozal Town; © 442-3329; www. corozal.net): The second-floor oceanfront rooms at this little hotel are the best bargains in Corozal Town. The hotel itself is just across the street from a small seaside promenade that fronts the beautiful Corozal Bay. See p. 122.
- **Ruby's** (Ambergris Caye; © 226-2063; www.ambergriscaye.com/rubys): Located right on the waterfront in the center of San Pedro, most of the rooms here overlook the ocean, and the best ones come with a balcony. This is one of the older and more historic hotels on the island, and you just can't do much better on Ambergris Caye for this price. See p. 140.
- **De Real Macaw** (Caye Caulker; © 226-0459; www.derealmacaw. com): This small and relatively new compound on Front Street in Caye Caulker is a great bargain. The hotel is close to all the action, and the rooms are clean, cool, and comfortable. There's plenty of shade and trees strung with hammocks for a well-deserved tropical siesta. See p. 158.

- **Tree Tops Guest House** (Caye Caulker; © 226-0240; www.tree topsbelize.com): While the best rooms here actually fall into the moderately priced category (and are some of the best rooms on Caye Caulker), the whole place offers such good value for your money that it's getting a listing in this category. The budget rooms here continue to set the standard on Caye Caulker, and the service is friendly, knowledgeable, and attentive. See p. 159.
- **Tipple Tree Beya** (Hopkins Village; ©/fax 520-7006; http://tippletree.net): There are just five simple rooms at this friendly hostel-like option at the southern end of Hopkins Village. However, if the rooms are full, you can also camp. The hotel sits on a lovely section of beach, and is within easy walking distance of the small Garífuna village of Hopkins. See p. 184.
- **Tradewinds** (Placencia; © 523-3122; www.placencia.com): Set on a curving spit of sand at the southern edge of Placencia, the individual cabins here are so close to the water's edge that I worry it's only a matter of time before the ocean reclaims them. But if you get here soon enough, and land one of them, you'll likely never want to leave. Each has a private front porch strung with a hammock, where you can swing and listen to the lapping waves. See p. 196.
- **Midas Tropical Resort** (San Ignacio, Cayo District; © 824-3172; www.midasbelize.com): Sure you can stay in San Ignacio for a little

less, but this collection of cottages and cabins is just a half-mile or so from downtown, right on the banks of the Macal River. You can also camp here. The whole thing has the feel of an isolated nature lodge, at a fraction of the cost. See p. 228.

- **Clarissa Falls Resort** (San Ignacio, Cayo District; ℂ/fax **824-3916**): Set on the banks of the

Mopan River at the foot of its namesake Clarissa Falls, this collection of cabins, rooms, a bunkhouse, and campsites is one of the most popular and vibrant budget options in the Cayo District. Owner Chena Glavez is as famous for her pleasing demeanor and attentive service as she is for her wholesome Belizean cooking. See p. 233.

13 The Best Restaurants

- **Harbour View** (Belize City; ℂ **223-6420**): Set on the water's edge overlooking the juncture of Haulover Creek and the Caribbean sea, this is the most creative and elegant restaurant in Belize City. Fresh seafood and local staples are cooked with fusion flare and some Asian accents. If the weather's right and you land one of the outdoor tables on the wraparound veranda, you will enjoy certainly the finest dining experience available in the city. See p. 90.
- **The Smokey Mermaid** (Belize City; ℂ **223-4722**): Less formal then the Harbour View, this place also serves up some excellent and eclectic cuisine in a lovely garden setting. This is also probably the best breakfast option in Belize City. See p. 91.
- **Wet Lizard** (Belize City; ℂ **223-2664**): Even less formal than either of the two Belize City restaurants mentioned above, this often-rowdy little restaurant and bar still serves up excellent fresh seafood and burgers, in an open-air setting overlooking the Swing Bridge and Belize Harbor. This is a great place to savor some late-afternoon conch fritters and a refreshing drink. See p. 91.
- **Le Café Kela** (Corozal Town; ℂ **422-2833**): If you're in

Corozal Town, you'll definitely want to eat here. Once you've tried it, you may not eat anywhere else in town. This place is casually elegant, with a wonderful menu and very reasonable prices. The menu ranges from thin-crust pizzas, as well as some French-inspired dishes, and Belizean classics. This is without a doubt the best restaurant in Northern Belize. See p. 123.
- **Elvi's Kitchen** (San Pedro, Ambergris Caye; ℂ **226-2176**): Elvia Staines has come a long way since she began selling hamburgers out of a takeout window over 30 years ago. Today her friendly and very popular restaurant oozes island charm. The restaurant is a thatched, screened-in building with picnic tables, with a large flamboyant tree growing up through the roof and a floor of crushed shells and sand. No visit to Ambergris Caye is complete without a meal here. See p. 145.
- **Palmilla** (Ambergris Caye; ℂ **226-2067**): This is easily the most elegant and finest dining to be had on Ambergris Caye, if not in all of Belize. Chef Amy Knox prepares the freshest of local ingredients with a creative blend of techniques, spices, and cuisines from around the world. The atmosphere is island formal, meaning

relaxed yet refined at the same time. When the weather's nice, you can dine under the stars by candlelight. See p. 147.

- **Mambo Cuisine** (Ambergris Caye; © 220-5010): These folks are serving up very creative and well-prepared fusion cuisine at this isolated beach resort. The menu is so wide and varied that you'll want to eat here with several friends, just to taste as many offerings as possible. Whatever you do, save room for their chocolate soufflé dessert. See p. 147.

- **Rasta Pasta Rainforest Café** (Caye Caulker; © 226-0358): This place is the epitome of funky island charm, but it's even better than that sounds. Sure you get your sand floor, your plastic lawn furniture, your view of the Caribbean Sea, and your fair dose of vegetarian and Rastafarian-influenced menu items. But you also get a wide and eclectic menu, huge portions, and excellent service. What's more, the food is delicious and the ambience is wonderful. See p. 160.

- **Luba Hati** (Placencia; © 523-3402): These folks have brought fusion cuisine to Belize's Southern Zone, and they've done it with style and flair. The menu features a wide range of very creative takes on typical Belizean and Central American fare. They also have an elegant martini bar and an excellent wine list. See p. 196.

- **Waluco's** (Punta Gorda; © 722-0196): This simple waterfront joint has quickly become the best and most popular dining option in Punta Gorda. Fresh fish, tasty conch, succulent barbecue, and cold drinks are the main draws here. What more could you ask for in this remote Southern Zone? See p. 207.

14 The Best After-Dark Fun

There's not really all that much in the way of nightlife in Belize. The capital city is small and relatively quiet by most international standards. In both the capital and the various tourist destinations, you'd be hard pressed to find a truly notable bar or club. Still, there are some unique after-dark destinations and activities that should not be missed in Belize.

- **Stargazing:** This is one of my favorite nighttime activities, but it is especially rewarding when there is no (or little) ambient light. Given its sparse development and low population density, Belize offers a wealth of opportunities for some truly spectacular stargazing. Your best spots are the isolated beach getaways of Belize's three mid-ocean atolls, but you can also enjoy the astronomical splendor from any number of deserted beaches or rural mountain getaways.

- **Night Diving:** If you've come to Belize to scuba dive, you should definitely try a night dive. Many creatures are nocturnal, and the reefs here come alive at night. Moreover, the brilliant colors of the coral and sea life really shine under the strong glare of an underwater light, and there's something truly eerie about the experience. All of the major dive destinations and resorts offer night diving. See chapter 3 and the destination chapters for more details.

- **Barefoot Iguana** (Ambergris Caye): This cavernous bar features everything from hot new DJs to mud wrestling to sporting events shown on a giant screen. The two-story hangar-sized space is hung with faux jungle plants and foliage, and it has quickly become the most happening nightspot in San Pedro. See "Ambergris Caye" in chapter 6.

- **Sugar Reef Lounge** (Placencia; ℂ **523-3289**): Placencia is a small village. On Wednesday nights, it seems like the entire town heads to the Sugar Reef Lounge for their karaoke night. On other nights of the week, this is also one of the better spots in town to hang out after the sun goes down. See "Placencia" in chapter 7.

- **Moon Rise at Tikal:** Watching the full moon rise from the top of Temple IV in Tikal is one of the highlights of my many travels to this region. You'll have to be staying at one of the hotels on-site to do this, and you may even have to persuade or bribe a park guard. You'll also have to time your visit with the moon phase. But if all these things come together, you're in for a memorable and awe-inspiring evening. See "Tikal" in chapter 9.

15 The Best Websites about Belize

- **Latin America Network Information Center** (www.lanic.utexas.edu/la/ca/cr): Hosted by the University of Texas Latin American Studies Department, this site houses a vast collection of diverse information about Belize. This is hands-down the best one-stop shop for Web browsing. There are helpful links to a wide range of tourism and general-information sites.

- **Belize By Naturelight** (www.belizenet.com): This is probably the single best collection of links to individual hotels, restaurants, and attractions. They also have featured links to the various regions and destinations within Belize, as well as links to most other major and important websites on the country.

- **The Belize Forums** (www.belizeforum.com): These are active and informative forums on living in

and traveling around Belize. Several regular posters are quite knowledgeable, and are generous with that knowledge.

- **Belize News** (http://belizenews.com): This site provides access to all of Belize's major online news sources, including all the major weekly print newspapers.

- **Belize Kriol** (www.kriol.org.bz): If you want to know about Belize's Kriol (creole) culture, this is the place to go. The site includes pages on Kriol history, culture, and language. There's a handy spelling guide and Kriol dictionary here as well.

- **Belize Tourist Board** (www.travelbelize.org): This is the official site of the Belize Tourist Board. It has its fair share of information and links, although you'll probably end up being directed to one of the other sites mentioned above.

2

Planning Your Trip to Belize

For such a small country, Belize offers a wealth of vacation options, ranging from sun and fun beach time, to dedicated scuba diving or fishing trips, to themed vacations exploring the ancient Mayan culture and archaeology. Moreover, given the compact size of the country, it's very possible to mix and match these options. Whatever your interests, this chapter, as well as the subsequent "Active Vacation Planner," will provide you with all the tools and information necessary to plan and book your trip.

1 The Regions in Brief

BELIZE CITY Belize City is a modest-size coastal port city located at the mouth of the Belize River. Although it's no longer the official governmental seat, Belize City remains the most important city—culturally, economically, and historically—in the country. It is also Belize's transportation hub, with the only international airport, an active municipal airport, a cruise-ship dock, and all the major bus line and water taxi terminals. Still, Belize City is of limited interest to most visitors, who quickly seek the more provincial and pastoral charms of the country's various tourist destinations and resorts. Belize City has a reputation as a rough and violent urban center, and visitors should exercise caution and stick to the most popular tourist areas of this small city.

NORTHERN BELIZE Anchored on the south by Belize City, this is the country's business and agricultural heartland. Towards the north lie Orange Walk Town and Corozal Town. Both of these small cities have a strong Spanish feel and influence, having been settled largely by refugees from Mexico's Caste War. The Maya also lived here, and their memories

live on at the ruins of Altun Ha, Lamanai, Cerros, and Santa Rita, all in this zone. This is a land that was once submerged and is still primarily swamp and mangrove. Where the land is cleared and settled, sugar cane is the main cash crop, although bananas, citrus fruits, and pineapples are also grown. Towards the western section of this region lies the Río Bravo Conservation Area, a massive tract of virgin forest, sustainable-yield managed forest, and recovering reforestation areas. Northern Belize has some of the country's premier isolated nature lodges, as well as some of the prime destinations for bird-watchers, including the Shipstern Nature Reserve and Crooked Tree Wildlife Sanctuary.

THE NORTHERN CAYES & ATOLLS This is Belize's primary tourist zone and attraction. Hundreds of palm-swept offshore islands lie between the coast of the mainland and the protection of the 185-mile (298km) Barrier Reef. The reef, easily visible from many of the cayes, offers some of the world's most exciting snorkeling, scuba diving, and fishing. The most developed cayes here, Ambergris Caye and Caye Caulker,

Belize

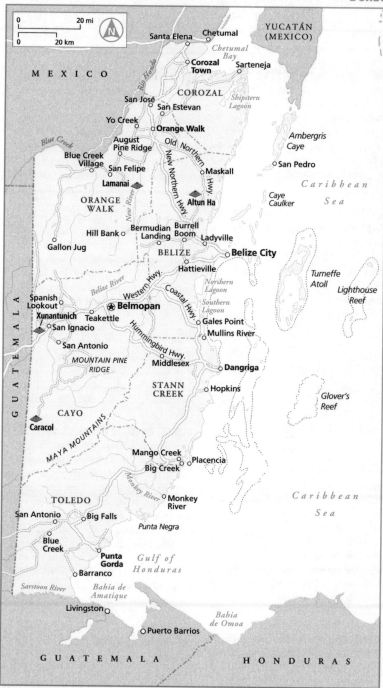

0   20 mi
0   20 km

N

YUCATÁN (MEXICO)

Santa Elena
Chetumal
Chetumal Bay

Corozal Town
Sarteneja

MEXICO

Río Hondo

COROZAL

San José
San Estevan
Shipstern Lagoon

Yo Creek
Orange Walk

August Pine Ridge
Old Northern Hwy.

Blue Creek Village
San Felipe
Maskall

Blue Creek

Lamanai

ORANGE WALK

New River

New Northern Hwy.

Altun Ha

Ambergris Caye

San Pedro

Caribbean Sea

Caye Caulker

Hill Bank
Bermudian Landing
Burrell Boom
Ladyville

Gallon Jug

BELIZE
Belize City

Hattieville

Belize River

Western Hwy.

Northern Lagoon

Turneffe Atoll

Lighthouse Reef

Spanish Lookout
Xunantunich
★ **Belmopan**
Teakettle
San Ignacio

Coastal Hwy.

Southern Lagoon

Gales Point
Mullins River

Hummingbird Hwy.

San Antonio

MOUNTAIN PINE RIDGE

Middlesex

STANN CREEK

Dangriga

Hopkins

Glover's Reef

CAYO

MAYA MOUNTAINS

Caracol

Monkey River

Mango Creek
Placencia
Big Creek

Caribbean Sea

TOLEDO

San Antonio
Big Falls

Monkey River

Punta Negra

Blue Creek

Punta Gorda
Barranco

Gulf of Honduras

Sarstoon River

Bahía de Amatique

Livingston

Bahía de Omoa

Puerto Barrios

GUATEMALA

GUATEMALA

HONDURAS

have numerous hotels and small resorts, while some of the less developed cayes maintain the feel of fairytale desert isles. In addition to the many cayes, there are two open-ocean atolls here, Turneffe Island Atoll and Lighthouse Reef Atoll. These unique rings of coral, limestone, and mangrove cayes each surround a central, protected saltwater lagoon.

For those whose main sport is catching rays, not fish, it should be mentioned that the cayes, and Belize in general, lack wide, sandy beaches. Although the water is as warm and clear blue as it's touted to be, most of your sunbathing will be on docks, deck chairs, or imported patches of sand fronting a seawall or seagrass patch of shallow ocean. Also, note that there are still no large-scale all-inclusive resorts like those found throughout much of the rest of the Caribbean.

SOUTHERN BELIZE Southern Belize encompasses two major districts, Stann Creek and Toledo. The former includes the Cockscomb Basin Wildlife Sanctuary and the coastal towns of Dangriga, Hopkins Village, and Placencia. Dangriga is the country's major center of Garifuna culture, and Placencia boasts what is arguably the country's best beach. Further south, the Toledo District is Belize's final frontier. The inland hills and jungles are home to numerous Kekchi and Mopan Mayan villages. Hidden in these hills are some lesser known and less visited Mayan ruins, including Lubaantun and Nim Li Punit. The Toledo District is also emerging as an ecotourism destination, with the country's richest, wettest, and most undisturbed rainforests. Off the shores of southern Belize lie more cayes and yet another mid-ocean atoll, Glover's Reef Atoll. The cayes down here get far less traffic and attention than those to the north, and are perfect for anyone looking for all of the same attractions, but fewer crowds.

THE CAYO DESTRICT & WESTERN BELIZE This mountainous district near the Guatemalan border has become Belize's second most popular destination. Here you'll find some of Belize's most beautiful countryside and most fascinating natural and man-made sights. The limestone mountains of this region are dotted with numerous caves, sinkholes, jagged peaks, underground rivers, and waterfalls. There are clear flowing aboveground rivers that are excellent for swimming and canoeing, as well as mile after mile of unexplored forest full of wild animals and hundreds of bird species. Adventurers, nature lovers, and bird-watchers will definitely want to spend some time in the Cayo District. This is also where you'll find Belize's largest and most impressive Mayan ruins. In the remote Mountain Pine Ridge section of the Cayo District lies Caracol, one of the largest known Classic Mayan cities ever uncovered. Closer to the main town of San Ignacio, you'll find Xunantunich, Pilar, and the smaller Cahal Pech.

TIKAL & GUATEMALA'S PETEN Just over Belize's western border lies Guatemala's Petén province, a massive and remote area of primary forest and perhaps Mesoamerica's most spectacular Mayan ruin, Tikal. The level of preservation, restoration, and rich rainforest setting make Tikal one of the true wonders of the world, and an enchanting stop for anyone even remotely interested in the ancient Maya or archaeology. The surrounding jungles and small Guatemalan villages are easily accessible from Belize and allow travelers the chance to add yet another unique adventure to any itinerary.

2 Visitor Information

The **Belize Tourism Board,** Central Bank Building, Gabourel Lane (PO Box 325) in Belize City, will mail you a basic information packet. You can order this packet on their website at **www.travelbelize.org**. Alternatively, folks in the United States and Canada can call the Belize Tourism Board toll free at © **800/624-0286.** Travelers from the United Kingdom, Australia, and New Zealand will have to rely primarily on the website, or dial direct to Belize (© **223-1913**), as the Belize Tourism Board does not have offices or a toll-free number in these countries.

In addition to the official website, you'll be able to find a wealth of Web-based information on Belize with a few clicks of your mouse. See "The Best Websites about Belize" in chapter 1 for some helpful suggestions on where to begin your online search.

3 Entry Requirements & Customs

ENTRY REQUIREMENTS

A current passport, valid through your departure date, is required for entry into Belize. Driver's licenses and birth certificates are not valid travel documents. In some cases you may be asked to show an onward or return plane ticket. No visas are required for citizens of the United States, Great Britain, Ireland, South Africa, Australia, or New Zealand. Nationals of certain other countries do need a visa or consular permission to enter Belize. For a current list, see the Belize Tourism Board website (www.travel belize.org) or call the nearest Belize consulate or embassy. For an up-to-date country-by-country listing of passport requirements around the world, go to the "Foreign Entry Requirement" website page of the U.S. State Department at **http://travel. state.gov/foreignentryreqs.html**.

Tourists are permitted a maximum stay of 30 days. The **Belize Department of Immigration and Nationality** in Belmopan (© **822-2423**) will sometimes grant a 30-day extension. These extensions are handled on a case-by-case basis and cost BZ$50 (US$25).

If you have additional travel or visa questions about Belize, you can contact any of the following Belizean embassies or consulates: in the **United** **States** or **Canada,** 2535 Massachusetts Ave. NW, Washington, DC 20008 (© **202/332-9636;** www. embassyofbelize.org); in **Great Britain,** Belize High Commission, 22 Harcourt House, 19 Cavendish Sq., London, W1G 0PL (© **020/7499-9728**). There are no Belizean embassies or consulates in Australia or New Zealand.

For information on how to get a passport, go to "Passports" in the "Fast Facts" section of this chapter—the websites listed provide downloadable passport applications as well as the current fees for processing passport applications.

CUSTOMS
WHAT YOU CAN BRING INTO BELIZE

Visitors to Belize may bring with them any and all reasonable goods and belongings for personal use during their stay. Cameras, computers, and electronic equipment, as well as fishing and diving gear for personal use, are permitted duty free. Customs officials in Belize seldom check arriving tourists' luggage.

WHAT YOU CAN TAKE HOME

It is expressly illegal to bring out any pre-Columbian artifact from Belize, whether you bought it, you discovered it, or it was given to you. Do not traffic in Mayan artifacts.

Tips Passport Savvy

Allow plenty of time before your trip to apply for a passport; processing normally takes 3 weeks but can take longer during busy periods (especially spring). And keep in mind that if you need a passport in a hurry, you'll pay a higher processing fee. When traveling, safeguard your passport in an inconspicuous, inaccessible place like a money belt and keep a copy of the critical pages with your passport number in a separate place. If you lose your passport, visit the nearest consulate or embassy of your native country as soon as possible for a replacement.

Returning **U.S. citizens** who have been away for at least 48 hours are allowed to bring back, once every 30 days, $800 worth of merchandise duty-free. You'll be charged a flat rate of duty on the next $1,000 worth of purchases. Any dollar amount beyond that is dutiable at whatever rates apply. On mailed gifts, the duty-free limit is $200. Be sure to have your receipts or purchases handy to expedite the declaration process. *Note:* If you owe duty, you are required to pay on your arrival in the United States by cash, personal check, government or traveler's check, or money order, and in some locations, by a Visa or MasterCard.

To avoid having to pay duty on foreign-made personal items you owned before you left on your trip, bring along a bill of sale, insurance policy, jeweler's appraisal, or receipts of purchase. Or you can register items that can be readily identified by a permanently affixed serial number or marking —think laptop computers, cameras, and CD players—with Customs before you leave. Take the items to the nearest Customs office or register them with Customs at the airport from which you're departing. You'll receive, at no cost, a Certificate of Registration, which allows duty-free entry for the life of the item.

With some exceptions, you cannot bring fresh fruits and vegetables into the United States. For specifics on what you can bring back, download the invaluable free pamphlet *Know Before You Go* online at **www.cbp.gov.** (Click on "Travel," and then click on "Know Before You Go! Online Brochure.") Or contact the **U.S. Customs & Border Protection (CBP),** 1300 Pennsylvania Ave. NW, Washington, DC 20229 (© **877/287-8667**), and request the pamphlet.

For a clear summary of **Canadian** rules, write for the booklet *I Declare,* issued by the **Canada Border Services Agency** (© **800/461-9999** in Canada, or 204/983-3500; www.ccra-asfc.gc.ca). Canada allows its citizens a C$750 exemption, and you're allowed to bring back duty-free one carton of cigarettes, one can of tobacco, 40 imperial ounces of liquor, and 50 cigars. In addition, you're allowed to mail gifts to Canada valued at less than C$60 a day, provided they're unsolicited and don't contain alcohol or tobacco (write on the package "Unsolicited gift, under $60 value"). All valuables should be declared on the Y-38 form before your departure from Canada, including serial numbers of valuables you already own, such as expensive foreign cameras. *Note:* The $750 exemption can only be used once a year and only after an absence of 7 days.

U.K. citizens returning from **a non-E.U. country** have a Customs allowance of: 200 cigarettes; 50 cigars; 250 grams of smoking tobacco; 2 liters of still table wine; 1 liter of spirits or strong liqueurs (over 22% volume); 2 liters of fortified wine, sparkling wine or other liqueurs; 60cc (ml) perfume; 250cc (ml) of toilet water; and £145 worth of all other goods, including gifts and souvenirs. People under 17 cannot have the tobacco or alcohol allowance. For more information, contact HM Customs & Excise at © 0845/010-9000 (from outside the U.K., 020/8929-0152), or consult their website at www.hmce.gov.uk.

The duty-free allowance in **Australia** is A$400 or, for those under 18, A$200. Citizens can bring in 250 cigarettes or 250 grams of loose tobacco, and 1,125 milliliters of alcohol. If you're returning with valuables you already own, such as foreign-made cameras, you should file form B263. A helpful brochure available from Australian consulates or Customs offices is *Know Before You Go.* For more information, call the **Australian Customs**

Service at © **1300/363-263,** or log on to www.customs.gov.au.

The duty-free allowance for **New Zealand** is NZ$700. Citizens over 17 can bring in 200 cigarettes, 50 cigars, or 250 grams of tobacco (or a mixture of all three if their combined weight doesn't exceed 250g); plus 4.5 liters of wine and beer, or 1.125 liters of liquor. New Zealand currency does not carry import or export restrictions. Fill out a certificate of export, listing the valuables you are taking out of the country; that way, you can bring them back without paying duty. Most questions are answered in a free pamphlet available at New Zealand consulates and Customs offices: *New Zealand Customs Guide for Travellers, Notice no. 4.* For more information, contact **New Zealand Customs,** The Customhouse, 17–21 Whitmore St., Box 2218, Wellington (© **0800/428-786** or 04/473-6099; www.customs. govt.nz).

4 Money

CURRENCY

The Belize dollar, abbreviated BZ$, is the official currency of Belize. The Belize dollar is pegged to the U.S. dollar at a ratio of 2 Belize dollars to 1 U.S. dollar. Both currencies are acceptable at almost any business or establishment around the country. As long as you have some U.S. dollars or U.S. dollar-based traveler's checks, it is entirely unnecessary to change for Belize dollars in advance of your trip. In fact, it is really unnecessary to change money at all. Once you are in Belize, the change you receive will most likely be in Belize dollars, although it is not uncommon for it to be a mix of both currencies. However, do try to have some small-denomination bills for paying taxis, modest meal tabs, and tips.

The branch of the **Belize Bank** (© **225-2107**) at the international

airport is only open Monday through Friday from 8:30am to 4pm. If you are flying out on a weekend, or outside of these hours, be sure to spend or exchange any Belize dollars beforehand.

Tip: Be careful to note whether or not the price you are being quoted is in Belize or U.S. dollars. Many hotels, restaurants, and tour operators actually quote in U.S. dollars. If in doubt, ask. At a two-to-one ratio, the difference can be substantial.

ATMs

The easiest and best way to get cash away from home is from an ATM (automated teller machine). **Belize Bank** ATMs were finally connected to the Cirrus and PLUS networks in 2004. It is expected that Scotiabank and Atlantic Bank will soon follow suit. The **Cirrus** (© **800/424-7787;** www.mastercard.com) and **PLUS**

The Belize Dollar, the U.S. Dollar, the Euro & the British Pound

BZ$	US$	Euro €	UK£
1.00	0.50	0.40	0.28
2.00	1.00	0.80	0.56
5.00	2.50	1.65	1.40
10.00	5.00	4.10	2.80
20.00	10.00	8.25	5.60
25.00	12.50	10.30	7.00
50.00	25.00	20.65	14.10
100.00	50.00	41.30	28.15
200.00	100.00	82.60	56.30
500.00	250.00	206.40	140.70
1,000.00	500.00	412.85	281.35
2,000.00	1,000.00	825.70	562.70
5,000.00	2,500.00	2,064.00	1,406.70

(© 800/843-7587; www.visa.com) networks span the globe; look at the back of your bank card to see which network you're on, then call or check online for ATM locations at your destination. Currently, in Belize, you will only find internationally accessible ATMs in Belize City, San Pedro, Placencia, San Ignacio, Belmopan, Dangriga, and Corozal Town, although this may change and increase soon. Given the limited number of internationally enabled ATMs in Belize and the relatively recent nature of their connection to the Cirrus and PLUS systems, I still advise you to think of your ATM as a backup measure. It's wise to bring enough spending cash, and charge the rest of your bills. Try not to rely on your ATM card for an emergency cash bailout.

Be sure you know your personal identification number (PIN) before you leave home, and be sure to find out your daily withdrawal limit before you depart. Also keep in mind that many banks impose a fee every time a card is used at a different bank's ATM, and that fee can be higher for international transactions (up to $5 or more) than for domestic ones (where they're rarely more than $1.50). On top of this, the bank from which you withdraw cash may charge its own fee. For international withdrawal fees, ask your bank.

You can also get cash advances on your credit card at an ATM. Keep in mind that credit card companies try to protect themselves from theft by limiting the funds someone can withdraw outside their home country, so call your credit card company before you leave home. And keep in mind that you'll pay interest from the moment of your withdrawal, even if you pay your monthly bills on time.

TRAVELER'S CHECKS

Traveler's checks are something of an anachronism from the days before the ATM made cash accessible at any time. Traveler's checks used to be the only sound alternative to traveling with dangerously large amounts of cash. They were as reliable as currency but, unlike cash, could be replaced if lost or stolen.

These days, traveler's checks are less necessary because most cities have 24-hour ATMs that allow you to withdraw small amounts of cash as needed. However, keep in mind that you will likely be charged an ATM withdrawal fee if the bank is not your own, so if you're withdrawing money every day, you might be better off with traveler's checks—provided that you don't mind showing identification every time you want to cash one. Traveler's checks are accepted at most hotels in Belize, but less frequently at restaurants.

You can get traveler's checks at almost any bank. **American Express** offers denominations of $20, $50, $100, $500, and (for cardholders only) $1,000. You'll pay a service charge ranging from 1% to 4%. You can also get American Express traveler's checks over the phone by calling © **800/221-7282;** Amex gold and platinum cardholders who use this number are exempt from the 1% fee.

Visa offers traveler's checks at Citibank locations nationwide, as well as at several other banks. The service charge ranges between 1.5% and 2%; checks come in denominations of $20, $50, $100, $500, and $1,000. Call © **800/732-1322** for information. AAA members can obtain Visa checks without a fee at most AAA offices or by calling © **866/339-3378. MasterCard** also offers traveler's checks. Call © **800/223-9920** for a location near you.

If you choose to carry traveler's checks, be sure to keep a record of their serial numbers separate from your checks in the event that they are

What Things Cost in Belize	BZ$	US$
Taxi from the airport to Belize City	35.00–40.00	18.00–20.00
Local taxi ride	2.00–5.00	1.00–2.50
Water taxi ride to Ambergris Caye	30.00	15.00
One-way flight to San Pedro from Municipal Airport	52.00	26.00
One-way flight to San Pedro from International Airport	93.00	47.00
Private villa at the Turtle Inn	500.00–600.00	250.00–300.00
Double room, expensive	340.00	170.00
Double room, moderate	130.00–150.00	65.00–75.00
Double room, inexpensive	70.00–100.00	35.00–50.00
Dinner for one without wine, expensive	60.00	30.00
Dinner for one without wine, moderate	30.00	15.00
Dinner for one, inexpensive	15.00	7.50
Bottle of Belikin beer	2.00–3.00	1.00–1.50
Bottle of Coca-Cola	1.50	0.75
Cup of coffee	1.00	0.50
Gallon of premium gas	8.25	4.15
Admission to most national parks	10.00	5.00
Admission to Belize Zoo	15.00	7.50
Two-tank dive with equipment	120.00–180.00	60.00–90.00
Exit tax	70.00	35.00

stolen or lost. You'll get a refund faster if you know the numbers.

CREDIT CARDS

Credit cards are a safe way to carry money. They also provide a convenient record of all your expenses, and they generally offer relatively good exchange rates. You can also withdraw cash advances from your credit cards at banks or ATMs, provided you know your PIN. If you've forgotten yours, or didn't even know you had one, call the number on the back of your credit card and ask the bank to send it to you; it usually takes 5 to 7 business days to arrive in the mail. Keep in mind that when you use your credit card abroad, most banks assess a 2% fee above the 1% fee charged by Visa or MasterCard or American Express for currency conversion on credit charges. But credit cards still may be the smart way to go when you factor in things like exorbitant ATM fees and higher traveler's check exchange rates (and service fees).

Most major credit cards are accepted in Belize, although Master-Card and Visa are somewhat more widely accepted than American Express,

especially by smaller hotels, restaurants, and tour operators. While there are some exceptions, Diners Club and Discover have made minimal inroads around Belize.

Some credit card companies recommend that you notify them of any impending trip abroad so that they don't become suspicious when the card is used numerous times in a foreign destination and block your charges. Even if you don't call your credit card company in advance, you can always call the card's toll-free emergency number (see "Lost & Found" in "Fast Facts," later in this chapter) if a charge is refused—a good reason to carry the phone number with you. But perhaps the most important lesson here is to carry more than one card with you on your trip; a card might not work for any number of reasons, so having a backup is the smart way to go.

IF YOUR WALLET IS LOST OR STOLEN

For tips and telephone numbers to call if your wallet is stolen or lost, go to "Lost & Found" in "Fast Facts," at the end of this chapter.

5 When to Go

Belize's high season for tourism runs from late November to late April, which coincides almost perfectly with the chill of winter in the United States, Canada, and Great Britain. The high season is also the dry season. If you want some unadulterated time on a tropical beach and a little less rain during your rainforest experience, this is the time to visit. During this period (and especially around the Christmas and Easter holidays), the tourism industry operates at full tilt—prices are higher, attractions are more crowded, and reservations need to be made in advance.

The weather in Belize is subtropical and generally similar to that of southern Florida. The average daytime temperature on the coast and cayes is around 80°F (27°C), although it can get considerably warmer during the day during the summer months. During the winter months, when northern cold fronts extend their grip south, it can get downright nippy. In fact, from late December to February, "northers" can hit the coastal and caye areas hard, and hang around for between 3 and 5 days, putting a severe crimp in any beach vacation. The best months for guaranteed sun and fun are March through May.

The rainy season runs from June to mid-November, while the hurricane season runs from July to October, with the most active months being August, September, and October. For the most part, the rainy season is characterized by a dependable and short-lived afternoon shower. However, the amount of rainfall varies considerably with the regions. In the south, there may be more than 150 inches of rain per year, while in the north there is rarely more than 50 inches per year. There is also usually a brief dry period in mid-August, known as the *mauger*. If you're skittish about rain and hurricanes, don't come to Belize between late August and mid-October, the height of both the rainy and hurricane seasons. However, if you do come, you should be able to land some good bargains.

The Cayo District and other inland destinations tend to be slightly cooler than the coastal and caye destinations, although since there is generally little elevation gain, the differences tend to be slight.

Average Monthly Temperatures & Rainfall in Belize

	Jan	Feb	Mar	Apr	May	June	July	Aug	Sep	Oct	Nov	Dec
Temp (°F)	73.4	76.1	77.9	79.7	81.5	81.5	81.5	81.5	80.6	78.8	75.2	74.3
Temp (°C)	23	24.5	25.5	26.5	27.5	27.5	27.5	27.5	27	26	24	23.5
Days of Rain	12	6	4	5	7	13	15	14	15	16	12	14

PUBLIC HOLIDAYS

Official holidays in Belize include **January 1** (New Year's Day), **March 9** (Baron Bliss Day), Good Friday, Holy Saturday, Easter Sunday, Easter Monday, **May 1** (Labour Day), **May 24** (Commonwealth Day), **September 10** (St. George's Caye Day), **September 21** (Independence Day), **October 12** (Pan American Day), **November 19** (Garífuna Settlement Day), **December 25** (Christmas Day), **December 26** (Boxing Day), and **December 31** (New Year's Eve).

Government offices and banks are closed on official holidays, transportation services are reduced, and stores and markets may also close.

BELIZE CALENDAR OF EVENTS

Some of the events listed here might be considered more of a community celebration or tradition than an event—there's not, for instance, a Deer Dance Festival PR Committee that readily dispenses information. If I haven't listed a contact number, your best bet is to call the **Belize Tourism Board** at ℂ **800/624-0286** in the U.S. and Canada, or 223-1913 in Belize, or visit www.travel belize.org for additional information.

January

Krem New Year's Cycling Classic. This New Year's Day road race starts in Corozal Town and ends in Belize City. The competitors are mostly Belizean, although Guatemalan and Mexican teams occasionally enter.

The winners usually take around 3½ to 4 hours to cross the finish line; crowds usually form at the start and finish points. January 1.

February

International Billfish Tournament. Hosted by the Radisson Fort George Hotel and Marina (© 800/333-3333 in the U.S., or 223-3333; www.radisson.com), this multiday event features cash prizes. Early February.

Carnival. Nationwide celebrations during the week before Lent. Larger towns have parades and dance competitions. In San Pedro, watch out for getting "painted."

March

La Ruta Maya Belize River Challenge. This 4-day canoe race begins in San Ignacio in the Cayo District and ends at the Swing Bridge in Belize City. For more details, visit www.bighjuices.com/rutamaya/vidal.htm. March 6 to 9.

Baron Bliss Day. The day is marked with nationwide celebrations of Belize's benefactor. The greatest festivities are held in Belize City, where there is a regatta, as well as horse and foot races. March 9.

May

Labour Day. After a national address by the prime minister or minister of labour (carried on all local radio and television stations), the rest of the day is filled with celebrations, regattas, and horse races. May 1.

Cashew Festival, Crooked Tree Village. Celebrating the cashew harvest, this weekend celebration features local booths selling everything possible under the sun made with this coveted nut, including cashew wine and cashew jelly. There's usually live music and general revelry. First weekend in May.

National Agriculture & Trade Show, Belmopan. This national fair is geared towards farmers, cattle ranchers, large-scale agro-business, and buyers, but it's still an interesting event to tour or visit if you're in the country at the time. See www.agriculture.gov.bz/nats.html for additional details. Mid-May.

June

Día de San Pedro, San Pedro, Ambergris Caye. This is a 3-day celebration of the island's patron saint, Saint Peter, or San Pedro. Boats are blessed, and there are parades and processions. June 27 to 29.

Lobster Festival, Placencia. During this extended weekend celebration of the opening of lobster season, this beach town pulls out all the stops. There's plenty of lobster to be had in a variety of preparations, at temporary outdoor stalls and restaurants around town. There are also concerts and dancing and an arts fair. Check www.placencia.com for the latest details. Late June.

July

Lobster Festival, Caye Caulker. Not to be outdone by Placencia, Caye Caulker also puts on a long weekend celebration of the start of lobster season. Food, music, and dancing are all served up in hearty portions around town. Early July.

August

Costa Maya Festival, San Pedro, Ambergris Caye. This is perhaps the largest festival in the country. Drawing participants from neighboring countries of El Salvador, Mexico, Guatemala, and Honduras, this celebration features a steady stream of live concert performances, street parades, beauty pageants, and water shows and activities. Early August.

Deer Dance Festival, San Antonio, Toledo District. This 9-day festival is celebrated in the small Mayan village of San Antonio. Costumed performances and dances are the highlight of this traditional Mayan festival. Late August to early September.

September

Independence Day. Patriotic parades and official celebrations are mixed with street parties, beauty pageants, and open-air concerts. September 21.

October

Pan American Day. Formerly known as Columbus Day, the day now celebrates mestizo and Mayan culture with parades, street fairs, and concerts. October 12.

November

Garífuna Settlement Day. The greatest celebration occurs in Dangriga, where Garífunas from across Belize and throughout the region gather to commemorate their arrival from St. Vincent in 1832. Street parades, religious ceremonies, and dance and drumming performances are all part of the celebrations throughout the southern coastal zone. November 19.

December

Boxing Day. While Christmas Day is predominantly for the family in Belize, Boxing Day is a chance to continue the celebration with friends, neighbors, and strangers. There are dances, concerts, horse races, and general festivities around the country. December 26.

6 Travel Insurance

Check your existing insurance policies and credit card coverage before you buy travel insurance. You may already be covered for lost luggage, cancelled tickets or medical expenses. In terms of Belize, given the off chance of a hurricane canceling or cutting short your vacation, you might consider purchasing travel insurance, especially if you are traveling here between July and October.

The cost of travel insurance varies widely, depending on the cost and length of your trip, your age and health, and the type of trip you're taking, but expect to pay between 5% and 8% of the vacation itself.

TRIP-CANCELLATION INSURANCE

Trip-cancellation insurance helps you get your money back if you have to back out of a trip, if you have to go home early, or if your travel supplier goes bankrupt. Allowed reasons for cancellation can range from sickness to natural disasters to the State Department declaring your destination unsafe for travel. (Insurers usually won't cover vague fears, though, as many travelers discovered who tried to cancel their trips in Oct 2001 because they were wary of flying.) In this unstable world, trip-cancellation insurance is a good buy if you're getting tickets well in advance—who knows what the state of the world, or of your airline, will be in 9 months? Insurance policy details vary, so read the fine print—and make sure that your airline or cruise line is on the list of carriers covered in case of bankruptcy. A good resource is **"Travel Guard Alerts,"** a list of companies considered high-risk by Travel Guard International (see website below). Protect yourself further by paying for the insurance with a credit card—by law, consumers can get their money back on goods and services not received if they report the loss within 60 days after the charge is listed on their credit card statement.

Note: Many tour operators, particularly those offering trips to remote or high-risk areas, include insurance in the cost of the trip or can arrange insurance policies through a partnering provider, a convenient and often cost-effective way for the traveler to obtain insurance. Make sure the tour company is a reputable one, however: Some experts suggest you avoid buying insurance from the tour or cruise company you're traveling with, saying it's better to buy from a "third party" insurer than to put all your money in one place.

For more information, contact one of the following recommended insurers: **Access America** (© 866/807-3982; www.accessamerica.com); **Travel Guard International** (© 800/826-4919; www.travelguard.com); **Travel Insured International** (© 800/243-3174; www.travelinsured.com); and **Travelex Insurance Services** (© 888/457-4602; www.travelex-insurance.com).

MEDICAL INSURANCE

Many health insurance policies cover you if you get sick away from home—but check, particularly if you're insured by an HMO. For travel overseas, most health plans (including Medicare and Medicaid) do not provide coverage, and the ones that do often require you to pay for services upfront and reimburse you only after you return home. Even if your plan does cover overseas treatment, most out-of-country hospitals make you pay your bills upfront, and send you a refund only after you've returned home and filed the necessary paperwork with your insurance company. As a safety net, you may want to buy travel medical insurance, particularly if you're traveling to a remote or high-risk area where emergency evacuation is a possible scenario. If you require additional medical insurance, try **MEDEX Assistance** (© 410/453-6300; www.medexassist.com) or **Travel Assistance International** (© 800/821-2828; www.travelassistance.com; for general information on services, call the company's Worldwide Assistance Services, Inc., at © 800/777-8710).

If you're coming to Belize specifically to scuba dive, you should check

out the policies and coverage offered by **The Divers Alert Network** (**DAN**; © 800/446-2671 or 919/684-8181; www.diversalertnetwork.org).

Some credit cards (American Express and certain gold and platinum Visa and MasterCards, for example) offer automatic flight insurance against death or dismemberment in case of an airplane crash if you charged the cost of your ticket.

The cost of travel medical insurance varies widely. Check your existing policies before you buy additional coverage. Also, check to see if your medical insurance covers you for emergency medical evacuation: If you have to buy a one-way same-day ticket home and forfeit your nonrefundable round-trip ticket, you may be out big bucks.

LOST-LUGGAGE INSURANCE

On international flights (including U.S. portions of international trips), baggage coverage is limited to approximately $9.07 per pound, up to approximately $635 per checked bag. If you plan to check items more valuable than the standard liability, see if your valuables are covered by your homeowner's policy, get baggage insurance as part of your comprehensive travel-insurance package, or buy Travel Guard's "BagTrak" product. Don't buy insurance at the airport, as it's usually overpriced. Be sure to take any valuables or irreplaceable items with you in your carry-on luggage, as many valuables (including books, money, and electronics) aren't covered by airline policies.

If your luggage is lost, immediately file a lost-luggage claim at the airport, detailing the luggage contents. For most airlines, you must report delayed, damaged, or lost baggage within 4 hours of arrival. The airlines are required to deliver luggage, once found, directly to your house or destination free of charge. If your bag is delayed or lost, the airline may reimburse you for reasonable expenses, such as a toothbrush or a set of clothes, but the airline is under no legal obligation to do so. Once you've filed a complaint, persist in securing your reimbursement; there are no laws governing the length of time it takes for a carrier to reimburse you.

Many platinum and gold credit cards cover you as well. If you choose to purchase additional lost-luggage insurance, be sure not to buy more than you need. Buy in advance from the insurer or a trusted agent (prices will be much higher at the airport).

7 Health & Safety

STAYING HEALTHY

The only major modern hospitals in Belize are located in Belize City, although there are smaller hospitals or clinics in every major town or city. In general, you should bring any prescription drugs you will need with you, although there are reasonably well-stocked pharmacies in most major towns and tourist destinations.

Contact the **International Association for Medical Assistance to Travelers** (IAMAT; ℂ **716/754-4883,** or 416/652-0137 in Canada; www.iamat. org) for tips on travel and health concerns in the countries you're visiting, and lists of local, English-speaking doctors. The United States **Centers for Disease Control and Prevention** (ℂ **800/311-3435;** www.cdc.gov) provides up-to-date information on health hazards by region or country and offers tips on food safety.

GENERAL AVAILABILITY OF HEALTHCARE

There are two major hospitals in Belize City: **Belize Medical Associates,** 5791 St. Thomas Kings Park (ℂ **223-0302;** www.belizemedical. com), a modern, 24-hour private hospital, with emergency care and numerous private-practice physicians; and the city's main public hospital, the **Karl Heusner Memorial Hospital** on Princess Margaret Drive (ℂ **223-1548**), which is also open 24 hours and has a wide range of facilities and services.

Most of the other towns and major tourist destinations either have a small

hospital or a local health clinic, in addition to private-practice doctors. Any foreign consulate can provide a list of area doctors. If you get sick, consider asking your hotel concierge or front desk staff to recommend a local doctor—even his or her own. I've listed hospitals and emergency numbers under "Fast Facts" in the regional destination chapters.

BEFORE YOU GO

If you suffer from a chronic illness, consult your doctor before your departure. For conditions like epilepsy, diabetes, or heart problems, wear a **MedicAlert identification tag** (ℂ **888/633-4298;** www.medicalert. org), which will immediately alert doctors to your condition and give them access to your records through MedicAlert's 24-hour hot line.

Pack **prescription medications** in your carry-on luggage, and carry prescription medications in their original containers, with pharmacy labels—otherwise they won't make it through airport security. Also bring along copies of your prescriptions in case you lose your pills or run out. Carry the generic name of prescription medicines, in case a local pharmacist is unfamiliar with the brand name. Don't forget an extra pair of contact lenses or prescription glasses.

If you worry about getting sick away from home, consider purchasing **medical travel insurance** and carry your ID card in your purse or wallet. In most cases, your existing health plan will provide the coverage you need. See the section on insurance, above, for more information.

COMMON AILMENTS

TROPICAL ILLNESSES None of the major tropical illnesses are epidemic in Belize, and your chance of contracting any serious tropical disease in Belize is slim. However, several mosquito-borne illnesses are present, particularly malaria and dengue.

Malaria is found in Belize, but it is far from epidemic. It is most common along the coastal lowlands, as well as in some of the more remote southern inland communities. Malaria prophylaxes are available, but several have side effects, and others are of questionable effectiveness. Consult your doctor as to what is currently considered the best preventive treatment for malaria. Be sure to ask whether a recommended drug will cause you to be hypersensitive to the sun—it would be a shame to come down here for the beaches and then have to hide under an umbrella the whole time. Because malaria-carrying mosquitoes usually come out at night, you should do as much as possible to avoid being bitten after dark. If you are in a malarial area, wear long pants and long sleeves, use insect repellent, and either sleep under a mosquito net or burn mosquito coils (similar to incense but with a pesticide).

Of greater concern may be **dengue fever,** which has had periodic outbreaks in Latin America since the mid-1990s. Dengue fever is similar to malaria and is spread by an aggressive daytime mosquito. This mosquito seems to be most common in lowland urban areas, and Belize City and Dangriga have been the hardest hit cities in Belize. Dengue is also known as "bone-break fever," because it is usually accompanied by severe body aches. The first infection with dengue fever will make you very sick but should cause no serious damage.

However, a second infection with a different strain of the dengue virus can lead to internal hemorrhaging and may be life-threatening. As with malaria, your best protection is to not get bit. Use plenty of repellent, and wear light long-sleeved shirts and long pants, especially on bird-watching tours or nature hikes.

Many people are convinced that taking B-complex vitamins daily will help prevent mosquitoes from biting you. I don't think the American Medical Association has endorsed this idea yet, but I've run across it in enough places to think there may be something to it.

Belize has been relatively free from the **cholera** epidemic that has spread through much of Latin America in recent years. This is largely due to an extensive public-awareness campaign that has promoted good hygiene and increased sanitation. Your chances of contracting cholera while you're here are very slight.

DIETARY DISTRESS Even though the water around Belize is generally safe, particularly in most of the popular tourist destinations, and even though you've been careful to buy and drink only bottled water, you still may encounter some intestinal difficulties. Most of this is just due to tender northern stomachs coming into contact with slightly more aggressive Latin American intestinal flora. In extreme cases of diarrhea or intestinal discomfort, it's worth taking a stool sample to a lab for analysis. The results will usually pinpoint the amoebic or parasitic culprit, which can then be readily treated with available over-the-counter medicines.

Vegetarians will frequently find their options limited, but even a hard-core vegan should be able to find sustenance around Belize. If you have any strict dietary restrictions, be it for health, religious, or ethical reasons, be sure to check with your hotel in advance to ensure that you don't starve while on vacation.

BUGS, BITES & OTHER WILD-LIFE CONCERNS Although Belize has Africanized bees (the notorious "killer bees" of fact and fable) and several species of venomous snakes, your chances of being bitten are minimal, especially if you refrain from sticking your hands into hives or under rocks in the forest. If you know that you're allergic to bee stings, consult your doctor before traveling.

Snake sightings, much less snakebites, are very rare. Moreover, the majority of snakes in Belize are nonpoisonous. If you do encounter a snake, stay calm, don't make any sudden movements, and do not try to handle it. If you're bitten, seek medical attention immediately—don't try to bleed the area of the wound or suck the poison out. As recommended above, avoid sticking your hand under rocks, branches, and fallen trees.

Scorpions, black widow spiders, tarantulas, bullet ants, and other biting insects can all be found in Belize. In general, they are not nearly the danger or nuisance most visitors fear. (If you're a serious arachnophobe, stick to the beach resorts.) Watch where you stick your hands; in addition, you might want to shake out your clothes and shoes before putting them on to avoid any unpleasant and painful surprises.

In fact, the most prevalent and annoying biting insect you are likely to encounter, especially on the cayes and along the coast, are sandflies or "no-see-ems." These tiny biting bugs leave a raised and itchy welt, but otherwise are of no significant danger. Sandflies and no-see-ems tend to be most active around sunrise and sunset, or on overcast days. Your best protection is to use light long-sleeved shirts and long pants when these bugs are biting.

TROPICAL SUN Limit your exposure to the sun, especially during the first few days of your trip and, thereafter, from 11am to 2pm. Use a sunscreen with a high protection factor and apply it liberally. Remember that children need more protection than adults do.

Also, drink plenty of water and other fluids to avoid dehydration.

STAYING SAFE

Belize City itself has a somewhat deserved reputation for being a dangerous city for travelers, especially after dark, and especially in neighborhoods off the beaten path. See "Safety" in "Fast Facts: Belize City," for more details. That said, in general, if you use basic common sense and take standard precautions, you should have no problems staying safe in Belize.

Despite a seemingly relaxed and open drug culture at some of the popular beach and caye destinations, visitors should be very careful, as drugs, including marijuana, are strictly illegal, even in small quantities, and the laws are applied firmly to foreigners.

8 Specialized Travel Resources

TRAVELERS WITH DISABILITIES

Most disabilities shouldn't stop anyone from traveling. There are more options and resources out there than ever before. However, in general, there are relatively few handicapped-accessible buildings or transport vehicles in Belize. A very few hotels offer wheelchair-accessible accommodations, and there are no public buses, commuter airlines, or water taxis thus equipped. In short, it's relatively difficult for a person with disabilities to get around in Belize.

Many travel agencies offer customized tours and itineraries for travelers with disabilities. **Flying Wheels Travel** (© **507/451-5005;** www.flyingwheelstravel.com) offers escorted tours and cruises that emphasize sports and private tours in minivans with lifts. **Access-Able Travel Source** (© **303/232-2979;** www.access-able.com) offers extensive access information and advice for traveling around the world with disabilities. **Accessible Journeys** (© **800/846-4537** or 610/521-0339; www.disabilitytravel.com) caters specifically to slow walkers and wheelchair travelers and their families and friends

Organizations that offer assistance to disabled travelers include **Moss-Rehab** (www.mossresourcenet.org), which provides a library of accessible-travel resources online; **SATH (Society for Accessible Travel & Hospitality;** © **212/447-7284;** www.sath.org; annual membership fees: $45 adults, $30 seniors and students), which offers a wealth of travel resources for all types of disabilities and informed recommendations on destinations, access guides, travel agents, tour operators, vehicle rentals, and companion services; and the **American Foundation for the Blind** (© **800/232-5463;** www.afb.org), a referral resource for the blind or visually impaired that includes information on traveling with Seeing Eye dogs.

For more information specifically targeted to travelers with disabilities, check out the quarterly magazine **Emerging Horizons** ($14.95 per year, $19.95 outside the U.S.; www.emerginghorizons.com), and *Open World* magazine, published by SATH (see above; subscription: $13 per year, $21 outside the U.S.). **Mobility International USA** (©541/343-1284; www.miusa.org) publishes *A World of Options*, a 658-page book of resources, covering everything from biking trips to scuba outfitters, and a biannual newsletter, *Over the Rainbow.* Annual membership is $35.

GAY & LESBIAN TRAVELERS

Belize is a small, conservative, and provincial country where public displays of same-sex affection are rare and considered somewhat shocking. In fact, homosexual sodomy is still illegal and even occasionally prosecuted here. There is virtually no open gay or lesbian bar or club scene in Belize City or any of the major tourist destinations. Gay and lesbian travelers should choose their hotels with care, and be discreet in most public areas and situations.

The **International Gay and Lesbian Travel Association** (© **800/448-8550** or 954/776-2626; www.iglta.org) is the trade association for the gay and lesbian travel industry, and offers an online directory of gay- and lesbian-friendly travel businesses; go to their website and click on "Members."

Many agencies offer tours and travel itineraries specifically for gay and lesbian travelers. **Above and Beyond Tours** (© **800/397-2681;** www.abovebeyondtours.com) is the exclusive gay and lesbian tour operator for United Airlines. **Now, Voyager** (© **800/255-6951;** www.nowvoyager.com) is a well-known San Francisco–based gay-owned and operated travel service. **Olivia Cruises & Resorts** (© **800/631-6277;** www.olivia.com) charters entire resorts and ships for exclusive lesbian vacations and offers smaller group experiences for both gay and lesbian travelers.

The following travel guides are available at most travel bookstores and gay and lesbian bookstores, or you can order them from **Giovanni's Room** bookstore, 1145 Pine St., Philadelphia, PA 19107 (© **215/923-2960;** www.giovannisroom.com); *Out and About* (© **800/929-2268;** www.outandabout.com), which offers guidebooks and a newsletter ($20 per year;

10 issues) packed with solid information on the global gay and lesbian scene; *Spartacus International Gay Guide* (Bruno Gmünder Verlag; www.spartacusworld.com/gayguide) and *Odysseus: The International Gay Travel Planner* (Odysseus Enterprises Ltd.), both good, annual English-language guidebooks focused on gay men; the *Damron* guides (www.damron.com), with separate, annual books for gay men and lesbians; and *Gay Travel A to Z: The World of Gay & Lesbian Travel Options at Your Fingertips* by Marianne Ferrari (Ferrari International; Box 35575, Phoenix, AZ 85069), a very good gay and lesbian guidebook series.

SENIOR TRAVEL

Mention the fact that you're a senior when you make your travel reservations. Although all of the major U.S. airlines except America West have cancelled their senior discount and coupon book programs, many hotels still offer discounts for seniors. While this practice is not widespread in Belize, it never hurts to ask.

Members of **AARP** (formerly known as the American Association of Retired Persons), 601 E St. NW, Washington, DC 20049 (© **888/687-2277**; www.aarp.org), get discounts on hotels, airfares, and car rentals. AARP offers members a wide range of benefits, including *AARP: The Magazine* and a monthly newsletter. Anyone over 50 can join.

Many reliable agencies and organizations target the 50-plus market. **Elderhostel** (© **877/426-8056;** www.elderhostel.org) arranges study programs for those aged 55 and over (and a spouse or companion of any age) in the U.S. and in more than 80 countries around the world, including Belize. Most courses last between 1 and 3 weeks, and many include airfare, accommodations in university dormitories or modest inns, meals,

and tuition. **ElderTreks** (© **800/741-7956;** www.eldertreks.com) offers small-group tours to off-the-beaten-path or adventure-travel locations including Belize, restricted to travelers 50 and older. **Interhostel** (© **800/733-9753;** www.learn.unh.edu/interhostel), organized by the University of New Hampshire, also offers educational travel for seniors. On these escorted tours, the days are packed with seminars, lectures, and field trips, with sightseeing led by academic experts. Interhostel takes travelers 50 and over (with companions over 40), and offers 1- and 2-week trips, mostly international.

Recommended publications offering travel resources and discounts for seniors include: the quarterly magazine *Travel 50 & Beyond* (www.travel50andbeyond.com); *Travel Unlimited: Uncommon Adventures for the Mature Traveler* (Avalon); *101 Tips for Mature Travelers,* available from Grand Circle Travel (© **800/221-2610** or 617/350-7500; www.gct.com); and *Unbelievably Good Deals and Great Adventures That You Absolutely Can't Get Unless You're Over 50* (McGraw-Hill) by Joann Rattner Heilman.

Due to its temperate climate, stable government, low cost of living, and friendly retiree incentive program, Belize is popular with retirees from North America. The country's retirement and incentive program is run by the **Belize Tourism Board** (© **800/624-0286** in the U.S. and Canada, or 223-1913 in Belize). They have a website dedicated to the subject at **www.belizeretirement.org**.

FAMILY TRAVEL

If you have enough trouble getting your kids out of the house in the morning, dragging them thousands of miles away may seem like an insurmountable challenge. But family travel can be immensely rewarding, giving you new ways of seeing the world through smaller pairs of eyes.

Hotels in Belize often give discounts for children under 12 years old, and children under 3 or 4 years old are usually allowed to stay for free. Discounts for children and the cutoff ages vary according to hotel, but in general, don't assume that your kids can stay in your room for free.

Many hotels, particularly on the cayes, offer rooms equipped with kitchenettes or full kitchen facilities. These can be a real money-saver for those traveling with children, and I've listed many of these accommodations in the destination chapters that follow.

Hotels offering regular, dependable babysitting service are few and far between. If you will need babysitting, make sure your hotel offers it before you make your reservation.

To locate those accommodations, restaurants, and attractions that are particularly kid-friendly, refer to the "Kids" icon throughout this guide, and check out "The Best Destinations for Families" in chapter 1.

Familyhostel (© 800/733-9753; www.learn.unh.edu/familyhostel) takes the whole family, including kids ages 8 to 15, on moderately priced domestic and international learning vacations. Lectures, field trips, and sightseeing are guided by a team of academics.

Recommended family travel Internet sites include **Family Travel Forum** (www.familytravelforum.com), a comprehensive site that offers customized trip planning; **Family Travel Network** (www.familytravelnetwork.com), an award-winning site that offers travel features, deals, and tips; **Traveling Internationally with Your Kids** (www.travelwithyourkids.com), a comprehensive site offering sound advice for long-distance and international travel with children; and **Family Travel Files** (www.thefamilytravelfiles. com), which offers an online magazine and a directory of off-the-beaten-path tours and tour operators for families.

STUDENT TRAVEL

Arm yourself with an **International Student Identity Card (ISIC),** which offers substantial savings on rail passes, plane tickets, and entrance fees. It also provides you with basic health and life insurance and a 24-hour help line. The card is available for $22 from **STA Travel** (© 800/781-4040 in North America; www.sta.com), the biggest student travel agency in the world. If you're no longer a student but are still under 26, you can get an **International Youth Travel Card (IYTC)** for the same price from the same people, which entitles you to some discounts (but not on museum admissions). (*Note:* In 2002, STA Travel bought competitors **Council Travel** and **USIT Campus** after they went bankrupt. It's still operating some offices under the Council name, but it's owned by STA.)

Travel CUTS (© 800/667-2887 or 416/614-2887; www.travelcuts.com) offers similar services for both Canadians and U.S. residents. Irish students may prefer to turn to **USIT** (© 01/602-1600; www.usitnow.ie), an Ireland-based specialist in student, youth, and independent travel.

SINGLE TRAVELERS

Many people prefer traveling alone. Unfortunately, the solo traveler is often forced to pay a punishing "single supplement" charged by many resorts, cruise lines, and tours for the privilege of sleeping alone. To avoid it, you can agree to room with other single travelers on the trip, or you can find a compatible roommate before you go from one of the many roommate locator agencies.

Travel Buddies Singles Travel Club (© 800/998-9099; www.travelbuddiesworldwide.com), based in Canada, runs small, intimate, single-friendly group trips and will match you with a roommate free of charge.

TravelChums (℗ 212/787-2621; www.travelchums.com) is an Internet-only travel-companion matching service with elements of an online personals-type site, hosted by the respected New York–based Shaw Guides travel service.

Many reputable tour companies offer singles-only trips. **Backroads** (℗ 800/462-2848; www.backroads. com) offers more than 160 active-travel trips to 30 destinations worldwide, including Belize, Bali, and Morocco.

For more information, check out Eleanor Berman's latest edition of *Traveling Solo: Advice and Ideas for More Than 250 Great Vacations* (Globe Pequot), a guide with advice on traveling alone, whether on your own or on a group tour.

9 Planning Your Trip Online

SURFING FOR AIRFARES

The "big three" online travel agencies, **Expedia.com, Travelocity.com,** and **Orbitz.com,** sell most of the air tickets bought on the Internet. (Canadian travelers should try Expedia.ca and Travelocity.ca; U.K. residents can go for Expedia.co.uk and Opodo.co.uk.). Each has different business deals with the airlines and may offer different fares on the same flights, so it's wise to shop around. Expedia and Travelocity will also send you **e-mail notification** when a cheap fare becomes available to your favorite destination. Of the smaller travel agency websites, **Side-Step** (www.sidestep.com) has gotten the best reviews from Frommer's authors. It's a browser add-on that purports to "search 140 sites at once," but in reality only beats competitors' fares as often as other sites do.

Also remember to check **airline websites,** especially those for low-fare carriers such as Southwest, JetBlue, WestJet, or Ryanair, whose fares are often misreported or simply missing from travel agency websites. Even with major airlines, you can often shave a few bucks from a fare by booking directly through the airline and avoiding a travel agency's transaction fee. But you'll get these discounts only by **booking online:** Most airlines now offer online-only fares that even their phone agents know nothing about. For the websites of airlines that fly to and from Belize, go to "Getting There," later in this chapter.

Great **last-minute deals** are available through free weekly e-mail services provided directly by the airlines. Most of these are announced on Tuesday or Wednesday and must be purchased online. Most are only valid for travel that weekend, but some (such as Southwest's) can be booked weeks or months in advance. Sign up for weekly e-mail alerts at airline websites or check mega-sites that compile comprehensive lists of last-minute specials, such as **Smarter Living** (http://smarterliving.com). For last-minute trips, **site59.com** and **lastminutetravel.com** in the U.S. and **lastminute.com** in Europe often have better air-and-hotel package deals than the major-label sites. A website listing numerous bargain sites and airlines around the world is **www.itravelnet.com**.

If you're willing to give up some control over your flight details, use what is called an **"opaque" fare service** like **Priceline** (www.priceline.com; www.priceline.co.uk for Europeans) or its smaller competitor **Hotwire** (www.hotwire.com). Both offer rock-bottom prices in exchange for travel on a "mystery airline" at a mysterious time of day, often with a mysterious change of planes en route. The mystery airlines are all major, well-known carriers, and the airlines' routing computers have gotten a lot better than they used to be.

But your chances of getting a 6am or 11pm flight are pretty high. Hotwire tells you flight prices before you buy; Priceline usually has better deals than Hotwire, but you have to play their "name our price" game. If you're new at this, the helpful folks at **Bidding-ForTravel** (www.biddingfortravel. com) do a good job of demystifying Priceline's prices and strategies. Priceline and Hotwire are great for flights within North America and between the U.S. and Europe. But for flights to other parts of the world, consolidators will almost always beat their fares. *Note:* Priceline recently added non-opaque service to its roster. You now have the option to pick exact flights, times, and airlines from a list of offers—or opt to bid on opaque fares as before.

SURFING FOR HOTELS

Shopping online for hotels is generally done one of two ways: by booking through the hotel's own website or through an independent booking agency (or a fare-service agency like Priceline; see below). These Internet hotel agencies have multiplied in mind-boggling numbers of late, competing for the business of millions of consumers surfing for accommodations around the world. This competitiveness can be a boon to consumers who have the patience and time to shop and compare the online sites for good deals—but shop they must, for prices can vary considerably from site to site. And keep in mind that hotels at the top of a site's listing may be there for no other reason than that they paid money to get the placement.

Of the "big three" sites, **Expedia** offers a long list of special deals and "virtual tours" or photos of available rooms so you can see what you're paying for (a feature that helps counter the claims that the best rooms are often held back from bargain booking websites). **Travelocity** posts unvarnished customer reviews and ranks its properties according to the AAA rating system. Also reliable are **Hotels. com** and **Quikbook.com.** An excellent free program, **TravelAxe** (www. travelaxe.net), can help you search multiple hotel sites at once, even ones you may never have heard of—and conveniently lists the total price of the room, including the taxes and service charges. Another booking site, **Travel-web** (www.travelweb.com), is partly owned by the hotels it represents (including the Hilton, Hyatt, and Starwood chains) and is therefore plugged directly into the hotels' reservations systems—unlike independent online agencies, which have to fax or e-mail reservation requests to the hotel, a good portion of which get misplaced in the shuffle. More than once, travelers have arrived at the hotel, only to be told that they have no reservation. To be fair, many of the major sites are undergoing improvements in service and ease of use, and Expedia will soon be able to plug directly into the reservations systems of many hotel chains—none of which can be bad news for consumers. In the meantime, it's a good idea to **get a confirmation number** and **make a printout** of any online booking transaction.

In the opaque website category, **Priceline** and **Hotwire** are even better for hotels than for airfares; with both, you're allowed to pick the neighborhood and quality level of your hotel before offering up your money. Priceline's hotel product even covers Europe and Asia, though it's much better at getting luxury lodging for moderate prices than at finding anything at the bottom of the scale. On the down side, many hotels stick Priceline guests in their least desirable rooms. Be sure to go to the BiddingForTravel website (see above) before bidding on a hotel room on Priceline; it features a fairly up-to-date list of hotels that Priceline uses in major cities. For both Priceline and

Frommers.com: The Complete Travel Resource

For an excellent travel-planning resource, we highly recommend **Frommers.com** (www.frommers.com), voted Best Travel Site by *PC Magazine*. We're a little biased, of course, but we guarantee that you'll find the travel tips, reviews, monthly vacation giveaways, bookstore, and online-booking capabilities thoroughly indispensable. Among the special features are our popular **Destinations** section, where you'll get expert travel tips, hotel and dining recommendations, and advice on the sights to see for more than 3,500 destinations around the globe; the **Frommers.com Newsletter,** with the latest deals, travel trends, and money-saving secrets; our **Community** area featuring **Message Boards,** where Frommer's readers post queries and share advice (sometimes even our authors show up to answer questions); and our **Photo Center,** where you can post and share vacation tips. When your research is done, the **Online Reservations System** (www.frommers.com/book_a_trip) takes you to Frommer's preferred online partners for booking your vacation at affordable prices.

Hotwire, you pay upfront, and the fee is nonrefundable. *Note:* Some hotels do not provide loyalty program credits or points or other frequent-stay amenities when you book a room through opaque online services.

SURFING FOR RENTAL CARS

For booking rental cars online, the best deals are usually found at rental-car company websites, although all the major online travel agencies also offer rental-car reservations services. Priceline and Hotwire work well for rental cars, too; the only "mystery" is which major rental company you get, and for most travelers the difference between Avis, Budget, and Thrifty is negligible.

10 The 21st-Century Traveler

INTERNET ACCESS AWAY FROM HOME

Travelers have any number of ways to check their e-mail and access the Internet on the road. Of course, using your own laptop—or even a PDA (personal digital assistant) or electronic organizer with a modem—gives you the most flexibility. But even if you don't have a computer, you can still access your e-mail and your office computer from cybercafes.

WITHOUT YOUR OWN COMPUTER

It's hard nowadays to find a city that *doesn't* have a few cybercafes. Although there's no definitive directory for cybercafes—these are independent businesses, after all—two places to start looking are at **www.cyber captive.com** and **www.cybercafe. com**. In Belize, you'll readily find cybercafes in most major destinations. Many of the more upscale isolated nature lodges also provide for guest connectivity in one form or another. However, you should try to avoid **hotel business centers** unless you're willing to pay exorbitant rates.

Most major airports now have **Internet kiosks** scattered throughout their gates. These kiosks, which you'll also see in shopping malls, hotel lobbies, and tourist information offices around the world, give you basic Web access for a per-minute fee that's usually higher than cybercafe prices. The kiosks' clunkiness and high price mean they should be avoided whenever possible.

To retrieve your e-mail, ask your **Internet Service Provider (ISP)** if it has a Web-based interface tied to your existing e-mail account. If your ISP doesn't have such an interface, you can use the free **mail2web** service (www.mail2web.com) to view and reply to your home e-mail. For more flexibility, you may want to open a free, Web-based e-mail account with **Yahoo! Mail** (http://mail.yahoo.com) or **Fastmail** (www.fastmail.fm). (Microsoft's Hotmail is another popular option, but Hotmail has severe spam problems.) Your home ISP may be able to forward your e-mail to the Web-based account automatically.

If you need to access files on your office computer, look into a service called **GoToMyPC** (www.gotomypc.com). The service provides a Web-based interface for you to access and manipulate a distant PC from anywhere—even a cybercafe—provided your "target" PC is on and has an always-on connection to the Internet (such as with Road Runner cable). The service offers top-quality security, but if you're worried about hackers, use your own laptop rather than a cybercafe computer to access the GoToMyPC system.

WITH YOUR OWN COMPUTER

Wi-Fi (wireless fidelity) is the buzzword in computer access, and more and more hotels, cafes, and retailers are signing on as wireless "hot spots" from where you can get high-speed connection without cable wires, networking hardware, or a phone line (see below). At press time, there was no Wi-Fi service in Belize, but that could change at any moment. Additionally, you may find the following information useful while you're en route to Belize.

You can get a Wi-Fi connection one of several ways. Many laptops sold in the last year have built-in Wi-Fi capability (an 802.11b wireless Ethernet connection). Mac owners have their own networking technology, Apple AirPort. For those with older computers, an 802.11b/**Wi-Fi card** (around $50) can be plugged into your laptop. You sign up for wireless access service much as you do for cellphone service, through a plan offered by one of several commercial companies that have made wireless service available in airports, hotel lobbies, and coffee shops, primarily in the U.S. (followed by the U.K. and Japan). **Boingo** (www.boingo.com) and **Wayport** (www.wayport.com) have set up networks in airports and some high-class hotel lobbies. IPass providers (see below) also give you access to a few hundred wireless hotel lobby setups. Best of all, you don't need to be staying at the Four Seasons to use the hotel's network; just set yourself up on a nice couch in the lobby. The companies' pricing policies can be byzantine, with a variety of monthly, per-connection, and per-minute plans, but in general you pay around $30 a month for limited access—and as more and more companies jump on the wireless bandwagon, prices are likely to get even more competitive.

There are also places that provide free wireless networks in cities around the world. To locate these free hot spots, go to **www.personaltelco.net/index.cgi/WirelessCommunities**.

In addition, major Internet Service Providers (ISP) have local access numbers around the world, allowing you to go online by simply placing a local call. Check your ISP's website or call its toll-free number and ask how you can use your current account away from home, and how much it will cost.

Digital Photography on the Road

Many travelers are going digital these days when it comes to taking vacation photographs. Not only are digital cameras left relatively unscathed by airport X-rays, but with digital equipment you don't need to lug armloads of film with you as you travel. In fact, nowadays you don't even need to carry your laptop to download the day's images to make room for more. With a **media storage card,** sold by all major camera dealers, you can store hundreds of images in your camera. These "memory" cards come in different configurations—from memory sticks to flash cards to secure digital cards—and different storage capacities (the more megabytes of memory, the more images a card can hold) and range in price from $30 to over $200. (**Note:** Each camera model works with a specific type of card, so you'll need to determine which storage card is compatible with your camera.) When you get home, you can print the images out on your own color printer or take the storage card to a camera store, drugstore, or chain retailer. Or have the images developed online with a service like **Snapfish** (www.snapfish.com) for something like 25¢ a shot.

If you're traveling outside the reach of your ISP, the iPass network has dial-up numbers in most of the world's countries. You'll have to sign up with an iPass provider, who will then tell you how to set up your computer for your destination(s). For a list of iPass providers, go to www.ipass.com and click on "Individual Purchase." One solid provider is **i2roam** (© 866/ 811-6209 or 920/235-0475; www. i2roam.com).

Wherever you go, bring a connection kit of the right power and phone adapters, a spare phone cord, and a spare Ethernet network cable—or find out whether your hotel supplies them to guests. Electricity in Belize is 110-volt AC and most outlets are either two- or three-prong U.S.-style outlets.

USING A CELLPHONE

The three letters that define much of the world's **wireless capabilities** are GSM (Global System for Mobiles), a big, seamless network that makes for easy cross-border cellphone use throughout Europe and dozens of other countries worldwide. In the U.S.,

T-Mobile, AT&T Wireless, and Cingular use this quasi-universal system; in Canada, Microcell and some Rogers customers are GSM, and all Europeans and most Australians use GSM.

If your cellphone is on a GSM system, and you have a world-capable multiband phone such as many Sony Ericsson, Motorola, or Samsung models, you can make and receive calls across much of the globe, from Andorra to Uganda. Just call your wireless operator and ask for "international roaming" to be activated on your account. Unfortunately, per-minute charges can be high—anywhere from US$1.50 to US$3.50 in Belize.

That's why it's important to buy an "unlocked" world phone from the get-go. Many cellphone operators sell "locked" phones that restrict you from using any other removable computer memory phone chip (called a **SIM card**) card other than the ones they supply. Having an unlocked phone allows you to install a cheap, prepaid SIM card in Belize. (Show your phone to the salesperson; not all phones work on all networks.) You'll get a local phone number—and much, much lower calling rates. Getting an already locked phone unlocked can be a complicated process, but it can be done; just call your cellular operator and say you'll be going abroad for several months and want to use the phone with a local provider.

In Belize, with the recent bankruptcy of Intelco, Belize Telecommunications Limited (BTL) and their cellular division **DigiCell** (② 227-2017; www.digicell.bz) have a virtual monopoly on cellular service in Belize. Luckily, DigiCell does have affordable packages for SIM card activation. If you have an unlocked 1900MHz GSM phone, they sell local pre-paid SIM cards in various denominations, although the initial activation costs BZ$50 (US$25), including BZ$10 (US$5) of calls. Prepaid phone card rates for local calls range from BZ$.30 to BZ$.90 (US15¢–US45¢). You can buy these cards at their desk at the airport, or at any number of outlets around Belize.

For many, **renting** a phone is a good idea. (Even worldphone owners will have to rent new phones if they're traveling to non-GSM regions.) While you can rent a phone from any number of overseas sites, including kiosks at airports and at car-rental agencies, we suggest renting the phone before you leave home. That way you can give loved ones and business associates your new number, make sure the phone works, and take the phone wherever you go—especially helpful for overseas trips through several countries, where local phone-rental agencies often bill in local currency and may not let you take the phone to another country.

Phone rental isn't cheap. You'll usually pay US$40 to US$50 per week, plus airtime fees of at least a dollar a minute. The bottom line: Shop around.

Two good wireless rental companies are **In Touch USA** (② 800/872-7626; www.intouchglobal.com) and **Roadpost** (② 888/290-1606 or 905/272-5665; www.roadpost.com). Give them your itinerary, and they'll tell you what wireless products you need. In Touch will also, for free, advise you on whether your existing phone will work overseas; simply call ② 703/222-7161 between 9am and 4pm Eastern Standard Time, or go to http://intouchglobal.com/travel.htm.

For trips of more than a few weeks spent in one country, **buying a phone** becomes economically attractive, as many nations have cheap, no-questions-asked prepaid phone systems. Once you arrive at your destination, stop by a local cellphone shop and get the cheapest package; you'll probably pay less than US$100 for a phone and a starter calling card. Local calls may be as low as US15¢ per minute, and in many countries incoming calls are free.

True wilderness adventurers, or those heading to an isolated lodge on a deserted mid-ocean caye, should consider renting a **satellite phone** ("satphone"), which are different from cellphones in that they connect to satellites rather than ground-based towers. A satphone is more costly than a cellphone but works where there's no cellular signal and no towers. You can rent satellite phones from **Roadpost** (② 888/290-1606 or 905/272-5665; www.roadpost.com). In Touch USA (see above) offers a wider range of satphones but at higher rates. Per-minute call charges can be even cheaper than roaming charges with a regular cellphone, but the phone itself is more expensive (up to $150 a week), and depending on the service you choose, people calling you may incur high long-distance charges. At press time, satphones were amazingly expensive to buy, so don't even think about it.

Online Traveler's Toolbox

Veteran travelers usually carry some essential items to make their trips easier. Following is a selection of handy online tools to bookmark and use.

- **Airplane Seating and Food.** Find out which seats to reserve and which to avoid (and more) on all major domestic airlines at www.seatguru.com. And check out the type of meal (with photos) you'll likely be served on airlines around the world at www.airline meals.com.
- **Intellicast** (www.intellicast.com) and **Weather.com** (www.weather. com). Gives weather forecasts for all 50 states and for cities around the world.
- **Mapquest** (www.mapquest.com). This best of the mapping sites lets you choose a specific address or destination, and in seconds, it will return a map and detailed directions.
- **Time and Date** (www.timeanddate.com). See what time (and day) it is anywhere in the world.
- **Travel Warnings** (http://travel.state.gov/travel_warnings.html, www.fco.gov.uk/travel, www.voyage.gc.ca, www.dfat.gov.au/consular/ advice). These government sites offer health and safety information for American, British, Canadian, and Australian travelers.
- **Universal Currency Converter** (www.xe.com/ucc). See what your dollar or pound is worth in more than 100 other countries.
- **Visa ATM Locator** (www.visa.com), for locations of PLUS ATMs worldwide, or **MasterCard ATM Locator** (www.mastercard.com), for locations of Cirrus ATMs worldwide.

11 Getting There

BY PLANE

Belize City's **Philip S. W. Goldson International Airport** (BZE) is serviced by several airlines out of major U.S. hubs. **American Airlines** (© 800/433-7300 in the U.S. and Canada, or 223-2522 in Belize; www. aa.com) has two daily flights out of Miami; **Continental** (© 800/525-0280 in the U.S. and Canada, or 227-8309 in Belize; www.continental. com) has one daily flight from Houston; **Grupo Taca** (© 800/535-8780 in the U.S. and Canada, or 227-7363 in Belize; www.grupotaca.com) has daily flights from its hub in El Salvador, which can be reached by a variety of daily flights from different major U.S. cities; and **US Airways** (© 800/428-4322 in the U.S. and Canada, or 225-3589 in Belize City; www.usairways.com) has daily direct flights from Charlotte, North Carolina. Flying time from Miami is just over 2 hours.

There are no direct flights to Belize from Europe, Australia, New Zealand, mainland Asia, or Africa. From Canada, the only direct flights are seasonal winter charters. To get to Belize from any of these points of origin, you will have to connect through one of the cities listed above.

GETTING INTO TOWN FROM THE AIRPORT

The **Philip S. W. Goldson International Airport** is located 10 miles (16km) northwest of the city on the Northern Highway. There is no public bus service or shuttle van service. However, taxis are there to meet every flight. A taxi into downtown will cost BZ$35 to BZ$40 (US$18–US$20).

GETTING THROUGH THE AIRPORT

With the federalization of airport security, security procedures at U.S. airports are more stable and consistent than ever. Generally, you'll be fine if you arrive at the airport **1 hour** before a domestic flight and **2 hours** before an international flight; if you show up late, tell an airline employee and she'll probably whisk you to the front of the line.

Bring a **current, government-issued photo ID** such as a driver's license or passport. Keep your ID at the ready to show at check-in, the security checkpoint, and sometimes even the gate. (Children under 18 do not need government-issued photo IDs for domestic flights, but they do for international flights to most countries.)

The Transportation Security Administration (TSA) has phased out **gate check-in** at all U.S. airports. And **e-tickets** have made paper tickets nearly obsolete. Passengers with e-tickets can beat the ticket-counter lines by using airport **electronic kiosks** or even **online check-in** from your home computer. Online check-in involves logging on to your airlines' website, accessing your reservation, and printing out your boarding pass—and the airline may even offer you bonus miles to do so! If you're using a kiosk at the airport, bring the credit card you used to book the ticket or your frequent-flier card. Print out your boarding pass from the kiosk and simply proceed to the security checkpoint with your pass and a photo ID. If you're checking bags or looking to snag an exit-row seat, you will be able to do so using most airline kiosks. Even the smaller airlines are employing the kiosk system, but always call your airline to make sure these alternatives are available. **Curbside check-in** is also a good way to avoid lines, although a few airlines still ban curbside check-in; call before you go.

Security checkpoint lines are getting shorter, but some doozies remain. If you have trouble standing for long periods of time, tell an airline employee; the airline will provide a wheelchair. Speed up security by **not wearing metal objects** such as big belt buckles. If you've got metallic body parts, a note from your doctor can prevent a long chat with the security screeners. Keep in mind that only **ticketed passengers** are allowed past security, except for folks escorting disabled passengers or children.

Federalization has stabilized **what you can carry on** and **what you can't.** The general rule is that sharp things are out, nail clippers are okay, and food and beverages must be passed through the X-ray machine—but that security screeners can't make you drink from your coffee cup. Bring food in your carry-on rather than checking it, as explosive-detection machines used on checked luggage have been known to mistake food (especially chocolate, for some reason) for bombs. Travelers in the U.S. are allowed one carry-on bag, plus a "personal item" such as a purse, briefcase, or laptop bag. Carry-on hoarders can stuff all sorts of things into a laptop bag; as long as it has a laptop in it, it's still considered a personal item. The TSA has issued a list of restricted items; check its website at www.tsa. gov for details.

Airport screeners may decide that your checked luggage needs to be searched by hand. You can now purchase luggage locks that allow screeners to open and re-lock a checked bag if

Travel in the Age of Bankruptcy

Airlines go bankrupt, so protect yourself by **buying your tickets with a credit card,** as the Fair Credit Billing Act guarantees that you can get your money back from the credit card company if a travel supplier goes under (and if you request the refund within 60 days of the bankruptcy.) **Travel insurance** can also help, but make sure it covers against "carrier default" for your specific travel provider. And be aware that if a U.S. airline goes bust mid-trip, a 2001 federal law requires other carriers to take you to your destination (albeit on a space-available basis) for a fee of no more than $25, provided you rebook within 60 days of the cancellation.

hand-searching is necessary. Look for Travel Sentry certified locks at luggage or travel shops and Brookstone stores (you can buy them online at www.brookstone.com). These locks, approved by the TSA, can be opened by luggage inspectors with a special code or key. For more information on the locks, visit www.travelsentry.org. If you use something other than TSA-approved locks, your lock will be cut off your suitcase if a TSA agent needs to hand-search your luggage.

FLYING FOR LESS: TIPS FOR GETTING THE BEST AIRFARE

Passengers sharing the same airplane cabin rarely pay the same fare. Travelers who need to purchase tickets at the last minute, change your itinerary at a moment's notice, or fly one-way often get stuck paying the premium rate. Here are some ways to keep your airfare costs down.

- If you can book your ticket **long in advance, stay over Saturday night,** or **fly midweek** or **at less-trafficked hours,** you may pay a fraction of the full fare. If your schedule is flexible, say so, and ask if you can secure a cheaper fare by changing your flight plans.
- You can also save on airfares by keeping an eye out in local newspapers for **promotional specials** or **fare wars,** when airlines lower prices on their most popular routes. You rarely see fare wars

offered for peak travel times, but if you can travel in the off-months, you may snag a bargain.

- Search **the Internet** for cheap fares (see "Planning Your Trip Online," earlier in this chapter).
- **Consolidators,** also known as bucket shops, are great sources for international tickets, although they usually can't beat the Internet on fares within North America. Start by looking in Sunday newspaper travel sections; U.S. travelers should focus on the *New York Times, Los Angeles Times,* and *Miami Herald.* For less-developed destinations, small travel agents who cater to immigrant communities in large cities often have the best deals. ***Beware:*** Bucket shop tickets are usually nonrefundable or rigged with stiff cancellation penalties, often as high as 50% to 75% of the ticket price, and some put you on charter airlines, which may leave at inconvenient times and experience delays. **Exito Travel (℗ 800/655-4053** in the U.S. and Canada, or 970/482-3019; www.exitotravel.net) is a good Latin American specialist. Several other reliable consolidators are worldwide and available on the Net. **STA Travel** (www.sta.com) is now the world's leader in student travel, thanks to their purchase of Council Travel. It also offers good fares for travelers of all

Flying with Film & Video

Never pack film—developed or undeveloped—in checked bags, as the new, more powerful scanners in U.S. airports can fog film. The film you carry with you can be damaged by scanners as well. X-ray damage is cumulative; the faster the film, and the more times you put it through a scanner, the more likely the damage. Film under 800 ASA is usually safe for up to five scans. If you're taking your film through additional scans, U.S. regulations permit you to demand hand inspections. In international airports, you're at the mercy of airport officials. On international flights, store your film in transparent baggies, so you can remove it easily before you go through scanners. Keep in mind that airports are not the only places where your camera may be scanned: Highly trafficked attractions are X-raying visitors' bags with increasing frequency.

Most photo supply stores sell protective pouches designed to block damaging X-rays. The pouches fit both film and loaded cameras. They should protect your film in checked baggage, but they also may raise alarms and result in a hand inspection.

You'll have little to worry about if you are traveling with **digital cameras.** Unlike film, which is sensitive to light, the digital camera and storage cards are not affected by airport X-rays, according to Nikon. Still, if you plan to travel extensively, you may want to play it safe and hand-carry your digital equipment or ask that it be inspected by hand. See "Digital Photography on the Road" on p. 41.

Carry-on scanners will not damage **videotape** in video cameras, but the magnetic fields emitted by the walk-through security gateways and handheld inspection wands will. Always place your loaded camcorder on the screening conveyor belt or have it hand-inspected. Be sure your batteries are charged, as you may be required to turn the device on to ensure that it's what it appears to be.

ages. **ELTExpress (Flights.com;** ℂ **800/TRAV-800;** www.elt express.com) started in Europe and has excellent fares worldwide, but particularly to that continent. **FlyCheap** (ℂ **800/FLY-CHEAP;** www.1800flycheap.com) is owned by package-holiday megalith MyTravel and so has especially good access to fares for sunny destinations. **Air Tickets Direct** (ℂ **800/778-3447;** www.airtickets direct.com) is based in Montreal and leverages the currently weak Canadian dollar for low fares; it'll also book trips to places that U.S. travel agents won't touch, such as Cuba.

• Join **frequent-flier clubs.** Accrue enough miles, and you'll be rewarded with free flights and elite status. It's free, and you'll get the best choice of seats, faster response to phone inquiries, and prompter service if your luggage is stolen, if your flight is canceled or delayed, or if you want to change your seat. You don't need to fly to build frequent-flier miles—**frequent-flier credit cards** can provide thousands of miles for doing your everyday shopping.

BY CRUISE SHIP

It is estimated that as many as one million tourists may stop in Belize as part of a cruise itinerary this year. All ships call at Belize City and offer a wide range of day-tour options around the country. Cruise lines that offer stops in Belize as part of their Caribbean and Panama Canal routes include **Crystal Cruises** (© 800/804-1500; www.crystalcruises.com), **Celebrity Cruises** (© 800/722-5941; www.celebritycruises.com), **Holland America** (© 877/932-4259; www.hollandamerica.com), **Norwegian Cruise Lines** (© 800/327-7030; www.ncl.com), **Princess** (© 800/421-0522; www.princess.com), **Royal Caribbean** (© 800/398-9819; www.rccl.com), **Radisson Seven Seas Cruises** (© 877/505-5370; www.rssc.com), and **Seabourn Yachts** (© 800/929-9391; www.seabourn.com). It might pay off to book through a travel agency that specializes in cruises; these companies buy in bulk and stay on top of the latest specials and promotions. Try either the **Cruise Company** (© **800/289-5505;** www.thecruisecompany.com) or **World Wide Cruises** (© **800/882-9000;** www.wwcruises.com).

12 Packages for the Independent Traveler

Before you start your search for the lowest airfare, you may want to consider booking your flight as part of a travel package. A package tour is not the same thing as an escorted tour. Package tours are simply a way to buy the airfare, accommodations, and other elements of your trip (such as car rentals, airport transfers, and sometimes even activities) at the same time and often at discounted prices—kind of like one-stop shopping. Packages are sold in bulk to tour operators—who resell them to the public at a cost that usually undercuts standard rates.

One good source of package deals is the airlines themselves. Most major airlines offer air/land packages, including **American Airlines Vacations** (© 800/321-2121; www.aavacations.com), **Delta Vacations** (© 800/221-6666; www.deltavacations.com), **Continental Airlines Vacations** (© 800/301-3800; www.covacations.com), and **United Vacations** (© 888/854-3899; www.unitedvacations.com). Several big **online travel agencies**—Expedia, Travelocity, Orbitz, Site59, and Lastminute.com—also do a brisk business in packages. If you're unsure about the pedigree of a smaller packager, check with the Better Business Bureau in the city where the company is based, or go online at www.bbb.org. If a packager won't tell you where they're based, don't fly with them. **Latin American Vacations** (© 877/471-3876 in the U.S. and Canada; www.latinamericavacations.com) usually has very good deals on package tours. **Capricorn Travel** (© 207/730-6216 in the U.K.; www.capricorntravel.co.uk) is a popular and prominent package tour operator in Great Britain.

Travel packages are also listed in the travel section of your local Sunday newspaper. Or check ads in the national travel magazines such as *Budget Travel, Travel + Leisure, National Geographic Traveler,* and *Condé Nast Traveler.*

Package tours can vary by leaps and bounds. Some offer a better class of hotels than others. Some offer the same hotels for lower prices. Some offer flights on scheduled airlines, while others book charters. Some limit your choice of accommodations and travel days. You are often required to make a large payment upfront. On the plus side, packages can save you money, offering group prices but allowing for independent travel. Some even let you to add on a few guided excursions or escorted day trips (also at prices lower than if you booked them yourself) without booking an entirely escorted tour.

Before you invest in a package tour, get some answers. Ask about the **accommodations choices** and prices for each. Then look up the hotels' reviews in a Frommer's guide and check their rates online for your specific dates of travel. You'll also want to find out what **type of room** you get. If you need a certain type of room, ask for it; don't take whatever is thrown your way. Request a nonsmoking room, a quiet room, a room with a view, or whatever you fancy.

Finally, look for **hidden expenses.** Ask whether airport departure fees and taxes, for example, are included in the total cost.

13 Escorted Tours

Escorted tours are structured group tours, with a group leader. The price usually includes everything from airfare to hotels, meals, tours, admission costs, and local transportation.

Most escorted tours to Belize focus on adventure travel such as scuba diving, sport fishing, or bird-watching, or on cultural or educational topics, such as Mayan ruin tours. For more information on operators offering these types of package trips, see chapter 3.

Many people derive a certain ease and security from escorted trips. Escorted tours—whether by bus, motor coach, train, or boat—let travelers sit back and enjoy their trip without having to spend lots of time behind the wheel or worrying about details. You know your costs upfront, and there are few surprises. Escorted tours can take you to the maximum number of sights in the minimum amount of time with the least amount of hassle—you don't have to sweat over the plotting and planning of a vacation schedule. Escorted tours are particularly convenient for people with limited mobility. They can also be a great way to make new friends.

On the downside, an escorted tour often requires a big deposit upfront, and lodging and dining choices are predetermined. You'll get little opportunity for serendipitous interactions with locals. The tours can be jam-packed with activities, leaving little room for individual sightseeing, whim, or adventure—plus they also often focus only on the heavily touristed sites, so you miss out on the lesser-known gems.

Before you invest in an escorted tour, ask about the **cancellation policy:** Is a deposit required? Can they cancel the trip if they don't get enough people? Do you get a refund if they cancel? If *you* cancel? How late can you cancel if you are unable to go? When do you pay in full? *Note:* If you choose an escorted tour, think strongly about purchasing trip-cancellation insurance, especially if the tour operator asks you to pay upfront. See the section on "Travel Insurance," earlier in this chapter.

You'll also want to get a complete **schedule** of the trip to find out how much sightseeing is planned each day and whether enough time has been allotted for relaxing or wandering solo.

The **size** of the group is also important to know upfront. Generally, the smaller the group, the more flexible the itinerary, and the less time you'll spend waiting for people to get on and off the bus. Find out the **demographics** of the group as well. What is the age range? What is the gender breakdown? Is this mostly a trip for couples or singles?

Discuss what is included in the **price.** You may have to pay for transportation to and from the airport. A box lunch may be included in an excursion, but drinks might cost extra. Tips may not be included. Find out if you will be charged if you decide to opt out of certain activities or meals.

Find out about the **accommodations options,** including what **type of room** you get. If you plan to travel alone, you'll need to know if a **single supplement** will be charged and if the company can match you up with a roommate.

14 Getting Around Belize

BY CAR

There are only four major roads in Belize, the Northern, Western, Southern, and Hummingbird highways. All are just two-lane affairs, and all actually have speed bumps as they pass through various towns and villages along their way. Belize is only 70 or so miles (113km) wide, and around 250 miles (403km) long. Renting a car is an excellent way to see the country. If you are going to the Mountain Pine Ridge area of the Cayo District, or to the Gallon Jug or Lamanai areas, you will certainly need a four-wheel-drive vehicle. However, if you're just visiting the major towns and cities of San Ignacio, Placencia, Corozal, or Punta Gorda, you'll probably be fine in a standard sedan. That said, it's always nice to have the extra clearance and off-road ability of a four-wheel-drive vehicle, particularly useful in the rainy season (June through mid-Nov).

The major car-rental companies in Belize are **Avis Rent A Car** (© 225-2385; www.avis.com); **Budget Rent A Car** (© 223-2435; www.budget-belize.com); **Crystal Auto Rental** (© 800/777-7777 toll free in Belize, or 223-1600; www.crystal-belize.com); and **Thrifty Car Rental** (© 207-1271; www.thrifty.com). Prices run between BZ$120 (US$60) and BZ$200 (US$100) per day for a late-model compact car to a compact SUV, including insurance. Most of the rental companies above have a 25-year-old minumum age requirement for renting, although Crystal Auto

Rental will rent to 21- to 24-year-olds, but with twice the deductible.

Note: It's sometimes cheaper to reserve a car in your home country than to book when you arrive in Belize. If you know you'll be renting a car, it's always wise to reserve it well in advance for the high season, as the rental fleet still can't match demand.

There are so few roads in Belize that you will probably be fine using the maps in this book, or the free maps given out at the airport or by your car rental agency. If you really want a more detailed map, the Belize map produced by the **International Travel Maps and Books** (www.itmb.com) is a good option. You can get this and other maps at many bookstores and gift shops in Belize, if you are unable to buy it in advance either online or at a bookstore near you. Alternatively, you can pick up a copy of Emory King's regularly updated *Driver's Guide To Beautiful Belize* (Tropical Books, 2003).

Despite having been a British colony and current member of the Commonwealth, cars drive on the right-hand side of the road, just as in the United States. Seatbelt use is mandatory in Belize, and failure to comply carries a BZ$25 (US$13) fine. Gas stations can be found in all the major towns and tourist destinations. At press time, a gallon of premium gas cost BZ$8.25 (US$4.15).

Note: It should go without saying, but you cannot rent a car on or drive to any of the cayes or outer atolls.

Road Distances from Belize City

Belmopan	52 miles (84km)
Benque Viejo	81 miles (130km)
Corozal Town	86 miles (138km)
Dangriga	72 miles (116km)
Orange Walk Town	55 miles (90km)
Placencia	150 miles (241km)
Punta Gorda	205 miles (330km)
San Ignacio	72 miles (116km)

CAR RENTAL INSURANCE (LOSS/DAMAGE WAIVER OR COLLISION DAMAGE WAIVER)

If you hold a private auto insurance policy, you probably are covered in the U.S., but not abroad, for loss or damage to the car, and liability in case a passenger is injured. The credit card you used to rent the car also may provide some coverage.

Car rental insurance probably does not cover liability if you caused the accident. Check your own auto insurance policy, the rental company policy, and your credit card coverage for the extent of coverage: Is your destination covered? Are other drivers covered? How much liability is covered if a passenger is injured? (If you rely on your credit card for coverage, you may want to bring a second credit card with you, as damages may be charged to your card and you may find yourself stranded with no money.) Car-rental insurance costs about BZ$28 to BZ$40 (US$14–US$20) per day with an average deductible of around BZ$1,500 (US$750), although sometimes for a few extra dollars per day you can get no-fault, no-deductible coverage.

Before driving off with a rental car, be sure that you inspect the exterior and point out to the rental-company representative every tiny scratch, dent, tear, or any other damage.

BY PLANE

Traveling around Belize by commuter airlines is common, easy, and relatively economical. Two local commuter airlines serve all the major tourist destinations around Belize, as well as Tikal, Guatemala. The carriers are **Maya Island Air** (© 226-2435; www.maya airways.com) and **Tropic Air** (© 226-2012; www.tropicair.com). Both

Car Rental Tips

While it's preferable to use the coverage provided by your home auto-insurance policy or credit card, check carefully to see if the coverage really holds in Belize. Many policies exclude four-wheel-drive vehicles and off-road driving—but good portions of Belize can in fact be considered off-road. While it's possible at some car-rental agencies to waive the insurance charges, you will have to pay all damages before leaving the country if you're in an accident. If you do take the insurance, you can expect a deductible of between $750 and $1,500. At some agencies, you can buy additional insurance to lower the deductible.

operate out of both the **Philip S. W. Goldson International Airport** and the Belize City **Municipal Airport.** In both cases, flights are considerably less expensive into and out of the Municipal Airport. See the destination chapters for specific details on schedules and costs.

BY BUS

Belize has an extensive network of commuter buses serving all of the major villages and towns, and tourist destinations in the country. However, this system is used primarily by Belizeans. Moreover, the buses tend to be a bit antiquated, and some recent buy-outs and bankruptcies within the industry have left the future status of the local bus network a little bit in limbo. See the destination chapters for specific details on schedules and costs, and be sure to check in advance, or as soon as you arrive, as schedules (and costs) do change regularly.

BY BOAT

While it's possible to fly to a few of the outer cayes, most travel between mainland Belize and the cayes and atolls is done by high-speed launch. There are regular water taxis between Belize City and Ambergris Caye, Caye Caulker, Caye Chapel, and St. George's Caye. Hotels and resorts on the other islands all either have their own boats, or can arrange transport for you. See the destination chapters for specific details on how to get to the cayes and atolls by boat.

15 Tips on Accommodations

Belize has no truly large-scale resorts or hotels. While the Radisson and Best Western chains have one property each in Belize City, there are no other chain hotels in Belize. Upscale travelers looking for over-the-top luxury have very few options here. True budget hounds will also find slim pickings, especially in the beach and caye destinations. What the country does have is a host of intimate and interesting **small to midsize hotels** and **small resorts.** Most of these are quite comfortable and reasonably priced by most international standards, although nowhere near as inexpensive as neighboring Mexico.

Belize is a noted ecotourism and bird-watching destination, and there are small nature-oriented **ecolodges** across the inland portion of the country. These lodges offer opportunities to see wildlife (including sloths, monkeys, and hundreds of species of birds) and learn about tropical forests. They range from spartan facilities catering primarily to scientific researchers to luxury accommodations that are among the finest in the country.

At the more popular beach and resort destinations, specifically Ambergris Caye, Caye Caulker, and Placencia, you might want to look into a renting a **condo** or efficiency unit, especially for longer stays.

Throughout this book, I've separated hotel listings into several broad categories: **Very Expensive,** $150 and up; **Expensive,** $100 to $150; **Moderate,** $50 to $100; and **Inexpensive,** under $50 double. *Rates given in this book do not include the 7% hotel tax.* This tax will add to the cost of your room, so do factor it in.

One item you're likely to want to bring with you is a beach towel. Your hotel might not provide one at all, and even if it does, it might be awfully thin.

SAVING ON YOUR HOTEL ROOM

The **rack rate** is the maximum rate that a hotel charges for a room. Hardly anybody pays this price, however, except in high season or on holidays. To lower the cost of your room:

- **Ask about special rates or other discounts.** Always ask whether a

---

Tips Speak Up

If you are booking directly with your hotel (either by phone, fax, or e-mail), remember that most hotels are accustomed to paying as much as 20% in commission to agents and wholesalers. It never hurts to ask if it will pass some of that on to you. Don't be afraid to bargain.

---

room less expensive than the first one quoted is available, or whether any special rates apply to you. You may qualify for corporate, student, military, senior, or other discounts. Mention membership in AAA, AARP, frequent-flier programs, or trade unions, which may entitle you to special deals as well. Find out the hotel policy on children—do kids stay free in the room or is there a special rate?

- **Book online.** Many hotels offer Internet-only discounts, or supply rooms to Priceline, Hotwire, or Expedia at rates much lower than the ones you can get through the hotel itself. Shop around. And if you have special needs—a quiet room, a room with a view—call the hotel directly and make your needs known after you've booked online.
- **Remember the law of supply and demand.** Resort hotels are most crowded and therefore most expensive on weekends, so discounts are usually available for midweek stays. Business hotels in downtown locations are busiest during the week, so you can expect big discounts over the weekend. Many hotels have high-season and low-season prices, and booking the day after high season ends can mean big discounts.
- **Look into group or long-stay discounts.** If you come as part of a large group, you should be able to negotiate a bargain rate, since the hotel can then guarantee occupancy in a number of rooms.

Likewise, if you're planning a long stay (at least 5 days), you might qualify for a discount. As a general rule, expect 1 night free after a 7-night stay.

- **Avoid excess charges and hidden costs.** When you book a room, ask whether the hotel charges for parking. Use your own cellphone, pay phones, or prepaid phone cards instead of dialing direct from hotel phones, which usually have exorbitant rates. And don't be tempted by the room's minibar offerings: Most hotels charge through the nose for water, soda, and snacks. Finally, ask about local taxes and service charges, which can increase the cost of a room by 15% or more. If a hotel insists upon tacking on a surprise "energy surcharge" that wasn't mentioned at check-in, or a "resort fee" for amenities you didn't use, you can often make a case for getting it removed.
- Consider the pros and cons of **all-inclusive** resorts and hotels. Belize doesn't have any of the type of large-scale all-inclusive resorts that are so common throughout the rest of the Caribbean, but many of the beach and caye resorts do offer all-inclusive options. The term "all-inclusive" means different things at different hotels. Many all-inclusive hotels will include three meals daily, sports equipment, spa entry, and other amenities; others may include all or most drinks. In general, you'll save money going the all-inclusive way—as long as you use the

---

Tips **Dial E for Easy**

For quick directions on how to call Belize, see the "Telephone" listing in the "Fast Facts" section at the end of this chapter or check out the "Telephone Tips" on the inside front cover of the book.

---

amenities provided. The downside is that your choices are limited and you're stuck eating and playing in one place for the duration of your vacation.

- Carefully consider your hotel's meal plan. If you enjoy eating out and sampling the local cuisine, it makes sense to choose a **Continental Plan (CP),** which includes breakfast only, or a **European Plan (EP),** which doesn't include any meals and allows you maximum flexibility. If you're more interested in saving money, opt for a **Modified American Plan (MAP),** which includes breakfast and one meal, or the **American Plan (AP),** which includes three meals. If you must choose a MAP, see if you can get a free lunch at your hotel if you decide to do dinner out.

- **Book an efficiency.** A room with a kitchenette allows you to shop for groceries and cook your own meals. This is a big money saver, especially for families on long stays.

16 Tips on Dining

Belizean cuisine is a mix of Caribbean, Mexican, African, Spanish, and Mayan culinary influences. Belize's strongest suit is its **seafood.** Fresh fish, lobster, shrimp, and conch are widely available, especially at the beach and island destinations. **Rice and beans** are a major staple, served as an accompaniment to almost any main dish. Often the rice and beans are cooked together, with a touch of coconut milk. In addition to seafood, and particularly inland, Belizeans also eat a fair amount of meat and poultry, as well as some more **interesting game.** Some of the more interesting game items you might see on a Belizean menu include gibnut and iguana. The former is actually a large rodent, or paca, which is often called "The Queen's Rat," because Queen Elizabeth was served gibnut on a visit here. The latter is frequently called "bamboo chicken," and it does actually taste a bit like chicken.

If there was such a thing as a national dish, it just might be **stew** **chicken,** and its close cousins stew beef and stew fish. These dark stews get their color from a broad mix of spices.

Perhaps the most distinctive and ubiquitous element of Belizean cuisine and dining is **Marie Sharp's Hot Sauce.** Almost no restaurant or home dining table is complete without the requisite bottle of Marie Sharp's.

Belizeans tend to eat three meals a day, in similar fashion and hours to North Americans. Breakfasts tend to be served between 6:30am and 9am; lunch between noon and 2pm; and dinner between 6 and 10pm. Most meals and dining experiences are quite informal. In fact, there are only a few restaurants in the entire country that could be considered semi-formal, and none require a jacket or tie, although you could certainly wear them.

I have separated restaurant listings throughout this book into three price categories based on the average cost per person of a meal, including tax and service charge. The categories are

Expensive, more than $20; **Moderate,** $10 to $20; and **Inexpensive,** less than $10. (Note, however, that individual items in the listings—entrees, for instance—do not include the sales or service taxes.) Keep in mind that there is an additional 8% sales tax, and a 10% service charge is often added on.

Belizeans rarely tip, but that doesn't mean you shouldn't. If the service was particularly good and attentive, you should probably leave a little extra.

For a more detailed discussion of Belizean cuisine and dining, see "Conch Fritters, Stew Fish & Belikin: Belizean Food & Drink" in appendix A.

17 Suggested Itineraries

There's a lot to see and do in Belize. Nevertheless, many folks come for a solid week of rest and relaxation, fishing and/or scuba diving at a beach resort, without ever getting to know the rest of the country. The following itineraries are very rough outlines to help you structure your time and get a taste of some of the country's must-see destinations. Other options include specialized itineraries focused on a particular interest or activity. Bird-watchers could design an itinerary that visits a series of prime bird-watching sites. Cave enthusiasts and spelunkers could design a trip to take in a series of Belize's explored caves and cave adventures.

10 Days in Belize for a First-Time Visitor

Day 1   Arrive and grab a connecting flight down to **Placencia.** Settle in to your hotel and then walk around the tiny village, choosing your diner restaurant according to what most strikes your fancy.

Days 2 & 3   Spend some time on the beach, but also be sure to take a snorkel trip, as well as a bird- and nature-watching excursion up the **Monkey River.** More adventurous souls can take an ultralight tour or a day trip to **Cockscomb Wildlife Sanctuary.**

Day 4   Fly back to Belize City and head out to the Cayo District by land. Stop at the **Belize Zoo** or for a **cave tubing** adventure near Jaguar Paw en route. If there's time, take an afternoon tour to the ruins at **Xuanantunich.**

Day 5   Wake up very early and head to **Caracol,** visiting the **Río On Pools** and **Río Frío Cave** on your way back to San Ignacio.

Day 6   Take a day trip to **Tikal.**

Days 7, 8 & 9   Head for the cayes. Choose between **Caye Caulker,** with its intimate funky charm, or **Ambergris Caye,** with its wide choice of hotels, resorts, and restaurants. There are a whole range of activities and adventures available for you here. Or you could just chill in the sun and sand. Be sure to try the snorkel trip to **Hol Chan Marine Reserve** and **Shark-Ray Alley.**

Day 10   Return to **Belize City** in time for your international connection.

Mayan Ruins Highlights Tour

There are dozens of known Mayan ruins of varying sizes and in varying states of excavation and exploration. The following itinerary hits most of the major ruins, and even gives you some time on the cayes. You could easily add on a side trip to the Northern or Southern zones, where there are several lesser-known ruins.

Days 1 & 2   Arrive and head to the **Lamanai** ruins, staying right next door at the Lamanai Outpost Lodge. If there's time, stop at **Altun Ha** on your way here.

Days 3 & 4   Head over to **Chan Chich Lodge** and spend a couple of nights on the grounds, and in the central plaza of a minor Mayan ruin. Take a day trip to **La Milpa,** a large site with an active and ongoing excavation.

Days 5, 6 & 7   Head to the **Cayo District** and stay at one of the lodges in San Ignacio or on the way to Benque Viejo. Visit **Xunantunich, El Pilar, Chechem Ha,** and **Cahal Pech.**

Days 8 & 9   Take a 2-day/1-night trip to **Tikal.** Stay at one of the lodges right at the ruins. Return to Belize, and head to the Mountain Pine Ridge area.

Day 10   Visit **Caracol.**

Days 11, 12 & 13   Unwind for a few days on Ambergris Caye or Caye Caulker. If you didn't get to visit **Altun Ha** during your inland portion, you can easily visit by boat and minivan from here. You can also arrange boat trips to the ruins of **Chac Balam** in the **Bacalar Chico National Park & Marine Reserve** or to **Cerros.**

Day 14   Return to **Belize City** in time for your international connection.

18 Recommended Books, Films & Music

There's currently no great readable history of Belize out on the market. Emory King, a longtime expatriate and all-around local legend, has put out two volumes of a projected four-volume history of the country. *The Great Story Of Belize Vols. I & II* (Tropical Books) can be ordered online directly from King at www.emoryking.com. Both are thin books and lively reads.

To prepare your eyes for possible sensory overload when you arrive in Belize, you may want to get your hands on a copy of Thor Janson's coffee table book of photography, *Belize: Land of the Free by the Carib Sea* ★★ (Bowen and Bowen Ltd., 2000). This book is chock-full of beautiful photos of Belizean countryside, wildlife, local festivities, and people.

If the wildlife and nature pictures in Janson's book move you and leave you anxious to see the real deal, there are a slew of books dedicated to observing the wonders of Belizean flora and fauna. Probably the best all-around field guide for first-timers and armchair naturalists is Les Beletsky's *Belize and Northern Guatemala: The Ecotravellers' Wildlife Guide* ★★ (Natural World Academic Press, 1999), which features descriptions and color plates of most of the commonly spotted mammals, birds, amphibians, reptiles, fish, and corals.

Bird-watchers should check out *Birds of Belize* (University of Texas Press, 2004), by H. Lee Jones and Dana Gardener. If you love to look at fish, or just prefer catching them, you might try finding *Fishes of the Continental Waters of Belize* (University Press of Florida, 1997), by David W. Greenfield and Jamie E. Thomerson. This book is available only in hardcover and may be difficult to find in stores, so you might check your local library first.

If you plan to stalk a wild cat, *Jaguar: One Man's Struggle to Establish the World's First Jaguar Preserve* (Island Press, 2000), by Alan Rabinowitz, is an account of the author's time in Belize studying and working to protect jaguars. As you might have already guessed from the title, Rabinowitz was a major force in the establishment of the world's first jaguar sanctuary, the Cockscomb Basin jaguar preserve.

Maya-philes will want to have some reference material handy when visiting the many Belizean ruins. *The Maya* ★ (Thames and Hudson, 1999), by Michael D. Coe, is a good primer on the history of this advanced and enigmatic culture. To delve into the intricacy and reasoning behind the Mayan aesthetic legacy, check out Mary Ellen Miller's book, *Maya Art and Architecture* (Thames and Hudson, 1999). Anabel Ford has published a helpful pamphlet/book entitled *The Ancient Maya of Belize: Their Society and Sites* that is available at many bookstores and gift shops in Belize.

The history of Ix Chel Farm, one of Belize's most popular eco-attractions, is chronicled in *Sastun: My Apprenticeship with a Maya Healer* (HarperSanFrancisco, 1994), by Rosita Arvigo, who spent years studying with Mayan bush doctor Don Elijio Panti. If this book on Belizean natural medicine doesn't satisfy your shamanistic tendencies, don't fret; there are several additional books on the subject. Check out the newly expanded and revised book *One Hundred Healing Herbs Of Belize* (Lotus Press, 1993), by Michael Balick et al.; or *Rainforest Home Remedies: the Maya Way to Heal Your Body and Replenish Your Soul* (HarperSanFrancisco, 2001), by Rosita Arvigo and Nadine Epstein.

Belize, A Novel ✦ (Xlibris, 1999), by Carlos Ledson Miller, is a lively novel covering four decades of life in a family, beginning with the disastrous consequences and events of Hurricane Hattie.

If you're bringing along the little ones, or even if you're leaving them behind but want to share a little bit of Mayan culture with them, look for Pat Mora's beautifully illustrated book *The Night the Moon Fell: a Maya Myth* ✦ (Groundwood Books, 2000).

Or, for a handy little picture book filled with photographs of Mayan daily life, check out *Hands of the Maya: Villagers at Work and Play* by Rachel Crandell (Henry Holt & Company, 2002). Older children and adults alike should read **Beka Lamb** ✦ (Heinemann, 1986), by Zee Edgell; it is a beautiful coming-of-age story by one of Belize's most prolific modern fiction writers.

Although it wasn't a box-office hit, you might want to rent a copy of *The Mosquito Coast* (1986), which was filmed in Belize. Starring Harrison Ford and River Phoenix and directed by Peter Weir, the film is about an inventor who relocates his family to the Central American jungle. Another film shot in Belize is *Dogs of War* (1980), which features Christopher Walken.

If you're taken by the pounding beat and lyrical melodies of Belize's own Punta Rock (a kind of reggae-rock fusion based on Garífuna rhythms), you can find a limited selection online; or, better yet, pick up cassette tapes and CDs around Belize. Look out for Andy Palacio, Pen Cayetano, the Garífuna Kids, Travesia Band, Peter Flores (aka Titiman), and Chico Ramos. The best online source I've found for Belizean music is http://music.calabashmusic.com. I'd avoid the various vendors selling bootleg cassettes and CDs on the side of the road, since the quality can be sketchy, and the artists don't receive a dime.

FAST FACTS: Belize

American Express American Express Travel Services is represented in Belize by **Belize Global Travel Services Ltd.**, 41 Albert St. (© 227-7363), which can issue traveler's checks and replacement cards, and provide other standard services. They are open Monday through Friday from 8am to noon and 1 to 5pm, and on Saturday from 8am to noon. To report lost or stolen Amex traveler's checks within Belize, call the number above, or call collect to (C) **801/964-6665.**

Area Codes The country code is 501. Belize has a unified seven-digit phone numbering system, with no local area or city codes.

ATM Networks Belize does not yet have an extensive network of ATMs. In fact, as of press time, only Belize Bank ATMs were linked to international networks. Belize Bank has ATMs in Belize City, at the Goldson International Airport, San Pedro, Corozal, Belmopan, and Orange Walk.

Business Hours Banks are generally open Monday through Friday from 8am to 4:30pm. However, in many small towns, villages, and tourist destinations, bank hours may be limited. In very few instances, banks have begun opening on Saturday. Belizean businesses tend to be open Monday through Friday from 8am to noon, and from 1 to 5pm. Some businesses do not close for lunch, and some open on Saturday.

Climate See "When to Go," earlier in this chapter.

Currency See "Money," earlier in this chapter.

Driving Rules See "Getting Around Belize," earlier in this chapter.

Drugstores There are a handful of pharmacies around Belize City, and in most of the major towns and tourist destinations. Perhaps the best-stocked pharmacy in the country can be found at **Belize Medical Associates,** 5791 St. Thomas Kings Park ((C) **223-0303;** www.belize medical.com).

Electricity Electricity is 110-volt AC, and most outlets are either two- or three-prong U.S. style outlets.

Embassies & Consulates The **United States Embassy** is located in Belize City at 29 Gabourel Lane ((C) 227-7161). The **Canadian Honorary Consul** is also located in Belize City at 83 North Front St. ((C) 223-1060). The **British High Commission** is located in Belmopan, at Embassy Square ((C) 822-2146).

Emergencies In case of any emergency, dial (C) **90** from anywhere in Belize. This will connect you to the police. I've listed the various numbers for fire departments, ambulances, and hospitals in the "Fast Facts" sections throughout the book.

Etiquette & Customs There are no overarching etiquette or customs concerns for visitors to Belize. This is a hot, humid tropical country, and dress is uniformly light and casual, except in business situations, where a suit or dressy women's clothing is appropriate.

Holidays See "Calendar of Events," earlier in this chapter.

Internet Access Cybercafes are becoming more and more common in Belize. You'll find cybercafes in most of the major towns and tourist destinations. Rates run between BZ$4 (US$2) and BZ$10 (US$5) per hour. Alternatively, **BTL** ((C) **0800/112-4636;** www.btl.net), the state Internet monopoly, sells pre-paid cards in BZ$10 (US$5), BZ$25 (US$13), BZ$50 (US$25), and BZ$100 (US$50) denominations for connecting your laptop to the Web via a local phone call. Some knowledge of configuring your computer's dial-up connection is necessary, and be sure to factor in the phone call charge if calling from a hotel.

Language English is the official language of Belize, and it is almost universally spoken. However, Belize is a very polyglot country, and you are also likely to hear and come across Spanish, Creole, and Garífuna. For some help in communicating in Spanish and Creole, see appendix B.

Laundromats Most folks rely on their hotel's laundry and dry-cleaning services, although these can be expensive. Where they exist, I've listed laundromats and laundry options in the "Fast Facts" sections of the destination chapters.

Liquor Laws The legal drinking age in Belize is 18 years old, although it is often not enforced. Beer, wine, and liquor are all sold in most supermarkets and small convenience stores Monday through Saturday. No liquor is sold on Good Friday or Easter Sunday. On Election Day, no liquor can be sold until 6pm.

Lost & Found Be sure to tell all of your credit card companies the minute you discover your wallet has been lost or stolen and file a report at the nearest police precinct. Your credit card company or insurer may require a police report number or record of the loss. Most credit card companies have an emergency toll-free number to call if your card is lost or stolen; they may be able to wire you a cash advance immediately or deliver an emergency credit card in a day or two. Most credit cards have a number that you can call collect from anywhere in the world 24 hours printed on the back. It's a good idea to write this down and carry it someplace separate from your wallet or credit cards. **Visa**'s emergency number is ⓒ **800/847-2911** toll-free in the U.S., or call 410/581-9994 collect from Belize. **American Express** cardholders and traveler's check holders should call ⓒ **800/221-7282** toll-free in the U.S., or ⓒ 336/393-1111 collect from Belize. **MasterCard** holders should call ⓒ **800/307-7309** toll-free in the U.S., or 636/722-7111 collect from Belize.

If you need emergency cash over the weekend when all banks and American Express offices are closed, you can have money wired to you via **Western Union** (ⓒ **227-0014**; www.westernunion.com), although the service charges are substantial.

Identity theft or fraud are potential complications of losing your wallet, especially if you've lost your driver's license along with your cash and credit cards. Notify the major credit-reporting bureaus immediately; placing a fraud alert on your records may protect you against liability for criminal activity. The three major U.S. credit-reporting agencies are **Equifax** (ⓒ **800/766-0008**; www.equifax.com), **Experian** (ⓒ **888/397-3742**; www.experian.com), and **TransUnion** (ⓒ **800/680-7289**; www.transunion.com). Finally, if you've lost all forms of photo ID, call your airline and explain the situation; they might allow you to board the plane if you have a copy of your passport or birth certificate and a copy of the police report you've filed.

Mail Most hotels will post a letter for you, and there are post offices in the major towns. It costs BZ$.60 (US30¢) to send a letter to the United States, and BZ$.75 (US38¢) to send a letter to Europe. Postcards to the same destinations cost BZ$.30 (US15¢) and BZ$.40 (US20¢) respectively.

If your postal needs are urgent, or you want to send anything of value, several international courier and express-mail services have offices in

Belize City, including **DHL,** 38 New Rd. (© 223-4350; www.dhl.com); **FedEx,** 1 Mapp St. (© 224-5221; www.fedex.com); and **Mail Boxes Etc.,** 166 North Front St. (© 227-6046; www.mbe.com). All can arrange pick up and delivery services to any hotel in town, and sometimes in the different outlying districts. *Beware:* Despite what you may be told, packages sent overnight to U.S. addresses tend to take 3 to 4 days to reach their destination.

Maps Belize is such a small and undeveloped country that you'll probably be fine with the maps contained in this book. The **Belize Tourism Board** (www.travelbelize.org) can provide you with good maps to both the city and various destinations around the country at either their kiosk at the international airport, or at their main offices in the Central Bank Building on Gabourel Lane. Alternatively, most gift shops sell maps of the country.

Newspapers & Magazines Belize has no daily newspaper. There are four primary weeklies, *Amandala, The Reporter, Belize Times,* and *The Guardian.* All come out on Friday, and all are relatively similar in terms of content, although with some differing (and usually obvious) political leanings and loyalties. *Belize First* is a periodic book-style magazine aimed at the tourist trade.

Passports **For Residents of the United States:** Whether you're applying in person or by mail, you can download passport applications from the U.S. State Department website at **http://travel.state.gov/passport_services. html.** To find your regional passport office, either check the U.S. State Department website or call the **National Passport Information Center** toll-free number at © **877/487-2778** for automated information.

   For Residents of Canada: Passport applications are available at travel agencies throughout Canada or from the central **Passport Office,** Department of Foreign Affairs and International Trade, Ottawa, ON K1A 0G3 (© **800/567-6868;** www.ppt.gc.ca).

   For Residents of the United Kingdom: To pick up an application for a standard 10-year passport (5-year passport for children under 16), visit your nearest passport office, major post office, or travel agency; or contact the **United Kingdom Passport Service** at © **0870/521-0410** or search its website at www.ukpa.gov.uk.

   For Residents of Ireland: You can apply for a 10-year passport at the **Passport Office,** Setanta Centre, Molesworth Street, Dublin 2 (© **01/ 671-1633;** www.irlgov.ie/iveagh). Those under age 18 and over 65 must apply for a €12 3-year passport. You can also apply at 1A South Mall, Cork (© **021/272-525**) or at most main post offices.

   For Residents of Australia: You can pick up an application from your local post office or any branch of Passports Australia, but you must schedule an interview at the passport office to present your application materials. Call the **Australian Passport Information Service** at © **131-232,** or visit the government website at www.passports.gov.au.

   For Residents of New Zealand: You can pick up a passport application at any New Zealand Passports Office or download it from their website. Contact the **Passports Office** at © **0800/225-050** in New Zealand or 04/474-8100, or log on to www.passports.govt.nz.

Pets The importing of pets falls under the jurisdiction of the **Belize Agricultural Health Authority** (© **822-0197**; baha@btl.net). In general, pet owners must provide a valid rabies certificate and international veterinary certificate, and the pet must pass an on-the-spot examination by a quarantine officer to be allowed into the country. Fees are BZ$50 (US$25).

Photographic Needs While I recommend bringing as much film as you foresee needing and waiting until you return to develop it, you can buy and develop film at most popular tourist destinations (but it's more expensive in Belize).

Police The police in Belize are generally rather helpful; there is a dedicated tourism police force in Belize City. Dial © **90** or **911** in an emergency. You can also dial © **227-2222**.

Restrooms There are very few public restrooms in Belize. About the only ones I know of are located at the little cruise-ship tourist village on Fort Street in the Fort George section of Belize City. However, most hotels and restaurants will let tourists use their facilities.

Safety See "Health & Safety," earlier in this chapter.

Smoking Belize has yet to pass any no-smoking legislation, and aside from a handful of hotels that are entirely nonsmoking, few others have true nonsmoking rooms or floors. Similarly, many restaurants don't have a nonsmoking section. Luckily, so much dining in Belize is alfresco that this may not be a problem, especially if you can snag an upwind seat.

Taxes There is a US$35 departure tax that must be paid in cash at the airport upon departure. There is a 7% hotel tax added on to all hotel bills, and there is an 8% sales tax on all goods and services. A 10% service charge is sometimes added on to restaurant bills. Take this into account when deciding how much to tip.

Telephones Belize has a standardized seven-digit phone numbering system. There are no city or area codes to dial from within Belize; use the country code, 501 (not to be confused with the area code for the state of Arkansas), only when dialing a Belizean number from outside Belize.

For directory assistance: Dial © **113** if you're looking for a number inside Belize, and for numbers to all other countries dial © **114** or **115** and (for a charge) an operator will connect you to an international directory assistance operator.

For operator assistance: If you need operator assistance in making a call, dial © **114** or **115**, whether you're trying to make a local or an international call.

Toll-free numbers: Numbers beginning with 0800 and 800 within Belize country are toll-free, but calling a 1-800 number in the States from Belize is not toll-free. In fact, it costs the same as an overseas call.

See "Telephone Tips" on the inside front cover of this guide for additional information.

Time Zone Belize is on Central Standard Time, 6 hours behind Greenwich mean time. Belize does not observe daylight saving time.

Tipping Most Belizeans don't tip. Many restaurants add a 10% service charge. However, if the service is particularly good, or if the service charge is not included, tipping is appropriate.

Useful Phone Numbers **U.S. Department of State Travel Advisory,** © 202/647-5225 (manned 24 hr.). **U.S. Passport Agency,** © 202/647-0518. **U.S. Embassy in Belize,** © 227-7161. **Canadian Embassy in Belize,** © 223-1061. **U.K. Embassy in Belize,** © 822-2146. **U.S. Centers for Disease Control International Traveler's Hot Line,** © 404/332-4559. **Time, date, and temperature,** © 121.

Water The water in most major cities and tourist destinations in Belize is ostensibly safe to drink. However, many travelers react adversely to water in foreign countries, and it is probably best to drink bottled water throughout your visit to Belize.

3

The Active Vacation Planner

Belize is an ideal destination for the active and adventurous traveler. The range of available options is wide; the quality of the adventures and local tour operators is high; and the fact that the country is so compact allows you to mix and match. Whether your interests are scuba diving, snorkeling, fishing, sailing, spelunking, mountain biking, horseback riding, or bird-watching, Belize has some fabulous terrain and opportunities that are perfect for you. I hope that the following chapter, combined with the regional and destination chapters that follow it, will help you design and enjoy your dream vacation.

1 Organized Adventure Trips

Because many travelers have limited time and resources, organized ecotourism or adventure-travel packages are a popular and efficient way of combining several activities. Bird-watching, cave explorations, and hiking can be teamed with, say, visits to classical Mayan ruins and a few days on an outlying caye for snorkeling and diving, sea kayaking, and more bird-watching.

Traveling with a group on an organized trip has several advantages over traveling independently. Your accommodations and transportation are arranged, and most (if not all) of your meals are included in the cost of a package. If your tour operator has a reasonable amount of experience and a decent track record, you should proceed to each of your destinations quickly without the snags and long delays that those traveling on their own can occasionally face. You'll also have the opportunity to meet like-minded souls who are interested in nature and active sports. Of course, you'll pay more for the convenience of having all your arrangements handled in advance.

In the best cases, group size is kept small (10–20 people), and the tours are conducted by knowledgeable guides who are either naturalists or biologists. Be sure to ask about difficulty levels when you're choosing a tour. While most companies offer "soft adventure" packages that those in moderately good (but not phenomenal) shape can handle, others focus on more hard-core activities geared toward only seasoned athletes or adventure travelers.

NORTH AMERICAN–BASED TOUR OPERATORS

These agencies and operators specialize in well-organized and coordinated tours that cover your entire stay. Many travelers prefer to have everything arranged and confirmed before arriving in Belize, and this is a good idea for first-timers and during the high season. *Note:* Most of these operators are not cheap, with 10-day tours generally costing in the neighborhood of US$2,000 to US$3,000 per person, not including airfare to Belize.

Bike Hike Adventures (© 888/805-0061, or 416/534-7401; www.bikehike. com) is a Toronto-based company specializing in multiday, multi-adventure tours for small groups. They have several different offerings in Belize. Their 9-day tour will have you horseback riding, mountain biking, cave tubing, and either snorkeling or diving. The cost is around US$1,700 per person, not including airfare to Belize.

Journeys International (© **800/255-8735** or 734/665-4407; www.journeys-intl.com) offers small-group natural history and adventure packages around Belize, including trips especially geared towards families. Their 8-day family trip costs US$2,295 per adult and US$1,295 to US$1,695 per child. Airfare to Belize is extra.

International Expeditions ⚕ (© **800/633-4734** or 205/428-1700; www.ietravel.com) specializes in independent programs and 10-day natural history group tours. They run a regular 10-day tour to Belize and Tikal that takes in several of the major Mayan sites and tropical ecosystems. The cost is US$3,000 per person, not including airfare to Belize.

Island Expeditions ⚕⚕ (© **800/667-1630,** or 604/452-3212; www.islandexpeditions.com) runs various adventurous multiday land and sea tours around Belize. Kayaking the atolls is one of their strong suits, but they also combine this with inland adventures. These trips usually involve some island camping. Prices run around US$1,300 for a 7-day trip, not including airfare to Belize.

Sierra Club ⚕ (© **415/977-5522;** www.sierraclub.org) leads at least one 10-day trip each year to Belize, with a side trip to Guatemala. The focus is on birdwatching and natural history, but you'll also visit several Mayan ruins and spend some time on Caye Caulker. The cost is between US$2,000 and US$2,300 per person, not including airfare to Belize.

Slickrock Adventures ⚕⚕ (© **800/390-5715** or 435/259-4225; www.slickrock.com) offers a variety of multiday land and sea tours around Belize. They specialize in a sea-kayak and dive extravaganza based out of their camp and lodge on the private Long Caye in Glover's Reef atoll. A full week with these folks, not including international airfare, costs around US$1,895.

U.K.-BASED TOUR OPERATORS

Adventure Bound (© **0800/316-2717** or 01473/667-337; www.adventurebound.co.uk) is a good-value operator specializing in budget student and group travel. Their offerings in Belize focus on the entire Mundo Maya, and usually also take in parts of southern Mexico and Guatemala. These trips range in duration from 9 to 22 days.

Journey Latin America ⚕ (© **020/8747-3108;** www.journeylatinamerica.co.uk) is a large British operator specializing in Latin American travel. They don't currently offer any set trips to Belize, but they do design custom itineraries, and they often have excellent deals on airfare.

BELIZEAN TOUR OPERATORS

Because many U.S.-based companies subcontract portions of their tours to established Belizean companies, some travelers like to set up their tours directly with these companies, thereby cutting out the middleman. While that means these packages are often less expensive than those offered by U.S. companies, it doesn't mean they are cheap. You're still paying for the convenience of having all your arrangements handled for you.

There are scores of tour agencies in Belize City and at all of the major tourist destinations around the country that offer a plethora of adventure options. These agencies, and the tour desks at most hotels, can arrange everything from cave tubing to Mayan ruins tours to scuba diving and snorkeling. While it's generally quite easy to arrange most of these popular tours and adventures at the spur of the moment during your vacation, some are offered only when there are enough interested people or on set dates. If you have a very specialized tour or activity in mind, it pays to contact the hotel you will be staying at or a few of the companies listed here before you leave home to find out what they might be doing when you arrive.

Action Belize (✆ **888/383-6319** in the U.S., or 223-2987; www.action belize.com) is a Belize City–based operation offering a vast array of package and custom tour options. They are especially good with fishing itineraries, but can arrange most adventure options available in the country.

Discovery Expeditions (✆ **223-0748;** www.discoverybelize.com) is a long-standing and well-respected Belizean company with a broad offering of soft adventure and natural history tours.

Jaguar Adventures Tours & Travel ✆ (✆ **223-6025,** www.jaguarbelize. com) offers a variety of packaged natural history, adventure, and Mayan ruin tours. They will also put together custom itineraries for group, individual, and family travel.

S & L Travel & Tours ✆ (✆ **227-7593;** www.sltravelbelize.com) is one of the original tour operators in Belize, with more than 25 years experience in both adventure and regular tours. It's still one of the best, with excellent on-staff guides and a good working relationship with all the hotels.

2 Activities A to Z

Each listing in this section describes the best places to practice a particular sport or activity and lists tour operators and outfitters. If you want to focus on only one active sport during your time in Belize, these companies are your best bets for quality equipment and knowledgeable service.

Adventure activities by their very nature carry certain risks. In the past couple of years there have been several deaths and dozens of relatively minor injuries in activities ranging from mountain biking to white-water rafting to canopy tours. I try to list only the most reputable and safest of companies. However, if you ever have any doubt as to the safety of the guide, equipment, or activity, it's better to be safe than sorry. Moreover, know your limits and abilities and don't try to exceed them.

BIKING

Belize is not a major biking destination. In fact there are only four or so major paved roads in the entire country—primarily the Northern, Western, Southern and Hummingbird highways. Except for the wild Maya Mountains and Mountain Pine Ridge areas, the country is almost entirely flat. It would be possible to tour Belize's major mainland destinations on a touring bike, but the heat and humidity are often oppressive, and those few highways get plenty of traffic and generally don't have very wide shoulders.

The options are slightly more appealing for mountain bikers and off-track riders, however. Fat-tire explorations are relatively new and underexploited in Belize. Just about every major hotel in the Cayo District and Southern Zone has mountain bikes for guest use or rental, or can hook you up with a local rental company. These bikes are fine for day trips and non-technical riding. However, if you plan to do any serious biking you might consider bringing your own rig, as quality mountain bike rentals are still a rarity in Belize. The **Mountain Pine**

> **Tips A Bird-Watcher's Bible**
>
> Any serious bird-watcher will want to pick up a copy of *Birds of Belize* (University of Texas Press) by H. Lee Jones. Published in January 2004, this dedicated guide to the birds of Belize was long overdue. The book is wonderfully illustrated by Dana Gardener, and includes 574 species of birds.

Ridge Forest Reserve and the area around it wins my vote as the best place for mountain biking in Belize. The scenery's great, with primary and secondary forests, waterfalls, and plenty of trails. Truly hearty bikers can make it all the way to Caracol. See "Mountain Pine Ridge & Caracol" in chapter 8 for details.

A TOUR OPERATOR

Western Spirit Cycling Adventures (© 800/845-2453, or 435/259-8732 in the U.S. and Canada; www.westernspirit.com) offers a 6-day guided group tour around the Cayo District for US$1,925 per person. These folks are based out of Moab, Utah, and their off-road credentials are stellar.

BIRD-WATCHING

With more than 550 species of resident and migrant birds identified throughout the country, and a wide variety of ecosystems and habitats, Belize abounds with great bird-watching sites. Even amateur bird-watchers should have little trouble checking off upwards of 100 species in a week's worth of watching.

Lodges with the best bird-watching include **Chan Chich Lodge** (p. 115), near Gallon Jug; **Lamanai Outpost Lodge** (p. 114) on the New River Lagoon; **Chaa Creek** (p. 231), **duPlooy's** (p. 232), or any of the nature lodges outside of San Ignacio; **Blancaneaux Lodge** (p. 239) or any of the lodges in the Mountain Pine Ridge area; **Lighthouse Reef Resort** (p. 165) on the Lighthouse Reef Atoll, **Pook's Hill** (p. 217) outside of Belmopan, and **The Lodge at Big Falls** (p. 206) in the Toledo District.

Some of the best parks and reserves for serious birders are **Cockscomb Basin Forest Reserve,** for scarlet macaws and a host of primary forest dwellers; **Shipstern Nature Reserve,** for scores of different sea and shore birds; **Crooked Tree Wildlife Sanctuary,** for large varieties of wading birds, including the jabiru stork; **Man-O-War Caye,** a major nesting site for the magnificent frigate; **Caracol** Mayan ruins and the **Chiquibil National Park,** for many different resident and migratory forest species; **Half Moon Caye,** for the vast nesting flocks of red-footed boobies; and the **Río Bravo Conservation Area,** for ocellated turkeys and trogons.

Bird-watchers staying on Ambergris Caye should certainly head to the **Bacalar Chico National Park & Marine Preserve.**

TOUR OPERATORS

Field Guides (© 800/728-4953 or 512/263-7295; www.fieldguides.com) is a specialty bird-watching travel operator. Its 9-day trip to Belize costs US$3,100, not including airfare. The trip focuses on the western mainland sections of Belize, and the accommodations are quite comfortable. Group size is limited to 14 participants.

Sierra Club (© 415/977-5522; www.sierraclub.org) leads at least one 10-day trip each year to Belize, with a side trip to Guatemala. The focus is on bird-watching and natural history, but you'll also visit several Mayan ruins and Caye Caulker. The cost is between US$2,000 and US$2,300 per person, not including airfare to Belize.

Victor Emanuel Nature Tours 🎯🎯 (© **800/328-8368** or 512/328-5221 in the U.S.; www.ventbird.com) is a very well-respected small-group tour operator specializing in bird-watching trips, and a pioneer of the genre in Belize. These tours focus primarily on the area around Chan Chich Lodge and Crooked Tree Wildlife Sanctuary, two of the country's prime bird-watching destinations. Their 9-day trip costs US$3,095 and is limited to 10 participants.

Wings 🎯 (© **888/293-6443** or 520/320-9868; www.wingsbirds.com) is also a specialty bird-watching travel operator with more than 28 years of experience in the field. Its 7-day Belize trip is also based at the remote and luxurious Chan Chich Lodge and costs around US$3,150, not including airfare. Trip size is usually between 6 and 14 people.

A BELIZEAN BIRDING COMPANY
In addition to the operator listed below, the **Belize Audubon Society** (© **223-4988;** www.belizeaudubon.org) is an active and informative organization worth contacting.

Paradise Expeditions 🎯 (© **824-2772;** www.birdinginbelize.com) specializes in bird-watching trips and adventures. Based in San Ignacio in the Cayo District, these folks offer small-group package tours and personalized guided and unguided itineraries to all of the major birding spots and lodges in Belize and western Tikal. A 7-day/6-night tour costs around US$1,200 per person.

CAVING
Belize is an excellent destination for spelunking. Whether you're passionate about cave exploration or you've never been underground in the dark, you should not leave Belize without venturing into one or more of its vast cave systems. The ancient Maya believed caves to be a mystical portal between the world of the living and the underworld of spirits and the dead. They called this mystical realm Xibalba. In almost every explored cave in Belize, some evidence of use by the Mayans has been uncovered. Fire pits, campsites, burial mounds, and ritual altars have all been found. Numerous pieces of pottery as well as skeletons, bones, and religious artifacts have also been encountered.

The aptly named **Caves Branch region,** just outside of Belmopan, is a prime (and certainly the most popular place) to go caving. The cave tube trips here, including the spectacular **Crystal Cave,** are excellent introductions to the underworld. There are also several great caves for exploring in the Cayo District, including the **Barton Creek Cave** and **Chechem Ha.** Perhaps the most adventurous and rewarding cave to explore is **Actun Tunichil Muknal.** For more information, see chapter 8.

TOUR OPERATORS
The premier cave adventure operator in Belize is **Ian Anderson's Caves Branch** 🎯🎯, Hummingbird Highway, Mile Marker 41½ (© **822-2800;** www.cavesbranch.com). The company has a lovely forested setting at a far upstream entrance to the Caves Branch River, and a wide variety of cave tours and explorations is offered; most full-day trips run from US$75 to US$105.

Jaguar Paw 🎯🎯, Western Highway, Mile Marker 37 (© **888/775-8645** or 820-2023; www.jaguarpaw.com), is a very comfortable lodge located at the prime entry and takeout point for the popular cave tubing tours. They are also basically at the entrance to the Crystal Cave, and the owners here have been instrumental in efforts to explore and preserve this amazing cave. A half-day at Crystal Cave or cave tubing costs US$45, a full day US$75.

CRUISING

Belize is blessed with some wonderful cruising grounds. Steady yet gentle trade winds, combined with protected internal passages and innumerable isolated islands and anchorages, make this a perfect place to explore by boat. Cruising options in Belize range from bareboat charters of modern catamarans and monohulls to funky converted Belizean fishing sloops pressed into the snorkel and sunset cruise market. Belize is also a major port of call for many Caribbean cruise lines. For information on the major cruise lines that ply the waters of Belize and make Belize City a port of call, see "By Cruise Ship" under "Getting There" in chapter 2.

Virtually any section of Belize's coast and its outlying cayes and barrier reef are perfect for sailing. At nearly every beach or dive destination, it is possible to get out on the water for a cruise. Given the choice, I'd say the more remote and isolated cayes of southern Belize are the best places to venture out to sea. The two operations listed below are by far your best bets for bareboat cruising.

YACHT OUTFITTERS

The Moorings ⚓ (℗ 888/952-8401 in the U.S. and Canada, or 523-3351; www.moorings.com) has bases in Placencia and on Ambergris Caye. They offer bareboat and crewed charters on both monohull and catamaran yachts. Depending on the season and boat size, rates for a bareboat run between US$2,000 and US$7,000 per week, and crewed charters cost from US$3,000 to US$8,000 per week.

Also with bases in both Placencia and Ambergris Caye, **TMM** ⚓ (℗ 800/633-0155 in the U.S., or 226-3026; www.sailtmm.com) offers mostly catamarans, and again your option is for either bareboat or crewed chartering. Rates for a bareboat run between US$2,000 and US$8,000 per week, depending on the season and the size of the boat; add about US$100 to US$150 per day for a captain, and another US$100 per day for a cook.

FISHING

Any angler worth his or her saltwater fly rod already knows that Belize is a world-class fishing destination. Fly-fishing on the flats for permit, tarpon, and bonefish is the main draw, and they are excellent all up and down the coast and on the saltwater flats the length of the barrier reef. Bonefish and permit fishing is good year-round, while tarpon are best sought from April to November, with July and August being the best months. The Southern Zone around Punta Gorda and Placencia is prime fishing grounds for permit, while the coastal mangroves and rivers are excellent spots to land lively snook.

Just beyond the barrier reef, anglers can land snapper, barracuda, jack, and grouper, while those who head further out can stalk sailfish and marlin.

Action Belize (℗ 888/383-6319 in the U.S., or 223-2987; www.action belize.com) is a Belize City–based operation offering a vast array of package and custom tour options. They are especially good with fishing itineraries, and even have their own boats and captains. A 7-day/6-night trip with 4 full days of fishing costs US$1,098 per person, double occupancy. A full day of fishing costs US$115 per person for cruise-ship passengers and independent travelers.

FISHING LODGES

The name of **Blue Marlin Lodge** ⚓ (South Water Caye; ℗ 800/798-1558 in the U.S., or 522-2243; www.bluemarlinlodge.com) says it all or, at least, it says a lot. These folks have good facilities for both flats and offshore fishing, as well as a lovely location on a small and isolated caye. See p. 177 for a complete review.

El Pescador South ★★ (Punta Gorda; © **800/242-2017** in the U.S., or 722-0050; www.elpescadorpg.com) is a new luxury lodge that's setting the standard for fishing (and comfort) down in the Southern Zone. They also have a sister lodge on North Ambergris Caye. See p. 205 for more details.

Turneffe Flats ★★ (Turneffe Island Atoll; © **800/815-1304,** or 605/578-1304 in the U.S.; www.tflats.com) is a beautiful dedicated fishing lodge with a privileged position right on the ring of the Turneffe Island Atoll and its extensive mid-ocean lagoon and open-water flats. See p. 164 for a complete review.

GOLF

Belize is not one of the world's great golfing destinations, but it does boast one beautiful oceanfront course that takes up almost an entire private little island. While relatively flat, the par-72 course features plenty of water and sand hazards, and an unmatched number of oceanfront holes. The steady trade winds often come into play here, so be prepared. However, there are never any crowds or waits on the course.

Caye Chapel Resort ★★ (© **226-8250**; www.belizegolf.cc) has luxury condominium units and private villas, as well as a marina, a pool, and tennis facilities. Rates run between BZ$460 and BZ$1,000 (US$230–US$500) per person per day, with all meals and unlimited golf included. Players not staying on the island can play with an advance reservation. Rates for a full day of unlimited golfing, including carts, club rental, and use of the resort's pool and beach area cost BZ$400 (US$200) per person.

HORSEBACK RIDING

Although Belize is very sparsely populated, and much of it is ideal for exploring on the back of a horse, this is still a rather undeveloped area of adventure travel here. The best place to grab a mount and explore is the Mountain Pine Ridge Forest Reserve, and the best outfitter to tour with here is **Mountain Equestrian Trails** (© **820-4041**; www.metbelize.com). A half-day trip (including lunch) costs US$60 per person, a full day US$85. Even if you're not staying here, most of the lodges in this area also offer horseback riding. For more information on riding in this region, see chapter 8.

A MONTANA COWBOY IN CENTRAL BELIZE

Banana Bank Lodge ★, Western Highway, Mile Marker 47½ (© **820-2020;** www.bananabank.com), is a rustic riverside lodge owned by a former cowboy from Montana. Horseback riding is a major attraction here, and a horse lover and avid rider would feel right at home. For more information on this hotel, see p. 216.

KAYAKING & CANOEING

Belize lacks the major white water necessary for serious rapid enthusiasts. Most of the rivers here are rated Class I, II or III. Still, many of these rivers are quite well suited for gentle canoe explorations and less technical kayaking adventures. The Macal and Mopan rivers in the Cayo District are perfect for these types of adventures, and most of the hotels and tour operators in the area offer a range of these types of tours. See chapter 8 for more information.

However, sea kayaking in Belize is excellent. The relatively calm waters and protection provided by the barrier reef and mid-ocean atoll lagoons, combined with a string of small, relatively closely spread cayes, make this a perfect place to tour and explore by sea kayak. **Glover's Reef Atoll** is probably the most popular and best place for a sea kayak adventure; see "Dangriga" in chapter 7 for more information.

OUTFITTERS

Island Expeditions ☆☆ (© **800/667-1630** or 604/452-3212 in the U.S.; www. islandexpeditions.com) run various multiday kayaking tours to the outer atolls, Glover's Reef Atoll, and the coral islands along the southern stretch of Belize's barrier reef. An 8-day/7-night excursion runs US$1,400 to US$1,800.

Slickrock Adventures ☆☆ (© **800/390-5715** or 435/259-4225 in the U.S.; www.slickrock.com) specializes in multiday kayak tours around Glover's Reef Atoll, and they even have their own, rustically comfortable base camp and lodge on a private caye here. An 8-day/7-night trip costs US$1,895 per person.

SCUBA DIVING & SNORKELING

Simply put, Belize is one of the world's top spots for scuba diving and snorkeling. I've said it before, and I'll probably say it again, but Belize has the second longest barrier reef in the world, as well as three spectacular mid-ocean atolls. The diving and snorkeling all along this reef and at the atolls is world-class. In general, the reef is in very healthy shape and the water quality and visibility are consistently excellent.

Amateur or casual divers and snorkelers should really be happy almost anywhere in Belize, and every major beach and island destination has easy access to some fabulous dive and snorkel sites. Truly dedicated divers will probably want to head to one of the outer atolls. **Glover's Reef, Turneffe Island,** and **Lighthouse Reef atolls** all offer outstanding diving opportunities. The Blue Hole and several other sites on Lighthouse Reef Atoll make it the top choice for scuba divers, amongst a crowded field. **Shark-Ray Alley** and **Hol Chan Marine Reserve** are two deservedly popular snorkel spots just off of Ambergris Caye, although over-popularity and overcrowding are threatening the experience there. And finally, only just becoming known to cognoscenti, the **Gladden Spit** area, off the coast from Placencia, is one of the top spots on the planet to snorkel or dive with giant whale sharks.

There are several dedicated dive resorts around Belize. Another option for hard-core divers is to stay on a live-aboard dive boat. These midsize vessels usually carry from between 10 to 20 divers in private staterooms. The boats feature fully equipped dive operations and a host of amenities. One of the advantages here is that you get to hit several of the top reef and atoll sites in a weeklong vacation.

There is information on snorkeling, scuba diving, and local operators in each of the destination chapters that follow. The fact is that almost every beach and island resort hotel in Belize, as well as most in Belize City, either has its own dive shop and operation, or can hook you up with a local crew. Below are listed a couple of live-aboard operations, and a couple of the best dedicated dive resorts in Belize.

Note: While many of the beach and island hotels and all of the dive shops in Belize have snorkeling and diving gear for rent, you might consider bringing your own. If nothing else, bring your own mask. A good, properly fitting mask is the single most important factor in predicting the success of a dive outing. Faces come in all sizes and shapes, and I really recommend finding a mask that

---

When a Package Isn't a Deal

While it's often tempting to purchase all-inclusive dive packages before coming to Belize, this limits your flexibility. For example, if the weather and water are really rough, you're already committed, even though you might prefer taking an inland tour to a Mayan ruin instead of a rough dive.

Tips Capturing It on Film

If you don't own your own underwater camera or video camera casing, you might want to bring one or more cheap, disposable waterproof or underwater cameras. Alternatively, many dive shops will rent professional or semi-professional underwater still and video cameras for about US$20 to US$35 per day.

---

gives you a perfect fit. Fins are a lesser concern, as most operators should have fins to fit your feet. As for your own snorkel, well, in this day and age, I think you should want your own. If you plan on going out snorkeling or diving more than a few times, the investment will more than pay for itself.

LIVE-ADOARD DIVE DOATS

Aggressor Fleet ★★ (© 800/348-2628 or 985/385-2628 in the U.S.; www. aggressor.com) has the 110-foot (34m) *Aggressor III,* a comfortable dive boat with deluxe staterooms. Rates cost around US$2,000 to US$2,400 per week.

Peter Hughes Diving ★★ (© 800/932-6237 or 305/669-9391 in the U.S.; www.peterhughes.com) runs the *Sundancer II,* a 138-foot (42m) yacht with 10 staterooms. Rates range from US$1,600 to US$2,100 per week.

Tip: Both boats are very comfortable and well equipped, with full dive and photo lab operations, rental equipment, attentive service, and plenty of deck and lounge areas. Each boat has one or two master staterooms with a queen-size bed for couples. The *Aggressor III* features TVs and VCRs in every stateroom, and even has a hot tub on the upper deck. However, I find the two separate single beds in the standard staterooms on the *Sundancer* to be more comfortable than the staggered, quasi-bunk bed arrangement on the *Aggressor III.*

DIVING RESORTS & OUTFITTERS

In addition to the folks listed below, check the listings at specific beach and island destinations in the regional chapters.

Hamanasi ★★ (© 877/552-3483 in the U.S., or 520-7073; www.hamanasi. com) is an excellent new dive resort located on a beautiful patch of beach south of Hopkins Village. The location grants good access to a wide range of dive sites, including the outer atolls. See p. 182 for a complete review.

Lighthouse Reef Resort ★★ (© 800/423-3114 or 863/439-6600 in the U.S.; www.scuba-dive-belize.com) is blessed with the prime location right on one of Belize's top dive destinations—Lighthouse Reef Atoll. What's more, the resort runs an excellent dive operation. See p. 165 for more information.

The Inn at Robert's Grove ★★ (© 800/565-9757 in the U.S., or 523-3565 in Belize; www.robertsgrove.com) is a pioneering luxury resort in Placencia with its own marina, an excellent dive operation, and two private cayes. See p. 192 for more details.

SPAS & RETREATS

So far the trend towards destination spas and yoga or tai chi retreats hasn't fully caught on in Belize. In fact, at press time, there were no true dedicated destination spas or retreats. However, I don't think it will be long before someone cashes in on the craze. In the meantime, the two places listed below do a pretty good job at what they do.

Primarily a nature lodge and ecotourism resort, **Chaa Creek** ★★, off the road to Benque Viejo in the Cayo District (© **824-2037;** www.chaacreek. com), does have a very nice full-service day spa offering a wide range of body and skin treatments. Multiday packages are available and can be designed to give the feel of a full destination spa experience. See p. 231 for a complete review of the resort.

Maruba Resort Jungle Spa ★★ (© **800/627-8227** in the U.S., 322-2199; www.maruba-spa.com) is a true spa, offering a wide range of treatments and packages. Their various massages, mud and exfoliating treatments, and the general sense of sensual overload and pampering, are all top-notch. However, they don't really offer any of the classes or active exercise programs that you would expect at a destination spa. For more information, see "The Old Northern Highway: Altun Ha & Maruba Resort Jungle Spa" in chapter 5.

WINDSURFING

The steady trade winds and calm waters make Belize a great place for beginning and intermediate windsurfers. More advanced boardsailers would probably want more extreme conditions, but this is a great place to learn and perfect your skills. That said, this is still a relatively minor activity in Belize. Your best bet for windsurfing is **Ambergris Caye,** and the folks at **Sail Sports Belize** (© **226-4488;** www.sail sportsbelize.com) are the best source for equipment rental and advice. They even offer classes and rent equipment for the new adventure craze of kite surfing.

3 Belize's Top Parks & Bioreserves

Belize has a broad mix of national parks, forest reserves, marine reserves, natural monuments, wildlife sanctuaries, archaeological reserves, and private reserves. All told, more than one-fifth of the country's landmass and much of its offshore waters are, to some extent, protected areas. In fact, the entire Belize barrier reef was declared a World Heritage Site by UNESCO in 1996.

Most of the national parks charge a BZ$10 (US$5) per-person per-day fee for any foreigner, although some have begun charging slightly more and a few slightly less. Belizeans and foreign residents often pay less. At parks where camping is allowed, there is usually an additional charge of around BZ$4 (US$2) per person per day. Fees at private reserves vary, but are similar to those listed above.

The following section is not a complete listing of all of Belize's national parks, protected areas, and private reserves, but rather a selective list of those parks that are of greatest interest and accessibility. They're the most popular, but they're also among the best. You'll find detailed information about food and lodging options near each of the individual parks in the regional chapters that follow.

NORTHERN BELIZE

CROOKED TREE WILDLIFE SANCTUARY   This swampy lowland is home to over 250 resident species of birds and serves as a resting spot for scores of migratory species. During a visit here you are sure to spot any number of interesting water birds. However, the sanctuary was established primarily to protect Belize's main nesting site of the endangered jabiru stork, the largest bird in the Western Hemisphere. Crocodiles, iguanas, coatimundi, and howler monkeys are all frequently sighted. There are six major lagoons here connected by a series of creeks, rivers, and wetlands. The best way to explore the preserve is by dugout canoe. **Location:** 33 miles (53km) northwest of Belize City. For more information, see "En Route North: Crooked Tree Wildlife Sanctuary" in chapter 5.

RIO BRAVO CONSERVATION AREA   This 260,000-acre (10,400-ha) tract is a mix of virgin forest, sustainable-yield managed forest, and recovering reforestation areas. The land is home to nearly 400 bird species and over 200 species of tropical trees. It also supports a healthy population of most of the New World cat species, and is one of the best areas in the Americas for spotting a jaguar, even better I think than Cockscomb Basin. La Milpa, one of Belize's largest known Mayan sites, is located within this reserve, and Río Bravo is bordered by some 250,000 acres (100,000 ha) of private reserve at Chan Chich, as well as the Kalakmul Reserve in Mexico and the Maya Biosphere Reserve in Guatemala, making it part of a massive regional biological and archaeological protected area. **Location:** 55 miles (89km) southwest of Orange Walk Town. For more information, see "Going West: Río Bravo Conservation Area, La Milpa & Chan Chich" in chapter 5.

SHIPSTERN NATURE RESERVE   The 22,000 acres (8,800 ha) of this reserve protects a variety of distinct ecosystems and a wealth of flora and fauna. Shipstern Nature Reserve is home to over 250 bird species, and its mangroves, lagoons, and flat wetlands are some of the best bird-watching sites in Belize. The lagoons and wetlands here are also home to manatees and Morelet's crocodiles. The reserve also has lowland tropical dry forest unique to Belize, as well as a butterfly breeding project. **Location:** 37 miles (60km) north of Orange Walk Town. For more information, see "Corozal Town" in chapter 5.

NORTHERN CAYES & ATOLLS

BACALAR CHICO NATIONAL PARK & MARINE RESERVE   This is one of the newest additions to Belize's national park system. In addition to being the home to scores of bird, animal, and plant species (many of which are endemic), the park also features several ancient Mayan ceremonial and trading sites. Nearly 200 species of birds have been spotted here, and the park allegedly contains all five wild cat species found in Belize, including the jaguar. The park is only accessible by boat, but once you get here, there are several trails. **Location:** On the far northern end of Ambergris Caye. For more details, see "Ambergris Caye" in chapter 6.

HALF MOON CAYE NATIONAL MONUMENT   This is a combined land and marine reserve. Half Moon Caye itself is the principal nesting ground for the red-footed booby, as well as for both hawksbill and loggerhead turtles. There is a visitor's center here, and overnight camping is permitted with prior arrangement. **Location:** On the southern tip of the Lighthouse Reef Atoll. For more information, see "The Outer Atolls" in chapter 6.

HOL CHAN MARINE RESERVE   *Hol chan* is a Mayan term meaning "little channel," which is exactly what you'll find here—a narrow channel cutting through the shallow coral reef. The reserve covers 5 square miles (8 sq. km) and is divided into three zones: the reef, the sea-grass beds, and the mangroves. The walls of the channel are popular with divers, and the shallower areas are frequented by snorkelers. Some of the exciting residents of the area are large green moray eels, stingrays, and nurse sharks (harmless). **Location:** 4 miles (6km) southeast of San Pedro on Ambergris Caye. For more details, see "Ambergris Caye" in chapter 6.

SOUTHERN BELIZE

COCKSCOMB BASIN WILDLIFE SANCTUARY   The world's first jaguar reserve, this place covers nearly 150 square miles (389 sq. km) of rugged forested mountains and has the greatest density of jaguars on the planet. Other resident

Belize's National Parks & Nature Reserves

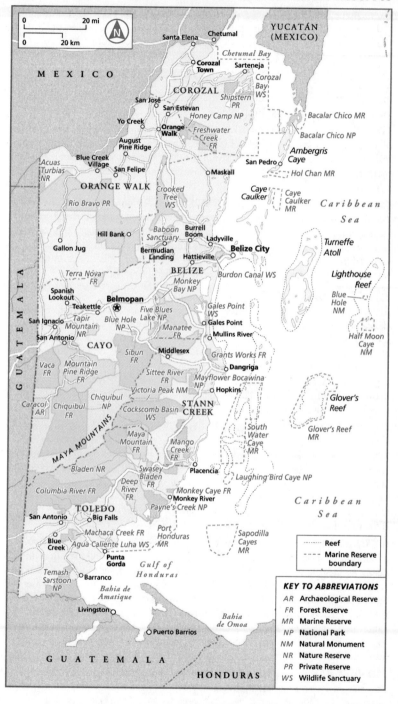

0   20 mi
0   20 km

YUCATÁN (MEXICO)

Santa Elena
Chetumal
Chetumal Bay
Corozal Town
Sarteneja
MEXICO
Corozal Bay WS
COROZAL
San José
Shipstern PR
San Estevan
Honey Camp NP
Yo Creek
Orange Walk
Freshwater Creek FR
Bacalar Chico MR
Bacalar Chico NP
August Pine Ridge
Ambergris Caye
Blue Creek Village
San Felipe
Maskall
San Pedro
Hol Chan MR
Acuas Turbias NR
ORANGE WALK
Crooked Tree WS
Caye Caulker
Caye Caulker MR
Caribbean Sea
Rio Bravo PR
Hill Bank
Baboon Sanctuary
Burrell Boom
Ladyville
Gallon Jug
Bermudian Landing
Hattieville
Belize City
Turneffe Atoll
BELIZE
Monkey Bay NP
Burdon Canal WS
Lighthouse Reef
Terra Nova FR
Spanish Lookout
Teakettle
Belmopan
Five Blues Lake NP
Gales Point WS
Blue Hole NM
San Ignacio
Tapir Mountain NR
Blue Hole NP
Gales Point
Manatee FR
Mullins River
San Antonio
CAYO
Sibun FR
Middlesex
Grants Works FR
Half Moon Caye NM
Vaca FR
Mountain Pine Ridge FR
Sittee River FR
Dangriga
Caracol AR
Chiquibul NP
Chiquibul FR
Victoria Peak NM
Mayflower Bocawina NP
Hopkins
STANN CREEK
Glover's Reef
Maya Mountain FR
Cockscomb Basin WS
South Water Caye MR
Glover's Reef MR
Bladen NR
Mango Creek FR
Swasey Bladen FR
Placencia
MAYA MOUNTAINS
Columbia River FR
Deep River FR
Monkey Caye FR
Monkey River
Laughing Bird Caye NP
Payne's Creek NP
Caribbean Sea
TOLEDO
San Antonio
Big Falls
Machaca Creek FR
Port Honduras MR
Sapodilla Cayes MR
Blue Creek
Agua Caliente Luha WS
Punta Gorda
Temash-Sarstoon NP
Barranco
Gulf of Honduras
Bahia de Amatique
Livingston
Bahia de Omoa
Puerto Barrios
GUATEMALA
HONDURAS

····· Reef
----- Marine Reserve boundary

KEY TO ABBREVIATIONS
AR Archaeological Reserve
FR Forest Reserve
MR Marine Reserve
NP National Park
NM Natural Monument
NR Nature Reserve
PR Private Reserve
WS Wildlife Sanctuary

mammals include tapirs, otters, coatimundis, tayra, kinkajous, deer, peccaries, anteaters, armadillos, and four other species of wild cats, as well as nearly 300 species of birds. The sanctuary is part of the even larger Cockscomb Basin Forest Reserve. Trails inside the park range from gentle and short to quite arduous and long. During the dry season, you can even climb Victoria Peak here, which at 3,675 feet (1,103m) is the country's highest mountain. **Location:** 6 miles (10km) west of the Southern Highway, at a turnoff 20 miles (32km) south of Dangriga. For more information, see "Dangriga" in chapter 7.

FIVE BLUES LAKE NATIONAL PARK   The main attraction here is a stunning cenote, whose various hues of blue give the park its name. All around the park lay forested lands and beautiful karst hill formations. **Location:** Mile Marker 32 on the Hummingbird Highway. For more information, see "Dangriga" in chapter 7.

GLOVER'S REEF ATOLL MARINE RESERVE   This stunning and isolated mid-ocean coral formation features an oval-shaped central lagoon nearly 22 miles (35km) long. The steep-walled reefs here offer some of the best wall diving anywhere in the Caribbean. The entire atoll was declared a World Heritage Site by the United Nations. **Location:** 75 miles (121km) southeast of Belize City; 28 miles (45km) east of Dangriga. For more information, see "Dangriga" in chapter 7.

THE CAYO DISTRICT & WESTERN BELIZE

BLUE HOLE NATIONAL PARK   This park gets its name from a crystal clear pool, or *cenote,* formed in a collapsed cavern. A short well-marked trail leads to the main attraction here. Dense jungle surrounds a small natural pool of deep turquoise. This park also features **St. Herman's Cave,** one of the largest and most easily accessible caves in Belize. The trail that connects them passes through lush and beautiful primary and secondary tropical forests that are rich in flora and fauna. **Location:** 12 miles (19km) south of Belmopan on the Hummingbird Highway. For more information, see "Belmopan" in chapter 8.

CARACOL ARCHAEOLOGICAL RESERVE   Caracol is the largest known Mayan archaeological site in Belize, and one of the great Mayan city-states of the Classic era. So far three main plazas with numerous structures and two ball courts have been excavated. Caracol is located deep within the **Chiquibil Forest Reserve,** which is a largely undeveloped tract of primary and secondary tropical rain and pine forests. The bird-watching here is excellent. **Location:** 50 miles (80km) from the Western Highway at a turnoff just south of San Ignacio. For more information, see "Mountain Pine Ridge & Caracol" in chapter 8.

GUANACASTE NATIONAL PARK   This 50-acre (20-ha) park is named for a huge old Guanacaste, or tubroos, tree that is found within the park. There are nearly 2 miles (3km) of well-marked and well-maintained trails in the park. The park is bordered on the west by Roaring Creek and on the north by the Belize River. Among the animals you might see are more than 120 species of birds, large iguanas, armadillos, kinkajous, deer, agoutis (large rodents that are a favorite game meat in Belize), and jaguarundis (small jungle cats). **Location:** 2 miles (3km) north of Belmopan, where the Hummingbird Highway turns off the Western Highway. For more information, see "Belmopan" in chapter 8.

MONKEY BAY   The combined Monkey Bay Wildlife Sanctuary and Monkey Bay Nature Reserve represent over 2,300 acres (920 ha) of private protected reserve of forest and wetlands. Over 250 species of birds have been recorded here so far, and the number is growing. There are hiking trails, as well as canoe tours on the Sibun River. **Location:** 31 miles (50km) west of Belize City, just off the Western Highway. For more information, see "Belmopan" in chapter 8.

TIKAL, GUATEMALA

TIKAL NATIONAL PARK   While it's obviously not in Belize, the close proximity and convenient access have earned this spectacular Guatemalan national park and ancient Mayan ceremonial city a place on this list and in this book. Surrounded by dense, virgin tropical rainforest, the Tikal ruins are perhaps the most spectacularly preserved and restored Mayan ruins yet uncovered. **Location:** 62 miles (100km) northwest of the Belize border; 40 miles (65km) north of Flores. For more information, see "Tikal" in chapter 9.

4 Tips on Health, Safety & Etiquette in the Wilderness

Much of what is discussed below is common sense. For more detailed information, see "Health & Safety" in chapter 2.

While most tours are safe, there are risks involved in any adventurous activity. Know and respect your own physical limits before undertaking any strenuous activity. Be prepared for extremes in temperature and rainfall and for wide fluctuations in weather. A sunny morning hike can quickly become a cold and wet ordeal, so it's usually a good idea to carry along some form of rain gear when hiking in the rainforest, or to have a dry change of clothing waiting at the end of the trail. Make sure to bring along plenty of sunscreen when you're not going to be covered by the forest canopy.

If you do any backcountry packing or camping, remember that it really *is* a jungle out there. Don't go poking under rocks or fallen branches. Snakebites are very rare, but don't do anything to increase the odds. If you do encounter a snake, stay calm, don't make any sudden movements, and *do not* try to handle it. Also, avoid swimming in major rivers unless a guide or local operator can vouch for their safety. Though white-water sections and stretches in mountainous areas are generally pretty safe, most mangrove canals and river mouths in Belize support healthy crocodile and caiman populations.

Bugs and bug bites will probably be your greatest health concern in Belize, and even they aren't as big a problem as you might expect. Mostly bugs are an inconvenience, although mosquitoes can carry malaria or dengue (see "Health & Safety" in chapter 2, for more information). A strong repellent and proper clothing will minimize both the danger and inconvenience; you may also want to bring along some cortisone or Benadryl cream to soothe itching. At the beaches, you'll probably be bitten by sand fleas, or "no-see-ems." These nearly invisible insects leave an irritating welt. Try not to scratch, as this can lead to open sores and infections. No-see-ems are most active at sunrise and sunset, so you might want to cover up or avoid the beaches at these times.

And remember: Whenever you enter and enjoy nature, you should tread lightly and try not to disturb the natural environment. There's a popular slogan well known to most campers that certainly applies here: "Leave nothing but footprints, take nothing but memories." If you must take home a souvenir, take photos. Do not cut or uproot plants or flowers. Pack out everything you pack in, and *please* do not litter.

Searching for Wildlife

Animals in the forests are predominantly nocturnal. When they are active in the daytime, they are usually elusive and on the watch for predators. Birds are easier to spot in clearings or secondary forests than they are in primary forests. Unless you have lots of experience in the tropics, your best hope for enjoying a walk through the forest lies in employing a trained and knowledgeable guide.

Here are a few helpful hints:

- **Listen.** Pay attention to rustling in the leaves; whether it's monkeys up above or coatis on the ground, you're most likely to hear an animal before seeing one.
- **Keep quiet.** Noise will scare off animals and prevent you from hearing their movements and calls.
- **Don't try too hard.** Soften your focus and allow your peripheral vision to take over. This way you can catch glimpses of motion and then focus in on the prey.
- **Bring your own binoculars.** It's also a good idea to practice a little first, to get the hang of them. It would be a shame to be fiddling around and staring into space while everyone else in your group oohs and aahs over a trogon or honeycreeper.
- **Dress appropriately.** You'll have a hard time focusing your binoculars if you're busy swatting mosquitoes. Light, long pants and long-sleeved shirts are your best bet. Comfortable hiking boots are a real boon, except where heavy rubber boots are necessary. Avoid loud colors; the better you blend in with your surroundings, the better your chances of spotting wildlife.
- **Be patient.** The jungle isn't on a schedule. However, your best shot at seeing forest fauna is in the very early-morning and late-afternoon hours.
- **Read up.** Familiarize yourself with what you're most likely to see. Most nature lodges and ecotourism-based hotels have copies of various wildlife field guides and bird books, although it's always best to have your own. The best of the bunch for most travelers would be Les Beletsky's *Belize & Northern Guatemala: The Ecotravellers' Wildlife Guide* (Academic Press, 1998). Also, bird-watchers will want to purchase a copy of the new *Birds of Belize* (University of Texas Press, 2004) by H. Lee Jones, since many lodges and guides in Belize still might not have a copy.

5 Ecologically Oriented Volunteer & Study Programs

Below are some institutions and organizations that are working on ecology and sustainable development projects.

Cornerstone Foundation *★★* (© 824-2373; www.peacecorner.org/cornerstone.htm), based in San Ignacio in the Cayo District, is an excellent and effective non-religious, non-governmental peace organization with a variety of volunteer and cultural exchange program opportunities. Programs range from

AIDS education to literacy campaigns to renewable resource development and use. Apart from the US$100 application fee, costs are extremely low, and reflect the actual costs of basic food, lodging, and travel in country.

Earthwatch Institute ⚲ (© 800/776-0188; www.earthwatch.org) organizes volunteers to go on research trips to help scientists collect data and conduct field experiments in a number of scientific fields and a wide range of settings. Current expeditions to Belize focus on the study and field research on manatees. Fees for food and lodging average around US$1,950 for a 2-week expedition, excluding airfare.

Habitat for Humanity International ⚲ (© 202/628-9171 in the U.S., or 227-6818; www.habitat.org) is a nonprofit, non-denominational Christian volunteer organization, specializing in building individual housing for needy folks around the world. Habitat has an independent chapter in Belize and sometimes runs organized Global Village programs here. It usually costs between US$1,200 and US$1,400 per person for a 2-week program, including room, board, and in-country transportation (but not airfare to Belize).

International Zoological Expeditions (© 800/548-5843; www.ize2belize.com) has two research and educational facilities in Belize, on South Water Caye and in Blue Creek Village. IZE organizes and administers a variety of educational and vacation trips to these two stations, for both school groups and individuals. A 12-day program usually costs about US$1,200 to US$1,600.

Maya Research Program at Blue Creek ⚲ (© 817/257-5943 in the U.S., or 233-0241; www.mayaresearchprogram.org) runs volunteer and educational programs at an ongoing Mayan archaeological dig. Two-week sessions allow participants to literally dig in and take part in the excavation of a Mayan ruin. The cost is US$1,250 for the 2-week program; discounts are available for longer stays.

Monkey Bay Wildlife Sanctuary ⚲ (© 820-3032; www.monkeybaybelize.org) is a private reserve and environmental education center that specializes in hosting study-abroad student groups. They also run their own in-house educational programs and can arrange a variety of volunteer stays and programs, including home-stays with local Belizean families. See "Belmopan" in chapter 8 for complete details.

Toledo Institute for Development and Environment ⚲ (© 722-2274; www.tidebelize.org) is a small, grassroots environmental and ecotourism organization working on sustainable development and ecological protection issues in the Toledo District. Contact them directly if you are interested in volunteering.

4

Belize City

Belize City is not the capital of Belize, although it once was. Still, as the only large city in the country (albeit with a pop. of just 70,000), it remains its business, transportation and cultural hub. Sooner or later you'll probably have to spend some time here, unless you do all your in-country traveling by air or have a very well-planned itinerary. In fact, since the country itself is so small, Belize City makes an excellent base for a host of interesting day trips to most of the country's major destinations and attractions.

Belize City is surrounded on three sides by water, and at high tide it is nearly swamped. It's a strange, dense warren of narrow streets and canals (the latter being little more than open sewers and pretty pungent in hot weather), modern stores, dilapidated shacks, and quaint wooden mansions, coexisting in a seemingly chaotic jumble.

The city was originally settled by the ancient Mayans, who settled up and down the coast here. By the mid-1600s, pirates were using the current site of Belize City as a hideout and provisioning spot. Soon after, the British arrived and set up a logging base here, fueled by slave labor. Logs were harvested inland and floated down the Belize River for milling and shipping. This logging base soon became a colonial settlement and the seat of Britain's colonial empire on the Central American isthmus. Belize City itself is said to sit on a foundation of wood chips, discarded ship's ballast, and empty rum bottles.

Belize City has historically been beset by tragedy. The entire population abandoned the city and moved to St. George's Caye in 1779 following a Spanish attack. The Baymen, as the British settlers called themselves, returned and resettled the city in 1784. Massive fires razed much of the city in 1804, 1806, and 1856. Deadly hurricanes inflicted heavy damage in 1931 and 1961. Between these events, the residents endured smallpox, yellow fever, and cholera epidemics. Belize City had been declared the capital of British Honduras in 1892, but after Hurricane Hattie struck in 1961, the country's capital was relocated inland to Belmopan. Nevertheless, Belize City continues to be the country's largest and culturally most important city.

Despite a reputation for crime and violence, periodic devastation from passing hurricanes, and the loss of its capital status, Belize City remains the urban heart and soul of Belize. Most visitors treat Belize City merely as a transition point and transportation hub. This is probably what you'll want to do too. But if you've got a day or two to burn on a layover here, Belize City is a good place to walk around, admire the fleet of working wooden fish sloops, do some craft and souvenir shopping, and stock up on Marie Sharp's Hot Sauce to bring home with you.

1 Orientation

ARRIVING

BY PLANE

All international flights into Belize land at the **Philip S. W. Goldson International Airport,** which is located 10 miles (16km) northwest of the city on the Northern Highway. See chapter 2 for details about airlines that service Belize City.

In the baggage claim area, there's an information booth maintained by the **Belize Tourist Board.** This booth supplies maps and brochures, and will often make a call for you if you need a hotel or car-rental reservation. Inside the international departure terminal is a branch of **Belize Bank,** open daily from 8:30am to 4pm. Across the parking lot, you'll find car-rental and tour agency desks, open daily from 8am to 9:30pm. A taxi into town will cost BZ$35 to BZ$40 (US$18–US$20).

If you fly in from somewhere else in Belize, you'll probably land at the **Municipal Airport,** which is on the edge of town. A taxi from here costs just BZ$5 (US$2.50). There's no bank or any other services at the municipal airport, although most car-rental agencies can arrange to have a car there for you.

There is no direct bus service to either airport.

BY BUS

If you arrive in town by bus, you'll probably end up at the main **Novelo's bus terminal** on West Collet Canal Street. This is an easy walk to downtown, but it is not recommended after dark. A taxi from the bus station to any hotel in town will cost around BZ$5 (US$2.50).

BY CAR

There are only two highways into Belize City: the Northern Highway, which leads to the Mexican border (103 miles/166km away), and the Western Highway, which leads to the Guatemalan border (82 miles/132km away). Both are well marked and in good driving condition. If you arrive by car from the north, stay on the road into town, paying close attention to one-way streets, and you'll end up at the Swing Bridge. If you're arriving on the Western Highway, stay on it after it becomes Cemetery Road, and you'll end up at the intersection with Albert Street, a block away from the Swing Bridge.

VISITOR INFORMATION

The **Belize Tourist Board,** Gabourel Lane (© **223-1913;** www.travelbelize. org), is housed in the new Central Bank Building. They have a basic information desk with regional brochures, basic maps, and a score of hotel and tour fliers; the office is open Monday through Friday from 8am to 5pm. Local travel agencies are another good source of information. Three in Belize City to try are **Action Belize,** at the Best Western Belize Biltmore Plaza, Northern Highway, Mile Marker 3½ (© **888/383-6319** in the U.S., or 223-2987; www.action belize.com); **Discovery Expeditions,** 5916 Manatee Dr., Buttonwood Bay (© **223-0748;** www.discoverybelize.com); and **S&L Travel and Tours,** 91 N. Front St. (© **227-7593;** www.sltravelbelize.com).

CITY LAYOUT

Belize City is surrounded on three sides by water, with the murky waters of the Haulover Creek dividing the city in two. The Swing Bridge, near the mouth of Haulover Creek, is the main route between the two halves of the city, as well as

Belize City

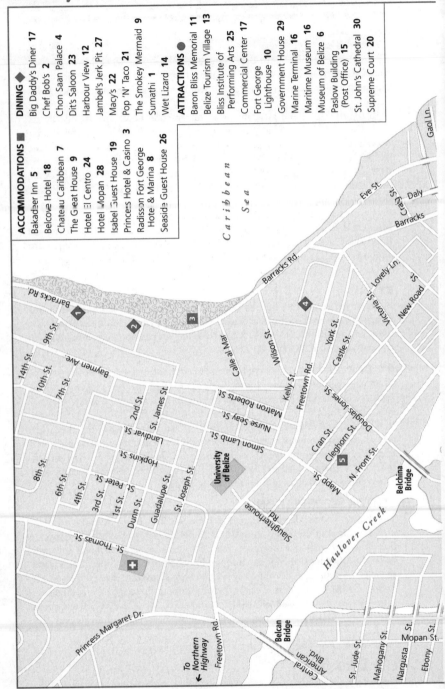

ACCOMMODATIONS ■
Bakadeer Inn **5**
Belcove Hotel **18**
Chateau Caribbean **7**
The Great House **9**
Hotel El Centro **24**
Hotel Mopan **28**
Isabel Guest House **19**
Princess Hotel & Casino **3**
Radisson Fort George
Hotel & Marina **8**
Seaside Guest House **26**

DINING ◆
Big Daddy's Diner **17**
Chef Bob's **2**
Chon Saan Palace **4**
Dit's Saloon **23**
Harbour View **12**
Jambel's Jerk Pit **27**
Macy's **22**
Pop 'N' Taco **21**
The Smokey Mermaid **9**
Sumathi **1**
Wet Lizard **14**

ATTRACTIONS ●
Baron Bliss Memorial **11**
Belize Tourism Village **13**
Bliss Institute of
Performing Arts **25**
Commercial Center **17**
Fort George
Lighthouse **10**
Government House **29**
Marine Terminal **16**
Maritime Museum **16**
Museum of Belize **6**
Paslow Building
(Post Office) **15**
St. John's Cathedral **30**
Supreme Court **20**

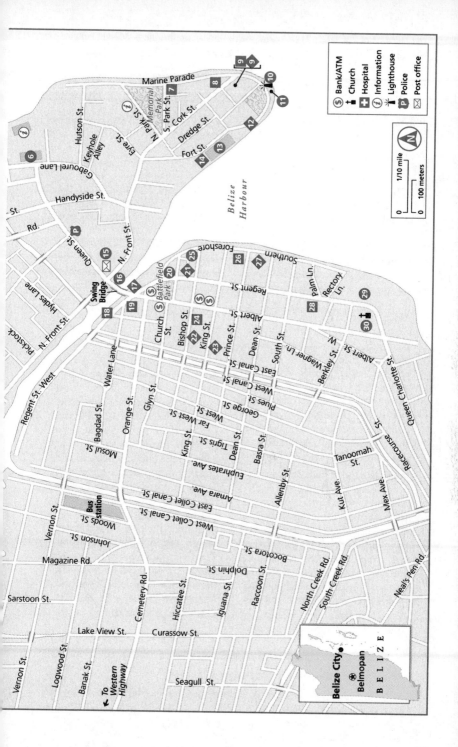

the city's principal landmark. At the south end of the bridge is Market Square and the start of Regent Street and Albert Street. This is where you'll find most of Belize City's shops and offices. To the west and east of these two major roads is a grid of smaller roads lined with dilapidated wooden houses. On the north side of the bridge and to the right is the Fort George area. From the southern side of the city, Cemetery Road heads out of town to the west and becomes the Western Highway, while from the northern side of the city, Freetown Road becomes Haulover Road and then the Northern Highway.

THE NEIGHBORHOODS IN BRIEF

North Side

Barracks Road   Located a mile or so north of downtown, Barracks Road runs along the Caribbean Sea for a good stretch before curving inland and becoming Princess Margaret Drive. This is where you'll find the Princess Hotel & Casino, as well as a couple of good restaurants. Much of the land on either side of Barracks Road is set aside as public park land, while just inland is an area that is made up mostly of modern middle-class homes. While not within easy walking distance of downtown, it's just a very short taxi ride away. The seaside setting and parks make this a relaxing option for those wanting to avoid the bustle of downtown.

Fort George   Anchored by the Fort George Lighthouse and Radisson Fort George Hotel & Marina at the eastern tip of the city, the Fort George neighborhood encompasses the area south of Queen Street, beginning at the northern side of the Swing Bridge, until it ends at Gabourel Lane. This neighborhood is easily the most upscale and picturesque in Belize City, with stately houses and mansions, generally kept in good repair. Most of the best hotels in the city and the U.S. Embassy are located here. It also includes the small triangular Memorial Park and the Belize Tourism Village, as well as the lovely seaside Marine Promenade. This area was originally an island, but was deliberately connected to the mainland with landfill. This area should probably be your first choice for a stay in Belize City.

South Side

Business District   Belize City's downtown business district runs from the south end of the Swing Bridge between East Canal Street and Southern Foreshore Road to the aptly named South Street. In addition to a busy mix of banks and businesses, this area is home to a host of inexpensive hotels, as well as the Supreme Court and the Bliss Institute. Just south of this area you will find the old Government House and St. John's Cathedral. This is a good option for budget travelers, but those with a little more money to spend will probably head across the river to the Fort George neighborhood.

(Fun Fact   Hauled Over Haulover

Haulover Creek is actually just what locals call the final few miles of the Belize River, before it joins the Caribbean Sea. It got its name as an outgrowth of common usage, as this is the area where goods and cattle used to be "hauled over" by early settlers, before a bridge was built.

2 Getting Around

BY FOOT

Belize City's downtown hub is compact and easy to navigate on foot. However, the rest of the city has a rather nasty reputation for being unsafe for visitors, and you'd be wise to stick to the busiest sections of downtown and obvious tourist districts. You can easily walk the entire Fort George neighborhood, as well as the compact business area just south of the Swing Bridge. If you need to venture any further, take a taxi. Be careful when you walk, as sidewalks are often in bad shape and sometimes quite narrow. And don't walk anywhere at night, except perhaps around the downtown hub of budget hotels and restaurants and the Fort George area.

BY TAXI

Taxis are plentiful and relatively inexpensive. A ride anywhere in the city should cost between BZ$5 and BZ$10 (US$2.50–US$5). There's no standardized look or color to taxis in Belize. Many are old, gas-guzzling American models, although newer Japanese sedans are starting to appear more frequently. Most taxis are clearly marked in some form or other, usually with a roof ornament. Very few taxis use meters, so be sure to negotiate your fare in advance. If you need to call a cab, ask at your hotel or try **Cinderella Plaza Taxi Stand** (© 223-0453), **Taxi Garage Services** (© 227-3031), or **Majestic Taxi** (© 224-4465).

BY CAR

There is little need to navigate Belize City in a car. If you do find yourself driving around Belize City, go slow, as pedestrians can appear out of nowhere, and pay attention to the general flow of traffic and a wealth of one-way streets. Despite being a former British colony, cars drive on the right-hand side of the road, and road distances are listed in miles.

Most rental car agencies are based at the Philip S. W. Goldson International Airport, although a couple have offices downtown or at the Municipal Airport, and almost all will arrange to deliver and pick up your vehicle at any Belize City hotel. The most reputable rental car agencies in Belize include: **Avis** (© 225-2385; www.avis.com); **Budget** (© 223-2435; www.budget-belize.com); **Crystal Auto Rental** (© 800/777-7777 toll-free in Belize, or 223-1600; www.crystal-belize.com); and **Thrifty** (© 207-1271; www.thrifty.com). Prices run between BZ$120 (US$60) and BZ$200 (US$100) per day for a late-model compact to a compact SUV, including insurance. For more information on renting a car in Belize, see chapter 2.

BY BUS

While Belize has an extensive network of bus connections to most cities and rural destinations, there is no metropolitan bus system in Belize City.

FAST FACTS: Belize City

American Express American Express Travel Services is represented in Belize by **Belize Global Travel Services Ltd.,** 41 Albert St. (© 227-7363), which can issue traveler's checks and replacement cards, and provide other standard services. They are open Monday through Friday from 8am to noon and 1 to 5pm, and on Saturday from 8am to noon. To report lost or stolen Amex traveler's checks within Belize, call the local number above, or call collect to © **801/964-6665.**

Airport See "Arriving," earlier in this chapter.

Babysitters Your hotel front desk is your best bet for finding a babysitter.

Bookstores Bibliophiles will be disappointed in Belize. You'd be best off purchasing any specific reading material, either for pleasure or research, before coming to Belize. Many gift shops carry a small selection of locally produced fiction and poetry, as well as guidebooks and maps. One decent bookstore in Belize City is **The Book Center,** 4 Church St. (© **227-7457**); it has a dependably well-stocked collection of local fare, but a very limited selection of U.S. and popular fiction and nonfiction titles.

Camera Repair Although your chances of having any serious repair work done are slim, your best bet is the **Belize Photo Lab,** 46 Bishop St. and East Canal (© **227-4991**).

Car Rentals See "Getting Around," above.

Cellphones **DigiCell** (© **227-2017;** www.digicell.bz) has a booth at the airport. If you have an unlocked 1900MHz GSM phone, they sell local prepaid SIM cards in various denominations, although the initial activation costs BZ$50 (US$25), including BZ$10 (US$5) of calls. You can buy these cards at their desk at the airport or at one of their outlets around Belize.

Currency Exchange Most banks will exchange money for a small service charge. It is virtually unnecessary to exchange U.S. dollars for Belize dollars while in Belize, as U.S. dollars are universally accepted at the official 2-to-1 exchange rate. The exception to this is upon leaving the country, when you will want to convert your remaining Belize dollars. There is a branch of **Belize Bank** (© **225-2107**) at the international airport, open Monday through Friday from 8:30am to 4pm. If you are flying out on a weekend, or outside of these hours, be sure to exchange any Belize dollars before hand.

Dentists Call your embassy, which will have a list of recommended dentists, or ask at your hotel.

Doctors Contact your embassy for information on doctors in Belize City, or see "Hospitals," below.

Drugstores There are a handful of pharmacies around Belize City. In downtown, try **Brodie James & Co. Ltd.,** Regent Street (© **227-7070**); it's open Monday through Friday from 8am to 6pm and Saturday from 9am to 2pm. Perhaps the best stocked pharmacy can be found at **Belize Medical Associates,** 5791 St. Thomas Kings Park (© **223-0303;** www.belize medical.com); it's open Monday through Friday from 8am to 7pm and Saturday from 8am to 2pm, and it makes emergency deliveries at any hour.

Embassies & Consulates See "Fast Facts: Belize" in chapter 2.

Emergencies In case of any emergency, dial © **90** from anywhere in Belize City. This will connect you to the police, fire department, and ambulance central switchboard. You can also call © **911.**

Express Mail Services Several international courier and express-mail services have offices in Belize City, including **DHL**, 38 New Rd. (© **223-4350**; www.dhl.com); **FedEx**, 1 Mapp St. (© **224-5221**; www.fedex.com); and **Mail Boxes Etc.**, 166 N. Front St. (© **227-6046**; www.mbe.com). All can arrange pickup and delivery services to any hotel in town. *Note:* Despite what you may be told, packages sent overnight to U.S. addresses tend to take 3 to 4 days to reach their destination.

Eyeglasses The **Hoy Eye Center** is a small nationwide chain of opticians and eyeglass stores. Their Belize City branch (© **223-0994**; www.hoyeye center.bz) is located at the corner of St. Thomas and St. Joseph streets.

Hospitals **Belize Medical Associates**, 5791 St. Thomas Kings Park (© **223-0302**; www.belizemedical.com), is a modern, 24-hour private hospital, with emergency care and numerous private practice physicians. The city's main public hospital, the **Karl Heusner Memorial Hospital**, Princess Margaret Drive (© **223-1548**), is also open 24 hours and has a wide range of facilities and services.

Internet Access Internet cafes are becoming increasingly common in Belize City. Rates run between BZ$4 and BZ$10 (US$2–US$5) per hour. **M-Business Solutions**, 13 Cork St., in the lobby of the Great House (© **223-6766**), has good high-speed connections and is open Monday through Friday from 8am to 5pm. Alternatively, **BTL** (© **0800/112-4636**; www.btl.net), the state Internet monopoly, sells pre-paid cards in denominations of BZ$10 (US$5), BZ$25 (US$13), BZ$50 (US$25), and BZ$100 (US$50) for connecting your laptop to the Web via a local phone call. Some knowledge of configuring your computer's dial-up connection is necessary, and be sure to factor in the phone charge if calling from a hotel.

Laundry & Dry Cleaning Most folks rely on their hotel's laundry and dry cleaning services, although these can be expensive. Alternatively, you can try the **C.A. Coin Laundromat**, 114 Barrack Rd. (© **203-3063**), or **Belize Dry Cleaners & Laundromat**, 3 Dolphin St. (© **227-3396**).

Maps The **Belize Tourist Board** (© **223-1913**) can provide you with good maps to both the city and country at either their kiosk at the international airport, or at their main office in the Central Bank Building on Gabourel Lane. Also, most gift shops sell maps of the country.

Newspapers & Magazines Belize has no daily newspaper. There are four primary weeklies: *Amandala, The Reporter, Belize Times,* and *The Guardian.* All come out on Friday, and all are relatively similar in terms of content, although with some differing and usually obvious political leanings. *Belize First* is a periodic book-style magazine aimed at the tourist trade.

Photographic Needs While I recommend bringing as much film as you foresee needing and waiting until you return home to develop it, if you'd rather not wait, your best bet is the **Belize Photo Lab**, 46 Bishop St. and East Canal (© **227-4991**).

Police The main Belize City station is at 9 Queen St.; the Tourist Police is a division of the small force. Dial © **90** or **911** in the case of emergency. You can also call © **227-2222**.

Post Office The main post office (© 227-2201) is located at the corner of Queen and North Front streets, across from the Swing Bridge. It costs BZ$0.60 (US30¢) to send a letter to the United States, and BZ$.75 (US38¢) to send a letter to Europe. Postcards to the same destinations cost BZ$.30 (US15¢) and BZ$.40 (US20¢) respectively.

Restrooms There are very few public restrooms in Belize City. The only ones I know of are located at the little cruise-ship tourist village on Fort Street in the Fort George neighborhood. Most hotels and restaurants will let travelers use their facilities, although they are happiest about providing the service to clients.

Safety Belize City has a reputation for being a rough and dangerous city. While things have improved somewhat, the reputation was earned for a reason. Tourist police do patrol the busiest tourist areas during the day and early evenings. Still, while most populous downtown areas and tourist attractions are quite safe during the daytime, travelers are strongly advised to not walk around very much at night, except in the best-lit and most popular sections of downtown. Basic common sense and street smarts are to be employed. Don't wear flashy jewelry or wave wads of cash around. Be aware of your surroundings, and avoid any people and places that make you feel uncomfortable.

Rental cars generally stick out and they are easily spotted by thieves, who know that such cars are likely to be full of expensive camera equipment, money, and other valuables. Don't ever leave anything of value in an unattended parked car.

Also, see "Safety" in "Fast Facts: Belize" in chapter 2.

Taxes There is a US$35 departure tax that must be paid in cash at the international airport upon departure; the land exit fee is US$19. There is a 9% hotel tax added on to all hotel bills, and there is a 9% sales tax on all goods and services. A 10% service charge is sometimes added on to restaurant bills. Take this into account when deciding how much to tip (if the service is really good, an extra 5%–10% is fine).

Taxis See "Getting Around," above.

Time Zone Belize City is on Central Standard Time, 6 hours behind Greenwich mean time. Belize does not observe daylight saving time.

Useful Telephone Numbers For directory assistance, call © 113; for an international operator and directory assistance, call © 114 or 115; for the exact time, date, and temperature, call © 121.

Water The water in Belize City is ostensibly safe to drink. However, many travelers react adversely to water in foreign countries, so it's probably best to drink bottled water during your visit to Belize.

Weather The weather in Belize City is subtropical, and generally similar to that of southern Florida. Average daytime temperature is around 80°F (27°C), although it can get considerably warmer during the summer months, while during the winter months, when northern cold fronts extend their grip south, it can get downright nippy. For more details, see "When to Go" in chapter 2.

3 Where to Stay

Belize City is small, and your options on where to stay are relatively limited, especially for a capital city. The most picturesque and safest neighborhood by far is the area around the Fort George Lighthouse. Here you'll find most of the city's best shopping, dining, and accommodations. Still, since the city is so compact, and it's not really recommended to walk around anywhere at night, you're best off choosing a hotel that best meets your needs, style, and budget. There are really only three large, modern hotels in town, and they're all listed below. If your tastes tend towards smaller, more intimate lodgings, there are several good options in different price ranges to choose from.

When getting a price quote from or negotiating with a hotel in Belize, be careful to be clear whether or not you are being quoted a price in Belize or U.S. dollars. There is a 9% tax on all hotel stays in Belize, which isn't included in the rates listed below.

FORT GEORGE
VERY EXPENSIVE

Radisson Fort George Hotel & Marina ☆☆ *Kids*   This is Belize City's top business-class and luxury hotel. The hotel is located in the quiet Fort George neighborhood fronting the ocean, out by the lighthouse, just 1 block from the cruise-ship tourist village. The best rooms here are located in the six-story Club Tower; those on the higher floors have the best views. All are quite spacious and modern, and feature marble floors and programmable safes. The Club Tower also has one junior suite on each floor. The Colonial rooms, all of which are nonsmoking, are also spacious and comfortable. Rooms on the ground floor come with a comfortable private garden terrace, while some of those on the higher floors offer enticing ocean views. The least expensive and least attractive rooms here are the misnamed "Villas," which are located in a separate building across the street from the principal facility. While these rooms are acceptable and most even have a private balcony, you'll want to either splurge a little for the better Club Tower or Colonial rooms mentioned above, or head to one of the more intimate hotel options listed below. The poolside bar here is one of the more popular spots in town, and often features live music. The hotel also features a full-service marina and dive shop.

2 Marine Parade, Belize City. © **800/333-3333** in the U.S., or 223-3333 in Belize. Fax 227-3820. www.radisson.com. 102 units. BZ$358–BZ$398 (US$179–US$199) double. Rates slightly lower in the off season. AE, DISC, MC, V. Free parking. **Amenities:** 3 restaurants; 2 bars; lounge; 2 midsize outdoor pools; small gym; concierge; tour desk; babysitting; laundry service; limited room service (6am–10:30pm); nonsmoking rooms. *In room:* A/C, TV, dataport, minibar, coffeemaker, hair dryer.

EXPENSIVE

The Great House ☆ *Finds*   This stately colonial-style small hotel is aptly named. Set a block from the water, near the Fort George lighthouse, this three-story converted mansion was originally built in 1927. It has been well maintained and restored. The three rooms on the top floor are my favorites, with high ceilings, wood floors, and a large, shared wraparound veranda. (In fact, all but one of the rooms feature wood floors.) While the rooms vary in size, most are quite spacious; room no. 1 is one of the largest. Throughout the building you'll find a mix of wicker, neo-colonial, and locally made modern wood furniture. The Smokey Mermaid restaurant (p. 91) is one of the best options in town.

13 Cork St. (opposite the Radisson Fort George), Belize City. © 223-3400. Fax 223-3444. www.greathouse belize.com. 16 units. BZ$240 (US$120) double. AE, MC, V. Free parking. **Amenities:** Restaurant; lounge; concierge; tour desk; small shopping arcade; laundry service; nonsmoking rooms. *In room:* A/C, TV, dataport, fridge, coffeemaker, hair dryer, safe.

MODERATE

Chateau Caribbean   This midsize hotel is set facing the sea. The rooms here are all carpeted, with comfortable double beds, modern furnishings, and cable TV. The third-floor deluxe rooms are somewhat misnamed; while they are huge and have excellent ocean views from their private balconies, I find them a bit threadbare and barren, with too much empty space taken up by little more than the worn carpeting. The second-floor dining room serves good moderately priced meals of Belizean and Chinese cuisine, with a wonderful view of the ocean.

6 Marine Parade (P.O. Box 947), Belize City. © 223-0800. Fax 223-0900. www.chateaucaribbean.com. 21 units. DZ$170 (US$09) double, DZ$210 (US$109) deluxe. AE, MC, V. Free parking. Amenities: Restaurant, tour desk; laundry service. *In room:* A/C, TV, dataport.

BARRACKS ROAD
EXPENSIVE

Princess Hotel & Casino 🍴   This is the largest hotel in Belize City, and the only one with a real resort feel to it. The massive lobby area lets out into the hotel's casino, two movie theaters, a shopping arcade, an eight-lane bowling alley, a salon, and various restaurants and bars. The hotel is set right on the water's edge a little bit north of downtown and is built as one long six-story structure so that every room has an ocean view. The rooms are all large and well equipped, with either one king bed or two full-size beds, a working desk, large bathrooms, and plush bathrobes. The junior suites are a little bit larger and have private oceanfront balconies. The casino here is definitely one of the prime nightlife attractions in the country. The Princess also has a full-service marina and dive shop. The Radisson definitely feels a bit more elegant and better maintained, but the Princess trumps it in terms of facilities and nightlife.

Barracks Rd., Belize City. © 800/233-9784 in the U.S., or 223-2670 in Belize. Fax 223-2660. www.princess belize.com. 181 units. BZ$240 (US$120) double; BZ$300–BZ$360 (US$150–US$180) suite; BZ$640 (US$320) presidential suite. Rates include breakfast buffet. AE, DISC, MC, V. Free parking. **Amenities:** 2 restaurants; 2 bars; lounge; large outdoor pool; fitness center; concierge; tour desk; salon; limited room service (7am–9pm); in-room massage; laundry service; nonsmoking rooms. *In room:* A/C, TV, dataport, hair dryer, safe.

BUSINESS DISTRICT
MODERATE

Hotel El Centro   Located in the heart of the business and shopping district, with several restaurants and the bus station within a few blocks, this hotel offers relatively comfortable and modern rooms, albeit with little in the way of charm or character. There is a lawn in back of the hotel, which is a rarity and pleasant surprise in this section of the city, but otherwise this place is rather uninspired and spartan. There's a simple, inexpensive, dependable restaurant downstairs here.

4 Bishop St. (P.O. Box 2267), Belize City. © 227-2413. Fax 227-4553. 13 units. BZ$80 (US$40) double. AE, MC, V. Free parking. **Amenities:** Restaurant; laundry service. *In room:* A/C, TV.

INEXPENSIVE

Belcove Hotel *Finds*   This funky canal-front hotel is my preferred budget choice in town. You just can't beat the charm of grabbing a seat on one of the upstairs balconies overlooking Haulover Creek and the Swing Bridge, especially at these prices. Sure, the rooms are simple and funky, but they are neatly kept with shiny varnished wood floors, while the old wooden building is kept in fresh yellow paint with blood red trim, yet still feels weathered and historic.

9 Regent St., Belize City. ✆ **227-3054.** Fax 227-5248. www.belcove.com. 12 units. BZ$40–BZ$80 (US$20–US$40) double. MC, V. Free street parking. *In room:* No phone.

Hotel Mopan   Located a block or so from the water towards the western end of Regent Street, this longstanding little hotel has received some long overdue remodeling. Everything is rather up-to-date now, and the hotel staff is as friendly and helpful as ever. The rooms are clean and comfortable, and about half of them currently have air-conditioning. Moreover, plans are to have air-conditioning and televisions in every room by the time you read this.

55 Regent St., Belize City. ✆ **227-7351.** Fax 227-5383. www.hotelmopan.com. 12 units. BZ$80–BZ$120 (US$40–US$60) double. MC, V. Free street parking. *In room:* No phone.

Isabel Guest House   The three rooms here are on the third floor of a prominent building, located above a hardware store just over the Swing Bridge on Albert Street. Inside, the rooms are spacious and kept quite clean. They feature painted wooden floors and angled ceilings from the numerous gables and dormers. Room no. 2 is cavernous, with a good view over Belize City's busiest intersection and the ubiquitous bridge. The hotel is located at a very busy intersection, and it can be noisy here, especially in the early morning when the city gets going.

3 Albert St., Belize City. ✆ **207-3139.** 3 units. BZ$50 (US$25) double. No credit cards. Free street parking. *In room:* No phone.

Seaside Guest House *Value*   One of Belize City's most popular low-budget lodgings, and deservedly so, the Seaside is located on a quiet street just off Southern Foreshore. Run by a local group of Quakers, this typical Caribbean wood-frame house is a haven for the backpacker crowd, and it's often booked well in advance. If you want to stay here, make a pre-paid reservation beforehand, if at all possible. There are only four double rooms, with two double beds each, and one dorm-style affair. All of them share a couple of very clean, communal bathrooms and showers. Breakfasts and light meals are served from 7am till around 10pm. The staff and bulletin board here are a wealth of information for budget travelers. There's also a bar, Internet access, a TV lounge, and a second-floor veranda with a view of the sea.

3 Prince St. (P.O. Box 2060), Belize City. ✆ **227-8339.** Fax 227-1689. seasidebelize@btl.net. 5 units, all with shared bathroom. BZ$60 (US$30) double; BZ$24 (US$12) per person in dorm room. DISC, MC, V. Free street parking. **Amenities:** Restaurant; bar; tour desk; laundry service. *In room:* No phone.

AROUND TOWN
MODERATE
Bakadeer Inn   Built in 1990, this inn has a pleasant pseudo-Tudor exterior, although inside, there's little in the way of old-world charm or character. Still, the rooms are clean and have cable TV. The rooms on the first floor are tiled, while those on the second floor are carpeted; I prefer the former, as the latter can get a tad musty at times. The hotel is located several blocks north of the downtown hub, in a somewhat quiet residential area. There's secure parking here, and if you don't have a car, a taxi to the center should cost you around BZ$6 (US$3).

74 Cleghorn St. (P.O. Box 512), Belize City. ✆ **223-0659.** mcfield@btl.net. 12 units. BZ$100 (US$50) double. AE, MC, V. Free parking. **Amenities:** Nonsmoking rooms. *In room:* A/C, TV, fridge.

Best Western Belize Biltmore Plaza   Located on the northern outskirts of the city, this chain hotel is simple and straightforward, but it lacks any sense of Caribbean or colonial charm. It's a decent choice if you want to be a little closer to the airport and avoid the crowds and commotion of downtown. The carpeted rooms are modern and comfortable and all face the hotel's central courtyard and pool area. The management here are the same folks from the formerly famous Fort Street Guesthouse and Restaurant. Their influence can be tasted in the excellent international cuisine served here. As at the Radisson and Princess hotels, the bar here is a popular meeting place for locals, after work and on weekends.

Northern Hwy., Mile Marker 3½. Belize City. © 223-2302. Fax 223-2301. www.belizebiltmore.com. 80 units. BZ$178–BZ$250 (US$89–US$125) double. AE, MC, V. Free parking. **Amenities:** Restaurant; 2 bars; small outdoor pool; small gym; tour desk; limited room service (6:30am–10pm); laundry service; nonsmoking rooms. *In room:* A/C, TV, hair dryer.

NEAR THE AIRPORT

The airport is located just 10 miles (16km) north of downtown Belize City, a 15- to 20-minute drive, depending on traffic. The area around the airport is decidedly undeveloped and of little interest to visitors. Few international flights arrive late enough or leave early enough to necessitate a stay near the airport. The only true airport hotel, the **Embassy Hotel** (© 225-3333; www.embassy hotelbelize.com), is a run-down and desultory affair, with no relation whatsoever to the Embassy Suites chain. In addition to the place listed below, the **Belize River Lodge** (© 888/275-4843 in the U.S., or 225-2002 in Belize; www.belizeriverlodge.com) is an upscale fishing lodge located on the banks of the Belize River, just a few miles from the airport.

MODERATE

Villa Boscardi 🐾   This small and elegant bed and breakfast is the plushest lodging you'll find near the airport. Housed in a converted private home, the rooms here are spacious and decorated with a sense of style. Most have interesting artwork and headboard treatments over the beds. The best room here is actually a detached cottage. The owners provide a nightly shuttle to downtown restaurants. The hotel is located on the very northern outskirts of Belize City, in a quiet neighborhood, just a block or so from the water.

6043 Manatee Dr., Buttonwood Bay, Belize City. ©/fax 223-1691. www.villaboscardi.com. 5 units. BZ$138 double (US$69). Rates include continental breakfast. AE, MC, V. Free parking. **Amenities:** Tour desk; massage; laundry service. *In room:* A/C, TV.

4 Where to Dine

Despite its small size, Belize City actually has an excellent and varied selection of dining options open to visitors. While Belizean cuisine and fresh seafood are most common, you can also get excellent Chinese, Indian, and other international fare at restaurants around the city.

Note: When the cruise ships are in town, the restaurants in the Fort George area can get extremely crowded, especially for lunch.

FORT GEORGE
EXPENSIVE

Harbour View 🐾🐾 INTERNATIONAL   This is probably the most expensive and creative restaurant in town. The menu here features some fusion touches you won't find at other Belize City restaurants. I like the Parasol of Reddened Shrimp, which are coated in an Asian-style sweet and pungent glaze and served atop a rice pilau. Another excellent choice is the Picasso Pork Tenderloin, which comes with a delicious jalapeno relish. You can also get thick cuts of steak, and a host of other dishes. The main dining room is a second-floor space with large picture windows opening onto Belize Harbour. However, when the weather's right, I recommend grabbing one of the outdoor tables on the wooden wraparound veranda, which will put you even closer to the water. There's often live jazz music in the evenings.

Fort St., next to the Belize Tourism Village. (C) **223-6420.** Reservations recommended. Main courses BZ$33–BZ$60 (US$17–US$30). AE, DISC, MC, V. Mon–Fri 11:30am–3pm; daily 5–11pm.

The Smokey Mermaid ★★ (Finds INTERNATIONAL   I love the open-air brick courtyard setting of this semi-elegant yet relaxed restaurant. There are a couple of raised decks and gazebos and a few fountains, spread out amongst heavy wooden tables and chairs under broad canvas umbrellas in the shade of large seagrape and mango trees and a wealth of other lushly planted ferns and flowers. An equally pleasant choice for breakfast, lunch, or dinner, the menu here ranges from Jamaican jerk pork to shrimp Thermidor to chicken Kiev. I personally prefer the yuca-crusted red snapper, although the rosemary lamb chops run a close second. The desserts here are excellent, with their signature sweet being the Original Decadent Ecstasy, a chocolate coconut pie swimming in ice cream, nuts, and chocolate sauce.

13 Cork St., in The Great House. (C) **223-4722.** Reservations recommended. Main courses BZ$22–BZ$40 (US$11–US$20). AE, MC, V. Daily 6:30am–10pm.

MODERATE

Wet Lizard ★★ (Finds BELIZEAN   Boasting an excellent setting on a second-floor covered deck overlooking the Swing Bridge and Belize City's little harbor, this raucous new restaurant has quickly become one of the most popular spots in town. The menu here is simple, with an emphasis on sandwiches, burgers, and American-style bar food. Start things off with some coconut shrimp, conch fritters, or fried calamari, before tackling one of the hearty sandwiches or wraps. You can also get tacos, nachos, fajitas, and quesadillas, as well as a daily special or two. If you like sweets, save room for the banana chimichanga. The best seats here are the small tables and high stools ringing the railing and overlooking the water. Everything is painted in bright primary colors, and the walls are quickly being covered with graffiti and signatures from guests. The practice is actually encouraged, so be sure to ask for a magic marker and add to the wall art. When the cruise ships are in town, this place is overrun and even serves a separate menu, so be sure to ask for their full menu.

1 Fort St. (C) **223-2664.** Reservations not accepted. Main courses BZ$10–BZ$17 (US$5–US$8.50). AE, MC, V. Tues–Sat 11am–9:30pm.

BARRACKS ROAD
EXPENSIVE

Chef Bob's ★★ INTERNATIONAL   Widely considered one of the best formal dining options in town, this place offers a wide array of salads, pita wraps, pasta, and perfectly prepared grilled meats and fresh fish. I particularly like the guava-marinated pork chops, and the Moroccan spice-crusted lamb chops. Be sure to start things off with the delicious blue cheese, walnut, and Port pâté. For lunch or brunch you can get a sandwich, salad, or hearty omelet. Chef Bob worked for many years as the executive chef at the Radisson and Princess hotels before setting out on his own.

164 Newtown Barracks Rd. © 227-6080. Reservations recommended. Main courses BZ$28–BZ$45 (US$14–US$23). AE, MC, V. Mon–Fri 11:30am–2pm; Mon–Sat 6–10:30pm.

MODERATE

Sumathi ® INDIAN   Formerly the Searock Café, this is still the best Indian restaurant in town. Currently located just up the road from the Princess Hotel, the restaurant is housed on the bottom floor of a hurricane-damaged three-story concrete monster. The service is semi-formal and attentive. The menu features a wide selection of northern Indian and tandoori specialties. If you're familiar with Indian cuisine, you won't be disappointed here. This is also an excellent option for vegetarians, who probably won't find as broad a selection to fit their dietary needs in any other restaurant in the country.

190 Newtown Barracks Rd. © 223-1172. Main courses BZ$10–BZ$22 (US$5–US$11). MC, V. Tues–Sun 11am–11pm.

BUSINESS DISTRICT
MODERATE

Jambel's Jerk Pit ® CARIBBEAN/BELIZEAN   An offshoot of its successful sister on Ambergris Caye, this simple cafe and restaurant serves spicy curries and jerk concoctions, alongside local specialties. The coconut curry chicken is excellent, as is the Grouper Cleopatra, fresh grilled grouper with a shrimp and garlic cream sauce. Still, the spicy Jamaican jerk is the signature here, and you might as well go for the Jerk Lobster (BZ$25/US$13). There are about five tables in the main dining room, but your best bet is to grab one of the tables in the outdoor courtyard, beneath the shade of a large Belikin umbrella, surrounded by banana, palm, and ficus trees and flowering heliconia.

2B King St. © 227-6080. Reservations not accepted. Main courses BZ$12–BZ$25 (US$6–US$13). MC, V. Mon–Sat 11:30am–3pm and 6–10pm.

INEXPENSIVE

Big Daddy's Diner BELIZEAN   Located in the two-story concrete Belize City market, just over the Swing Bridge, Big Daddy's is a clean and comfortable cafeteria-style restaurant. A breakfast here of scrambled eggs and fry jacks is filling and inexpensive. For lunch there are always several salads, rice dishes, vegetables, and main courses to choose from, and the portions are large. There are great views of the sailboats in the river from the restaurant's big windows.

2nd floor, Commercial Center, Booth 54. © 227-0932. Main courses BZ$5–BZ$20 (US$2.50–US$10). MC, V. Mon–Sat 7am–5pm.

Dit's Saloon BELIZEAN   This popular local joint is part coffee shop, part simple restaurant, and part bar. At its core, Dit's serves simple meals of Belizean rice and beans, fried and stewed chicken and fish, and hamburgers, although it's equally well known for its tempting daily assortment of fresh-baked cakes, pies, and pastries. You'll usually find cow's foot soup on the menu here, and this is as good a place to try it as any. Still, while this little restaurant does serve beer and drinks, the "saloon" part of its name is a bit of a stretch.

50 King St. © 227-3330. Main courses BZ$4–BZ$12 (US$2–US$6). No credit cards. Mon–Sat 7am–9pm; Sun 8am–4pm.

Macy's *(Finds)* BELIZEAN   For authentic Belizean cooking and a down-home funky vibe, you can't beat this tiny local place. The food is good, the service is friendly, the prices are right, and the dining room is cool and cozy. Order a fish filet with rice and beans, or curried chicken for BZ$10 (US$5), or be more daring and try one of their daily wild game chalkboard specials, which could feature anything from armadillo and deer to wild pig or gibnut. Macy's no longer serves turtle or other endangered species. There are only five tables, and each is set with a plastic tablecloth and plastic place mat, under a strategically placed overhead fan.

18 Bishop St. © 207-3419. Main courses BZ$10–BZ$25 (US$5–US$13). No credit cards. Mon–Sat 11:30am–9pm.

Pop 'N' Taco CHINESE Despite its Mexican name, the menu at this small local joint is heavy on Chinese standards. Although this place is an utter dive, it's quite popular with folks from the surrounding neighborhood (which happens to house several budget hotels). There are only a few tables in the simple restaurant, but you can also get your food to go. In addition to simple tacos and burritos, you can get a range of Cantonese rice, chicken, and noodle dishes.

24 Regent St. © 227-3826. Main courses BZ$3–BZ$18 (US$1.50–US$9). No credit cards. Mon–Sat 8am–3pm and 5–9:30pm.

AROUND TOWN
MODERATE
Chon Saan Palace 🦟 CHINESE If you're in the mood for Chinese food in Belize City, you can't do better than this local favorite. The room and the menu are immense. You'll find plenty of chow mein and Cantonese dishes, but there's also a substantial Szechuan section and a show-stopping sizzling steak that comes hissing and screaming to your table. If you're in the mood for seafood, you'll love the large fish tanks stocked with live lobster (in season), shrimp, and the daily catch. This is a great place to come with a group, as there are plenty of large round tables with built-in lazy susans, just perfect for sharing food and a good time. Don't take the easy way out and head to the more conveniently located New Chon Saan Palace—it's worth the short taxi ride to eat at the original.

1 Kelly St. © 223-3008. Main courses BZ$9–BZ$30 (US$4.50–US$15). MC, V. Mon–Sat 11am–3pm and 5–11:30pm; Sun 5–11pm. Closes even later Fri–Sat nights.

5 What to See & Do

There really isn't much reason to take a guided tour of Belize City. The downtown center is extremely compact and lends itself very easily to self-directed exploration. There are only a handful of interesting attractions, and all are within easy walking distance of the central Swing Bridge. Below you'll find reviews of the most interesting attractions, as well as a walking tour of the city.

If you really feel the need for a guided tour of the city, ask at your hotel desk for a recommendation, or call **Action Belize** (© 223-2987; www.actionbelize. com), **Discovery Expeditions** (© 223-0748; www.discoverybelize.com), **Jaguar Adventures** (© 223-6025; www.jaguarbelize.com), or **S & L Travel and Tours** (© 227-7593; www.sltravelbelize.com). A half-day city tour should cost around BZ$100 (US$50) per person, but can easily be combined with a visit to one of the several popular nearby attractions. All the above companies offer a whole range of day trips and combinations to the attractions close to the city and even further afield (see "Attractions Outside Belize City," below, and "Side Trips from Belize City," later in this chapter).

SUGGESTED ITINERARIES

If You Have 1 Day

If you have a full day, you can get an early start and visit the **Belize**

Zoo, before it gets too hot or crowded. Spend the afternoon exploring the downtown and doing some shopping. Have a sunset drink and some conch fritters at the **Wet Lizard,** and then dinner at whichever of the restaurants listed in this chapter that most strikes your fancy. If you've still got energy, try your luck at the **Princess Casino,** or see if there's any live music at the poolside restaurant at the **Radisson Fort George Hotel.**

If You Have 2 Days

On day 2, you're probably best off taking one of the day trips outside of Belize City described below. Alternatively, you could spend the day further exploring the capital.

This is a good time to visit the **Belize Zoo,** if you didn't squeeze it in on your first day.

If You Have 3 Days

On day 3, head out to **Altun Ha** or **Lamanai** for the day, or try a caving adventure out in the **Caves Branch** area. It's also easy to visit either **Caye Caulker** or **Ambergris Caye** for the day, where you can do a snorkel trip to **Shark-Ray Alley** and **Hol Chan Marine Reserve.**

If You Have 4 Days or More

Get out of Belize City. Do a 1- or 2-night trip to the **Cayo District,** **Placencia,** or one of the **cayes.**

THE TOP ATTRACTIONS

Belize City is very light on true attractions. The museums mentioned below are quite quaint and provincial by most international standards, although they are worth a visit if you are spending a day getting to know the city, residents, and local history.

Bliss Institute of Performing Arts ⋆   Totally rebuilt and recently reopened, the Bliss Institute is a busy little complex that promises to become the cultural heart of Belize City. Housing a performing arts space, rehearsal halls, a cafeteria, the National Institute of the Arts, and a couple of gallery spaces, this is the place to check for live performances of theater, dance, and music while you're in town. It's also a good place to stop and see if there's an interesting exhibit of art or photography. The main building's circular design takes advantage of the complex's setting, with large picture windows overlooking the Belize Harbour.

Southern Foreshore, between Church and Bishop sts. ℭ 227-2110. Free admission. Mon–Fri 8:30am–5pm.

Maritime Museum   Located adjacent to and over the Marine Terminal, where you catch the ferry boats to Caye Caulker and Ambergris Caye, this modest little museum features a few different types of exhibits relating to the various aspects of the country's marine heritage and natural history. There are collections of shells, corals, and marine animals, as well as an interesting 3-D model of the Belize barrier reef. You'll also find numerous photos and models of the various types of vessels used commercially and for pleasure, dating from the Mayan period to the present. Allow 1 to 2 hours for your visit.

N. Front St. and Queen St. ℭ 203-1969. Admission BZ$4 (US$2). Mon–Sat 7:30am–5:30pm.

Museum of Belize   Housed in what was once "Her Majesty's Prison," this museum features a collection of historical documents, photographs, and artifacts, alongside exhibits of Mayan pottery and archaeological finds. There are also traveling exhibits, and a room featuring attractively mounted insects from Belize. Just so you won't forget the building's history, a prison cell has been restored to its original condition. The museum takes up the two floors of this historic old brick building. Plan on spending between 1 and 2 hours here.

Gaborurel Lane, in front of the Central Bank building. ℭ 223-4524. Admission BZ$10 (US$5), BZ$4 (US$2) for students, free for children. Mon–Fri 8am–5pm.

> **Fun Fact Swingin'**
>
> The Swing Bridge opens twice a day at 6am and 5:30pm, Monday through Saturday, to let tall masted sailboats pass through. The entire process takes around 20 minutes, and in addition to being a minor spectacle, it is a major traffic hassle.

St. John's Cathedral ⊛   This old brick church is the oldest Anglican cathedral in Central America, and the oldest standing structure in Belize. Built in 1812, by slaves using bricks brought over as ballast, it is also the only Anglican church outside of England where kings have been crowned—during the 1800s four Mosquito Indian kings held their coronation ceremonies here.

At the corner of Albert and Regent sts. ✆ 227-2137. Free admission. Mon–Fri 8:30am–5pm.

A WALKING TOUR

The following walking tour covers both the north and south sides of Belize City, which together comprise the entire historic downtown center. For most of its length, you'll be either right on the water or just a block or two away. As described, the walking tour should take you anywhere from 2 to 4 hours, depending on how much time you take visiting the various attractions. The only major attraction not right on the route below is the Museum of Belize, although it's only a 4-block detour east from the Paslow Building. The route laid out on this walking tour is pretty safe during daylight hours, but should not be attempted after dark.

Begin your stroll at the **Fort George Lighthouse** and **Baron Bliss Memorial,** out on the northeastern tip of the city. A small slate stone marks the grave of Henry Edward Ernest Victor Bliss (see "Baron Bliss" on p. 96). After soaking up the view of the Caribbean and some fresh sea air, head towards downtown on Fort Street. On your left, you'll find the new **Belize Tourism Village** (✆ 223-2767; www.belizetourismvillage.com), which was built to accommodate the rising tide of cruise-ship passengers. Stop in and shop, or just browse the variety of local and regional arts and crafts.

As you continue, Fort Street becomes North Front Street. On your right, just before reaching the Swing Bridge, you'll find the main post office, housed in the **Paslow Building.** Thomas Paslow was a well-to-do 19th-century Bayman who figured prominently in the 1878 Battle of St. George's Caye. Across the street, you'll find the **Maritime Museum** (p. 94).

Now, cross the **Swing Bridge** and head south. On your left is the **Commercial Center.** Wander through the stalls of fresh vegetables, butcher shops, and fish stands. You'll also find some gift shops and souvenir stands here.

The **Supreme Court building,** off the small **Battlefield Park** (or Market Square) just a block south of the Swing Bridge, is a real prize of English colonial architecture with the city's only clock tower. Walk around the four sides and see if any are accurately telling the time.

Down at the southern end of Regent Street, you'll find the **Government House** and **St. John's Cathedral,** above, also known by its more officious-sounding moniker, the Anglican Cathedral of St. John the Baptist. Both of these buildings were constructed with slave labor in the early 19th century, and they remain the most prominent reminders of the 3 centuries of British colonial presence here. The Government House has recently been converted into a **House of**

Baron Bliss

Henry Edward Ernest Victor Bliss, the fourth Baron Bliss of the Kingdom of Portugal, anchored his yacht *Sea King* off of Belize City on January 14, 1926. Within 2 months, the baron would be dead, never having stepped foot on Belizean soil. Nonetheless, the eccentric Baron Bliss is this tiny country's most beloved benefactor. His time spent anchored in Belize Harbour was enough to convince him to rewrite his will and leave a large chunk of his estate—nearly $2 million at the time—to the country of Belize (then known as British Honduras). The trust he set up stipulated that the principal could never be touched, and only the interest was to be used. The ongoing bequest has funded numerous public works projects around the country, and today it's hard to miss the baron's legacy. There's the Baron Bliss Memorial, Baron Bliss Nursing School, Bliss Institute, and the Bliss (Fort George) Lighthouse. Every year on March 9, a large regatta is held in Belize Harbour in honor of the baron.

Culture, with the mission of encouraging and sponsoring local participation in the arts, music, and dance.

For your return to downtown, head towards the water and come back on the Southern Foreshore Road, stopping in at the **Bliss Institute** (p. 94) to see if there's an interesting exhibit on display or a performance scheduled for later in the evening.

ATTRACTIONS OUTSIDE BELIZE CITY

The attractions listed below are within an hour of Belize City; both can be reached by public transportation. In addition, the Mayan ruins of **Altun Ha** and **Lamanai** and the **Crooked Tree Wildlife Sanctuary** are all easily accessible from Belize City. All are popularly sold as day tours, often in various mix-and-match combinations. If you're interested in visiting one or more of these attractions as part of an organized tour, ask at your hotel, or call **Action Belize** (© 223-2987; www.actionbelize.com), **Discovery Expeditions** (© 223-0748; www.discoverybelize.com), **Jaguar Adventures** (© 223-6025; www.jaguarbelize.com), or **S & L Travel and Tours** (© 227-7593; www.sltravel belize.com). Prices range from about BZ$90 to BZ$220 (US$45–US$110) per person, depending on the tour, means of transportation, and the attraction(s) visited. Tours, especially those to Altun Ha and Crooked Tree, are often combined with lunch and an optional spa treatment at Maruba Resort Jungle Spa. For more information on Altun Ha, Lamanai, Crooked Tree Wildlife Sanctuary, and Maruba Resort Jungle Spa, see chapter 5.

BELIZE ZOO   Founded in 1983 as part of a last-ditch and improvised effort to keep and care for a host of wild animals that were being used in a documentary film shoot, the **Belize Zoo,** Western Highway, Mile Marker 29 (© 220-8004; www.belizezoo.org), is a national treasure. Gentle paths wind through some 29 acres (12 ha) of land, where the zoo houses over 125 animals, all native Belizean species. According to their own promotional materials, "The zoo keeps animals which were either orphaned, born at the zoo, rehabilitated animals, or sent to The Belize Zoo as gifts from other zoological institutions."

Walking around the zoo, you'll see several species of Belizean cats, "April" the tapir, and other wild animals in idealized natural surroundings. The animals here are some of the liveliest and happiest looking that I've ever seen in a zoo. It's obvious that they're well cared for. All the exhibits have informative hand-painted signs accompanying them. It's best to visit early in the morning or close to closing time, when the animals are at their most active and the Belizean sun is at its least oppressive.

Adjacent to the zoo is a new sister project, the **Tropical Education Center** (© **220-8003**). Set on 84 acres (34 ha) of untouched savannah, the center has a nature trail, observation platform, classroom, and some simple guest rooms. An overnight stay here costs between BZ$60 and BZ$70 (US$30–US$35) for double occupancy plus meals. While most of the beds here are in dormitory-style rooms, a couple of private cabins are definitely worth the few extra dollars. Folks who stay here can take a nocturnal tour of the zoo for BZ$20 (US$10).

The entrance is a couple of hundred yards in from the Western Highway. Any bus traveling between Belize City and Belmopan or San Ignacio will drop you off at the zoo entrance. Admission is BZ$15 (US$7.50), and the zoo is open daily from 9am to 5pm.

COMMUNITY BABOON SANCTUARY ⚡   No, there aren't really baboons in Belize; this is just the local name for the black howler monkeys who reside in this innovative sanctuary. The sanctuary is a voluntary program run by local landowners in eight villages to preserve the local population of these vociferous primates. The howlers found here are an endangered endemic subspecies found only in Belize. There's a visitor's center and natural history museum in the village of Bermudian Landing, and it is here that you pay your BZ$10 (US$5) admission fee, which includes a short guided hike. If you want a longer guided hike, you should hire one of the many local guides for a modest fee. The preserve stretches for some 20 miles (32km) along the Belize River, and there are several trails that wind through farmland and secondary forest. You will undoubtedly hear the whooping and barking of the howler monkeys as they make their way through the treetops feeding on fruits, flowers, and leaves. In addition to the nearly 1,500 howler monkeys that make their home in the sanctuary, there are also numerous other bird and mammal species to be spotted here. With your guide's help, you should be able to spot the monkeys and, if you're lucky, any combination of peccaries, anteaters, pacas, and coatimundi. Bring binoculars if you have them.

At the visitor's center, you can also hire a canoe for a leisurely paddle and float on the Belize River. The cost is around BZ$35 (US$18) per person. Finally, the several small villages that comprise the conservation project are wonderful examples of rural Creole villages. Be sure to visit one or two, stroll around, talk to the residents, and see what kind of craftwork and food you can find. In each village, there are families that rent out simple rooms.

Bermudian Landing village, site of the sanctuary's visitor center, is about 20 miles (32km) west of Belize City. If you are driving, head north on the Northern Highway and watch for the Burrel Boom Road turnoff. Buses to Bermudian Landing leave Belize City Monday through Saturday at noon and 5pm from the corner of Orange and Mosul streets, and at noon and 4pm from Cairo Street near the corner of Orange Street and Euphrates Avenue. Buses return to Belize City at 6am and 3pm. The one-way fare is BZ$4 (US$2).

6 Outdoor Activities

Due to the crime, chaos, and often oppressive heat and humidity, you'll probably want to get out of the city, or on to the water, before undertaking anything
too strenuous. But if you want to brave the elements, there are a few outdoor
activities for you to try in and around Belize City. See chapter 3 for more information on adventure sports in Belize.

CAVING   The **Caves Branch** region is about a 50- to 90-minute drive from
Belize City, depending on where you enter the cave systems. Several tour operators offer a variety of hiking and tubing trips through an extensive network of
caves here. Both hiking and tubing are interesting ways of exploring the eerie
world of caves. Hiking allows more time for close examination of the formations
and Mayan relics. The **Crystal Cave,** located adjacent to the Jaguar Paw Jungle
Resort, is one of the more spectacular caves you will ever visit, with numerous
stalactites, stalagmites, and pillars encrusted with the glimmering quartz crystals
that give the cave its name. The **Caves Branch River** is a slow meandering river
that should probably be called a creek. Nevertheless, it passes through a series of
long caves, making it perfect for a slow float on an inner tube through a dark
and mysterious world. Most tour operators and tour desks in Belize City can
arrange these trips, or you can call **Jaguar Paw Jungle Resort** (© 820-2023;
www.jaguarpaw.com) or **Ian Anderson's Caves Branch Adventure Company**
(© 822-2800; www.cavesbranch.com) directly. See "Belmopan" in chapter 8 for
more information on the Caves Branch region.

FISHING   While most serious fishermen head to one of the cayes or southern
Belize destinations, it's possible to line up fishing charters out of Belize City. The
marinas at both the **Fort George Radisson Hotel & Marina** (© 223-3333)
and **Princess Hotel & Casino** (© 223-2670) have regular sport charter fleets
and can arrange a variety of options. You could also check in with **Captain
Charles Usher** aboard the *Big Dipper* (© 225-2967; charlesush@btl.net).
Expect to pay around US$1,200 to US$1,600 per day for a boat that can
accommodate up to four fishermen. See "Corozal Town," in chapter 5, and
chapter 7 for more information on longer charter options.

GOLF & TENNIS   Your options are limited if you want to play golf or tennis in Belize. There's only one regulation golf course in Belize and it's located on
Caye Chapel, a little island in the middle of the Caribbean Sea. Luckily, Caye
Chapel is only a 30-minute water taxi ride or an even shorter commuter flight
from Belize City. The course at the **Caye Chapel Island Resort** (© 226-8250;
www.belizegolf.cc) is flat and often very windy. Still it's rather gorgeous, with
stunning views, plenty of water and sand hazards, and the ocean bordering the
entire length of many holes. Non-guests on Caye Chapel can play the course
with advance reservations only. The rate is US$200 per person per day for
unlimited golf, cart, clubs, lunch, and use of the resort's pools and beach.

There are no public tennis courts in Belize City, and none of the major hotels
have courts.

JOGGING   Belize City is not very amenable to jogging. If you must run, you
could try a loop around the Fort George neighborhood, hugging the coast from
the Fort George Lighthouse to Memorial Park, then heading to Fort Street,
which will bring you back to the lighthouse. It's best to jog very early, before
there's much street traffic and before it gets too hot. Another nice stretch for jogging is on the sidewalk and parks that line Barracks Road where it fronts the sea.

SAILING The waters off Belize Harbour are theoretically perfect for day sailing excursions, although currently no one is consistently offering this option. The two main charter companies, **The Moorings** and **TMM Charters,** are both based outside of Belize City, the former in Placencia, the latter in both Placencia and San Pedro. However, if you're interested in trying to line up a day sail, ask at your hotel desk or check in with the marinas at the **Fort George Radisson Hotel & Marina** (© 223-3333) and **Princess Hotel & Casino** (© 223-2670). See chapters 6 and 7 for details on longer charter options.

SCUBA DIVING & SNORKELING The Belize barrier reef lies just off the coast from Belize City. It's a short boat ride to some excellent scuba diving and snorkeling. While most serious divers chose to stay out on one of the cayes for really close proximity to the reefs, it is still possible to visit any number of excellent sites on day trips from Belize City, including the Blue Hole and Turneffe and Lighthouse atolls. Check in with **Hugh Parkey's Belize Dive Connection** (© 223-5086; www.belizediving.com).

SPAS & GYMS **Best Western Belize Biltmore Plaza** (p. 90) and **Princess Hotel & Casino** (p. 88) have small gym facilities and offer basic spa services. However, neither of these hotels allows non-guests use of their facilities.

If your hotel doesn't offer massage and you want some pampering, check in with the folks at **Oltsil Day Spa** (© 223-7722; oltsil@yahoo.com), which is located on Barracks Road about 2 blocks south of the Princess Hotel & Casino.

SWIMMING A few of the higher-end hotels in Belize City have pools. Of these, only **Princess Hotel & Casino,** Barracks Road (© 223-2670), allows nonguests to use their pool facilities for a small charge.

7 Shopping

You won't be bowled over by shopping options here in Belize City, and very few people come to Belize specifically to shop. You will find a modest handicraft industry, with different specialties produced by the country's various ethnic communities. The Creole populations of the coastal area and outer cayes specialize in coral and shell jewelry, as well as woodcarvings with maritime (dolphins, turtles, and ships) themes. Remember, coral is a very delicate, rapidly disappearing living organism that grows very slowly; please avoid buying coral jewelry, as it just feeds demand and inevitably leads to the destruction of the spectacular Belizean reefs. The Belizean Mayan population produces replicas of ancient petroglyphs and different modern designs on varying sized pieces of slate. Finally, the Garífuna peoples of the southern coastal villages are known for their small dolls.

My favorite gift item in Belize continues to be **Marie Sharp's Hot Sauce** ✷✷, which comes in several heat gradations, as well as some new flavors. The original blend of habanero peppers, carrots, and vinegar is one of my all-time favorite hot sauces. The company also produces mango chutney and an assortment of pepper jams. You can pick up Marie Sharp products at any supermarket and most gift shops; I recommend you stick to the supermarkets, though, to avoid price gouging.

Please do not buy any kind of sea-turtle products (including jewelry); wild birds; lizard, snake, or cat skins; corals; or orchids (except those grown commercially). No matter how unique, beautiful, insignificant, or inexpensive it may seem, your purchase will directly contribute to the further hunting of endangered species.

THE SHOPPING SCENE

Most shops in the downtown district are open Monday through Saturday from about 8am to 6pm. Some shops close for lunch, while others remain open (it's just the luck of the draw for shoppers).

SHOPPING A TO Z

ART

Fine Arts ✮✮   This is the best gallery I've found in Belize. They have a large selection of original art works in a variety of styles, formats, and sizes. Browse primitivist works by Walter Castillo and Pen Cayetano, alongside more modern abstract pieces, traditional still lifes, and colorful representations of Belize's marine, natural, and human life. 1 Fort St., next to the Belize Tourism Village. ✆ 223-7773. www.fineartsbelize.com.

HANDICRAFTS & SOUVENIRS

In addition to housing the best collection of fine art for sale in the city, **Fine Arts** (see "Art," above) also features some of the best handicrafts and handmade jewelry. The quality and selection are a definite step above what you'll find at most other gift shops and tourist traps in town.

Go-Tees ✮   This longstanding design and production company has moved to a larger facility and shop on the northern outskirts of the city. The shop and factory produces and carries an extensive collection of T-shirts, visored hats, and local textiles. They also sell a range of handmade jewelry, Guatemalan textiles, Mexican hammocks, and Belizean crafts. 6238 Park Ave., Buttonwood Bay. ✆ 223-4660. www.gotees.net.

National Handicraft Center   This place still houses a wide selection of local and regional crafts and souvenirs all under one roof, but it's no longer the main game in town. In fact it's lost a lot of its luster and traffic to the newer Belize Tourism Village. Still, you'll find a decent selection of Mayan stone carvings, coconut shell jewelry, and wooden knickknacks, as well as some oil paintings, prints, and a small selection of books. Moreover, the prices here are slightly better than those at the Belize Tourism Village, and if you see something you really like, you might even be able to bargain for it. 2 S. Park St. ✆ 223-3636.

Walkingstick Fine Art & Sculpture Gallery   This place features the wooden sculptures of Stephen Okeke. Okeke works in both large and small formats, in one-off and commissioned designs. He carves wood directly, but also puts out limited editions of molded pieces made from a combination of sawdust and resin. The gallery also carries a wide selection of mass-produced wooden sculptures and craft items, as well as a smaller collection of assorted local crafts and jewelry. Northern Hwy., Mile Marker 3½. ✆ 223-1369. www.sculptgentech.com.

LIQUOR

Your best bet for liquor shopping are local supermarkets, or the duty-free shop at the airport. There are several brands of Belizean rum available; the best is **One Barrel,** which has a hint of coconut. Other brands produce some more heavily flavored coconut rums. The **Prestige** brand aged rum is also pretty good, if you're looking for a straight dry rum. Belize doesn't produce any wines or other spirits of note.

MARKETS

The only real market of note is the Commercial Center located just over the Swing Bridge, on the southern side of the city. This two-story modern concrete structure houses a mix of stalls and enclosed storefronts. The first floor is predominantly devoted to fresh produce, fish stalls, and butcher shops, but you'll also find stands selling flowers, fresh herbs, and some souvenir shops. There are more souvenir shops and some restaurants, including Big Daddy's, on the second floor. The Commercial Center is open daily from 7:30am to 5pm.

MUSIC

Punta Rock is the most Belizean of music styles. A close cousin to soca and calypso, Punta is upbeat dance music. Popular proponents include Andy Palacios, Chico Ramos, Pen Cayetano, the Garífuna Kids, Travesia Band, and Peter Flores (aka Titiman). For a taste of traditional Creole folk music, try to track down a copy of *Mr. Peters' Boom & Chime.* You also might be able to find some traditional Garífuna music, which tends to be ceremonial dance music, very similar to traditional West African music.

The best place to find Belizean music is a gift shop. Still, these are very hit or miss. Check at the **Belize Tourism Village,** 8 Fort St. (© **223-2767;** www. belizetourismvillage.com). You might also try online music stores; the best online source I've found for Belizean music is **www.calabashmusic.com**. I'd avoid the various vendors selling bootleg cassettes and CDs on the side of the road, since the quality can be sketchy, and the artists don't receive a dime.

8 Belize City After Dark

Again, Belize City is a tiny, provincial town in an underdeveloped country, so don't expect to find a raging nightlife scene. The most popular nightspots—for both locals and visitors alike—are the bars at the few high-end hotels in town.

THE PERFORMING ARTS

It's really the luck of the draw as to whether or not you can catch a concert, theater piece, or dance performance—they are the exception, not the norm. To find out if anything is happening, ask at your hotel, read the local papers, or check in with the **Bliss Institute** (© **227-2110**).

THE BAR SCENE

The bar and club scene in Belize City is rather lackluster. Travelers and locals alike tend to frequent the bars at the major hotels and tourist traps. The liveliest of these are the bars at the **Radisson Fort George Hotel & Marina** (p. 87), the **Best Western Belize Biltmore Plaza** (p. 90), and the **Princess Hotel & Casino** (p. 88), all of which often have a live band on weekend nights. Of these, I prefer the **Club Calypso** (© **223-2670**), an open-air affair built over the water at the Princess Hotel & Casino, although it's sort of a crapshoot as to which bar will be really going off on any given night.

THE GAY & LESBIAN SCENE

Belize is a small and conservative Central American nation. Homosexuality is generally stigmatized. Whatever gay and lesbian community there is, is quite small and insular. There are currently no publicly known or advertised gay and lesbian bars or clubs in Belize City.

CASINOS

The **Princess Hotel & Casino** is the only game in town, and the casino here is large, modern, and well equipped. While it's not on the scale of Vegas or Atlantic City, the casino is certainly respectable, with enough gaming tables, slots and other attractions to make most casual gamblers quite happy to drop a few dollars.

9 Side Trips from Belize City

Given the fact that Belize is so small, it is possible to visit any of the country's major tourist destinations and attractions as a side trip from Belize City. Most are easily reached in less than 2 hours by car, bus, or boat taxi. Other attractions are accessible by short commuter flights. All in all, you can visit any destination or attraction described in this book as a day trip, except for the far southern zone.

For a listing of active adventures that make good day trips, see "Outdoor Activities," earlier in this chapter; for a description of the most popular attractions within close proximity to Belize City, see "What to See & Do," earlier in this chapter. Other possible destinations for side trips out of Belize City include **Caye Caulker** and **Ambergris Caye,** dive excursions to the nearby reefs, and even to the more isolated dive destinations like the **Blue Hole** and the **Lighthouse** and **Turneffe atolls.** You can also visit the Mayan ruins of **Altun Ha, Lamanai, Xunantunich, Cahel Pech,** and even **Caracol** and **Tikal.** All of the popular side-trip destinations out of Belize City are discussed in more depth in "What to See & Do," earlier in this chapter, or in the subsequent destination chapters.

Most hotels can arrange any of the day trips suggested above. In addition, you can check in with **Action Belize** (② 223-2987; www.actionbelize.com), **Discovery Expeditions** (② 223-0748; www.discoverybelize.com), **Jaguar Adventures** (② 223-6025; www.jaguarbelize.com), or **S & L Travel and Tours** (② 227-7593; www.sltravelbelize.com).

Note: Most of the tours and activities mentioned here and in "Outdoor Activities," earlier in this chapter, are also sold to visiting cruise-ship passengers. When the cruise ships are in town, a cave tubing adventure, snorkel trip to Hol Chan Marine Reserve and Shark Ray Alley, or a visit to either Altun Ha or Lamanai ruins can be a mob scene. It's often possible to avoid these crowds by starting your tour or activity very early, or in the late afternoon. If you are organizing your tour or activity with a local operator, be very specific in having them schedule your trip so as to avoid the cruise-ship groups, if at all possible.

5

Northern Belize

Northern Belize is often overlooked by travelers who fly into the country and head quickly to the cayes, the Cayo District, the southern beaches, or the Mayan Mountains. Even those who enter by land from Mexico frequently make a beeline to Belize City and bypass the region. Still, northern Belize has its charms, not least of which is the fact that it has such an undiscovered and undeveloped feel. It's here that you'll find some of the country's larger biological reserves, including the **Crooked Tree Wildlife Sanctuary,** the **Shipstern Wildlife Reserve,** and the **Río Bravo Conservation Area.** With over 400 species of birds and 250 species of orchids, naturalists will definitely want to spend some time here. The region was also an important and strategic part of the Mayan Empire, and ancient ruins abound. Most notably, it is here that you will find the **Altun Ha** and **Lamanai** ruins, two of the country's most popular and important Mayan sites. Lesser sites like **Cuello, Cerros, Santa Rita,** and **Noh Mul** are also possible stops for true aficionados. Finally, northern Belize is home to three very unique and isolated lodges: **Maruba Resort Jungle Spa, Chan Chich Lodge,** and **Lamanai Outpost Lodge,** all of which are described in detail below.

For our purposes, "northern Belize" refers to the northern section of the Belize District, as well as the entire Orange Walk and Corozal districts. The land here is low and plain, with massive sugar cane, citrus, soybean, and pineapple plantations set amidst large swaths of forests, swamps, lagoons, and slow steamy jungle rivers. Belize's Northern Highway runs from Belize City to the Mexican border, a little over 100 miles (161km) away. The road is not in good shape and the scenery tends to be flat and monotonous. There are few people and fewer population centers. There are only two cities of any note along the way, and both are actually designated as towns, **Orange Walk Town** and **Corozal Town.** Of these, only Corozal, with its seaside setting and proximity to the Mexican border and Shipstern Wildlife Reserve, is a destination with much appeal to travelers. Orange Walk, for its part, serves mainly as a gateway to the Lamanai ruins and the Río Bravo Conservation Area.

Much of this area was originally settled by immigrants fleeing southern Mexico's Yucatán peninsula during the Caste Wars of the mid–19th century. This is undoubtedly the most Spanish region in Belize. However, it is also the region with the largest concentration of Mennonite communities. Members of this somewhat radical and oft persecuted Christian order have thrived in this farming area. You can't miss the Mennonites in their heavy garb and horse-drawn carriages.

1 Along the Old Northern Highway: Altun Ha ⋆ & Maruba Resort Jungle Spa ⋆⋆

The Old Northern Highway is in rough shape. The narrow, paved road is in dire need of repair; it's riddled with potholes and washed out in many sections. Still, it is the only route to one major attraction and one unique resort. Aside from these two places, there's not much else along this highway, except for a few tiny communities and the occasional roadside restaurant or bar. To get here, take Freetown Road out of Belize City to connect with the Northern Highway. The turnoff to the Old Northern Highway is to the right just past Sand Hill; watch for signs for Altun Ha and Maruba Resort Jungle Spa.

ALTUN HA ⋆

Altun Ha is a small, well-preserved Mayan ruin. Only a few of the most imposing temples, tombs, and pyramids have been uncovered and rebuilt; hundreds more lie under the jungle foliage. Still, there are two large central plazas surrounded by midsize pyramids and mounds, as well as the beginnings of the excavation of residential areas. While nowhere near as extensive as some other sites, the quality and detail of the excavation and restoration at Altun Ha is admirable. Sections of different structures have been left in various states of repair and restoration, which gives a good sense of the process involved. Moreover, while the climb to the top of the tallest pyramids here is rather easy by Mayan standards, the views are still wonderful. The site was named after the village in which it's situated—Rockstone Pond, the literal Mayan translation meaning "stone water." At the back of the site, behind Plaza B, is the namesake pond. Archaeologists theorize that the pond is an example of a pre-Columbian water works project and a demonstration of the ingenuity of Mayan engineering.

Despite its somewhat diminutive size, Altun Ha was a major trade and ceremonial center. In its prime, during the Classic Period, Altun Ha supported a population of about 10,000. Many jade, pearl, and obsidian artifacts have been discovered here, including the unique jade-head sculpture of **Kinich Ahau** (the Mayan sun god), the largest well-carved jade from the Mayan era. Today, it's kept in a bank vault in Belmopan, out of public view, although you can see a replica at the Museum of Belize (p. 94). Some of the pieces found here show a direct link the great Mexican city of Teotihuacan.

The largest (though not the tallest) temple here is the **Temple of the Masonry Altars,** which fronts Plaza B. It has been well restored, and the pathway to the top is well maintained and even features handrails. However, if you're fairly fit and not acrophobic, I recommend you climb the almost entirely unrestored **Temple A-6,** which is truly the tallest building here. A climb to the top of Temple A-6 affords an excellent panorama of the entire site. Be careful climbing down; the Mayans were a society run by priests and holy men, not lawyers. A more litigious society would have never permitted the construction of such steep and treacherous stairways.

The site is open daily from 9am to 5pm. Admission is BZ$10 (US$5) for adults, free for children under 12. There is no public transportation to Altun Ha, so you'll need to take a tour, a taxi, your own wheels, or hitchhike. If you're driving, Altun Ha is located about 30 miles (48km) north of Belize City on the Northern Highway. Once you're on the Old Northern Highway, it's 11 miles (17km) to the Altun Ha road. From the highway, it's another bumpy 2¼ miles (4km) to the ruins.

Half-day tours to Altun Ha from Belize City cost between BZ$60 and BZ$90 (US$30–US$45). Full-day tours can be combined with visits to Crooked Tree Wildlife Sanctuary (see "En Route North: Crooked Tree Wildlife Sanctuary," below) or the Community Baboon Sanctuary (see "What to See & Do" in chapter 4) and should run between BZ$150 and BZ$200 (US$75–US$100). Many of the tours include lunch and an optional spa treatment at Maruba Resort Jungle Spa.

AN ISOLATED JUNGLE SPA

Maruba Resort Jungle Spa ★★ *Finds* Decadent, sensual, and exotic are the words most often used to describe this small resort, and for good reason. The whole place is an imaginative jungle fantasy where health, hedonism, and happiness are the primary goals. The accommodations are a collection of uniquely designed and decorated rooms and private villas, set in a patch of densely planted gardens and forest. Artistic touches abound and range from the many interesting architectural details to the eclectic mix of decorations and furnishings from Africa, Asia, the Caribbean, the Middle East, and, of course, Belize. The best rooms here are the private suites. Of these, the Chapel Suite is my favorite, with a large, enclosed private sitting area featuring a floor of loose stones, a two-person hot mineral bath with Jacuzzi jets, and heavy wooden Indonesian chaise lounges. The Jungle Villa Suite also has its own private mineral bath, as well as a private enclosed garden area. The standard rooms are certainly up to snuff, but I think it's worth the splurge for one of the suites.

There are two outdoor pools here, as well as a separate hot mineral pool. The spa facilities and services are wonderfully done and reasonably priced. Don't leave here without trying one of their treatments. The Mood Mud Massage is their signature offering, and I highly recommend it. The food at the restaurant here is excellent, featuring a creative mix of international and fusion cuisine. This place is very popular with day-trippers from the cayes and Belize City, as well as cruise-ship passengers. Luckily, one of the pools is reserved for hotel guests, and once the day tours clear out, you'll have the place to yourself. In addition to the spa treatments, a host of tours, activities, and adventures are offered here.

Old Northern Hwy., Mile Marker 40½. Maskall Village. (✆) 800/627-8227 in the U.S., or 322-2199. Fax 220-1049. www.maruba-spa.com. 16 units. BZ$550 (US$225) double; BZ$540–BZ$1,200 (US$270–US$600) suite. Rates include full breakfast. AE, MC, V. **Amenities:** Restaurant; bar; lounge; 2 outdoor swimming pools; spa; tour desk; car-rental desk; laundry service. *In room:* A/C, hair dryer, no phone.

2 En Route North: Crooked Tree Wildlife Sanctuary ★

33 miles (53km) NW of Belize City

Crooked Tree Wildlife Sanctuary is a swampy lowland that is home to over 250 resident species of birds and serves as a resting spot for scores of migratory species. During a visit here you are sure to spot any number of interesting water birds, including kites, hawks, ducks, grebes, pelicans, ospreys, egrets, and herons. However, the preserve was established primarily to protect Belize's main nesting site of the endangered jabiru stork, the largest bird in the Western Hemisphere. The jabirus arrive every November and pass the winter in these warm lowland climes. The jabiru is an impressive bird, standing nearly 5 feet (1.5m) tall, with a wingspan that can reach up to 12 feet (3.6m). Crooked Tree has rapidly become known as an excellent place to spot other endangered wildlife as well. Crocodiles, iguanas, coatimundi, and howler monkeys are all frequently sighted. There are six major lagoons here connected by a series of creeks, rivers, and wetlands.

The best way to explore the preserve is by dugout canoe. Ask in town or at the sanctuary's visitor's center and administrative building for a local who will paddle you around in a dugout for a few hours. The going rate is around BZ$15 to BZ$20 (US$7.50–US$10) per person for a 2- to 3-hour paddle tour of the lagoons. Or, if you're in the mood for a little exercise, Bird's Eye View Lodge (see below) offers canoe rental for BZ$10 (US$5) per person per hour. All visitors must first register at the visitor's center and pay the BZ$8 (US$4) admission fee.

Crooked Tree is also home to a thriving cashew industry. Each year during the first weekend of May, Crooked Tree village hosts its annual Cashew Festival. In addition to an abundance of the raw and roasted nuts, this is a great chance to sample some cashew wine, cashew jelly, and a whole plethora of dishes cooked around or including the local nut.

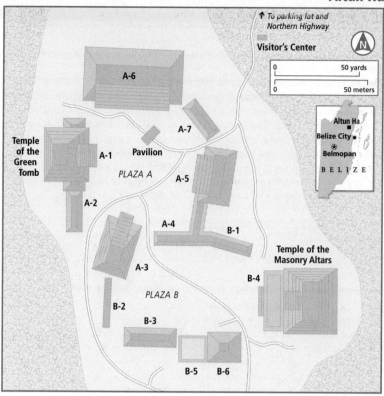

If you'd like to spend the night, accommodations can be arranged with a local family for around BZ$20 to BZ$40 (US$10–US$20), double occupancy. Meals should run you an additional BZ$20 (US$10) per person per day. Or, if you want to stay in a comfortable new lodge right on the edge of a lagoon, check out the **Bird's Eye View Lodge** ✰ (© **203-2040;** www.birdseyeviewlodge.com), where a double costs between BZ$60 and BZ$80 (US$30–US$40).

Crooked Tree is located 33 miles (53km) northwest of Belize City. If you are driving, head up the Northern Highway and watch for the turnoff to Crooked Tree. From the turnoff, it's another 3 miles (5km) on a well-graded dirt road.

Buses leave for Crooked Tree Village from the Novelo's bus terminal on West Collet Canal Street in Belize City Monday through Friday at 4pm, returning at 6am the following day. Jex bus company leaves from the bus terminal on Regent Street West in Belize City on Saturday at 11am. Or catch a ride to Crooked Tree with a Jex bus that departs from Belize City at Pound Yard Bridge, Monday through Friday at 4:30 and 5:15pm, and leaves Crooked Tree for Belize City at 6:30 and 7am. The fare is BZ$4.50 (US$2.25).

Half-day tours to Crooked Tree cost between BZ$60 and BZ$80 (US$30–US$40). A full-day trip combining Crooked Tree and Altun Ha, including transportation, guide, and lunch, should cost between BZ$150 and BZ$200 (US$75–US$100).

3 Orange Walk Town

55 miles (89km) N of Belize City; 31 miles (50km) S of Corozal

Between Belize City and Corozal Town, the only settlement of any size is Orange Walk Town, a bustling agricultural and business community with a population nearing 20,000. This is the heart of Belize's sugar cane industry, and some locals still call the town "Sugar City." Originally called Holpatin by the ancient Maya, the town's riverside location has insured its status as a trade center for over 2,000 years. The town's current name comes from the many citrus groves once planted alongside the New River here. Orange Walk Town's residents are a very heterogeneous mix of mestizos, Mayans, Chinese, and Black Creoles. There's not too much of interest to travelers in the town, but this is the gateway to several of the surrounding attractions of note, including the Lamanai ruins and the Río Bravo Conservation Area to the west.

ESSENTIALS
GETTING THERE & DEPARTING
BY PLANE   Although there's a small airstrip here, there is no regularly scheduled commuter traffic to Orange Walk Town. The closest active airports are those in Corozal Town (see "Corozal Town," later in this chapter), and the Philip S.W. Goldson International Airport outside of Belize City (see chapter 4).

BY BUS   **Northern Transport** buses (© **207-2025** in Belize City, 302-2858 in Orange Walk Town) leave throughout the day, roughly every hour between 6am and 6pm. Morning buses leave from the Novelo's terminal on West Collet Canal Street, and afternoon buses leave from the old Venus bus station on Magazine Road, 2 blocks west of the Novelo's station. Catch any bus going to Corozal Town or Chetumal. The Orange Walk Town bus station (© **302-2858**) is right on the Northern Highway in the center of town near Town Hall. You can pick up a return bus here to Belize City, or continue onward to Corozal. Buses can be either direct or local, and they vary in age and comfort. You'll pay more for a comfortable direct or express bus. The fare is BZ$7 to BZ$12 (US$3.50–US$6) between Belize City and Orange Walk Town, and BZ$8 to BZ$10 (US$4–US$5) between Orange Walk Town and Corozal Town.

BY CAR   Orange Walk is on the Northern Highway about 55 miles (89km) from Belize City. Take Freetown Road out of Belize City to connect with the Northern Highway. The highway is also known in this area as the Belize-Corozal Road, and Queen Victoria Avenue right in the heart of town. After passing through the small downtown section of Orange Walk Town, the highway continues on north to Corozal.

There's a tollbooth where the Northern Highway crosses the New River a few miles south of Orange Walk Town. The fee is BZ$.80 (US40¢) per car.

GETTING AROUND
Orange Walk is pretty compact, and the city center is just a few blocks wide in either direction. Still, a few taxis can be had around town. If you can't flag one down, call © **322-2050,** or head to the little park across from Town Hall.

Fun Fact
"Orange walk" is the Creole term for "orange orchard" or "orange grove," just as "sugar walk" would be the Creole version of "sugar plantation."

ACCOMMODATIONS ■
D*Victoria Hotel **6**
Mi Amor Hotel **5**
St. Christopher's Hotel **3**

DINING ◆
The Diner **1**

ATTRACTIONS ●
Banquitas House
 of Culture **2**
Godoy's Orchid Garden **1**
La Inmaculada Church **4**

⑤ Bank/ATM
♦ Church
Ⓟ Police
✉ Post office

ORIENTATION

The Northern Highway runs right through the heart of Orange Walk Town. Several gas stations are located on the outskirts of either end of town. As you're traveling north, the New River and "downtown" district will be to your right, while the Town Hall and Sports Ground are right on the highway, on your left.

FAST FACTS If you need to call the **police,** dial ✆ **322-2022;** for the **fire department,** dial ✆ **322-2090;** and for medical emergencies, call the **Orange Walk Hospital** at ✆ **322-2072.**

There's a **Belize Bank** (✆ **322-2019**) at the corner of Main and Park streets, and a **Scotia Bank** (✆ **322-2194**) down the block on the corner of Park Street and Lover's Lane. If you need film or developing, head to **Belicolor Photo Services,** 22 Lover's Lane (✆ **322-2819**).

SEEING THE SIGHTS

If you're staying in Orange Walk Town, you might want to visit the **Banquitas House of Culture,** at Main and Bautista's streets (✆ **322-0517**), which features a small collection of artifacts and historic displays from the Mayan, logging, and colonial eras. You might also want to stop at **Godoy's Orchid Garden,** 4 Trial Farm Rd. (✆ **322-2969**). Commercial growers and exporters, the Godoy family also offers visitors a stunning and informative tour of their extensive collection. In

Mennonites in Belize

Mennonites are a Protestant branch of the 16th-century Anabaptist movement, which also gave birth to the Amish and Hutterites. Believing that the New Testament is the sole word of God and that children should not be baptized, the Mennonites also believe that true Christians should not hold political or public office or serve in the military. Modern Mennonites are somewhat split as to the use of electricity and the internal combustion engine.

Mennonites get their name from Menno Simons, a Dutch Catholic priest who converted to Anabaptism and went on to lead the budding movement. From the start, the Anabaptists were severely persecuted and repeatedly forced into exile. Mennonites first migrated to Belize from Mexico in 1958. While the initial wave of immigrants was small, the Mennonites quickly settled in, buying large tracts of land and establishing very successful dairy farming and agricultural enterprises. The early Mennonite settlers were successful in negotiating certain strategic concessions and guarantees from the government, including that of religious freedom and exemption from military service and some forms of taxation.

While there are Mennonites throughout Belize, the Orange Walk District and northern Belize has one of the highest concentrations in the country, with large communities in Shipyard, Blue Creek Village, Little Belize, and Spanish Lookout. Most Mennonites, even in Belize, speak an archaic form of German. They are easily recognized, with their fair skin and blond hair, especially when they're traveling in their low-riding, horse-drawn carriages. The women often wear puffy cloth bonnets and simple cotton dresses, while the men sport broad-rimmed straw hats and dark jeans.

the center of town you'll find **La Inmaculada Church,** one of the few colonial Spanish churches in the country.

Two of the most popular tours out of Orange Walk Town are to **Crooked Tree Wildlife Sanctuary** (see "En Route North: Crooked Tree Wildlife Sanctuary," above) and the **Lamanai ruins** (see "Corozal Town," later in this chapter).

If you're looking for some nearby outdoor adventure and a refreshing dip, head to **Honey Camp Lagoon,** which features an unlikely sandy beach ringed by palm trees next to a spring-fed freshwater swimming hole. Honey Camp Lagoon is located about a 20-minute drive south from Orange Walk Town, via the Old Northern Highway.

If your hotel can't hook you up and you want a local guide for any of the aforementioned tours or trips to any of the nearby ruins, call **J. Avila & Sons River Tours,** 42 Riverside St. (© **322-3068**), or **Jungle River Tours** ⚛, 20 Lovers Lane (© **302-2293**).

A COUPLE OF LESSER MAYAN SITES NEARBY

CUELLO   This small site is located just over 3 miles (5km) from Orange Walk Town, near the Cuello Rum Distillery. It is named after the family that owns the land and distillery, and permission to visit the site must be obtained in advance.

Fun Fact

The original Mayan name for the New River, Dzuilhuinicob, translates roughly as "River of Strange People."

While very small and little excavated, Cuello is nonetheless one of the oldest-known Mayan sites in Belize, showing evidence of occupation as far back as 2600 B.C., in the Early Pre-Classic period.

There are two main plazas on the site, surrounded by small temples and ceremonial structures. Very little has been excavated and restored so far. There is evidence that this minor ceremonial city was razed on more than one occasion during distinct warring periods.

Permission to visit Cuello can be obtained by stopping at the rum distillery at the entrance to the site, or by calling in advance (© 322-2183). If you ask, you will probably be able to get a quick tour of the distillery as well. You might also be able to arrange for a guided tour by asking around Orange Walk Town. To get here, take the San Antonio Road out of Orange Walk Town towards Yo Creek.

NOH MUL   Noh Mul means "great mound," and this site boasts the largest Mayan structure in the Orange Walk District. Noh Mul was active in two distinct periods, the Late Pre-Classic era from around 350 B.C. to A.D. 250, and during the Late Classic era from A.D. 600 to 900. At the time, it was a major ceremonial center and supported a massive residential community that extended for nearly 8 square miles (21 sq. km). One of the more interesting features here is the fact that the two major ceremonial plazas are connected by a raised walkway, or *sacbe*. Crude excavation techniques, pillaging, and local agriculture have combined to limit the amount of restoration and conservation in evidence at Noh Mul.

Noh Mul is located about 1 mile (1.6km) west of the small village of San Pablo, which itself is about 9 miles (14km) north of Orange Walk Town. Any non-express bus running the northern line to Corozal and Chetumal can drop you off at San Pablo. However, your best bet for visiting Noh Mul is to try to arrange a tour in advance in Orange Walk Town or Belize City. You should have permission to visit Noh Mul; to get permission in San Pablo, check in with **Esteban Itzab** (no phone), whose house is located across from the water tower in the heart of the village. There are no facilities on-site, so bring some food and water with you.

WHERE TO STAY & DINE

There are few good dining options in Orange Walk Town. Your best bet is **The Diner,** 37 Clark St. (© 322-3753), which actually serves slightly more adventurous and varied dishes than its simple name implies. For a taste of Orange Walk Town's nightlife, see if there's anything happening at either the **D*Victoria Hotel** (see below) or the somewhat seedier **Mi Amor Hotel,** 19 Belize-Corozal Rd. (© 322-2031).

INEXPENSIVE

D*Victoria Hotel   This has long been the hotel of choice in Orange Walk Town. Spacious, clean rooms with tile floors await you at this surprisingly comfortable oasis set right on the side of a dreary section of road. You'll also find a cool swimming pool with a tiled patio around it. The higher-priced rooms here feature air-conditioning. The restaurant serves decent Belizean and Chinese food at reasonable prices. Between the raucous bar here on weekends and the every-day street noise, this is not exactly a quiet spot.

40 Belize-Corozal Rd., Orange Walk. ⓒ 322-2518. Fax 322-2847. www.dvictoria.com. 31 units. BZ$60–BZ$90 (US$30–US$45) double. MC, V. **Amenities:** Restaurant; bar; small outdoor pool; tour desk; limited room service (7am–10pm); laundry service. *In room:* TV, no phone.

St. Christopher's Hotel   Painted bright pink and named after the patron saint of world wanderers, this is the best choice in Orange Walk Town. It's still a better bet than the D*Victoria, although St. Christopher's is not nearly as well known and it lacks a swimming pool. The rooms and bathrooms are spacious, clean, and comfortable, and the hotel is on a quiet street, right across from the New River.

10 Main St., Orange Walk. ⓒ/fax 302-1064. rowbze@btl.net. 20 units. BZ$60–BZ$101 (US$30–US$51) double. MC, V. **Amenities:** Restaurant; tour desk; laundry service. *In room:* TV, no phone.

4 The Submerged Crocodile: Lamanai ★★

Lamanai is one of the more interesting and picturesque Mayan ruins to visit in Belize. Set on the edge of the New River Lagoon, it is one of the largest Mayan sites in Belize and features three large pyramids, a couple of residential areas, restored stelae, and open plazas, as well as a small and unique ball court that featured a large round stone set flush in its center. In addition, nearby are the ruins of two churches built by the Spanish during the 16th century; just off these ruins are the rusting remains of an abandoned sugar mill, which was set up and settled by U.S. Confederate soldiers who chose exile after the Civil War.

Lamanai was occupied continuously from around 1500 B.C. until the Spanish arrived in the 16th century and supported non-Mayan populations into the 19th century. Because it was still occupied by the Maya when the Spanish arrived, Lamanai is one of the few sites to retain its traditional name. Lamanai translates as "submerged crocodile" in Mayan; one of the principal rulers here was Lord Smoking Shell, who claimed he was the descendant of the spirit of a crocodile. Numerous crocodile images have been found in the stelae, carvings, and pottery here. And there are still plenty of live crocs in the lagoon.

Lamanai was an important and powerful pre-Classic trading city. As at Altun Ha, relics here can be traced to various cities throughout the early Mayan, Aztec, and Olmec worlds. It's a steep and scary climb to the top of the **High Temple,** but the view over the treetops and the lagoon is well worth it. The site's most striking feature just may be the **Mask Temple,** which features a series of 12-foot-high (3.6m) stone-and-mortar faces set into its sides. One of these faces is quite well restored and shows a distinct Olmec influence.

While many of the temples and ruins here have been cleared and restored to varying degrees, they are still surrounded by dense rainforest. The trails leading between temples offer excellent bird and wildlife watching opportunities.

When I last visited, the small museum and collection of artifacts was about to receive a modern new home on-site. The collection, though small, is quite interesting as it shows chronologically the distinct styles and influences present over the long history at Lamanai.

Lamanai is open daily from 8am to 4pm. Admission is BZ$10 (US$5). Although you can drive or fly here, the most common way to reach Lamanai is via boat up the New River. A host of different boats leave from docks just south of Orange Walk. The trip on the river is an hour of naturalist heaven as you cruise

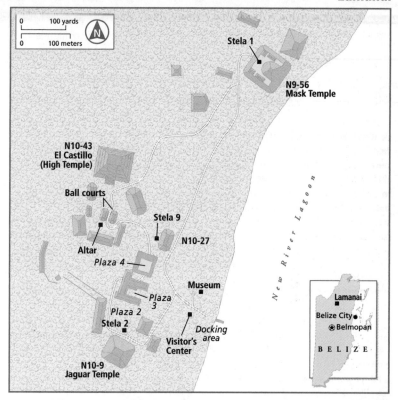

between narrow and densely forested banks, and alongside flooded marshes and wetlands. Eventually, the river opens on to the New River Lagoon, with the ancient Mayan city perched strategically atop some small limestone cliffs.

Most of the year it's possible to drive to Lamanai if you have a four-wheel-drive vehicle. During the heavy part of the rainy season, the road may become impassable. To drive here, take the Northern Highway into Orange Walk Town. Turn left near the center of town onto San Antonio Road. Follow signs to Yo Creek and San Felipe. There's an intersection at San Felipe; follow the signs to Indian Church and Lamanai. The total distance from Orange Walk Town is just about 30 miles (48km), but it will take you at least an hour to drive there on the rough dirt road. There's also a small airstrip in the neighboring village of Indian Church, and charter flights can be arranged through Lamanai Outpost Lodge.

While most folks either go on a guided tour or have a reservation at the Lamanai Outpost Lodge (see review below), it is possible to drive yourself to the boat docks, just south of the Toll Hill Bridge over the New River a few miles before Orange Walk, and pick up a boat there. Expect to pay around BZ$60 (US$30) per person for a boat to take you upriver to the ruins. The boats tend to leave for Lamanai between 8 and 10am, returning between 2 and 5pm. Many are booked in advance by large tour groups, although it's almost always possible to find a few spaces available with a boat departing in short order. Parking is safe near the docks, and the boat companies will usually watch your car for free or a nominal fee.

Take Your Time

With the rise in cruise-ship traffic, many of the new operators run massive speedboats between Orange Walk and Lamanai. Not only are these noisier and more impersonal, they also remove almost all of the opportunity to enjoy the bird- and wildlife viewing along the way. Be sure to try to book a smaller, slightly slower boat—you'll enjoy the trip much more.

A NEIGHBORING NATURE LODGE

Lamanai Outpost Lodge ★ *(Finds)* This rustic yet very comfortable lodge is set on a gentle hillside on the banks of the New River, just about a mile from the Lamanai ruins. The rooms here are all quite spacious and made of heavy local hardwoods, with high thatch roofs and ceilings. A ceiling fan is all you have—and all you will need—to cool things off. All the rooms have a private or semi-private balcony or veranda; most of these come with a hammock all ready for your afternoon siesta. There's also a separate open-air palapa strung with a series of hammocks, if your room is unequipped. While all the rooms are very similar in comfort and design, you'll want to ask for a riverfront room to be able to catch the sunrise from your front porch.

A wide range of tours and activities are available here, and the guides are excellent. The family-style meals (included in the rates) are hearty and well-prepared, and the long communal tables encourage guests and groups to mix it up, although some smaller tables are also available for honeymooners, families, and others wanting privacy. Down by the river there's a swimming and sunbathing dock. There are also canoes here that guests can take out on the New River at any time.

Indian Church Village, on the New River (P.O. Box 63, Orange Walk). © **800/733-7864** in the U.S., or 322-2199. Fax 727/864-4062 in the U.S. www.lamanai.com. 17 units. BZ$290 (US$145) double. Rates lower in the off season. Multiday packages available. AE, MC, V. **Amenities:** Restaurant; bar; lounge; tour desk; laundry service; nonsmoking rooms. *In room:* No phone.

---

5 Going West: Río Bravo Conservation Area, La Milpa & Chan Chich

The far western section of Orange Walk District is a wild area of virgin forest, remote farmlands, and under-explored Mayan ruins. It is also home to one of the country's premier and most unique nature lodges, Chan Chich Lodge. Dirt roads head west out of Orange Walk Town to the places listed below.

RIO BRAVO CONSERVATION AREA ★

Administered by the nonprofit **Programme for Belize,** this 260,000-acre (104,000 ha) tract is a mix of virgin forest, sustainable-yield managed forest, and recovering reforestation areas. The goal of the project is to combine sustainable management techniques with educational and tourism uses in a model that can prove the practical benefits of forest preservation and conservation. The land is home to nearly 400 bird species and over 200 species of tropical trees. It also supports a healthy population of most of the New World cat species, and is one of the best areas in the Americas for spotting a jaguar—although these sightings are far from common or easy to come by.

LA MILPA ★

Located inside the Río Bravo Conservation Area, La Milpa is the third largest Mayan site in Belize, behind Caracol and Lamanai. Enshrouded in jungle and just barely beginning to be excavated, La Milpa is a great site for budding archaeologists and those looking for a sense of what it must have been like to discover and begin uncovering an ancient Mayan city. Set on a high ridge, La Milpa was once a great ceremonial city. So far, at least one **Great Plaza,** numerous smaller plazas and courtyards, and two ball courts have been uncovered. The main plaza is one of the largest such public spaces yet discovered in the Mayan world. Polychrome pottery from various periods as well as numerous carved stelae have been uncovered. In 1996, excavation of a royal tomb here revealed a male skeleton buried with an elaborate and beautiful jeweled necklace. Ongoing archaeological research is being led by Boston University, in conjunction with the National Geographic Society and Programme for Belize.

A visit to La Milpa ruins is usually combined with a stay at **La Milpa Field Station** (see below), although it is possible to do it as a day trip from Orange Walk or on your way driving to or from Chan Chich Lodge. In any event, you will need permission and a reserved guide arranged in advance by calling the **Programme for Belize** (✆ 227-5616 or 227-1020; www.pfbelize.org). Ask for Verla Neal, the Tourism Development Officer, to arrange a visit.

WHERE TO STAY
INSIDE RIO BRAVO
La Milpa Field Station   Run by the Programme for Belize, this simple lodge is located in the heart of the wild Río Bravo Conservation Area and just 3 miles (5km) from La Milpa ruins. This working biological and archaeological field station also offers rooms, meals, and tours for travelers, students, and volunteers. The private thatch-roof cabins, while still relatively rustic, do feature private bathrooms and a sense of being at a more typical nature lodge. For their part, the dormitory rooms and shared bathrooms are kept quite clean, and would certainly please even the most discerning backpacker or budget traveler. The dorm rooms and shared bathrooms use solar power and hi-tech composting toilets. Guided tours are always available, and educational packages, sometimes including fieldwork, are often offered.

La Milpa section of Río Bravo Conservation Area, Orange Walk district. ✆ 227-5616. Fax 227-5635. www. pfbelize.org. 8 double-room cabins, 30 dormitory beds. BZ$230 (US$115) per person for cabins; BZ$200 (US$100) per person for dormitories. Rates include 3 meals and 2 guided tours daily. MC, V. **Amenities:** Restaurant; laundry service; nonsmoking rooms. *In room:* No phone.

RUINS OF YOUR OWN
Chan Chich Lodge ★★ *Finds*   Set in the central plaza of a minor Mayan ceremonial city, Chan Chich is one of the most unique jungle lodges in Mesoamerica. The low hills that surround 12 individual bungalows are all unexcavated pyramids and temples. The rooms feature high-pitched thatch roofs and wraparound wooden decks, and are all spacious, clean, and quite comfortable. Most come with two queen beds, made up with heavy comforters and lots of pillows. The deluxe bungalows are slightly larger, especially in the bathroom area, and feature king-size beds and some Japanese-style decor. My only complaint is that given the restricted size of the central plaza, most of the bungalows are quite close to each other. Behind one of the overgrown temple mounds, there's a refreshing screened-in pool and Jacuzzi area with its own bar. Some 9 miles (14km) of well-groomed trails lead off from the central plaza, and a host of guided tours and hikes are available. Wildlife viewing here is excellent, with over 350 bird species identified nearby. They also claim to average 50 to 80 daylight jaguar sightings per year. You can also go horseback riding, visit nearby agricultural communities,

Barry Bowen, Belikin Beer, Coca-Cola & Chan Chich

Building a modern nature lodge in the central plaza of an ancient Mayan ceremonial city is bound to be controversial. Some see it as a desecration and outrage. However, most recognize that the construction and operation of Chan Chich Lodge has served as a wonderful safeguard against looters, and a strong tool for raising awareness and money to support conservation and excavation efforts.

First discovered in 1938 by J. Eric Thompson, the site was originally named Kaxil Uinic, before being renamed by Barry Bowen in 1987. Bowen, owner of the Belikin Beer company and exclusive distributor for Coca-Cola in Belize, had bought over 750,000 acres (500,000 ha) of land (about one-sixth of the country) in western Orange Walk District in 1984. When Bowen and his workers rediscovered Chan Chich, the site had been severely looted, and many of the mounds and temples showed signs of active looting trenches.

Chan Chich sits on some 250,000 acres (10,000 ha) of private reserve, and is bordered to the north by the 262,000 acres (104,800 ha) of the Río Bravo Conservation Area. Since Bowen bought the land, a total hunting ban has been enacted, and if these protected lands are connected to the Kalakmul Reserve in Mexico and the Maya Biosphere Reserve in Guatemala, they may one day form a major Mesoamerican environmental and archaeological mega-reserve spanning three countries.

or canoe and swim at Laguna Verde. Day trips to Lamanai, La Milpa, and other Mayan sites can also be arranged.

A meal package will run you an extra BZ$110 (US$55) per day. The food here is excellent, which is a good thing, since you have no other options. You can either drive here or take a charter flight to nearby Gallon Jug; if you choose the charter, Chan Chich can arrange the flight and pick you up at the airport. If you choose to drive, it takes about 4 hours from Belize City, much of it on dirt roads, so a four-wheel-drive vehicle is recommended. If you are driving here, you will need permission to pass through the Programme for Belize's lands; call the lodge in advance to arrange this. When I last visited, there was talk of opening the rough road between Chan Chich and Spanish Lookout, connecting to the Western Highway and the Cayo District. This road would cut down drive time somewhat and allow for an interesting loop connecting Belize City, Orange Walk, Lamanai, Chan Chich, and the Cayo District.

Gallon Jug, Orange Walk District (mailing address in the U.S.: P.O. Box 1088, Vineyard Haven, MA 02568). 𝄢 800/343-8009 in the U.S., or 𝄢/fax 223-4419 in Belize. www.chanchich.com. 12 units. BZ$400–BZ$460 (US$200–US$230) double. Rates lower in the off season. Multiday packages are available. AE, MC, V. **Amenities:** Restaurant; bar; lounge; small pool; Jacuzzi; tour desk; laundry service; nonsmoking rooms. *In room:* Coffeemaker, no phone.

6 Corozal Town

8 miles (13km) N of Belize City; 31 miles (50km) N of Orange Walk Town; 8 miles (13km) S of the Mexican border

Corozal is a quiet seaside town, located just south of the Río Hondo (Hondo River), which forms the border between Mexico and Belize. Set on a crystal clear

ACCOMMODATIONS ■
Casa Blanca Hotel **1**
Copa Banana **8**
Corozal Bay Inn **9**
Hok'ol K'in Guesthouse **5**
Tony's Inn & Beach Resort **7**

DINING ◆
Cactus Plaza **6**
Corozal Bay Inn Restaurant **9**
Le Café Kela **2**
Y-Not Bar & Grill **7**

ATTRACTIONS ●
Corozal Cultural Museum **4**
Manuel Villamor Reyes's mural **3**

*Bay of Chetumal
(Corozal Bay)*

ⓘ Information
🅿 Police
✉ Post office

bay, Corozal was an important point on the early Mayan trading routes, and the evidence remains in the ruins of **Cerros** and **Santa Rita.** During the mid-1800s the modern town was settled with a large population of refugees from Mexico's Caste War. In 1955, Hurricane Janet paid a visit and left few of the town's wooden buildings standing. The rebuilding relied heavily on cement and cinderblock construction. Today, Corozal is home to a growing expatriate community. While not part of the traditional tourist circuit, Corozal Town makes a great base for fishing excursions in the calm bay, bird, and wildlife viewing tours into nearby **Shipstern Nature Reserve,** shopping trips to neighboring **Chetumal, Mexico,** and explorations of the aforementioned Mayan ruins.

ESSENTIALS
GETTING THERE & DEPARTING
BY PLANE All flights to and from Corozal Airport connect through San Pedro Airport on Ambergris Caye. There are numerous flights connecting San Pedro to both of Belize City's airports, as well as other destinations around the country.

Maya Island Air (ⓒ **226-2435** in Belize City, or 422-2333 in Corozal; www.mayaairways.com) has four daily flights between Corozal and San Pedro, leaving San Pedro at 7 and 10:30am, and at 1:30 and 4:30pm, and returning at

7:30 and 11am, and 2:30 and 5pm. Flight duration is 25 minutes. The fare is BZ$70 (US$35) each way.

Tropic Air (© **226-2012** in Belize City, or 422-0356 in Corozal; www.tropic air.com) has five daily flights departing from San Pedro at 7, 9 and 11am, and at 3 and 5pm. The flights return to San Pedro at 7:30, 9:30, and 11:30am, and at 3:30 and 5:30pm. Flight duration is 20 minutes. The fare is BZ$70 (US$35) each way.

See chapters 4 and 6 for more information on flights between San Pedro and Belize City, and other destinations around the country.

BY BUS **Northern Transport** buses (© **207-2025** in Belize City, 402-3034 in Corozal) leave throughout the day, roughly every hour between 4am and 7pm from their main terminal on West Collet Canal Street. Catch any bus going to Corozal Town or Chetumal. The Corozal Town bus station is located 2 blocks west of the small central plaza and Town Hall. You can pick up a return bus here to Belize City, or onward to the Mexican border and Chetumal. The fare is BZ$10 to BZ$15 (US$5–US$7.50) between Belize City and Corozal Town; BZ$8 to BZ$10 (US$4–US$5) between Orange Walk Town and Corozal Town; and around BZ$4 (US$2) between Chetumal and Corozal Town.

BY CAR Corozal Town is the last town on the Northern Highway before you reach the Mexican border. Take Freetown Road out of Belize City to connect with the Northern Highway. If you're driving in from Mexico, you'll reach a fork in the road 3 miles (5km) from the border; bear left and follow the signs to reach Corozal Town.

BY BOAT The *Thunderbolt* leaves from San Pedro on Ambergris Caye for Corozal every day at 7am. It leaves Corozal Town for a return trip daily at 3:30pm. Fare is BZ$40 (US$20) one-way.

GETTING AROUND

Corozal Town is very compact and it's easy to walk anywhere in the entire downtown and waterfront areas. However, if it's just too hot, you're too tired, or you're heading further afield, you can have your hotel call a taxi. Or try **Corozal Taxi Association** (© **422-2642**) or **Venus Taxi Service** (© **422-2720**).

ORIENTATION

Corozal is located right on a beautiful section of Corozal Bay. The town is laid out more or less in a grid, with avenues running roughly north-south and streets running east-west. The avenues run up numerically in order beginning with the waterfront 1st Avenue. The streets run in parallel but separate numerical order north and south from the town's central plaza, so that 3rd Street North and 3rd Street South are two distinct roads, one located 3 blocks north of the central plaza, the other 3 blocks south. The Northern Highway from Belize City and Orange Walk enters the town from the south. If you bear right and stay close to the water, you will be on 1st Avenue. If you bear left, you will be on 7th Avenue, the town's busiest thoroughfare, which skirts the western edge of downtown, before passing the bus terminal and continuing on to Chetumal and the Mexican border.

The post office and Town Hall front the small central plaza. Most banks and business are within a 2-block radius in either direction.

FAST FACTS If you need to call the **police,** dial © **422-2303;** for the **fire department,** dial © **422-2105;** and for medical emergencies, call the **Corozal Hospital** at © **422-2076.**

Travel Tip: He who finds the best hotel deal has more to spend on facials involving knobbly vegetables.

Hello, the Roaming Gnome here. I've been nabbed from the garden and taken round the world. The people who took me are so terribly clever. They find the best offerings on Travelocity. For very little cha-ching. And that means I get to be pampered and exfoliated till I'm pink as a bunny's doodah.

travelocity®

1-888-TRAVELOCITY / travelocity.com / America Online Keyword: Travel

There are several banks in Corozal Town: **Atlantic Bank,** 1 Park St. (© **422-3473**); **Scotiabank,** 4th Avenue (© **422-2046**); and **Belize Bank,** 5th Avenue and 1st Street South (© **422-2087**). All of these change U.S. dollars, Belize dollars, and Mexican pesos, as well as provide cash advances on your credit card. You can also head over to **M&D Casa de Cambio,** 36 5th Ave. (© **422-2175**), if you're looking for a slightly quicker, less bureaucratic money exchange experience.

If your hotel doesn't have a tour desk or good connections, and you want to visit any of the sites mentioned below or take an organized tour in this region, call **Jal's Travel Agency** (© **422-2163**). Also, the **Belize Tourism Board** (© **422-3176**) has an office in Corozal Town, on the waterfront near the Hok'ol K'in Guesthouse at 89 4th Ave.

WHAT TO SEE & DO

There isn't much to see or do in Corozal Town. It's mostly just a stopping point for weary travelers. However, it sits on the shores of a beautiful, quiet bay with amazing turquoise-blue water that is officially the **Bay of Chetumal,** but locally dubbed **Corozal Bay.** If you want to split hairs, the small bay just off Corozal Town could be considered a separate entity from the larger Bay of Chetumal that it sits in.

If you've just come from Mexico, you can take a day or two to walk around town and marvel at the difference between Mexican culture and Belizean culture. The countries are so close and yet worlds apart. Belize is truly a Caribbean country, with frame houses built on high stilts to provide coolness, protection from floods, and shade for sitting.

The heart of Corozal Town is the small plaza between 1st Street North and 1st Street South and 4th and 5th avenues. This is a good place to grab a bench and watch the locals go about their daily business. If you're hanging out here, it's worth a quick visit to the **Town Hall** to see the historical **mural** painted by Belizean-Mexican artist Manuel Villamor Reyes. The mural covers the local history from the Mayan era to the days of sugar cane plantations. However, if you want a real inviting park bench, I recommend heading a couple of blocks east to tiny parks and public lands you'll find all along the bayfront. Just off the town's waterfront market area, there's the little **Corozal Cultural Museum** (© **422-3176**). While it's far from impressive, you can glean a little bit of the area's history by touring its simple exhibits. Originally built in 1886 as the town's Custom's House, the museum has a collection of Mayan artifacts, as well as natural history exhibits and photos, documents, and relics from the town's more recent history. The museum is open daily from 8am to 5pm; admission is BZ$10 (US$5).

MAYAN RUINS

If you haven't yet had your fill of Mayan ruins, there are a couple to visit in the area. If you look across the water from the shore in Corozal Town, you can see **Cerros** or **Cerro Maya** on the far side of the Bay of Chetumal. "Cerro" means hill in Spanish, and the site is that little bump in the forest you can see across the bay. (Up close it seems much larger.) Cerros was an important coastal trading center during the Late Pre-Classic period. Some of the remains of this city are now under the waters of the bay, but there's still a 70-foot-tall (21m) **pyramid** built right on the water's edge that you can climb for a wonderful view of the bay. Ask around town to find someone willing to take you by boat to the ruins. Or you can drive, by heading out of town to the south and catching the free ferry across the New River; this will connect you with the road to Cerros.

Right on the outskirts of town you'll find some of the remains of another ancient city many believe was the Mayan trading center of **Chactemal** (Chetumal). It is currently called **Santa Rita.** Corozal Town is actually built on the ruins of Santa Rita, which was an important Late Post-Classic Mayan town and was still occupied at the time of the Spanish Conquest. The only excavated building is a small temple across the street from the Coca-Cola bottling plant. To reach it, head north past the bus station and, at the curve to the right, take the road straight ahead that leads up a hill. You'll see the building 1 block over to the right.

TWO NEARBY NATURE RESERVES

Bird-watchers and naturalists will want to visit the nearby **Shipstern Nature Reserve** *&*. The reserve's 22,000 acres (8,800 ha) protects a variety of distinct ecosystems and a wealth of flora and fauna. Managed by the Swiss International Tropical Conservation Foundation and the Belize Audubon Society, Shipstern Nature Reserve is home to over 250 bird species, and its mangroves, lagoons, and flat wetlands are excellent bird-watching sites. The massive network of lagoons and wetlands are home to manatees and Morelet's crocodiles. The reserve also has lowland tropical dry forest unique to Belize, as well as a butterfly breeding project. The reserve is open daily from 8am to 5pm. Admission is BZ$10 (US$5) per person and includes a short guided hike. It is possible to spend the night in some simple accommodations or pitch a tent inside of Shipstern Nature Reserve; rates are around BZ$20 (US$10) per person for a room and BZ$10 (US$5) for camping. There's no restaurant here, but kitchen facilities are available at the rooms. To make a reservation, call the ranger station at © **423-2247.**

Tip: The wetlands here are a major insect breeding ground. This is a bonanza for the birds and bats, but you might want to bring along plenty of insect repellent, and probably lightweight long-sleeved shirts and pants.

Three miles (5km) beyond Shipstern Nature Reserve, on the edge of the peninsula, lies the tiny lobster and fishing community of **Sarteneja.** In Sarteneja, you can stay at **Fernando's Seaside Guesthouse** (© **423-2085;** www.cybercayecaulker.com/sarteneja.html). Fernando is an excellent guide, and he can arrange everything from fishing or snorkeling trips to Mayan ruin excursions and night tours of the Shipstern Nature Reserve.

To drive to Shipstern Nature Reserve and Sarteneja, you used to have to first drive down to Orange Walk Town and take the Sarteneja Highway through San Estevan and Little Belize. There is now another route that cuts some time and distance off this trip. Heading south out of Corozal, stick close to the bay. Just outside of Corozal, take the small barge ferry over the New River, which then connects to the roads to Copper Bank, Progresso, and Shipstern and on to Sarteneja.

Several buses daily connect Shipstern Nature Reserve and Sarteneja to Orange Walk, Corozal Town, Chetumal, and Belize City. Alternatively, you can hitch a ride on the *Thunderbolt* (see "By Boat" under "Essentials," above) heading to San Pedro, or hire a boat on the docks in Corozal for around BZ$150 (US$75). The price is for the entire boat, and most can carry as many as 10 passengers. This is by far the quickest route.

The **Bacalar Chico National Park & Marine Reserve** lies about an hour's boat ride away from Corozal Town. This is a great spot for snorkeling and wildlife viewing. Ask around town or at the docks; you should be able to hire a

Crossing into Mexico

While Corozal Town is a sleepy little burg with a village feel to it, Chetumal, its nearby Mexican neighbor, is a bustling little border city, with a lively shopping and nightlife scene. Chetumal is also the gateway to the beaches and Mayan ruins of the Yucatán Peninsula.

Chetumal is the capital of Quintana Roo, the Mexican state that makes up much of the Yucatán Peninsula and is home to the resort towns of Cancún, Cozumel, Playa del Carmen, and Isla Mujeres, as well as the Mayan sites of Tulúm and Cobá.

In Chetumal, you can visit the **Museo de la Cultura Maya** ⚓, Avenida de los Héroes, between avenidas Colón and Gandhi (© **983/832-6838**), which offers a much more extensive museum representation of Mayan history, art, and archaeology than you will find anywhere in Belize. The museum is open Tuesday through Sunday from 9am to 7pm (it stays open 1 hr. later Fri–Sat). Admission is US$3.

Just 25 miles (40km) north of Chetumal lies the beautiful **Bacalar Lagoon.** This natural area is also known as Las Lagunas de los Siete Colores (The Lagoons of Seven Colors), and is a good place to have lunch and admire the views.

Frequent buses run between Corozal and Chetumal. The ride takes about 1 hour, including the formalities of the border crossing. The actual border is at the Belizean city of Santa Elena on the Hondo River, 8 miles (13km) north of Corozal Town. You don't need a visa in advance, but you will have to pay BZ$28 (US$14) in departure fees.

Alternatively, you can head to Chetumal by boat, a quick 10-minute hop away.

Tip: Your best bet for changing money from U.S. or Belize dollars are the money changers on the Belize side. Alternatively, there's widespread compatibility between ATMs in Chetumal and other Mexican destinations and most PLUS and Cirrus debit and credit cards.

For more on the area, pick up a copy of *Frommer's Cancún, Cozumel & the Yucatán* or *Frommer's Mexico.*

boat for around BZ$150 (US$75), and the snorkeling equipment and a bag lunch will probably run an extra BZ$30 to BZ$50 (US$15–US$25) per person. For more information on Bacalar Chico National Park & Marine Reserve, see chapter 6.

WHERE TO STAY
MODERATE
Casa Blanca Hotel ⚓ *(Finds)*   This is the place to come if you really want to get away from it all. Casa Blanca is located in Consejo Village, a small but growing retirement and vacation community located on Corozal Bay about 7 miles (11km) north of Corozal Town. The best rooms here are the second-floor suites with sea views. All rooms are attractively decorated with local textiles and crafts and feature handmade wooden and rattan furniture. The doors are all hand-carved with Mayan motifs in local mahogany. Hammocks and Adirondack

chairs are set beside the sea, where you can choose to either take the sun or rest in the shade of a thatch-roof palapa.

Consejo Village (P.O. Box 212), Corozal District. (✆) **423-1018.** Fax 423-1003. www.casablancabelize.com. 10 units. BZ$130 (US$65) double. AE, MC, V. **Amenities:** Restaurant; tour desk; laundry service. *In room:* A/C, TV, no phone.

Copa Banana   The five suites here are actually located in two side-by-side residential-style homes. Each has a full-service communal kitchen for guest use, and if you take two or three (or five) rooms, you can have one or both of the houses to yourself. Rooms are clean, bright, and spacious and come with either one queen bed or two twin beds. Several have sea views, although the hotel is located just across a small street and vacant lot from the water. Both houses have large living rooms, and one has a dining room if you decide to cook dinner. Guests have free use of the hotel's bicycles, which is a nice plus. All rooms and buildings are nonsmoking.

409 Corozal Bay Rd. (P.O. Box 226), Corozal Town. (✆) **422-0284.** Fax 422-2710. www.copabanana.bz. 5 units. BZ$110 (US$55) double. MC, V. **Amenities:** Complimentary bike use; nonsmoking rooms. *In room:* A/C, TV, no phone.

Corozal Bay Inn ⟨ℛ⟩   Ten individual thatch-roof cabins are spread around the grounds of this seaside hotel. If you're looking for amenities, this is the place to stay in Corozal Town. Each room has two double beds under mosquito netting, as well as a 27-inch flat-screen TV. There's a somewhat spartan feel to things, and the white walls could sure use some artwork. Still, the bathrooms are large and feature hand-painted Mexican ceramic sinks. The Corozal Bay Inn boasts Corozal's only swimming pool, and they also have a broad sandy area that they call their beach, although on the water's edge it's held in by a seawall, and the best saltwater swimming is at the end of their 600-foot (180m) pier. The hotel even has installed a Wi-Fi network, so that you can connect wirelessly to the Internet from your room. If your laptop or PDA isn't so equipped, guests can use the hotel's computer and Internet connection for free.

Corozal Bay Rd., Corozal Town. (✆) **442-2691.** Fax 800/836-9188 in the U.S. and Canada. www.corozal bayinn.com. 10 units. BZ$140 (US$70) double. AE, MC, V. **Amenities:** Restaurant; outdoor pool; tour desk; laundry service. *In room:* A/C, TV, minifridge, coffeemaker, hair dryer, no phone.

Tony's Inn & Beach Resort   This beachfront hotel has long been the lodging and meeting-place of choice in Corozal, but it's starting to face some competition. The rooms are all housed in a two-story L-shaped building, and feature clean tile floors, either one king bed or two double beds, a small sitting area, and 21-inch television sets. The second-floor rooms are all nonsmoking and have a shared veranda overlooking a grassy garden area. As at the neighboring Corozal Bay Inn, there's a sandy area by the water's edge here that can sort of be considered a beach, although the best swimming is of the end of the private pier. The Y-Not Bar & Grill (p. 123) serves lunch and dinner, and breakfast is served in a dining room just off the hotel lobby.

Corozal Bay Rd. (P.O. Box 12), Corozal Town. (✆) **800/447-2931** in the U.S. and Canada, or 442-2055. Fax 422-2829. www.tonysinn.com. 24 units. BZ$110 (US$55) double; BZ$150 (US$75) deluxe double. Rates slightly lower in the off season. AE, MC, V. **Amenities:** 2 restaurants; bar; tour desk; laundry service. *In room:* TV.

INEXPENSIVE

Hok'ol K'in Guesthouse   There are a handful of budget hotels in Corozal Town, but this is definitely the best of the bunch. The rooms here are located in a two-story building located right across the street from the bay and its little seaside promenade. Rooms are simple and a bit cramped, but everything's kept sparkling clean. Those on the second floor have small private balconies, most with pretty sea views. Some of the rooms have televisions, although you'll pay extra for them. The restaurant here serves good Belizean and international fare at reasonable prices.

89 4th Ave. (P.O. Box 145), Corozal Town. © 442-3329. Fax 422-3569. www.corozal.net. 10 units. BZ$60–BZ$110 (US$30–US$55) double. MC, V. **Amenities:** Restaurant; tour desk; laundry service. *In room:* No phone.

WHERE TO DINE

For such a small town, you'll find several good dining options. In addition to the places listed below, the restaurant at the Corozal Bay Inn is also quite good, and a popular hangout for the local expatriate community.

MODERATE

Y-Not Bar & Grill ☆ BELIZEAN/INTERNATIONAL   This open-air joint is the principal restaurant and bar at Tony's Inn & Beach Resort. It has a lovely setting on the water's edge under a high-pitched thatch roof. There's a loft area with seating in the main restaurant, but my favorite tables on a warm starry night are located on an uncovered little wooden deck built right over the water. Start things off with some conch fritters or coconut-battered shrimp. The chicken and beef fajitas are the most popular items here, but if you want something more substantial, try a T-bone or rack of barbecue ribs. There's also always plenty of fresh seafood, simply prepared.

At Tony's Inn & Beach Resort (p. 122), Corozal Bay Rd. © 422-2055. Main courses BZ$7–BZ$24 (US$3.50–US$12). AE, MC, V. Daily 11am–11pm.

INEXPENSIVE

Cactus Plaza *Value* MEXICAN   Serving basic Mexican fare in a pleasant open-air setting, this is perennially one of the most popular restaurants in Corozal Town. The menu here is simple: Get some tacos, tostados, or *salbutes,* and maybe a side of rice and beans. My favorite seats are on the canvas shaded rooftop patio, although you can also grab a seat at the small counter or at heavy tables on the ground floor.

6 6th St. S. © 422-0394. Reservations not accepted. Main courses BZ$1.50–BZ$4 (US75¢–US$2). MC, V. Mon–Sat 11:30am–10pm.

Le Café Kela ☆☆ *Finds* FRENCH/BELIZEAN/PIZZA   This simple yet elegant cafe serves excellent fresh seafood and delicious thin-crust pizzas, as well as some French-inspired dishes and Belizean classics. One of my favorite dishes here, the Antilles chicken, comes in a coconut milk and curry sauce. In addition to the ample menu, you can usually get some fresh fish or seafood made to order. Set on the edge of Corozal Bay, this open-air thatch-roof restaurant is hands-down the best restaurant in northern Belize. The restaurant is named after the owner's two children, Kevin and Lela.

37 1st Ave. © 422-2833. Main courses BZ$2–BZ$14 (US$1–US$7). MC, V. Daily 11:30am–3pm and 6–10pm.

COROZAL TOWN AFTER DARK

Corozal Town is a pretty quiet place. If you're looking for anything resembling action, forget about it. If you want to meet some locals, fellow travelers, or expatriates, head to the bars at either **Tony's Inn & Beach Resort** (p. 122) or the **Corozal Bay Inn** (p. 122). They're side-by-side, so if one's not happening, you can just walk next door.

6

The Northern Cayes & Atolls

The cayes (pronounced "keys") are the heart and soul of Belize's tourism industry and the country's primary attraction. Numerous small islands are strung along the length of the country's barrier reef, set amidst waters that are at once crystal clear and brilliantly turquoise. You've probably seen the photos; they're standard promotional fare. You might just think there's some fancy airbrush work and embellishment going on. If anything, the postcards, brochures, and magazine covers are understatements. Flat approximations. Seen firsthand, there's something truly mesmerizing and almost unbelievable about the clarity and color of this water. But as they say around here: "You betta Belize it."

With the reef providing protection from the open ocean, the cayes are literally islands of tranquillity in a calm blue sea. Aside from sunbathing and slow strolling, scuba diving, snorkeling, and fishing are the main attractions in the cayes. They are all world class. From the bustling mini-resorts of **Ambergris Caye** to the funky Rastafarian charm of tiny **Caye Caulker** to the deserted-isle feel of the **Turneffe Islands** and **Lighthouse Reef atolls,** it's the idyllic combination of sun and sea, as well as adventure and relaxation, that attract and captivate most visitors to Belize.

Jacques Cousteau put Belize on the diving map back in 1971, with his explorations of the **Blue Hole.** The country has almost 200 miles (322km) of continuous barrier reefs and visibility of up to 200 feet (60m) on some days. It's hard to open a diving magazine without finding an article on diving in Belize. For those sticking a little closer to the surface, the snorkeling is just as rewarding, with **Hol Chan Marine Reserve** and **Shark-Ray Alley** considered two of the best snorkeling experiences on the planet.

On the plentiful flats found inside the reefs and up in nearby estuaries, anglers find action with tarpon, snook, permit, and feisty bonefish. There's more tarpon as well as giant snapper and grouper found along the reefs, while out on the open ocean the tackle and game get bigger, with marlin, sailfish, tuna, and wahoo as the principal prey.

While Belize is very far from being considered a golf destination, there is one very pretty little course laid out on the small island of **Caye Chapel.**

Most of the cayes are small enough to walk from one end to the other in under 20 minutes. On others, it won't take you nearly as long.

1 Ambergris Caye ★★

36 miles (58km) N of Belize City; 40 miles (64km) SE of Corozal Town

Long before the British settled Belize, and long before the sun-seeking vacationers and zealous reef divers discovered Ambergris Caye, the Maya were here. In fact, the Maya created Ambergris Caye when they cut a channel through the long thin peninsula that extended down from what is now Mexico. The channel

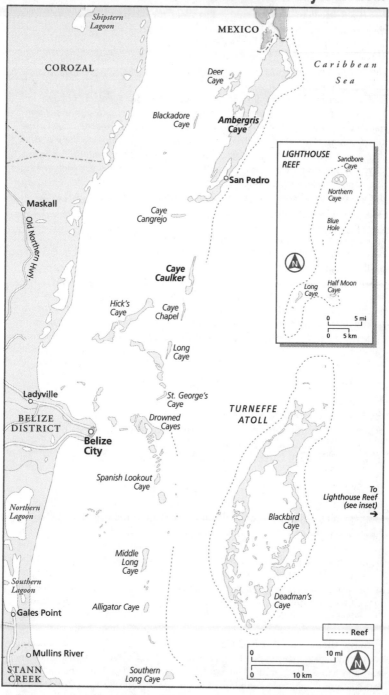

Shipstern Lagoon

MEXICO

COROZAL

Caribbean Sea

Deer Caye

Blackadore Caye

Ambergris Caye

LIGHTHOUSE REEF

Sandbore Caye

Northern Caye

Blue Hole

San Pedro

Maskall

Caye Cangrejo

Half Moon Caye

Long Caye

0   5 mi

0   5 km

Caye Caulker

Hick's Caye

Caye Chapel

Long Caye

Ladyville

St. George's Caye

TURNEFFE ATOLL

BELIZE DISTRICT

Drowned Cayes

Belize City

Old Northern Hwy.

Spanish Lookout Caye

Northern Lagoon

To Lighthouse Reef (see inset) →

Blackbird Caye

Middle Long Caye

Southern Lagoon

Deadman's Caye

Gales Point

Alligator Caye

- - - - Reef

0   10 mi

0   10 km

Mullins River

STANN CREEK

Southern Long Caye

was cut to facilitate coastal trading and avoid the dangerous barrier reef that begins not too far north of San Pedro. Today Ambergris Caye is 25 miles (40km) long and only a half-mile (1km) wide at its widest point.

For some time now, the town of San Pedro has been Belize's principal sun-and-fun destination, and it is here that you'll find the country's largest concentration of hotels and resorts. The compact "downtown" area is a jumble of small hotels, souvenir shops, restaurants, dive shops, and tour agencies. Though San Pedro continues to attract primarily scuba divers and fishermen, it is today popular with a wide range of folks who like the slow-paced atmosphere, including an increasing number of expatriates and retirees. People compare the island to the Florida Keys 40 or 50 years ago, though it is rapidly catching up. Ambergris Caye still has no paved streets, but golf carts and automobiles are proliferating and constantly force pedestrians and bicycle riders to the sides of the road. In the wake of rapid construction, wooden Caribbean houses are giving way to concrete and cinder-block buildings, and even a small strip mall or two. Development has reached both ends of Ambergris Caye, and steady construction appears destined to fill in the blanks from north to south. Still, most of the resorts located north or south of San Pedro are isolated and tranquil retreats, set on the shores of crystal-clear waters.

Despite the fact that much of the island is seasonally flooded mangrove forest, and despite laws prohibiting the cutting of mangroves, developers continue to clear this marginal land. Indiscriminate cutting of the mangroves is already having an adverse effect on the nearby barrier reef: Without the mangroves to filter the water and slow the impact of waves, silt is formed and carried out to the reef where it settles and kills the coral. There is still spectacular diving to be had just off the shore here, but local operators and long-term residents claim to have noticed a difference and are expressing concern.

ESSENTIALS
GETTING THERE & DEPARTING
You've got two options for getting to and from Ambergris Caye: sea or air. The trip is usually beautiful by either means. When the weather's rough it's bumpy both ways, although it's certainly quicker by air, and you're more likely to get wet in the boat.

BY PLANE There are dozens of daily flights between Belize City and San Pedro Airport (SPR) on Ambergris Caye. Flights leave from both Philip S.W. Goldson International Airport and Municipal Airport roughly every half-hour. Most stop en route at Caye Caulker to drop off and pick up passengers, and at Caye Chapel when there is demand. If you're coming in on an international flight and heading straight for San Pedro, you should book a flight from the international airport. If you're already in Belize City or in transit around the country, it's cheaper to fly from the municipal airport, which is also closer to downtown, and quicker and cheaper to reach by taxi. During the high season, and whenever possible, it's best to have a reservation. However, you can usually just show up at the airport and get a seat on a flight within an hour.

Maya Island Air (© 226-2435 in Belize City, or 226-2485 in San Pedro; www.mayaairways.com) has 12 flights daily between Goldson International Airport and San Pedro Airport. The first flight leaves at 6:55am and the last flight is at 5:40pm. Flight time is around 15 minutes; the fare is BZ$93 (US$47) each way. These flights actually originate at the Belize City Municipal Airport 10 minutes earlier. From the municipal airport, the fare is just BZ$52 (US$26)

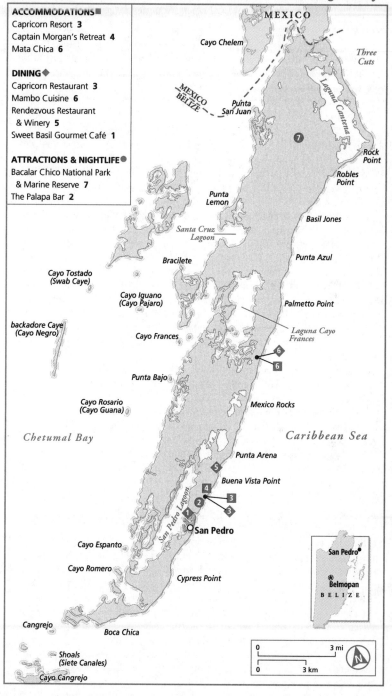

Ambergris Caye

ACCOMMODATIONS■
Capricorn Resort **3**
Captain Morgan's Retreat **4**
Mata Chica **6**

DINING◆
Capricorn Restaurant **3**
Mambo Cuisine **6**
Rendezvous Restaurant
 & Winery **5**
Sweet Basil Gourmet Café **1**

ATTRACTIONS & NIGHTLIFE●
Bacalar Chico National Park
 & Marine Reserve **7**
The Palapa Bar **2**

MEXICO

Cayo Chelem

Three
Cuts

MEXICO
BELIZE

Punta
San Juan

Laguna Cantena

Rock
Point

Robles
Point

Punta
Lemon

Basil Jones

Santa Cruz
Lagoon

Bracilete

Punta Azul

Cayo Tostado
(Swab Caye)

Cayo Iguano
(Cayo Pajaro)

Palmetto Point

backadore Caye
(Cayo Negro)

Cayo Frances

Laguna Cayo
Frances

Punta Bajo

Cayo Rosario
(Cayo Guana)

Mexico Rocks

Chetumal Bay

Caribbean Sea

Punta Arena

Buena Vista Point

Cayo Espanto

San Pedro Lagoon

San Pedro

Cayo Romero

Cypress Point

San Pedro

Belmopan
BELIZE

Cangrejo

Boca Chica

0   3 mi
0   3 km

Shoals
(Siete Canales)

Cayo Cangrejo

Tips Add It Up

Because a taxi into Belize City from the international airport costs BZ$35 to BZ$40 (US$18–US$20), and the boat to Ambergris Caye costs BZ$30 (US$15), it is only slightly more expensive to fly if you are heading directly to the cayes after arriving on an international flight.

---

each way. These flights take around 30 minutes, because they stop en route to pick up passengers at the international airport, and then at Caye Caulker to drop off passengers. When you're ready to leave, Maya Island Air flights from San Pedro to Belize City run from 6am to 5pm. Most of these flights stop first at Caye Caulker and then at the international airport, before continuing on to the municipal airport.

Tropic Air (© 226-2012; www.tropicair.com) has 11 flights daily between the Goldson International Airport and San Pedro. The first flight leaves at 7:40am and subsequent flights leave every hour thereafter until 5:40pm. The fare is BZ$93 (US$47) each way. These flights originate at the Belize City Municipal Airport 10 minutes earlier. From the municipal airport, the fare is BZ$52 (US$26) each way. These flights take around 30 minutes, because they stop en route to pick up passengers at the international airport, and then at Caye Caulker to drop off passengers. Tropic Air flights from San Pedro to Belize leave every hour on the hour between 6am and 5pm. Most of these flights stop first at Caye Caulker and then at the international airport, before continuing on to Municipal Airport.

Almost any of the above Tropic Air and Maya Island Air flights can be used to commute between Caye Caulker and San Pedro. Flight duration is just 10 minutes, and the fare is BZ$52 (US$26).

Tropic Air has five daily flights between Corozal Town and San Pedro leaving Corozal Town at 7:30, 9:30 and 11:30am, and at 3:30 and 5:30pm. Flights from San Pedro to Corozal Town leave at 7, 9 and 11am, and at 3 and 5pm.

Maya Island Air has four daily flights from Corozal Town to San Pedro leaving at 7:30 and 11am, and at 2:30 and 5pm. Flights from San Pedro to Corozal Town return at 7 and 10:30am, and at 1:30 and 4:30pm. The fare on either airline is BZ$70 (US$35) each way, and the flight duration is 20 minutes.

Connections to and from all the other major destinations in Belize can be made via the municipal and international airports in Belize City.

BY BOAT   Regularly scheduled boats ply the route between Belize City and Ambergris Caye. All leave from somewhere near the Swing Bridge. Most boats leave directly from the **Marine Terminal,** which is located right on North Front Street just over the Swing Bridge; and the boats are associated with the **Caye Caulker Water Taxi Association** (© 226-0992; www.cayecaulkerwatertaxi.com). Most are open speedboats with one or two very powerful engines. Most carry between 20 to 30 passengers, and make the trip in about 75 minutes. Almost all of these boats drop off and pick up passengers in Caye Caulker on their way, and on St. George's Caye and/or Caye Chapel when there's demand. If you're going to Ambergris from Caye Caulker, or either St. George's Caye or Caye Chapel, these boats will pick you up. Find out on Caye Caulker just where and when they stop. The schedule is subject to change, but boats for Ambergris Caye leave the Marine Terminal roughly every 90 minutes beginning at 8am, with the last

San Pedro

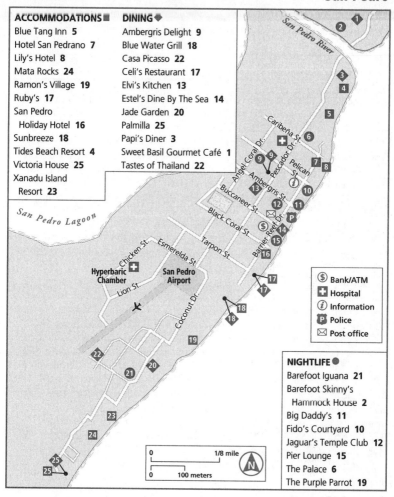

ACCOMMODATIONS ■

Blue Tang Inn **5**
Hotel San Pedrano **7**
Lily's Hotel **8**
Mata Rocks **24**
Ramon's Village **19**
Ruby's **17**
San Pedro
  Holiday Hotel **16**
Sunbreeze **18**
Tides Beach Resort **4**
Victoria House **25**
Xanadu Island
  Resort **23**

DINING ◆

Ambergris Delight **9**
Blue Water Grill **18**
Casa Picasso **22**
Celi's Restaurant **17**
Elvi's Kitchen **13**
Estel's Dine By The Sea **14**
Jade Garden **20**
Palmilla **25**
Papi's Diner **3**
Sweet Basil Gourmet Café **1**
Tastes of Thailand **22**

San Pedro River
San Pedro Lagoon
Caribeña St.
Angel Coral Dr.
Pescador Dr.
Pelican St.
Ambergris St.
Buccaneer St.
Black Coral St.
Esmerelda St.
Chicken St.
Tarpon St.
Barrier Reef Dr.
Hyperbaric Chamber
San Pedro Airport
Lion St.
Coconut Dr.

Bank/ATM $
Hospital ✚
Information ⓘ
Police P
Post office ✉

0   1/8 mile
0   100 meters
N

NIGHTLIFE ●

Barefoot Iguana **21**
Barefoot Skinny's
  Hammock House **2**
Big Daddy's **11**
Fido's Courtyard **10**
Jaguar's Temple Club **12**
Pier Lounge **15**
The Palace **6**
The Purple Parrot **19**

boat leaving at 4:30pm. The fare is BZ$30 (US$15) one-way, BZ$55 (US$28) round-trip between Belize City and Ambergris Caye; and BZ$20 (US$10) one-way between Caye Caulker and San Pedro. (See "Two Small Cayes on the Way" on p. 162 for more details about St. George's Caye and Caye Chapel.)

It is possible to purchase a seat in advance by visiting the Marine Terminal personally. This is a good idea in the high season, although in most cases, you'll need to purchase the ticket in cash upfront. Some Belize City hotels provide this service or can get you a confirmed reservation by phone.

In addition to the Caye Caulker Water Taxi Association, the *Triple J* (© 223-3464) leaves from a pier near the courthouse every morning at 9am, returning from the Texaco dock on Ambergris Caye at 3pm. The *Andrea II* (© 226-2656) departs daily from a pier in front of the former Bellevue Hotel on Southern Foreshore at 3pm. It leaves San Pedro for Belize City at 7am. The rates for these boats are the same as those listed above.

All the boats dock on Shark's Pier, near the center of town.

GETTING AROUND

The downtown section of San Pedro is easily navigated by foot. Some of the hotels located on the northern or southern ends of the island can be quite isolated, however.

Most hotels arrange pickup and drop off for guests, whether they are arriving or departing by air or sea. Taxis are waiting for all flights that arrive at the airport, and are available for most trips around the island. If your hotel can't call you one, try **Felix Taxi** (© 226-2041) or **Island Taxi** (© 226-3125). Fares run between BZ$4 and BZ$6 (US$2–US$3) for most rides.

Ubiquitous golf carts are available for rent from several outlets on the island. Rates run around BZ$100 to BZ$140 (US$50–US$70) per day for a four-seat cart, and BZ$140 to BZ$220 (US$70–US$110) for a six-seat cart. Hourly rates are between BZ$10 and BZ$40 (US$5–US$20). One of the largest and most dependable outfits is **Moncho's Rental** (© 226-3262; www.monchos rentals.com). Other dependable options include **Ambergris Golf Cart Rental** (© 226-3455) and **Island Auto Golf Cart Rental** (© 226-2790).

You can also rent scooters. **Island Scooters** (© 226-2119) has a couple of stands and outlets around the island. A scooter should run you around BZ$60 to BZ$80 (US$30–US$40) per day.

I personally think the best way to get around is on a bicycle. Most hotels have their own bikes, either available for free or a small rental fee. If your hotel doesn't have a bike, call or head to **Joe's Bike Rental** on the south end of Pescador Drive (© 226-4371). Rates run around BZ$20 to BZ$24 (US$10–US$12) per day.

Depending on where your hotel is located, a water taxi may just be your best means for commuting between your accommodations and the restaurants and shops of San Pedro. **San Pedro Water Taxi** (© 226-2194) and **Island Ferry** (© 226-3231) both run regularly scheduled launches that cover the length of the island, cruising just offshore from north to south and vice versa. The launches are in radio contact with all the hotels and restaurants, and they stop to pick up and discharge passengers as needed. Rates run around BZ$10 to BZ$20 (US$5–US$10) per person for a jaunt, depending on the length of the ride. Chartered water taxis are also available, and usually charge around BZ$40 to BZ$60 (US$20–US$30) depending on the length of the ride and size of your group.

ORIENTATION

San Pedro (the only town on the island of Ambergris Caye) is just three streets wide. The streets, from seaside to lagoonside, are Barrier Reef Drive (Front St.), Pescador Drive (Middle St.), and Angel Coral Street (Back St.). The airport is at the south end of the busy little downtown. The island stretches both north and south of San Pedro. Less than a mile north of San Pedro there is a small channel, or cut, dividing the island in two. The northern section of the island is much less developed, and is where you will find more of the higher-end isolated resorts.

A regular hand-drawn ferry runs 24 hours on demand between the two halves of the island. People, bicycles, mopeds, and golf carts can cross on the ferry, but cars cannot. The fare is BZ$2 (US$1) per person each way, with or without a bicycle, and BZ$10 (US$5) round-trip for golf carts.

Note: The ferry is tiny. Sometimes demand is quite high, and you will have to wait for it to make several trips before you can get on. When I last visited, the town council had begun a bidding process to build a bridge over the cut. However, I suspect it will be several years before any bridge is up and functional.

International Costa Maya Festival

Begun as the San Pedro Sea & Air Festival, the annual **International Costa Maya Festival** 🌟🌟 is the largest public celebration on Ambergris Caye, even larger and more popular than Carnival. Celebrated from a Thursday to Sunday in early August, the festival offers a steady stream of live concert performances, street parades, beauty pageants, and water shows and activities. When the festivities reinvented themselves several years ago, they had been transformed into a regional affair, honoring and inviting the peoples from around the Mayan world. Performers, participants, and festivalgoers come from around Belize, as well as from Mexico, Honduras, El Salvador, and Guatemala, the five countries that comprise the Mundo Maya. San Pedro's football field is converted into the fairgrounds, and a large stage is set up at one end. Food stalls and arts and crafts booths are set up as well. Admission to most events is free, and a party atmosphere envelops the entire island.

FAST FACTS   For the local **police,** dial ⓒ 911, or 226-2022; for the **fire department,** dial ⓒ 226-2372. In the case of a medical emergency, call the **San Pedro Health Clinic** (ⓒ 226-2536). If you want to attend an **AA Meeting,** call Natalie at ⓒ 226-4464.

Atlantic Bank (ⓒ **226-2195**) and **Belize Bank** (ⓒ **226-2482**) are both located on Barrier Reef Drive in downtown San Pedro. The **post office** (ⓒ **226-2250**) is located on Barrier Reef Drive; it's open Monday through Friday from 8am to noon and from 1 to 5pm. There are several Internet cafes on the island, and several hotels provide connections. If your hotel doesn't offer the service, try **Caribbean Connection Internet Café,** 55 Barrier Reef Dr. (ⓒ **226-4664**).

Most hotels provide laundry service, but pricing varies widely, so ask first. **Nellie's Laundromat** (ⓒ **226-2454**) is located on Pescador Drive toward the south end of town. They charge BZ$12 (US$6) per load, and they even offer pick-up and delivery service.

WHAT TO SEE & DO

Even though there's not much beach to speak of, this is a beach resort destination, of sorts. Snorkeling, scuba diving, and fishing are the main draws here. All are consistently spectacular.

However, before you book your vacation, you should be aware that there really isn't any beach to speak of on Ambergris Caye: There is a narrow strip of sand for much of the length of the island, where the land meets the sea, but even at low tide it isn't wide enough for you to unroll a beach towel on in most places. Try walking north or south from town along the water to find a more secluded spot where you can sit and stare out to sea. Otherwise, the beachfront hotels create their own beaches by building retaining walls and filling them in with sand. You'll find the best of these at the resorts on the north half of the island, and at Victoria House.

Likewise, swimming is not what you might expect. For 100 yards or more out from shore, the bottom is covered with sea grass. In a smart move that prioritizes the environment over tourism, the local and national government has decided to protect the sea grass, which supports a wealth of aquatic life. Beneath the grass is a layer of spongy roots and organic matter topped with a thin layer

---

Take Care
There is a lot of boat traffic (some of it quite fast and furious) running up and down the coast of Ambergris Caye, so do not try to swim or snorkel from shore out to the reef. Unfortunately, over the years, more than one swimmer or snorkeler has been run over by a speeding motorboat.

---

of white sand. Walking on this spongy sand is somewhat unnerving; there's always the possibility of a sea urchin or stingray lurking, and it's easy to trip and stumble. Swimming is best off the piers, and many of the hotels here have built long piers out into the sea, with steps down into the water, and usually a roped-off little swimming area. Beyond this, good swimming can be had from boats anchored out in the turquoise waters between the shore and the reef, or by taking a kayak offshore a little ways.

FUN IN THE WATER
Scuba Diving & Snorkeling
So why do people bother to come here if there is no beach and you can't go swimming right off the shore? They come for the spectacular coral reef, turquoise waters, and seemingly endless visibility. Less than a quarter-mile off-shore is the longest coral reef in the Western Hemisphere. The Belize Barrier Reef is second only to Australia's Barrier Reef.

Within a 10- to 20-minute boat ride from the piers lie scores of **world-class dive sites** ⋆⋆, including **Mexico Rocks, Mata Rocks, Tackle Box, Tres Cocos,** and **Rocky Point.** A day's diving will almost always feature a mix of steep wall drops and coral caverns and tunnels. You'll see brilliant coral and sponge formations, as well as a wealth of colorful marine life. On good dives, you might see schools of spotted eagle rays, watch an octopus slither amongst the coral and rocks, or have the chance to swim face to face with a sea turtle. Nurse sharks, moray eels, and large barracuda are also commonly sighted.

There are scores of dive operators in San Pedro, and almost every hotel can arrange a dive trip, either because they have their own dive shop or they subcontract out. Rates are pretty standardized, but you should be able to get deals on multiday, multi-dive packages. While it's often tempting to purchase all-inclusive dive packages before coming to Belize, this limits your flexibility; for example, if the weather and water are really rough, you're already committed, although you might prefer taking an inland tour to a Mayan ruin over a rough dive.

For reliable scuba-diving service and reasonable rates, contact **Amigos del Mar** (② 226-2706; www.amigosdive.com), **Aqua Dives** (② 800/641-2994 in the U.S. and Canada, or 226-3415; www.aquadives.com), **The Blue Hole Dive Center** (② 226-2982; www.bluedive.com), **Gaz Cooper's Dive Belize** (② 226-5206; www.divebelize.com), **Hustler Tours** (② 800/523-3350 in the U.S. and Canada, or 226-4137; www.scubadivingbelize.net), or **Patojo's Scuba Center** (② 226-2283; patojos@btl.net). Most of these companies, as well as the individual resorts, charge BZ$90 to BZ$110 (US$45–US$55) for a two-tank dive, with equipment rental running around BZ$40 (US$20) for a complete package, and BZ$10 (US$6) for a mask, snorkel, and fins.

For more adventurous and truly top-rate diving, you'll probably want to head out to the **Turneffe Island Atoll, Lighthouse Reef,** and **Blue Hole.** For more information on these sites, see section 3, later in this chapter. Most of the dive operations on the island offer this trip, or will subcontract it out. It's about a 2-to 3-hour ride each way (in a fast boat) over sometimes rough seas. You'll definitely want to choose a seaworthy, speedy, and comfortable boat. Most day trips out to Turneffe Island or Lighthouse Reef and Blue Hole run around BZ$280 to BZ$370 (US$140–US$185) per person, including transportation, two or three dives, and tanks and weights, as well as lunch and snacks. However, since these atoll islands and reefs are such a significant boat ride away, and since the diving here is so spectacular, it is really best to do overnight and multiday trips to these sites. All the above-mentioned operators offer multiday trips to the outer atoll islands and reefs. Prices average around BZ$500 to BZ$600 (US$250–US$300) for a 2-day trip, BZ$700 to BZ$800 (US$350–US$400) for a 3-day trip.

If you've always dreamed of learning to scuba dive and plan on spending any time on Ambergris Caye, you should consider taking a course here. Resort courses will give you a great 1-day introduction into the world of scuba diving, including a very controlled shallow-water boat dive. These courses cost BZ$200 to BZ$300 (US$100–US$150). In 3 to 4 days, however, you can get your full open water certification. These courses run between BZ$650 and BZ$750 (US$325–US$375), including all equipment rentals, class materials, and the processing of your certification, as well as four open water and reef dives. All of the above-mentioned dive centers, as well as many of the individual resorts here, offer these courses.

If you're hesitant to take a tank plunge, don't miss a chance to at least snorkel. There's good snorkeling all along the protected side of the barrier reef, but some of the best is at **Shark-Ray Alley** 𝒦𝒦 and **Hol Chan Marine Reserve** 𝒦𝒦, which are about 4 miles (6km) southeast of San Pedro. Shark-Ray Alley provides a nice adrenaline rush for all but the most nonchalant and experienced divers. Here you'll be able to snorkel above and between schools of nurse sharks and stingrays. *Hol chan* is a Mayan term meaning "little channel," which is exactly what you'll find here—a narrow channel cutting through the shallow coral reef. The walls of the channel are popular with divers, and the shallower areas are frequented by snorkelers. Some of the exciting residents of the area are large green moray eels, stingrays, and nurse sharks (harmless). The reserve covers 5 square miles (13 sq. km) and is divided into three zones: the reef, the sea-grass beds, and the mangroves. Most combination trips to Shark-Ray Alley and Hol Chan Marine Reserve last about 2½ to 3 hours, and cost around BZ$50 to BZ$60 (US$25–US$30). There is a BZ$10 (US$5) charge for diving at Hol Chan, which may or may not be included in the price of boat excursions to the reserve.

There are a host of boats offering snorkeling trips, and most of the above dive operators also offer snorkel trips and equipment rental. Trips to other sites range in price from BZ$25 to BZ$60 (US$13–US$30) for short jaunts to half-day outings, and BZ$100 to BZ$120 (US$50–US$60) for full-day trips. One of the operators who specializes in snorkeling trips here is the very personable Alfonse Graniel and his launch *Li'l Alfonse* (© **226-3537**). Snorkel gear is available from most of the above operators and at several other sites around town. A full set of mask, fins, and snorkel will usually cost between BZ$6 and BZ$14 (US$3–US$7) per person per day.

Tip: Hol Chan and Shark-Ray Alley are extremely popular. If you really want to enjoy them, try to find a boat leaving San Pedro at or before 8am, and head first to Shark-Ray Alley. Most boats dive Hol Chan first, and this is the best way to get a dive with the greatest concentration of nurse sharks and stingrays. By all means, avoid snorkeling or diving these sites at times when the cruise ships are running excursions there. Alternatively, you may want to consider visiting a different snorkeling site, such as Mexico Rocks Coral Gardens, Tres Cocos, or Mata Rocks, where the snorkeling is just as good, if not better, and you're more likely to have the place to yourself.

COMBINING SNORKELING WITH MANATEE VIEWING Another trip that has recently become popular is a day trip to see manatees and do some snorkeling at remote cayes. These trips include a leisurely tour of manatee feeding sites on the way to the isolated Goff's and Sergeant's cayes, which are little more than football field–size patches of sand, with a few palm trees. These trips include all transportation, lunch on one of the cayes, and several snorkeling stops, and cost around BZ$80 to BZ$150 (US$40–US$75). Most hotels and tour agencies in town offer this trip; or check with **Hustler Tours** (© **800/523-3350** in the U.S. and Canada, or 226-4137; www.scubadivingbelize.net).

GLASS-BOTTOM BOATS If you really don't want to take a plunge of any sort, you can still get a good view of the reef and its undersea wonders aboard a glass-bottom boat. There are a few glass-bottom boats working Ambergris Caye. Most hotels and tour agencies on the island can book them for you, or you can contact the *Reef Seeker* (© **226-2802**) direct. Rates run between BZ$50 and BZ$80 (US$25–US$40) depending on the length of the tour, and whether or not a meal or drink is involved. Most of the glass-bottom boat tours allow time for a snorkeling break as well.

Sailing

The crystal-clear waters, calm seas, and isolated anchorages and snorkeling spots all around Ambergris Caye make this an excellent place to go out for a sail. Your options range from crewed yachts and bareboat charters for multiday adventures, to day cruises and sunset sails.

A day cruise, including lunch, drinks, and snorkeling gear should run between BZ$200 to BZ$300 (US$100–US$150) per person. Most hotels and tour operators around town can hook you up with a day sail or sunset cruise.

The *Me Too* is a 44-foot (13m) catamaran that makes daily trips to Caye Caulker. For BZ$100 (US$50) per person, you get a pleasant sail, with several snorkel stops, drinks, and a lunch stop on Caye Caulker (lunch and snorkel equipment extra). The *Me Too* also does regular sunset cruises, leaving at around 4:30pm. The trip costs BZ$70 (US$35) per person, and includes drinks and light snacks. You can book the *Me Too* through **Hustler Tours** (© **800/523-3350** in the U.S. and Canada, or 226-4137; www.scubadivingbelize.net).

The *Winnie Estelle* (© **226-2394**; winnie_estelle@yahoo.com), a 66-foot (20m) island trader motor-sailer operated by Capt. Robert Smith, does a similar trip for BZ$110 (US$55). This boat can also be chartered for longer trips to the outer atolls, or southern cayes.

One of my favorite boats is the *Rum Punch,* a 32-foot (10m) classic Belizean gaff-rigged sloop. The *Rum Punch* runs full- and half-day tours, including snorkeling, and can be booked by most hotels and agencies around the island, or via **Island Guides Tours** (© **206-2222**).

If you're looking for a longer and more adventurous time on the high seas, **The Moorings** (© **888/952-8401** in the U.S. and Canada, or 523-3351; www.moorings.com) and **TMM** (© **800/633-0155** in the U.S., or 226-3026; www.sailtmm.com) are two large-scale charter companies with operations on Ambergris Caye. Options include monohulls, catamarans, and trimarans of varying sizes. Given the shallow draft, increased interior space, and reduced drag, a multihull is your best bet. All of the boats are well equipped and sea-worthy. Rates for a weeklong charter run between BZ$3,700 and BZ$13,000 (US$1,850–US$6,500) depending on the size of the boat. You can charter these boats, either solo or with a captain and crew.

Fishing

Sport fishing for tarpon, permit, and bonefish is among the best in the world around these cayes and reefs, and over the years a few record catches have been made. If you prefer deep-sea fishing, there's plenty of tuna, dolphin, and marlin to be had beyond the reefs. **Fishing San Pedro** (© 206-2191; www.fishingsan pedro.com), **Hustler Tours** (© 800/523-3350 in the U.S. and Canada, or 226-4137; www.scubadivingbelize.net), and **Island Guides Tours** (© 206-2222) all have respectable guides and equipment. A half-day reef trolling, casting, or fly-fishing for bonefish or tarpon runs around BZ$250 to BZ$350 (US$125–US$175), a full day BZ$400 to BZ$500 (US$200–US$300). Deep-sea trolling for larger game costs between BZ$800 and BZ$1,200 (US$400–US$600) for a half-day, and between BZ$1,600 and BZ$2,400 (US$800–US$1,200) for a full day. These prices are per boat for two to four fishermen and usually include drinks, tackle, and lunch.

Hard-core fishermen might want to check out one of the dedicated fishing lodges, like **El Pescador** ★ (© 800/242-2017 in the U.S. and Canada, or 226-2938; www.elpescador.com) on Ambergris Caye; or **Turneffe Flats** ★★ (© 800/815-1304, or 605/578-1304 in the U.S.; www.tflats.com) out on the Turneffe Island Atoll.

Windsurfing, Parasailing & Watercraft

Ambergris Caye is a good place for beginning and intermediate windsurfers. The nearly constant 15- to 20-knot trade winds are perfect for learning on and easy cruising. The protected waters provide some chop, but are generally pretty gentle on beginning board sailors. If you're looking to do some windsurfing, or to try the latest adrenaline boost of kiteboarding, your best bet is to check in with the folks at **Sail Sports Belize** (© 226-4488; www.sailsportsbelize.com). Board rentals run around BZ$40 to BZ$50 (US$20–US$25) per hour, or BZ$100 to BZ$150 (US$50–US$75) per day. Weekly rates are also available.

If you want a bird's-eye view of Ambergris Caye, try parasailing off the back of a speedboat. Head to **Fido's Watersports** (© 226-2056), where you can get a 15- to 20-minute ride for BZ$80 (US$40).

Most resort hotels here have their own collection of all or some of the above-mentioned watercraft. Rates run around BZ$30 to BZ$40 (US$15–US$20) per hour for a Hobie Cat, small sailboat, or wind surfer; and BZ$50 to BZ$60 (US$25–US$30) per hour for a jet ski. If your hotel doesn't have these, head to **Fido's Watersports** (© 226-2056), on the water behind Fido's Courtyard, near the center of town.

FUN ON DRY LAND

Truth be told, aside from sun bathing, shopping, reading, and relaxing, there's not an awful lot to do on dry land on Ambergris Caye.

Golf

There's no golf on Ambergris Caye, but guests here can arrange to play the course on nearby **Caye Chapel** ★ (© 226-8250; www.cayechapel.com). The course is almost entirely flat, but it features a lot of water and sand hazards, as well as some stunning views. Rates for a full day of unlimited golfing, including carts, club rental, and use of the resort's pool and beach area run BZ$400 (US$200) per person. Reservations are absolutely necessary. Transportation can be arranged by air, chartered water taxi, or regularly scheduled water taxi.

For a less challenging trip around the links, families might want to head to **Island Mini Golf,** a very basic minigolf course located just south of downtown. This place also features a soft-serve ice cream shop.

Bodywork

While there are no full-scale resort spas or high-end facilities on Ambergris Caye, you can certainly get sore muscles soothed and a wide array of pampering treatments at a series of day spas and independent massage therapy storefronts. The best of these include **The Art of Touch,** at the entrance to the Sunbreeze Hotel (© **226-3357**), and **Tropical Touch,** across from Fido's Courtyard, on the third floor (© **226-4666;** www.tropicaltouchspa.com). Rates run around BZ$140 (US$70) for an hour-long massage.

If you want to work out, there's a modest health club and gym at the Isla Bonita Tennis Club (see below). These folks also offer aerobic, Pilates, and yoga classes.

Tennis

This is very far from a tennis destination, and very few hotels have courts. You'll find two lit courts at the **Isla Bonita Tennis Club,** on the west side of San Pedro (© **226-2683**). You'll want to play early in the morning or late afternoon or evening, as it's just too hot to play tennis most days during the heat of the day.

OTHER ATTRACTIONS

Bacalar Chico National Park & Marine Reserve

Occupying the northern end of Ambergris Caye and its surrounding waters, **Bacalar Chico National Park & Marine Reserve** ⚓ is one of the newest additions to Belize's national park system. In addition to being the home to scores of bird, animal, and plant species (many of which are endemic), the park also features several ancient Mayan ceremonial and trading sites. The ranger station is, in fact, located at the diminutive Chac Balam ruins. Bacalar Chico is the name of the channel cut 1,500 years ago by the Maya to facilitate coastal trading. Just across the channel is Mexico. Nearly 200 species of birds have been spotted here, and the park allegedly contains all five wildcat species found in Belize, including the jaguar—although your odds of seeing a cat are remote at best. However, you've got decent odds of seeing a crocodile or wild deer, and of course numerous bird species. The park is only accessible by boat. All of the local tour outfits offer half- and full-day trips to Bacalar Chico. Depending on your needs, these trips usually provide a mix of bird- and nature-watching, snorkeling, and Mayan ruin explorations. Specialist guides can be hired around San Pedro, if you want to focus primarily on any one of these pursuits. Admission to the park is BZ$10 (US$5).

Excursions Farther Afield

If you've been on the island for a while or just want to see more of Belize, a host of tour operators on Ambergris Caye offer excursions to all of the major attractions and destinations around the country, including Altun Ha, Lamanai, Xunantunich, Mountain Pine Ridge, and even Tikal. You can also go cave tubing in the Caves Branch region. Most of these tours involve a flight in a small charter plane.

One of the most popular day trips is to the Mayan ruins at Altun Ha. This is also one of the most economical, as it doesn't require a flight. This begins on a powerful little boat that will whisk you over to the mainland. You'll then take a taxi to the ruins and have lunch before returning to San Pedro. Most operators offering the Altun Ha trip include a lunch stop at Maruba Resort, with the option of adding on a decadent jungle spa treatment. Prices for these trips run around BZ$120 to BZ$140 (US$60–US$70). A similar trip by boat, land, and boat is offered to the ruins at Lamanai.

For trips involving a flight, pries range from BZ$200 to BZ$400 (US$100–US$200) per person, depending on the distance traveled and amount of activities and attractions crammed into 1 day. Most hotels on the island can book these tours, or you can contact **Excalibur Tours** (© 226-3235), **Hustler Tours** (© 800/523-3350) in the U.S. and Canada, or 226-4137; www.scuba divingbelize.net), or **SEAduced** at Vilma Linda Plaza (© 226-2254).

For detailed descriptions of these various destinations and attractions, see the respective regional chapters in this book.

SHOPPING

Most of the shopping on Ambergris Caye is typical tourist fare. You'll see tons of T-shirts and tank tops, with dive logos and silk-screen prints of the Blue Hole. Beyond this, the best buy on the island is handmade jewelry sold by local Belizean artisans from makeshift display stands along Barrier Reef Drive. I'd be wary of black coral jewelry, though. Black coral is extremely beautiful, but as with every endangered resource, increased demand just leads to increased harvesting of a slow-growing coral.

Inside Fido's Courtyard at **Belizean Arts** ⭐ (© 226-3019; www.belizean arts.com), you'll find the island's best collection of original paintings and crafts. Of special note are the prints and paintings of co-owner Walter Castillo, a Nicaraguan-born artist whose simple, but bold, style captures the Caribbean color and rhythm of Belize.

Another shop at Fido's Courtyard worth checking out is **Ambar** ⭐⭐ (© 226-3101). The owner and artisan here sells handmade jewelry, with a specialty in amber. The stuff here is a significant cut above the wares you'll find in most other souvenir shops and street stands.

You can find some interesting locally made casual wear at **Isla Bonita Designs,** North Barrier Reef Drive (© 226-4258; www.islabonitadesigns.com). While I find the stuff here well designed, it is a bit pricey.

To get your fill of jade, head to the small **Ambergris Maya Jade & History Museum,** Barrier Reef Drive (© 226-3311), which has a nice collection of jade artifacts and jewelry, and really functions as the draw to get folks into their retail store.

If you're a diver, you might want to bring home a video reminder of those infamous Belizean blues. For BZ$120 (US$60), **Belize Underwater Video** (© 226-2276) will accompany and film you on two reef dives. Underwater wedding videos, night dive videos, and outer atoll dive videos are also available.

WHERE TO STAY
IN SAN PEDRO

There's a score of hotel options right in the heart of San Pedro town. Most are geared towards budget travelers, although a few of these are quite comfortable and charming. Most of the more upscale resorts are located a little bit further north or south of town. See below for these options.

Gonna Wash That Paint Right Out of My Hair

A modest version of the traditional Caribbean Carnival or Mardi Gras is celebrated in San Pedro—with an odd twist—over the weekend preceding Ash Wednesday and the period of Lent. Sure, there are colorful and lively *comparsa* parades, with marching drum bands and costumed dancers. But, over the years a tradition of painting has developed. This tradition predates paintball by decades. In times past, this was a fun and frivolous game between roaming bands of local residents using flour-based homemade "paints." Tourists were usually asked before being painted and their demurrals respected. Over the years, however, the painting fever has skyrocketed and gotten more aggressive: Fresh eggs and the occasional oil-based paint were introduced as weapons, and tourists are now often painted despite pleas to the contrary. My small daypack still proudly bears its mark. It's definitely fun and a good way to meet some locals. If you get to a shower relatively quickly, it'll wash off without much hassle. Still, if you go out during Carnival, expect to get painted, and dress accordingly.

Tip: Almost every hotel on Ambergris Caye, and certainly all of the resorts, offers scuba packages. If you plan to do a lot of diving, this is the way to go, as these packages can sometimes provide substantial savings over paying as you go. However, you can also buy dive packages from many of the individual dive operators, either in advance or upon arrival on the caye.

Very Expensive

Ramon's Village 🍀   This place is one of the original resorts on Ambergris Caye, and it's grown over the years. Originally begun by local son Ramón Núñez, this place is appropriately named, as there is a small-village feel to the collection of thatch-roofed bungalows and suites. At the center of the complex is a small but inviting free-form pool, surrounded by palm trees and flowering plants. Rooms vary a bit in size, and are classified as beachfront, seaside, and garden-view, with the beachfront units having the best unobstructed views of the water. Some of the older units are a bit dark and too close to the road for my taste. All are clean, modern, and comfortable, with colorful print bedspreads and dark varnished wood trim. Most have a private or shared balcony with a sitting chair or hammock. There are a few suites, which are larger and provide more room to roam and relax. Room nos. 58 and 61 are large second-floor suites set right near the edge of the sea. A few open-air thatch palapas are spread around the grounds and hung with hammocks.

Ramon's has one of the longer and prettier beaches to be found in San Pedro, as well as a very long dock jutting into the sea, and a wide range of watersports equipment and activities to choose from. This place also manages Steve & Becky's Cute Little Hotel, which is across the street slightly inland, but allows guests to use all of the facilities at Ramon's. Still, all things considered, I think you can do much better in this price range.

Coconut Dr. (southern edge of town), San Pedro, Ambergris Caye. ℂ **800/624-4215** or 601/649-1990 in the U.S., or 226-2067 in Belize. Fax 226-2214. www.ramons.com. 60 units. BZ$330–BZ$370 (US$165–US$185) double; BZ$450–BZ$780 (US$225–US$390) suite. Rates slightly higher during peak weeks, lower in the off season. AE, MC, V. **Amenities:** Restaurant, bar, small outdoor pool, full-service dive shop, watersports equipment rental; bike and golf cart rental; tour desk; limited room service (6:30am–10pm); laundry service. *In room:* A/C, no phone.

Expensive

Blue Tang Inn ⚐ *(Value)*   This intimate option features all-suite accommodations. Housed in a three-story plantation-style building, the rooms are modern, comfortable, and spacious, and all feature a kitchenette, making them an excellent option for extended stays. The prized rooms here are the third-floor oceanfront suites, which feature king beds, wood floors, arched ceilings, and Jacuzzi bathtubs. However, all rooms are up to snuff. The hotel is located right on the waterfront, just north of the heart of downtown San Pedro. While there is no restaurant here, they do serve morning coffee and fruit, and even if you choose to skip cooking on your own, a score of restaurants is just a few steps away.

Sand Piper St., San Pedro, Ambergris Caye. ✆ 866/881-1020 in the U.S. and Canada, or 226-2326 in Belize. Fax 226-2358. www.bluetanginn.com. 14 units. BZ$200–BZ$320 (US$100–US$160) double. AE, MC, V. **Amenities:** Small outdoor pool; tour desk; laundry service. *In room:* A/C, TV, kitchenette, no phone.

San Pedro Holiday Hotel ⚐ *(Finds)*   You can't miss this brilliantly white three-building complex with painted purple and pink trim in the center of town. Every room comes with air-conditioning, and most have excellent ocean views and small refrigerators. Get a room on the second floor and you'll have a wonderful balcony—you won't want to leave. Celi McCorkle opened this hotel over 35 years ago, the first on the island, and it's continued to keep pace with the times and tourism boom. There's a full-service dive shop, a popular bar and restaurant, and a small gift shop here. The whole operation has a festive and lively air to it. This hotel lacks some of the amenities of other options in this price range—there are no televisions and no swimming pool—but it makes up for that with its funky island vibe.

Barrier Reef Dr. (P.O. Box 61), San Pedro, Ambergris Caye. ✆ 226-2014. Fax 226-2295. www.sanpedro holiday.com. 18 units. BZ$206–BZ$226 (US$103–US$113) double. AE, MC, V. **Amenities:** 2 restaurants; bar; full-service dive shop; watersports equipment rental; bike rental; tour desk; laundry service. *In room:* A/C, no phone.

Sunbreeze ⚐   For my money, this is one of the best options right in San Pedro. This two-story seafront hotel is built in a horseshoe around a simple garden area, with a small pool at its core. The superior rooms are all spacious, recently remodeled, and nonsmoking. The standard rooms have slightly small and dated bathrooms, but are otherwise quite acceptable. The five deluxe units feature Jacuzzi tubs, nicer furnishings, and the best views. Room no. 225 is the best of the bunch, a corner deluxe unit, with a large balcony facing the Caribbean Sea. On the other end of the horseshoe, no. 201 is the best standard room in the house. This hotel is very ideally located in the center of town, with its own dive operation and a small arcade of shops. The hotel's Blue Water Grill (p. 144) serves excellent international fare. One of the nicest features here is a covered open-air hammock area built over the restaurant and bar. The hotel is directly across from the airstrip, and quite convenient if you are arriving and departing by air.

Coconut Dr. (P.O. Box 14) San Pedro, Ambergris Caye. ✆ 800/688-0191 in the U.S., or 226-2191 in Belize. Fax 226-2346. www.sunbreeze.net. 39 units. BZ$220–BZ$260 (US$110–US$130) double; BZ$320 (US$160) deluxe; rates lower in the off season. AE, MC, V. **Amenities:** Restaurant; bar; small outdoor pool; full-service dive shop; watersports equipment rental; bike rental; tour desk; limited room service (6:30am–9pm); laundry service; nonsmoking rooms. *In room:* A/C, TV.

Moderate

Lily's Hotel Lily's is on the beach, toward the north end of Front Street. While this was one of the pioneering budget options on the island, it's received regular remodeling and upgrades over the years. In fact, it's actually nudged itself right out of the budget price range, and I consider the rooms a tad pricey for what you get, although for Ambergris Caye, these are arguably reasonable rates for a waterfront room. Get your money's worth by watching the sun rise every morning and listening to the waves lap at your doorstep after the sun sets.

The rooms are simple yet well maintained and feature air-conditioning, minifridges, and modern furnishings. Not all of the rooms here have a water view—be sure to ask for one. The best rooms are those on the second floor, enjoying a wonderful seaview shared veranda. Those on the ground floor also have ocean views, although you need to be prepared for a fare amount of pedestrian traffic, as they are set right on the island's main pedestrian and bicycle thoroughfare. There's a relaxed vibe throughout the operation here, and you'll definitely enjoy the lounge chairs set on the sand for the guests' use.

On the beach, San Pedro, Ambergris Caye. © 206-2059. Fax 226-2623. www.ambergriscaye.com/lilys. 10 units. BZ$130–BZ$150 (US$65–US$75) double. MC, V. **Amenities:** Restaurant; bar; tour desk; laundry service. *In room:* Minifridge, no phone.

Tides Beach Resort 🟊 *Finds* Although it's actually rather new, this three-story oceanfront hotel has a worn and weathered feel, with its wood construction and gingerbread trim. The hotel and sister dive operation are owned and operated by the highly respected and personable local couple of Patojo and Sabrina Paz. All of the rooms are oceanfront, and have either a shared or small private veranda or balcony. They feature wood floors, simple furnishings, and either two double beds or one king bed. Most rooms are air-conditioned, but you'll have to pay a BZ$40 (US$20) surcharge to use it. Patojo runs one of the better dive operations on the island, and this place is popular with scuba divers and dive groups. This hotel is located on the north end of San Pedro town.

Boca del Río Dr., San Pedro, Ambergris Caye. © 226-2283. Fax 226-3797. www.ambergriscaye.com/tides. 12 units. BZ$160 (US$80) double. AE, MC, V. **Amenities:** Bar; full-service dive shop; watersports equipment rental; bike and golf cart rental; tour desk; laundry service. *In room:* Minifridge, no phone.

Inexpensive

There are quite a few budget options on Ambergris Caye, and almost all of them are concentrated in the compact downtown area of San Pedro. True budget hounds should just walk around and see who's got the best room for the best price. I list a couple of my personal favorites below.

Hotel San Pedrano Although few of the rooms here have ocean views, they do have nice wooden floors, a single bed, and a double bed in every room, and clean bathrooms with tubs. A few of the rooms even have air-conditioning. The best views can be enjoyed from the wide veranda that looks out over the rooftops of adjacent buildings, a great place to gather with fellow travelers or simply sit and read a book.

Barrier Reef Dr., San Pedro, Ambergris Caye. © 226-2054. Fax 226-2093. 7 units. BZ$50–BZ$70 double (US$25–US$35). Add BZ$20 (US$10) for A/C. AE, MC, V. **Amenities:** Restaurant; tour desk; laundry service. *In room:* No phone.

Ruby's *Value* Walking towards the ocean and into town from the airstrip, one of the first things you'll see is a three-story blood-red building, with white gingerbread trim. Most of the rooms at Ruby's overlook the water. The best ones have air-conditioning and a private balcony overlooking the sea. The floors are wooden, the rooms are simply furnished with a couple of beds and little else, and the showers and bathrooms are clean. You can't beat the location at this price in San Pedro. Downstairs you'll find Ruby's Deli (daily 5am–1:30pm), which is a good place for breakfast or a casual midday meal. These folks recently opened a separate hotel on the lagoon side of the island, with clean, spacious, simple rooms at even lower prices. After years of mixed messages, it seems like the owners here have settled on spelling Ruby's with a "y" and not "ie" at the end.

Barrier Reef Dr. (P.O. Box 56), San Pedro, Ambergris Caye. (C) **226-2063**. Fax 226-2434. www.ambergris caye.com/rubys. 21 units. BZ$70–BZ$100 (US$35–US$50) double. MC, V. **Amenities:** Restaurant; tour desk; laundry service. *In room:* No phone.

SOUTH OF SAN PEDRO
Very Expensive
Victoria House 🌴🌴🌴 *Finds*   This elegant and exclusive island retreat features a varied collection of rooms, suites, and villas. Everything is done with a refined sense of style and attention to detail. The resort is set on an expansive piece of land a couple of miles south of San Pedro, with lush tropical gardens and a surprisingly good section of soft white sand fronting it. My favorite accommodation here is the Rainforest Suite, which is a private villa set close to the water, with large wraparound deck overlooking the beach and sea. Inside, you'll find a spacious suite with a four-poster bamboo bed. The plantation rooms and suites are spread through two buildings, while there are 10 individual casitas aligned in a crescent around a grassy lawn. These latter feature high-pitched thatch roofs, tile floors, and wide French doors letting on to a private balcony. A private five-bedroom villa features its own swimming pool, and it can be rented whole or divided up. Service is attentive yet understated. A full range of tours and activities are offered, and the Palmilla Restaurant here (p. 147) is one of the finest on the island.

Beachfront, 2 miles (3km) south of San Pedro (P.O. Box 22, San Pedro), Ambergris Caye. (C) **800/247-5159** or 713/344-2340 in the U.S., or 226-2067 in Belize. www.victoria-house.com. 35 units. BZ$340 (US$170) double; BZ$520 (US$260) casita; BZ$540–BZ$780 (US$270–US$390) suite; BZ$1,350–BZ$2,800 (US$675–US$1,400) villa. Rates slightly higher during peak weeks, lower in the off season. AE, MC, V. **Amenities:** 2 restaurants; bar; lounge; midsize outdoor pool; full-service dive shop; watersports equipment rental; bicycle rental; tour desk; laundry service. *In room:* A/C, safe, no phone.

Expensive
Mata Rocks 🌴 *Finds*   The blinding white paint and angular architecture of this intimate hotel conjures up images of the Greek isles. All of the rooms here have at least a partial ocean view. The best is no. 53, a second-floor unit fronting the sea, with a large private balcony. There are six suites and 11 standard rooms. All are clean, modern, and cheery. The suites come with a fully equipped kitchenette, king bed and sofa bed, and small sitting area. At the center of the hotel is a small free-form pool that is fed via a small artificial "stream," which is in turn fed by a small fountain. Purple and lavender Adirondack chairs provide splashes of color. There is an intimate and relaxed air about the whole operation. A complimentary continental breakfast buffet is served in the open-air beachfront palapa bar, as are snacks and light lunches. This place is located about 1½ miles (2.4km) south of San Pedro town.

Oceanfront, southern end of Ambergris Caye. (C) **888/628-2757** in the U.S. and Canada, or 226-2336 in Belize. Fax 226-2349. www.matarocks.com. 17 units. BZ$250 (US$125) double; BZ$300–BZ$330 (US$150–US$165) suite. Rates include continental breakfast. Rates slightly lower in the off season. AE, MC, V. **Amenities:** Bar; small outdoor pool; complimentary bike use; tour desk; laundry service. *In room:* A/C, TV, minifridge, no phone.

Xanadu Island Resort ★★ *(Kids)* The two- and three-story thatch-roof buildings of this small resort are of sturdy construction, and are promoted as being hurricane-proof. They are set in a semi-circle around a central pool area. All of the units here are quite large, and loaded with amenities. In fact, all are classified as suites, although most have the feel of independent apartments or condo units. This isn't a bad thing, and it makes this a good choice for extended stays and for families. They even give you a complimentary BZ$5 (US$2.50) local calling card to get you started. Each unit features a full kitchen or a kitchen and spacious living room. Each comes with a private balcony or front porch. There are single-bedroom as well as two- and three-bedroom units available. The resort has a long pier jutting into the ocean, with a wonderful swimming platform at the end. There's no restaurant here, but several are within close proximity, and the town of San Pedro is just a mile (1.6km) away.

Oceanfront (P.O. Box 109, San Pedro Town), southern end of Ambergris Caye. © 226-2814. Fax 226-3409. www.xanaduresort-belize.com. 15 units. BZ$320–BZ$420 (US$160–US$210) double; BZ$540–BZ$620 (US$270–US$310) 2-bedroom; BZ$660–BZ$720 (US$330–US$360) 3-bedroom. Rates slightly lower in the off season; slightly higher during peak periods. AE, MC, V. **Amenities:** Small outdoor pool; complimentary bike use; tour desk; laundry service. *In room:* A/C, TV, dataport, kitchenette, coffeemaker, hair dryer, safe.

ON NORTH AMBERGRIS CAYE

This is where you'll find most of the larger, more isolated, and more upscale resorts on Ambergris Caye. If you stay here, you will have to rely on your hotel or on the local water taxis to get to and from San Pedro town.

In addition to the hotels listed below, **El Pescador Fly Fishing Resort** ★ (© 800/242-2017 in the U.S. and Canada, or 226-2398; www.elpescador.com) is a lovely and luxurious resort geared towards hard-core fishermen and women.

Very Expensive

Capricorn Resort ★ *(Finds)* If you're looking for an intimate getaway on the northern section of Ambergris Caye, you'd be hard pressed to find anything better than this elegant little hotel and restaurant. There are just three individual cabins here. Each features high vaulted ceilings, a large tile shower, and a private front deck with a hammock. The walls are painted bold primary colors, and artistic touches—in the form of local, Guatemalan, and other ethnic arts and crafts—abound. The cabins come with either one queen bed or two full beds; all come with mosquito netting. Cabin no. 1 is the closest to the ocean, and would be my first choice. The restaurant here (p. 147) is one of the best on Ambergris Caye.

Oceanfront (P.O. Box 247, San Pedro), 2½ miles (4km) north of the cut on northern end of Ambergris Caye. © 226-2809. Fax 226-5091. www.ambergriscaye.com/capricorn. 3 units. BZ$350–BZ$370 (US$175–US$185) double. Rates include full breakfast, and transfers to and from San Pedro airport. Rates lower in the off season. AE, MC, V. **Amenities:** Restaurant; bar; complimentary kayak use; tour desk; limited room service (8am–9pm); laundry service. *In room:* A/C, no phone.

Captain Morgan's Retreat ★★ *(Kids)* Featured in the campy reality show *Temptation Island,* Captain Morgan's is a large, lively, and well-equipped resort on a long and lovely section of beach. The rooms are either individual beachfront casitas (little houses), or one- or two-bedroom suites set in a series of two-story units. All feature thatch roofs and wood construction, as well as attractive Guatemalan bedspreads and varnished wood furnishings. Every room comes with a private balcony or veranda, and all are modern, comfortable, and plenty spacious. I prefer the casitas, which are named after famous pirate captains, for their sense of privacy, although if you want more space and amenities, choose one of the second-floor suites. The suites all come with a fully equipped kitch-enette. When I last visited, they were building a series of new suites, as well as a second pool area. Comfortable lounge chairs and hammocks are spread along the beach and in shady spots on the grounds, and a host of aquatic and land-based activities and tours are offered.

Oceanfront, 3 miles (5km) north of the cut on northern end of Ambergris Caye. C 888/653-9090 or 307/ 587-8914 in the U.S., or 226-2207 in Belize. Fax 226-4171. www.belizevacation.com. 26 units. BZ$498 (US$249) casita; BZ$480 (US$240) 1-bedroom suite; BZ$760 (US$380) 2-bedroom suite. Rates substantially lower in the off season; slightly higher during peak periods. AE, MC, V. **Amenities:** Restaurant; 2 bars; lounge; 2 outdoor pools; full-service dive shop; spa services; watersports equipment rental; complimentary bike use; tour desk; laundry service. *In room:* A/C, minifridge, safe.

Mata Chica ★★ This is one of the more northern resorts on Ambergris Caye, and in many ways it's the hippest. There's a sense of rustic luxury throughout. Artistic touches abound, with an eclectic mix of fabrics, sculptures, ceramics, and paintings from around the world. Every room here is actually a private bun-galow or villa, and all can be considered junior suites or better. My favorites are the "casitas," which are the closest to the ocean, and feature a large sitting area, a king bed on a raised platform, and an interior garden shower. The four "bun-galows" are listed as having sea views, but they are set back a bit, and that view is mostly a glimpse through foliage and the gaps between the casitas. Set back even further, but set high on raised stilts, are two very large villas, and one immense "mansion." The latter is over 5,000 square feet (465 sq. m), and fea-tures three bedrooms, a full kitchen, three full bathrooms, a huge living room, and ample deck areas and views. There's no pool here, but the large oceanfront Jacuzzi is quite popular, especially at night. There's a small spa, with a full list of treatments and cures, as well as a full-service tour desk. The hotel has a new mar-tini-slash-Internet bar, as well as one of the better restaurants on Ambergris Caye (Mambo Cuisine; see p. 147 for a complete review).

Oceanfront, northern end of Ambergris Caye. C 226-5010. Fax 226-5012. www.matachica.com. 14 units. BZ$460–BZ$650 (US$230–US$325) double; BZ$1,300–BZ$1,900 (US$650–US$950) villas. Rates include con-tinental breakfast and transfers to and from San Pedro airport. Rates slightly lower in the off season. AE, MC, V. **Amenities:** Restaurant; bar; large oceanfront Jacuzzi; small spa; complimentary kayak use; tour desk; laun-dry service. *In room:* A/C, coffeemaker, no phone.

AN ISLAND OF YOUR OWN
Cayo Espanto ★★★ Whether you're a bona-fide member of the jet set or you just want to feel like one, this is the place for you in Belize. Five individual bungalows are spread across this private island. Each bungalow is luxurious and elegantly appointed and set on the edge of the Caribbean Sea, and each comes with a private butler. Four of the five have private plunge pools, while the smaller unit, Casa Morada, skimps by with an outdoor Jacuzzi. All have wide French doors and windows that open on to private decks and verandas and stun-ning views. Several have private piers jutting into the ocean. A couple of the bungalows are set up to accommodate two couples or a small family. Service is very attentive and pampering, and the food is excellent. A minimum stay of 5 nights is required most of the year—it gets bumped up to a solid week during peak periods, although this is somewhat negotiable, depending upon demand. You can also rent the entire island for BZ$16,000 (US$8,000) per night. Cayo Espanto is located just off the western tip of Ambergris Caye.

Cayo Espanto. C 888/666-4282 in the U.S. and Canada. BZ$1,990–BZ$3,300 (US$995–US$1,650) double. Rates include 3 meals, all drinks (except wine and champagne), all non-motorized watersports equipment usage, and transportation to and from San Pedro during daylight hours. Rates slightly higher during peak weeks. AE, MC, V. **Amenities:** Restaurant; bar; lounge; 4 small outdoor pools; small exercise room; spa services; tour desk; laundry service. *In room:* A/C, TV, minifridge, coffeemaker, hair dryer, safe.

WHERE TO DINE
IN SAN PEDRO

Seafood is, of course, the most popular food on the island, and there's plenty of it around all year. However, please keep in mind that there are seasons for lobster and conch (because sea turtles are endangered, never order turtle). Officially, lobster season runs from July 15 to February 14, while conch is available from October 1 to June 30. Recently, local restaurants and fishery officials have struck a deal to allow lobster to be served in the off season. Supposedly this is lobster caught and frozen during the open season, and not while they are mating in the formerly closed season.

In addition to the restaurants listed below, **Ruby's Cafe** and **Celi's Deli,** on the ground floors of Ruby's Hotel (p. 140) and the San Pedro Holiday Hotel (p. 139) respectively, are good places to pick up a light meal, and both specialize in fresh baked breads and pastries, and sandwiches to go. The folks from the excellent Rasta Pasta Rainforest Café on Caye Caulker (p. 160) have recently opened **Rasta Pasta 2** (© 226-3512) in Coconuts Hotel, on Coconut Drive south of the airstrip.

Two local coffeehouses, **Café Olé** (© 226-2907) and **Sweet Du Monde Café** (© 226-3264) are also good options for a coffee break and light lunch. The latter is a New Orleans–influenced venture and has excellent beignets. Café Olé is located next to the Sunbreeze Hotel; Sweet Du Monde is in a two-story commercial center on Tarpon Street.

If you're staying for an extended period of time, or have a room equipped with a kitchenette, you'll find several good markets around town. The largest, most modern, and best stocked of these is **Island Supermarket** (© 226-2972), located on Coconut Drive.

Expensive

Blue Water Grill ★★ Finds INTERNATIONAL/ASIAN   This hotel restaurant has a broad and extensive menu, as well as a lovely setting overlooking the ocean and piers from the waterfront in the heart of San Pedro. While there's a good selection of pizzas, pastas, and such hearty dishes as grilled beef tenderloin with a Creole mustard and black pepper sauce; or chicken breasts served with fresh herbs, walnuts, and blue cheese, the real reason to come here is for their inspired Asian fare. Start things off with shrimp cakes served with an orange-sesame-miso dipping sauce infused with scallion oil. For a main course, I recommend the fresh snapper in a hot sesame butter, or the mixed seafood grill. These folks also have "sushi nights" every Tuesday and Thursday. If you come for sushi, be sure to try their spicy scallop hand roll.

At the Sunbreeze Hotel, on the waterfront. © 226-3347. Reservations recommended. Main courses BZ$36–BZ$56 (US$18–US$28). AE, MC, V. Daily 6:30am–9:30pm.

Moderate

Casa Picasso ★★ INTERNATIONAL/TAPAS   Housed on the second floor and outdoor deck of a converted residential house, this stylish little place is probably the hippest little restaurant in San Pedro. The menu features a wide selection of tapas, both traditional and more modern choices. I particularly recommend the chicken marinated in sangria and served with an orange-raisin-walnut salsa, as well as the medallions of pork tenderloin accompanied by two very distinct sauces, a mango chutney and a spicy Argentine chimichurri. If you want heartier fare, there are several pasta dishes to choose from. Casa Picasso advertises the widest selection of desserts on the island, and I definitely advise you to save room for their coffee-flavored crème brûlée and flourless chocolate cake. They also have an extensive list of creative martinis and coffee drinks, as well as a good selection of French, Italian, Chilean, and South African wines.

Sting Ray St., south of town on lagoon side of island. ℂ 226-4507. Tapas BZ$6–BZ$20 (US$3–US$10); main courses BZ$16–BZ$24 (US$8–US$12). MC, V. Daily 5:30–11pm.

Celi's Restaurant ⭐ SEAFOOD/BELIZEAN   This simple restaurant serves dependable local fare in a cheery setting. You can either dine indoors, or with your feet in the sand in the restaurant's screened-in outdoor dining area. Stick to the seafood, which is plentiful, reasonably priced, and expertly prepared. Freshly caught fish, shrimp, and conch are prepared in a variety of sauces, and lobster and stone crabs are offered seasonally. For dessert, be sure to try some of Celi's "Caye Lime Pie." The neighboring Celi's Deli is a good choice for sandwiches and light meals, especially if you're planning a picnic on some deserted beach or caye.

On the beach at the San Pedro Holiday Hotel. ℂ 226-2014. Reservations recommended. Main courses BZ$15–BZ$28 (US$7.50–US$14); burgers and sandwiches BZ$10–BZ$15 (US$5–US$7.50); lobster priced according to size and market. AE, MC, V. Thurs–Tues 11am–2pm and 5:30–9pm.

Tastes of Thailand ⭐ THAI   Once you get past the rather tacky decor— featuring mermaids and roses painted on the walls, interspersed with plastic Thai artworks, and vinyl tablecloths topped with glass centerpieces of swans and dolphins—you'll discover an excellent and authentic Thai restaurant in the heart of the Belizean cayes. There are only six tables here, so reservations are necessary in the high season. The extensive menu has all the Thai classics. Pork, beef, fish, and seafood specials are prepared as curries or with combinations of lemon grass, basil, hot chiles, and peanuts, either with rice or over rice noodles. There are quite a few good vegetarian options as well. I'm a bit of a traditionalist, but if you venture away from the pad thai, satay, and kaeng paneng, you will not be let down by the chef's Hurricane Hits, an original concoction blending various Thai sauces with the full range of available fresh seafood.

Sea Grape Dr., San Pedro. ℂ 226-2601. Reservations recommended. Main courses BZ$19–BZ$42 (US$9.50–US$21). MC, V. Mon–Sat 6–11pm.

Inexpensive

Ambergris Delight ⭐ *Finds* BELIZEAN   Located a block north of Elvi's (see below), Ambergris Delight is popular with locals and offers excellent and inexpensive seafood, burgers, and even some vegetarian plates. A big blackboard serves as the menu and includes occasional specials such as conch soup or crab claws. The pizzas here are also excellent. If you've been out fishing, these folks will cook up your catch for you. The ambience is down-home and funky. A television over the bar usually has news programming or even some sports. Ambergris Delight also delivers.

35 Pescador Dr., San Pedro. ℂ 226-2464. Reservations recommended. Main courses BZ$11–BZ$28 (US$5.50–US$14); burgers and sandwiches BZ$8–BZ$14 (US$4–US$7); lobster priced according to size and market. MC, V. Daily 11am–2pm and 6–10pm.

Elvi's Kitchen ⭐⭐ *Finds* BELIZEAN/SEAFOOD/INTERNATIONAL Local legend Elvia Staines began selling burgers out of a takeout window in 1974. Today, Elvi's is the most popular and renowned restaurant on Ambergris

Caye, with a word-of-mouth reputation built on the happy bellies of thousands of diners. Even after having enlarged the dining room, they still can't keep up with the dinner crowds that flock here for the attentive service, substantial servings, fresh ingredients, and food cooked to order. The restaurant is a thatched, screened-in building with picnic tables, a large flamboyant tree growing up through the roof, and a floor of crushed shells and sand. You can get everything from Belizean stewed chicken to shrimp in watermelon sauce. For lunch, there are still burgers, including traditional beef burgers, although I prefer the shrimp and fish burgers. There's live music most nights, with Caribbean night on Thursday, Mayan night on Friday, and Mexican night on Saturday. Food specials complement the musical selections.

Pescador Dr., San Pedro. ⓒ 226-2176. Reservations recommended. Main courses BZ$14–BZ$30 (US$7–US$15); fresh fish, seafood, and lobster priced according to market. AE, MC, V. Mon–Sat 11am–2pm and 5:30–10pm.

Estel's Dine By the Sea ⚘ SEAFOOD/INTERNATIONAL   If you want to dine right by the water, it's hard to get much closer than Estel's. This casual place has a sand floor with heavy wooden tables and plastic chairs inside the main dining room, and a sand terrace outside with pure plastic patio furniture. A broad range of memorabilia and antiques line the walls, and there's a piano in one corner. This is a popular place to start your day, with excellent *huevos rancheros* and breakfast burritos. The dinner menu features plenty of fresh seafood and fish simply prepared, as well as a host of Mexican and Belizean standards. Hosts Charles and Estella Worthington are usually on hand—they live upstairs. In general, it's a mellow scene, with great music on the stereo and occasional live performances.

Barrier Reef Dr., San Pedro. ⓒ 226-2019. Main courses BZ$8–BZ$36 (US$4–US$18). MC, V. Wed–Mon 6am–9pm.

Jade Garden CHINESE   Located in a large contemporary house south of the airport, Jade Garden has long been one of San Pedro's more popular restaurants. Wicker chairs, overhead fans, high ceilings, and a balcony overlooking the sea and garden create the atmosphere, and the kitchen serves up a long menu of well-prepared Chinese standards with the emphasis on seafood and Cantonese cuisine. There are also several non-Chinese specialties such as surf-and-turf kabobs, broiled lobster, and T-bone steak, as well as a good selection of vegetarian dishes. After a big dinner, you can walk back to your hotel and burn up a few calories.

1¼ miles (2km) south of airstrip. ⓒ 226-2506. Reservations recommended. Main courses BZ$9–BZ$36 (US$4.50–US$18). AE, MC, V. Daily 11am–2pm and 6–10pm.

Papi's Diner ⚘ *Value* BELIZEAN/SEAFOOD   This popular local joint is the epitome of funky island eating. A few tables are scattered around a simple room, with hot pink cloth tablecloths topped with white plastic place mats and some plastic flowers. There are a couple of tables under a plywood awning out front, but if any traffic passes it will kick up some dust to add spice to your dining pleasure. The food here is simple and well prepared, with a mix of local cuisine, fresh seafood, and some Mexican dishes. Your best bet is to get fresh snapper sautéed in garlic and wine, or a couple of the grilled seafood kabobs. However, you can also order some BBQ ribs or a T-bone steak. For breakfast, I recommend the breakfast burrito or *huevos rancheros*. This place is located on the north end of San Pedro Town, on the middle street a block or so away from the hand ferry.

Lagoon Dr., Boca del Río, San Pedro. ✆ 226-2047. Main courses BZ$7.50–BZ$35 (US$3.75–US$18); hamburgers and sandwiches BZ$3.75–BZ$8.50 (US$1.90–US$4.25). AE, MC, V. Thurs–Tues 7–10am and 11:30am–10pm.

SOUTH OF SAN PEDRO
Very Expensive
Palmilla ★★★ *Finds* INTERNATIONAL/FUSION   This is hands-down the most elegant and refined dining experience to be had on Ambergris Caye. Executive chef Amy Knox was awarded the Best Chef of 2003 in the Taste of Belize competition. Chef Knox prepares the freshest of local ingredients with a creative blend of techniques, spices, and cuisines from around the world. The menu changes nightly, but might include chile-seared snapper or grilled lobster with chipotle butter. You can choose a table in the formal dining room, with its orgy of white linens, walls, and orchids, or dine alfresco by candlelight at one of the heavy wooden tables on the outdoor poolside deck. Save room for dessert, as the molten chocolate cake and banana chimichangas are both to die for.

At Victoria House, south of downtown San Pedro. ✆ 226-2067. Reservations required. Main courses BZ$24–BZ$52 (US$12–US$26). AE, MC, V. Daily 6:30–9pm.

ON NORTH AMBERGRIS CAYE
Despite its relative isolation, the northern section of Ambergris Caye has perhaps the island's greatest concentration of truly excellent eateries. If you're staying in San Pedro or on the southern half of the island, you'll need to take a water taxi. Most of these restaurants will usually be able to arrange this for you, usually at a reduced rate from the going fare.

Very Expensive
Capricorn Restaurant ★★ INTERNATIONAL/SEAFOOD   Grab one of the outdoor tables here on the wraparound seafront veranda of this boutique hotel's little restaurant. If these are all filled, don't despair, as you'll also be able to watch the water through the wide windows of the small dining room, which are almost always thrown wide open. Although under new management, this intimate restaurant has maintained its quality and reputation. The menu is deceptively simple, but even the traditional stewed chicken is one of the tastier dishes you'll find anywhere in Belize. Start things off with some fresh ceviche and a few slices of rosemary-infused focaccia. Be sure to ask about the nightly specials. There's always fresh fish, and conch, stone crabs, scallops, or lobster depending on season and availability, as well as a handful of steak, chicken, and pork entrees.

At Capricorn Resort, on northern end of Ambergris Caye. ✆ 226-2809. Reservations recommended. Main courses BZ$38–BZ$58 (US$19–US$29). AE, MC, V. Thurs–Tues 10am–2pm and 6–9pm.

Mambo Cuisine ★★★ *Finds* FUSION/INTERNATIONAL   The eclectic menu here touches on a wide range of world cuisines. From the seared scallops in Jamaican jerk sauce to the filet mignon with blue cheese crust drizzled with an orange-balsamic reduction, the food and presentation here are top-notch. I also enjoyed the mango and ginger glazed pork chops, while the warm chocolate soufflé was perhaps the best dessert I tasted in Belize. The restaurant features an excellent and extensive wine list. And for those who want to keep on enjoying the finer things in life after dinner, these folks also offer a selection of Cuban cigars and cognacs. Service is attentive and professional, and the ambience is elegant without being stuffy.

At Mata Chica, on northern end of Ambergris Caye. ✆ 220-5010. Reservations required. Main courses BZ$32–BZ$60 (US$16–US$30). AE, MC, V. Daily noon–2:30pm and 6–10pm.

Rendezvous Restaurant & Winery 🌟 FRENCH/THAI   This refined restaurant serves a mix of French- and Thai-inspired dishes. You'll find Thai classics, such as pad thai and cold beef salad, right alongside escargot and bouillabaisse. I like to start things off with their light and tasty shrimp and salmon mousse. There's a relaxed semi-formal air to the whole operation, which is decorated with tablecloths, subdued lighting, and cushioned rattan chairs. They vint a few wine varieties right on-site, with imported grape juices. Unfortunately, I found these to be quite immature and thin; you'd do much better to buy an imported bottle off their more traditional wine list.

4½ miles (7km) north of cut, on the northern section of Ambergris Caye. ✆ **226-3426.** Reservations recommended. Main courses BZ$36–BZ$58 (US$18–US$29). MC, V. Daily 11:30am–2pm and 6–9pm.

Moderate

Sweet Basil Gourmet Café 🌟 INTERNATIONAL   This breezy, two-story wood-frame house with a bright paint job and gingerbread trim just may be my favorite lunch spot on Ambergris Caye. A wide range of specialty items and imported goods, from cheeses to olives to deli meats, are used to create an extensive menu of interesting salads, sandwiches, and pasta dishes. There is also a daily selection of main dishes. While there's seating on the first floor, you'll definitely want to grab a seat on the open-air second-floor veranda, with views to both the lagoon and Caribbean Sea. Sweet Basil will serve dinner upon request, if your group is big enough and you give them enough warning.

Just across the cut, on the northern section of Ambergris Caye. ✆ **226-3870.** Reservations recommended during high season. Sandwiches BZ$15–BZ$26 (US$7.50–US$13); pastas BZ$20–BZ$28 (US$10–US$14); salads BZ$20–BZ$32 (US$10–US$16). AE, MC, V. Tues–Sun 10am–5pm.

AMBERGRIS CAYE AFTER DARK

Ambergris Caye is a popular beach and dive destination, and as such it supports a fairly active nightlife and late-night bar scene. I recommend starting things off at one of the beachside bars such as the **Pier Lounge** at the Spindthrift Hotel, or a bar built out over the water like **The Palapa Bar,** located about a mile (1.6km) north of the cut on the northern half of the island. Two other popular choices are **Fido's Courtyard** and **The Purple Parrot** in Ramon's Village; the latter claims to be a favorite haunt of Jimmy Buffet. When I last visited, the new **Barefoot Skinny's Hammock House,** located just across the cut, was getting good live music and open jam sessions most weekends.

If you're looking for a dance club and late-night action, your best bets are the two traditional San Pedro discos, **Jaguar's Temple Club** and **Big Daddy's,** both of which are within a stone's throw of each other on Barrier Reef Drive, near the basketball court and the church. Just south of downtown on Coconut Drive, you might try the huge **Barefoot Iguana** 🌟, which features everything from hot new DJs, to mud wrestling, to sporting events shown on a giant screen.

If you're the betting type, try **The Palace,** at the corner of Caribeña and Pescador Drive (✆ **226-3570**). It's a small casino, but it's got a few blackjack and poker tables and one-armed bandits, as well as a sports book.

2 Caye Caulker 🌟🌟🌟

20 miles (32km) N of Belize City; 10 miles (16km) S of Ambergris Caye

The word is definitely out. Caye Caulker is no longer the secret hideaway of a handful of happy hippie backers and a few chosen cognoscenti. But this is still

Caye Caulker

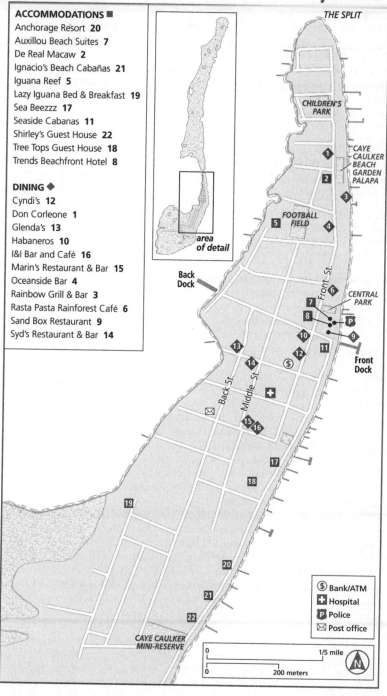

ACCOMMODATIONS ■
Anchorage Resort **20**
Auxillou Beach Suites **7**
De Real Macaw **2**
Ignacio's Beach Cabañas **21**
Iguana Reef **5**
Lazy Iguana Bed & Breakfast **19**
Sea Beezzz **17**
Seaside Cabanas **11**
Shirley's Guest House **22**
Tree Tops Guest House **18**
Trends Beachfront Hotel **8**

DINING ◆
Cyndi's **12**
Don Corleone **1**
Glenda's **13**
Habaneros **10**
I&I Bar and Café **16**
Marin's Restaurant & Bar **15**
Oceanside Bar **4**
Rainbow Grill & Bar **3**
Rasta Pasta Rainforest Café **6**
Sand Box Restaurant **9**
Syd's Restaurant & Bar **14**

THE SPLIT

CHILDREN'S PARK

CAYE CAULKER BEACH GARDEN PALAPA

FOOTBALL FIELD

Back Dock

Front St.

CENTRAL PARK

Front Dock

Back St.

Middle St.

CAYE CAULKER MINI-RESERVE

area of detail

$ Bank/ATM
+ Hospital
P Police
✉ Post office

0   1/5 mile
0   200 meters

N

the epitome of a small, isolated, and laid-back Caribbean getaway. Unlike neighboring San Pedro, you won't be constantly run off the road by cars and golf carts. In fact, Caye Caulker has no cars, and the golf cart traffic is still rather light. Let's hope it stays that way.

Nevertheless, behind the scenes battles are brewing, as developers covetously eye dormant land and pristine mangroves. Hopefully the island will not become as overbuilt and shadeless as San Pedro. When I last visited, there was quite a bit of cleared land around the airport, all laid out for development, although with little apparent action underway.

ESSENTIALS
GETTING THERE & DEPARTING

As with Ambergris Caye, you've got two options for getting to and from Caye Caulker: sea or air. When the weather's rough it's bumpy both ways, although it's certainly quicker by air, and you're more likely to get wet in the boat.

BY PLANE   There are dozens of daily flights between Belize City and Caye Caulker Airport (CUK). Flights leave from both Philip S. W. Goldson International Airport and Municipal Airport roughly every half-hour. Most will stop en route at Caye Chapel Airport (CYC), when there is demand. If you're coming in on an international flight and heading straight for Caye Caulker, you should book a flight from the international airport. If you're already in Belize City or in transit around the country, it's cheaper to fly from the municipal airport, which is also closer to downtown, and quicker and cheaper to reach by taxi. During the high season, and whenever possible, it's best to have a reservation. However, you can usually just show up at the airport and get a seat on a flight within an hour.

Maya Island Air (© 226-2435 in Belize City, or 226-0112 in Caye Caulker; www.mayaairways.com) has 12 flights daily between Goldson International Airport and Caye Caulker. The first flight leaves at 6:55am and the last flight is at 5:40pm. Flight time is around 10 minutes; fare is BZ$93 (US$47) each way. These flights actually originate at the Belize City Municipal Airport 10 minutes earlier. From the municipal airport, the fare is just BZ$52 (US$26) each way. These flights take around 20 minutes, because they stop en route to pick up passengers at the international airport. When you're ready to leave, Maya Island Air flights from Caye Caulker to Belize City run roughly every hour from 6:05am to 5:05pm. Most of these flights stop first at the international airport, before continuing on to Municipal Airport.

Tropic Air (© 226-2012 or 226-0040; www.tropicair.com) has 11 flights daily between Goldson International Airport and Caye Caulker. The first flight leaves at 7:40am, and subsequent flights leave every hour thereafter until 5:40pm. Fare is BZ$93 (US$47) each way. Flight duration is 10 minutes. These flights actually originate at the Belize City Municipal Airport 10 minutes earlier. From the municipal airport, the fare is just BZ$52 (US$26) each way. These flights take around 20 to 25 minutes, because of the stop en route to pick up passengers at the international airport. Tropic Air flights from Caye Caulker to Belize leave every hour on the hour between 6:10am and 5:10pm. Most of these flights stop first at the international airport, before continuing on to Municipal Airport.

Almost all of the above flights originating in Belize City continue on to San Pedro on Ambergris Caye. Similarly, almost all the return flights originate in San Pedro. The flight between the two islands takes 10 minutes, and the fare is BZ$52 (US$26).

Fun Fact What's in a Name?

The Spanish called this little island "Cayo Hicaco." *Hicaco* is Spanish for the coco plum palm. There are some who say the name comes from the fact that ships used to be caulked in the shallow calm waters off the back-side of this island, hence Caye Caulker. However, a third theory is based on the fact that the island appears as Caye Corker on several early British maps. This line of reasoning claims that early sailors and pirates stopped to fill and then "cork" their water bottles with the abundant fresh water found here.

Connections to and from all the other major destinations in Belize can be made via the municipal and international airports in Belize City.

BY BOAT   Regularly scheduled boats ply the route between Belize City and Caye Caulker. All leave from somewhere near the Swing Bridge. Most boats leave directly from the **Marine Terminal** (which is located right on North Front St. just over the Swing Bridge) and are associated with the **Caye Caulker Water Taxi Association** (© 226-0992; www.cayecaulkerwatertaxi.com). Most are open speedboats with one or two very powerful engines. Most carry between 20 to 30 passengers, and make the trip in about 45 minutes. Almost all of these boats stop to drop off and pick up passengers on St. George's Caye or Caye Chapel, when there's demand. If you're going to Ambergris, St. George's, or Caye Chapel from Caye Caulker, these boats all continue on and will take you there. Find out on Caye Caulker just where and when they stop. The schedule is subject to change, but boats for Caye Caulker leave the Marine Terminal roughly every 90 minutes beginning at 8am, with the last boat leaving at 5:30pm. The fare is BZ$20 (US$10) one-way and BZ$35 (US$18) round-trip between Belize City and Caye Caulker; and BZ$20 (US$10) one-way between Caye Caulker and San Pedro. (See "Two Small Cayes on the Way" on p. 162 for more details about St. George's Caye and Caye Chapel.)

In addition to the Caye Caulker Water Taxi Association, the *Triple J* (© 223-3464) leaves from a pier near the courthouse every morning at 9am, returning from the back bridge dock at 3:30pm. The *Andrea II* (© 226-2656) departs daily from a pier in front of the former Bellevue Hotel on Southern Foreshore at 3pm. It leaves San Pedro for Belize City at 7am, stopping at the front dock at around 7:30am. The rates for these boats are the same as those listed above.

It is possible to purchase a seat in advance by visiting the Marine Terminal personally. This is a good idea in the high season, although in most cases, you'll need to purchase the ticket in cash, upfront. Some Belize City hotels provide this service, or they can get you a confirmed reservation by pone.

GETTING AROUND

Caye Caulker is small. You can easily walk from one end of the island to the other in around 20 minutes. If you want to cover more ground quickly, a bicycle is your best bet. Many hotels have their own for guests to use free of charge or for a slight rental fee. If not, you can rent a bicycle in town. There are several places on Front Street that rent bicycles. **Mary Jo's Bike Rental & Deli** is a good choice. Rates run around BZ$20 to BZ$24 (US$10–US$12) per day.

While I think it's really unnecessary, you can also rent a golf cart from **Island Rental** (© 226-0229) or **Jasmine Cart Rentals** (© 206-0212). Rates run

---

FYI

The unofficial yet increasingly common motto on Caye Caulker is "Go Slow."

---

around BZ$100 to BZ$140 (US$50–US$70) per day for a four-seat cart. Hourly rates run between BZ$10 and BZ$40 (US$5–US$20).

ORIENTATION

Most boats dock at the newly remodeled and expanded pier jutting off Front Street at a spot called Front Bridge—so named because this is the front side of the island facing the reef (east). The town extends north and south from here. As you debark, if you kept walking straight ahead, you'd soon come to the western side of the island and the Back Bridge or dock, where some of the boats dock. Caye Caulker consists of two main north-south sand roads (Front and Back sts.), a few cross streets, and numerous paths. As the island has grown, there's now another, as yet unnamed, north-south road behind, or west of, Back Street. The small Caye Caulker airstrip is located on the southern outskirts of the town. At the north end of town you'll find the Split or Cut, the town's prime swimming and sunbathing spot.

Much of Caye Caulker is uninhabited. The small town and inhabited sections are quite concentrated. However, when I last visited, there was some movement towards building on the part of the island just north of the split.

Though Caye Caulker is still a relatively safe place, it is not advisable to leave money or valuables in your hotel room, except in a safe.

FAST FACTS   For the local **police,** dial ℂ 911, or 226-2022; for the **fire department,** dial ℂ 226-0353. In the case of a medical emergency, call the **Caye Caulker Health Clinic** (ℂ 226-2166).

Atlantic Bank (ℂ 226-0207) is located on Back Street, near the center of the island. The **post office** (ℂ 226-2325) is also located on Back Street; it's open Monday through Friday from 8am to noon and from 1 to 5pm. There are several **Internet cafes** on the island; just walk along Front Street and find one with an open terminal.

Most hotels provide laundry service, but pricing varies widely, so ask first. There's a small coin-operated **laundromat,** on the cross street connecting Front and Back bridges near the center of town, that will wash, dry, and fold for you, or allow you to do it on your own. Alternatively, you can check the bulletin boards around town or ask a few locals, and you should find an islander who'll do your laundry for a reasonable rate.

WHAT TO SEE & DO

The main activities on Caye Caulker itself are strolling up and down the sand streets, and swimming and sunbathing off the docks. The most popular spot is at the north end of the island by the **Split** ℛ. The Split was formed in 1961 when Hurricane Hattie literally split the island in two. You'll find the water's edge rimmed with a nice wooden dock and there's even a decent little patch of beach and a roped-off swimming area. The water is very calm by the Split, making it a good place to practice if you're an inexperienced snorkeler. Take care when swimming off the docks here. The split is an active channel with regular boat traffic. At least one swimmer was killed by a boat, so stick to designated swimming areas and out of obvious boat channels. Also, when the tides are running strong, there's quite a bit of current through the split and it's easy to get dragged along for a few hundred yards or so. If you do get caught in this current, treat it like any rip tide: Don't panic, and swim diagonally across the current to get out of it.

Aside from the split, and as on Ambergris Caye, there is not much beach to speak of on the rest of the island. There is a narrow strip of sand for much of the length of the island, where the land meets the sea, but even at low tide it isn't wide enough for you to unroll a beach towel on in most places. In fact, along most of its length this is a small bike and footpath that is probably the busiest thoroughfare on Caye Caulker. Just off the coast, for 100 yards or more out from shore, the bottom is covered with sea grass. Beneath the grass is a layer of spongy roots and organic matter topped with a thin layer of white sand. Walking on this spongy sand is somewhat unnerving, as you might encounter a sea urchin or stingray, and it's easy to trip and stumble.

Several of the hotels have built long piers out into the sea, with steps down into the water, and swimming is best here. Beyond this, some of the best swimming can be had from boats anchored out in the turquoise waters between the shore and the reef, or by taking a kayak offshore a little ways.

As on Ambergris Caye, snorkeling, scuba diving, and fishing are the main draws here. All are excellent.

IN THE WATER
Scuba Diving & Snorkeling ★★★
There's excellent diving and snorkeling close to Caye Caulker. Within a 5- to 20-minute boat ride from the pier lie a couple of world-class dive sites, including **Caye Caulker North Cut, Coral Gardens, Pyramid Flats, Sponge Avenue,** and **Amigos Wreck.** As on Ambergris Caye, a day's diving here will almost always feature a mix of steep wall drops and coral caverns and tunnels. In addition, in Caye Caulker you can dive on the wreck of a 50-foot (15m) boat, and amongst huge canyons of coral. You'll see brilliant coral and sponge formations, as well as a wealth of colorful marine life. The wreck and canyons are prime spots to spot giant grouper, and rays and turtles are fairly common here as well.

There are several dependable dive operators on Caye Caulker. Rates are pretty standardized, and you should be able to get deals on multiday, multi-dive packages. The best dive operations on the island are **Belize Diving Services** (© 226-0143; www.belizedivingservices.com), **Big Fish Dive Center** (© 226-0450; www.bigfishdive.com), **Frenchie's Diving** (© 226-0234; www.frenchiesdiving.com), and **Paradise Down Scuba** ℞ (© 226-0437; www.paradisedown.com). All of these operators charge BZ$90 to BZ$110 (US$45–US$55) for a local two-tank dive, with equipment rental running around BZ$40 (US$20) for a complete package, and BZ$10 (US$6) for a mask, snorkel, and fins.

For more adventurous diving, you'll probably want to head out to the **Turneffe Island Atoll, Lighthouse Reef,** and **Blue Hole.** All of the dive operations on Caye Caulker offer this trip or will subcontract it out. It's about a 2- to 3-hour ride each way (in a fast boat) over sometimes rough seas. Most day trips out to Turneffe Island or Lighthouse Reef and Blue Hole run around BZ$280 to BZ$370 (US$140–US$185) per person, including transportation, two or three dives, tanks, and weights, as well as lunch and snacks. For more information on these dive sites, see section 3, later in this chapter.

Caye Caulker is another excellent place to learn how to scuba dive. Resort courses will give you an excellent 1-day introduction into the world of scuba diving, including a very controlled shallow-water boat dive. These courses cost BZ$200 to BZ$300 (US$100–US$150). In 3 to 4 days, however, you can get your full open-water certification. These courses cost between BZ$650 and BZ$750 (US$325–US$375), including all equipment rentals, class materials, and the processing of your certification, as well as four open-water and reef dives. All of the above-mentioned dive operations offer these courses.

There are a host of boats on Caye Caulker offering snorkeling trips, and most of the above dive operators also offer snorkeling trips and equipment rental. Snorkeling tours range in price from BZ$25 to BZ$60 (US$13–US$30) for short jaunts to half-day outings, and BZ$100 to BZ$120 (US$50–US$60) for full-day trips. A full set of mask, fins, and snorkel will usually cost from BZ$6 to BZ$14 (US$3–US$7) per person per day.

All of the Caye Caulker dive and snorkel operators also offer trips to **Shark Ray Alley** ⟨⟨ and **Hol Chan Marine Reserve** ⟨⟨. These trips cost between BZ$70 and BZ$220 (US$35–US$110) per person, depending on whether it is a snorkel or scuba dive trip, how long the tour lasts, and whether or not there is a stop on Ambergris Caye. Many of these include a stop for lunch and a quick walk around town in San Pedro. See "What to See & Do" in section 1, earlier in this chapter, for more information and a detailed description of Shark-Ray Alley and Hol Chan Marine Reserve.

One of my favorite options for snorkelers is a day-cruise to Shark-Ray Alley and Hol Chan with **Raggamuffin Tours** (© 226-0348; www.raggamuffin tours.com) aboard a classic wooden Belizean sloop. The trip makes three distinct snorkel stops, and includes lunch on board the boat, snorkeling gear, and the park entrance fee for just BZ$70 (US$35) per person.

Sailing ⟨⟨

The crystal-clear waters, calm seas, and excellent snorkeling spots around Caye Caulker make this an excellent place to go out for a sail. Unlike on Ambergris Caye, there's no organized bareboat charters available here, but you can go out on any number of different vessels for a half- or full-day sail, a sunset cruise, a moonlight cruise, or a combined sailing and snorkeling adventure.

A day cruise, including lunch, drinks, and snorkeling gear should run between BZ$200 and BZ$300 (US$100–US$150) per person; a half-day tour including drinks, a snack, and snorkeling gear should cost between BZ$70 and BZ$110 (US$35–US$55). Most hotels and tour operators around town can hook you up with an appropriate captain and craft.

One of my favorite boats is the **Stone Crab** (no phone; stonecrab2@hotmail. com), captained by local son Ras Jimmy. A traditional Belizean sloop, the Stone Crab is available for half- and full-day cruises, as well as longer charters. Another good option is **Raggamuffin Tours** (© 226-0348; www.raggamuffintours.com).

Fishing

Although not nearly as developed or popular on Caye Caulker, sport fishing for tarpon, permit, and bonefish is still excellent around the caye, and on the reefs and flats. There are several dedicated fishing guides on the island, and almost every hotel, tour operator, or dive shop can hook you up with a captain and crew for some angling. If you're looking for a specific recommendation, check out Gabriel at **Gabriel's Fishing Trips** (© 206-0131) or **Porfilio Guzmán** (© 226-0152); both are excellent guides.

Chocolate & the Manatees

Sure you can get candy bars and cakes and a whole host of products derived from the fruit of the cacao tree here. But on Caye Caulker, when someone mentions "Chocolate" (using the Spanish pronunciation of "choh-coh-*lah*-teh"), they are almost inevitably referring to pioneering guide and boat captain Lionel "Chocolate" Heredia. Chocolate began his career as a fisherman, but he soon dedicated himself to the fledgling business of taxiing folks by speedboat back and forth between Belize City and Caye Caulker. This business soon expanded to include guided tours, snorkeling outings, and fishing adventures. Chocolate was also probably the first guide to introduce the popular day trip to see manatees and do some snorkeling at remote cayes. He and his wife Annie also led the battle to protect these gentle sea mammals and their feeding grounds, finally seeing the dedication of the Swallow Caye Manatee Reserve in 1999.

When I last visited, Chocolate had unfortunately been laid rather low by illness, but his company and others on Caye Caulker still lead the manatee and snorkel tours. These tours begin with a stop at the manatee-feeding site on Swallow Caye, before heading to either Goff's or Sergeant's cayes, which are little more than football field–size patches of sand with a few palm trees. The afternoons are usually spent snorkeling in the clear waters off these cayes, and lunching on the sand. These trips include all transportation, lunch on one of the cayes, and several snorkel stops, and cost between BZ$80 and BZ$130 (US$40–US$65).

A half-day reef trolling, casting, or fly-fishing for bonefish or tarpon costs between BZ$250 and BZ$350 (US$125–US$175), a full day between BZ$400 and BZ$500 (US$200–US$300). Deep-sea trolling for larger game runs around BZ$800 to BZ$1,200 (US$400–US$600) for a half-day, BZ$1,600 to BZ$2,400 (US$800–US$1,200) for a full day. These prices are per boat for two to four fishermen and usually include drinks, tackle, and lunch.

Kayaks & Other Watercraft

The calm protected waters just offshore are wonderful for any number of watersports vehicles. Several hotels and tour operators around Caye Caulker have one or more of the above craft for guest use, or general rental. Rates run around BZ$24 to BZ$30 (US$12–US$15) per hour for a kayak; BZ$30 to BZ$40 (US$15–US$20) per hour for a Hobie Cat, small sailboat, or windsurfer; and BZ$50 to BZ$60 (US$25–US$30) per hour for a jet ski.

FUN ON DRY LAND

Aside from sun bathing, reading, and relaxing, there's very little to do on Caye Caulker. However, you should be sure to head south of town to the **Caye Caulker Mini-Reserve.** Located on the southern outskirts of the town, the term "mini" is certainly fitting. Nevertheless, this local endeavor features a few gentle and well-cleared paths through a small stand of littoral forest. More serious birdwatchers might want to grab a boat and a guide and head to the northern half of the island, where 100 acres (40 ha) on the very northern tip have been declared the **Caye Caulker Forest Reserve.** As of yet, no admission fees are being charged at either of these reserves, but that could change. In all, over 130 species of resident and migrant birds have been spotted on and around Caye Caulker. Another option for bird-watchers and nature lovers is to rent a kayak for paddling around on the lagoon and mangrove side of the island.

EXCURSIONS ON THE MAINLAND

If you've got island fever or Caye Caulker is your only destination, and you want to see more of Belize, several tour operators on Caye Caulker offer excursions to all of the major attractions and destinations around the country, including Altun Ha, Lamanai, Xunantunich, Mountain Pine Ridge, and Tikal. You can also go cave tubing in the Caves Branch region. Most of these tours involve a flight or two in a small charter plane.

The most popular and economical tours are to the Mayan ruins of Altun Ha or Lamanai. These trips begin with a short boat ride to the mainland, followed by a minibus ride to the ruins. Lunch is usually included, and often these tours visit the spa at Maruba Jungle Resort, with spa treatments costing extra. Prices for these trips run from BZ$120 to BZ$140 (US$60–US$70).

For trips involving a flight, prices range from BZ$200 to BZ$400 (US$100–US$200) per person, depending on the distance traveled and amount of activities and attractions crammed into 1 day. Any hotel or tour agency on the island can help you arrange any number of these tours. In most cases, these trips are subcontracted out to an operator based either in Belize City or on Ambergris Caye.

For detailed descriptions of these various destinations and attractions, see the respective regional chapters throughout this book.

SHOPPING

In terms of shopping, you'll be amazed by the number of small gift shops and makeshift souvenir stands lining the few streets here. As on Ambergris Caye, much of the shopping on Caye Caulker is typical tourist fare. Mostly what you'll be able to buy are T-shirts and jewelry made by local artisans. **Chocolate's Boutique** (© 226-0151) has slightly higher quality goods, including reasonably priced Guatemalan and Indonesian textiles, as well as some lovely silver and stone jewelry.

Another good shop is **Caribbean Colors Art Gallery** (© 206-0206; www. caribbean-colors.com), which features some interesting original artwork and hand-painted silk by artist Lee Vanderwalker-Kroll.

As I recommend elsewhere in this book, please avoid buying black coral jewelry. Black coral is extremely beautiful, but as with every endangered resource, increased demand just leads to increased harvesting of a slow-growing coral.

WHERE TO STAY

Accommodations on Caye Caulker have improved over the years. But there are still no resorts or real luxury options to be had. In my opinion, this adds to the charm of the place. Budget and mid-range lodging options are abundant, and some of these are quite comfortable.

If you plan on staying any period of time, you should look into renting a small cottage, condo, or apartment. Look around for signs or bulletin boards, or check with Amanda at **Caye Caulker Rentals** (©/fax 226-0029; www.caye caulkerrentals.com). Rates run from BZ$700 to BZ$1,400 (US$350–US$700) per week for a fully equipped beachfront apartment. When demand is low, these units can usually be rented per night.

Camping is allowed at **Vega Inn & Gardens** (✆ **226-0142;** www.vega. com.bz), where BZ$20 (US$10) per day gets you a beachfront campsite and use of communal bathrooms and showers.

EXPENSIVE

Auxillou Beach Suites ✿✿   These modern, fully equipped one-bedroom suites are some of the best-equipped and -located rooms on Caye Caulker. Each comes with a kitchenette, a large front living room with a futon couch, an equally large bedroom, and a private balcony. A couple of the older units lack any real windows and natural light in the bedroom, but this has been resolved in the newer rooms. The best rooms are those on the second floor, just because the seclusion and view from their oceanfront balconies are that much better. These folks also rent a private house, and are related by blood to several other hotel and house rental owners around the island.

On the waterfront, in the center of town (P.O. Box 51), Caye Caulker. ✆ **226-0370.** Fax 226-0371. www. auxilloubeachsuites.com. 8 units. BZ$238 (US$119) double. Rates slightly higher during peak weeks, lower during the off season. DISC, MC, V. *In room:* A/C, TV, kitchenette, coffeemaker, no phone.

Iguana Reef ✿   This is probably the closest thing to a resort hotel on Caye Caulker, yet it still doesn't even have its own restaurant. The spacious rooms are housed in several two-story concrete block structures. Most rooms come with two queen beds, although some come with just one queen bed and a foldout futon couch. All include air-conditioning, a stocked minibar, and a programmable safe. The deluxe units have a sitting area, a stereo CD player, and a semi-private veranda. Although there's no restaurant here, a continental breakfast is served in a pleasant open-air dining area overlooking the water. Iguana Reef, which is on the lagoon or back side of the island, has a large and comfortable sandy area for lounging, with a pier leading off this to a nice swimming spot. When I last visited, they were talking about possibly adding a swimming pool.

Back St. (P.O. Box 31), Caye Caulker. ✆ **226-0213.** Fax 226-0087. www.iguanareefinn.com. 12 units. BZ$214–BZ$264 (US$107–US$132) double. Rates include continental breakfast. Rates slightly higher during peak weeks, lower during the off season. AE, MC, V. **Amenities:** Bar; tour desk; laundry service. *In room:* A/C, stocked minifridge, safe, no phone.

MODERATE

When I last visited, the folks at **Seaside Cabanas** ✿ (✆ **226-0498;** www.seaside cabanas.com) were in the midst of a major rebuilding effort, following a disastrous fire. The new hotel promises to be one of the most modern and comfortable options on the island, and should feature the first swimming pool on Caye Caulker.

Anchorage Resort   Set on a couple of sandy acres fronting the beach, this three-story concrete hotel building lacks much in the way of local character and style. Still, it is well located, clean, and one of the newer options on Caye Caulker. This is, in fact, a totally new incarnation of the former very rustic Anchorage Cabanas. The rooms have cable televisions, a small refrigerator, and either one king bed or two double beds. Each room also comes with a private balcony, and those on the third floor have excellent views and privacy. However, the rooms don't have air-conditioning, just ceiling fans.

On the waterfront south of Front Bridge (P.O. Box 25), Caye Caulker. ✆ **226-0304.** Fax 226-0391. www. anchorageresort.com. 18 units. BZ$130 (US$65) double. Rates higher during peak weeks, lower during the off season. MC, V. *In room:* TV, minifridge, no phone.

Lazy Iguana Bed & Breakfast ✦ Housed in an interesting four-story octag-
onal building, this little bed-and-breakfast offers comfortable rooms in a quiet
setting on the backside of the island. Three of the rooms have queen beds, and
just one comes with two twin beds. All of the rooms are spacious and immaculate. Breakfasts always include a couple of freshly baked items, and plenty of
fresh fruit and strong coffee. One of the nicest features here is the open-air
fourth-floor thatched terrace, which offers excellent 360-degree views of the
island, and has a couple of hammocks perfect for an afternoon siesta. Guests
have free use of bicycles, and there's a small lounge with a lending library and
cable television.

2 blocks north of the airstrip on the lagoon side (P.O. Box 59), Caye Caulker. © 226-0350. Fax 226-0320.
www.lazyiguana.net. 4 units. BZ$190 (US$95) double. Rates include full breakfast. Rates higher during peak
weeks, lower during the off season. MC, V. *In room:* A/C, minifridge, no phone.

INEXPENSIVE

There are literally scores of budget options on Caye Caulker. I list my favorite
and the most dependable options below.

De Real Macaw *(Value* This new place is located just north of the center of
town, across from a little sandy park and the ocean on Front Street. The hotel is
its own little compound, around a central sandy central garden area, with a few
tall shade trees hung with hammocks. The two "beachfront" rooms are the nicest
rooms here, but all are very clean and well kept, with tile floors, tiny television
sets, and a front porch or balcony. There's one two-bedroom "condo" unit here
that comes with a full kitchen and even a washing machine.

Front St., north of Front Bridge, Caye Caulker. © 226-0459. Fax 226-0497. www.derealmacaw.com. 7 units.
BZ$80–BZ$120 (US$40–US$60) double; BZ$220 (US$110) condo. Rates lower in the off season. MC, V. *In
room:* TV, minifridge, safe, no phone.

Ignacio's Beach Cabañas Located just south of the Anchorage, the cabañas
here are brightly painted purple little wooden boxes built on high stilts. You'll definitely want one of the front line units set practically on the ocean's edge. The
rooms themselves are quite small and rustic, with soft beds, cold-water showers,
and virtually no amenities, but all come with a fan and feature a small balcony. If
you're looking for funky charm and budget prices, this place just might be heaven
for you. The owner, Ignacio, is one of the island's more colorful characters.

On the waterfront, south of Front Bridge, Caye Caulker. © 226-0212. 15 units. BZ$28–BZ$44
(US$14–US$22) double. No credit cards. *In room:* No phone.

Sea Beezzz *(Finds* Gray buildings with white trim give this place a bit of Cape
Cod styling and feel. Two of the rooms are housed off the main building and
small restaurant here, while the others are in two separate duplexes in back of
this. The rooms themselves are all quite simple and spartan, and some are beginning to show their age. To make up for this, the grounds and gardens are kept
in stunning shape, and you are only steps from the water. Moreover, the owners
really do make you feel immediately like part of the family. The hotel has its own
swimming pier built into the sea, and a broad second-floor veranda for sitting
and reading, or enjoying the view. Sea Beezzz's restaurant serves excellent local
cuisine and fresh seafood, and the bar features tasty margaritas. The hotel is only
open November through April.

Oceanfront, just south of Front Bridge (P.O. Box 812, Belize City), Caye Caulker. © 226-0176 in Belize, or
631/668-9212 in the U.S. Fax 226-0276. www.geocities.com/seabeezzz. 6 units. BZ$90 (US$45) double. AE,
MC, V. **Amenities:** Restaurant; bar; tour desk; laundry service. *In room:* No phone.

Shirley's Guest House These picturesque white cabins with green trim are set on well-manicured grounds facing the ocean, just north of the airstrip. They're set on stilts and are shaded by coconut and casuarina palms. The setting is idyllic, safe, and quiet. The rooms have varnished floors and quilted bedspreads, and some come with a small refrigerator. Although they are a little on the expensive side for what you get, they are worth it for the location and the fairly large and comfortable rooms. Only adults are allowed here.

Close to the airstrip on the ocean side (P.O. Box 13), Caye Caulker. ℂ **226-0145** or 600-0069. Fax 226-0264. www.shirleysguesthouse.com. 5 units (3 with private bathroom). BZ$100 (US$50) double with shared bathroom, BZ$130–BZ$160 (US$65–US$80) double with private bathroom. Rates lower in the off season. MC, V. Children not accepted. *In room:* No phone.

Tree Tops Guest House ★ *(Value)* It's hard to beat this place for location and value on Caye Caulker. Set just off the ocean in the heart of town, this converted three-story home offers clean, spacious, and cool rooms. There are four rooms located on the ground floor. Each comes with tile floors, high ceilings, standing fan, cable television, and small refrigerator. Two of these share a common bathroom down the hall, but each has a vanity sink in the room itself. However, the choicest rooms here are the two new top-floor suites. Each of these comes with a king bed, cable television, air-conditioning, minifridge, telephone, and private balcony. The "Sunset Suite" is the best of these, with the largest balcony, and views to both the lagoon and the ocean. If you opt for one of the standard rooms, however, you can still enjoy the view from the new rooftop lounge area, which features several hammocks hung under a shade roof. Though the hotel is set back about 50 yards from the shore, the only thing between you and the ocean are some shady coconut palms.

On the waterfront south of Front Bridge (P.O. Box 29), Caye Caulker. ℂ **226-0240**. Fax 226-0115. www.tree topsbelize.com. 6 units (4 with private bathroom). BZ$75–BZ$90 (US$38–US$45) double; BZ$150 (US$75) suite. MC, V. *In room:* TV, minifridge, no phone.

Trends Beachfront Hotel Set right off the water and just off the main pier at Front Bridge, the rooms here are housed in a two-story wooden building painted in tropical pastel colors. The rooms are large, clean, bright, and airy, and it's hard to beat the location. There's also a separate, private bungalow, which is the closest unit to the water, and the best room in the house. These folks also run a separate hotel on Front Street a few blocks away. The rooms here are actually somewhat more modern, and most have air-conditioning; however, they lack the charm, character, and proximity to the water you'll enjoy at the beachfront option. The Sand Box Restaurant here (p. 161) is one of the most popular on the island.

Beachfront in the center of town, Caye Caulker. ℂ **226-0094**. Fax 226-0097. www.trendsbze.com. 7 units. BZ$60–BZ$70 (US$30–US$35) double; BZ$80 (US$40) bungalow. AE, MC, V. **Amenities:** Restaurant; bar; tour desk; laundry service. *In room:* No phone.

WHERE TO DINE

In addition to the places listed below, when I last visited, I was getting good reports about a new, upscale Italian restaurant, **Don Corleone** (ℂ **226-0025**), located on Front Street, a few blocks north of Front Bridge.

Do remember to abide by the seasons on lobster and conch, and don't order turtle soup or steaks (sea turtles are endangered). Recently, local restaurants and fishery officials have struck a deal to allow lobster to be served in the off season. Supposedly this is lobster caught and frozen during the open season, and not while they are mating in the formerly closed season.

About the Water

Much of the water on Caye Caulker is collected rainwater. While it's usually safe to drink, and most locals are used to it, I advise visitors to stick to bottled water.

MODERATE

Habaneros ★★ INTERNATIONAL   Although the name suggests a Mexican joint, the menu here goes beyond standard Mexican fare. You can get homemade pastas and Thai coconut curries, as well as Brazilian pork. You can also get spicy fajitas made of beef, chicken, or jerk pork. The nightly specials tend to be inventive takes on whatever fresh fish and seafood has been caught that day. Heavy wooden tables are spread across the pleasant open-air wraparound veranda of this raised-stilt wooden home right on Front Street. There's also indoor seating, but you'll really want to try to grab one of the outdoor spots. They open in the afternoon with a reduced menu heavy on appetizers and bar food, geared towards their popular happy hour. Margaritas and sangria are served by the pitcher, and there's a pretty good wine list for Caye Caulker.

On Front St., near the center of town. ✆ 226-0487. Reservations recommended during the high season. Main courses BZ$14–BZ$40 (US$7–US$20). MC, V. Wed–Sun 2–10pm.

Rainbow Grill & Bar ★ (Finds SEAFOOD/INTERNATIONAL   Built over the water near the center of town, this is a great place to dine to the sound of water lapping against the pilings below your feet. A dozen or so wooden tables with plastic chairs are set around the screened-in restaurant. The screen comes in handy, especially when the bugs are biting. Try to grab a table by the outer railing, closest to the water. Chicken, fish, conch, shrimp, and lobster are all offered in a variety of preparations from simply grilled or fried, or served with sauces ranging from lemon-ginger to Cajun. All are very well prepared and tasty. The lunch menu is much simpler and less expensive. I particularly like the conch fajitas.

Over the water on Front St., near the center of town. ✆ 226-0281. Reservations recommended during the high season. Main courses BZ$12–BZ$40 (US$6–US$20); lunch BZ$5–BZ$18 (US$2.50–US$9). MC, V. Tues–Sun 10:30am–4pm and 6–10pm.

Rasta Pasta Rainforest Café ★★★ (Finds INTERNATIONAL   This is easily my favorite restaurant on Caye Caulker. The food is excellent, the menu eclectic, the portions huge, the prices right, and the service friendly and efficient. What's more, the setting is idyllic—in the heart of town, just steps from the water. Tables are set in the sand under palm trees, or in the sand-floored open-air covered dining area. Appetizers include fabulous conch fritters and deep-fried crab rolls. There are several namesake pasta dishes, as well as Thai curries, and everything from chicken to conch and lobster is served grilled, blackened, or with a spicy Jamaican jerk sauce. Vegetarians are well cared for here as well, with various dishes to choose from. Whatever you do, save room for some of their B-52 Cheesecake, flavored with Bailey's and Kahlúa and baked in an Oreo cookie crust. Breakfasts here are huge and hearty. If you like the food, be sure to pick up some of their homemade spice packages.

Front St., on the waterfront, near the center of town. ✆ 206-0356. Reservations recommended during the high season. Main courses BZ$12–BZ$30 (US$6–US$15). MC, V. Thurs–Tues 7:30am–10pm.

Sand Box Restaurant 🛪 SEAFOOD/INTERNATIONAL This place gets its name from the fact that it features a sand floor, both inside and (obviously) out. I prefer the outdoor tables in the shade of broad-leafed seagrape trees. Either way, you'll be able to choose from an extensive menu of Belizean and international dishes. Seafood is the strong suit here, but you can also get chicken or meat dishes. You can have your fresh fish filet served with an almond and garlic butter sauce, or spicy banana chutney. Budget hounds can fill up on burgers, burritos, and quesadillas. The daily happy hour (3–6pm) is quite popular here.

Front St., on the waterfront, near the center of town. © 226-0200. Main courses BZ$6–BZ$28 (US$3–US$14). AE, MC, V. Daily 7am–9pm.

INEXPENSIVE

In addition to the places listed below, there are several simple local restaurants serving fresh fish, seafood, and Belizean standards at very economical rates. The best of these are **Syd's Restaurant & Bar** (© 206-0294) and **Marin's Restaurant & Bar** (© 226-0104), both located on Middle Street, near the center of town.

If you're staying for an extended period of time and have a kitchenette, or you just want to throw together a picnic lunch, you'll want to head to **Chan's Mini-Market,** on Back Street near the center of town (© 226-0165).

Cyndi's 🛪 BREAKFAST This quaint and simple breakfast joint is giving Glenda's (see below) a slight run for it, although if you're here for more than a couple of days, you can certainly enjoy both, as well as some of the other heartier breakfast options in town. Freshly baked brownies, banana bread, and whole-wheat breads are the mainstay here, served alongside strong coffee, cappuccino, or a fresh fruit smoothie. You can also get granola with yogurt and fresh fruits, scrambled eggs, and even bagels on most weekends. Perhaps the best thing about Cyndi's is the fact that its few tables are set on an open-air deck overlooking Front Street, so you get to watch Caye Caulker as it slowly wakes up and gets going.

Front St., near the center of town. No phone. Reservations not accepted. Main courses BZ$2–BZ$7 (US$1–US$3.50). No credit cards. Tues–Sun 7am–noon.

Glenda's *Value* BELIZEAN/MEXICAN This humble establishment is one of Caye Caulker's longest-standing traditions and most popular spots. The menu is written on a chalkboard on your left as you walk up to the open window into Glenda's house. Order here, and the meal will be brought to your table, but don't sit down and expect to be waited on. They specialize in simple Mexican fare, including *garnaches,* burritos, and rice and beans. Breakfasts feature eggs and johnnycakes, but the star attractions here are the freshly baked cinnamon rolls and freshly squeezed orange juice. There are only a few wooden tables with either plastic lawn chairs or folding metal card chairs. The best ones are on the small, screened-in porch. Come early for breakfast if you want a decent seat.

In back of Atlantic Bank, Caye Caulker. © 226-2148. Main courses BZ$.50–BZ$6 (US25¢–US$3). No credit cards. Mon–Sat 7–10am and noon–3pm.

CAYE CAULKER AFTER DARK

For evening entertainment, you can stargaze, go for a night dive, or have a drink in one of the island's handful of bars. Periodically, one of the bars will crank up the music, and *voilà*—a disco. In general, the scene is so small that most folks will congregate at one or two bars. Which one or two bars is happening might shift from night to night; ask a local or two, and you'll certainly be directed to the current hot spot. My favorite bar is the open-air **I&I Bar and Cafe** 🛪, which

Two Small Cayes on the Way

Between Belize City and the popular tourist destinations of Caye Caulker and Ambergris Caye lie scores of small islands and cayes. Of these, two are of interest to travelers, **St. George's Caye** 🎿🎿 and **Caye Chapel** 🎿. Each has its own charm and attractions. St. George's Caye offers easy access to Belize City and some excellent scuba diving and snorkel options. For its part, Caye Chapel is home to the only 18-hole golf course in Belize.

St. George is the closest resort caye to Belize City, just 9 miles (14km) offshore. This tiny island played a crucial role in the country's history. From 1650 until 1784, St. George's Caye was the first capital city for the early Baymen colonists, and it was also the site and namesake of the pivotal 1798 sea battle between the Baymen and a hostile Spanish fleet. Today, it is mostly a getaway for a handful of wealthy Belizeans, who have vacation cottages on the caye. There are also two small hotels here. The best of these is **Pleasure Island Resort** 🎿 (© **209-4020** or 610-1290; www.stgeorgescayepleasure.bz), a simple yet charming collection of wooden cabins and duplexes.

There's only one option for staying on Caye Chapel, and that is the **Caye Chapel Resort** 🎿🎿 (© **226-8250**; www.belizegolf.cc), a collection of luxury condominium units and private villas. Rates run between BZ$460 and BZ$1,000 (US$230–US$500) per person per day, with all meals and unlimited golf included. While relatively flat, the par-72 course has plenty of water and sand hazards, and an unmatched number of oceanfront holes. The frequent steady trade winds here provide further challenge. There are never any crowds or waits on the course, and only a maximum of 50 overnight guests on the caye at any one time.

Any of the water taxis going to Caye Caulker or Ambergris Caye will drop off and pick up passengers at either St. Georges Caye or Caye Chapel en route. Moreover, there is an airstrip on Caye Chapel, and any of the **Maya Island Air** (© **226-2435**; www.mayaairways.com) or **Tropic Air** (© **226-2012**; www.tropicair.com) flights to Caye Caulker or Ambergris Caye will similarly stop to drop off or pick up passengers on Caye Chapel upon demand. The fare is BZ$93 (US$47) to or from Goldson International Airport, and BZ$52 (US$26) each way to or from Municipal Airport. See "Essentials" in "Ambergris Caye" and "Caye Caulker," earlier in this chapter, for more details.

features rustic wooden plank swings for most of its seating. The bar itself takes up the second and third floors of this thatch-roofed wooden structure and is located on a cross street on the southern end of town. Right in the center of town on Front Street, the **Oceanside Bar** has been featuring live music fairly regularly. That's about it for nightlife on Caye Caulker.

3 The Outer Atolls ★★★

25–50 miles (40–80km) E of Belize City

Roughly due east, out beyond the barrier reef, lie two of Belize's three open ocean atolls, Turneffe Island Atoll and Lighthouse Reef Atoll. These reef and island rings of tranquillity in the midst of the Caribbean Sea are stunning and pristine places.

These outer island atolls are popular destinations for day trips out from Belize City, Ambergris Caye, and Caye Caulker. However, if you really want to experience and enjoy their unique charms, you should stay at one of the few small lodges located right on the edge of one of them, or on one of the live-aboard dive boats that ply these waters.

GETTING THERE & DEPARTING

These are remote and isolated destinations. Aside from the lodges, which all offer their own transportation, there is no regularly scheduled transportation out here. However, private water taxis and charter flights can be arranged.

BY PLANE   The only airstrip located on these outer atolls is the private airstrip of the Lighthouse Reef Resort on Big Northern Caye. The resort includes round-trip private charter flights with all its package tours. Guests wanting more flexibility can charter their own plane, with advance arrangements made through the lodge.

BY BOAT   Turneffe Island Atoll is a 1½- to 2-hour boat ride from Belize City. The lodges listed below provide their own transportation to and from Belize City as part of their vacation packages.

EXPLORING THE ATOLLS

Unlike Pacific Ocean atolls, which are often the crater rings of extinct volcanoes, these atolls were formed over millions of years by a combination of plate tectonics, rising water levels following the last ice age, and millennia of mid-ocean coral growth. Many of the atoll walls drop off steeply for over a thousand feet, while in the central lagoons, the water depths average only 10 to 40 feet (3–12m).

Most folks come out here to do one of two things: fish or dive. Some do both. Both activities are truly world-class. In broad strokes, fishermen should head to Turneffe Island Atoll, while dedicated and serious divers would probably want to choose Lighthouse Reef Atoll, although there's great diving to be had off Turneffe.

TURNEFFE ISLAND ATOLL

This is the largest of Belize's three ocean atolls, and the largest in the Caribbean Sea. Both the diving and fishing here are excellent, but the fishing gets a slight nod. The extensive mangrove and saltwater flats are perfect territory for stalking permit, bonefish, snook, and tarpon. Most fishing is done with fly rods, either wading in the flats or from a poled skiff.

Turneffe Island Atoll also boasts scores of world-class wall, coral, and sponge garden, and drift dive sites. Most of these sites are located around the southern tip of the atoll. Perhaps the most famous dive site here is **The Elbow,** a jutting coral point with steep drop-offs, huge sponges, and ample fish life. Another popular site is **Rendezvous Point,** which features several grottoes that divers can swim in and out of, and there's a small modern wreck, the *Sayonara,* sitting in about 30 feet (9m) of water.

LIGHTHOUSE REEF ATOLL

Boasting nearly 50 miles (81km) of wall and reef diving, including some of the best and most coveted dive sites in all of the Caribbean, this is a true scuba-diving mecca. This is the atoll farthest from shore, and the waters here are incredibly clear and pristine. The central lagoon of this atoll is some 30 miles (48km) long and around 8 miles (13km) wide at its widest point. In the center, you'll find the world-famous **Blue Hole,** a perfectly round mid-atoll sinkhole that plunges straight down to a depth of over 400 feet (120m). You'll see postcards, photos, and T-shirts all over town showing off aerial views of this perfectly round hole in the ocean. Nearly 1,000 feet (300m) across, the Blue Hole's eroded limestone karst walls and stalactite formations make this a unique and justifiably popular dive site. However, some of the wall and coral garden dives around the outer edges of the atoll are even better. Of these, **Half Moon Caye Wall** and **North Long Caye Wall** are consistently considered some of the best clear-water coral wall dives in the world.

Towards the southeastern edge of the atoll is **Half Moon Caye National Monument** ⨳⨳, a combined island and marine reserve. Half Moon Caye itself is the principal nesting ground for the beautiful and odd-looking red-footed booby. These birds are always here in massive numbers. The island is also a prime nesting site for both hawksbill and loggerhead turtles. **The Belize Audubon Society** (© **223-4988;** www.belizeaudubon.org) has constructed a small visitor center here, and a wonderful viewing platform near the center of the island. They also allow overnight camping, with prior arrangement. The admission fee is BZ$10 (US$5).

Water conditions here are amazingly consistent, with an average water temperature of around 80°F (27°C), while visibility on the outer atoll walls and reefs easily averages over 100 feet (30m).

There is only one lodge located on Lighthouse Reef Atoll (see below), although it is a popular destination for day-trippers and live-aboard dive boats (see chapter 3 for more details).

WHERE TO STAY & DINE ON TURNEFFE ISLAND ATOLL
EXPENSIVE
Turneffe Flats ⨳   This is a very well-run fishing resort geared towards dedicated flat water fly-fishing. Everything here is simple, yet rustically luxurious. The rooms are all beachfront and housed in a couple of long, low buildings raised off the sandy ground just a bit on some wooden pilings. The rooms each come with one queen bed and one twin bed, large bathrooms, and a common shared veranda. Meals are served family-style in the main lodge or, weather permitting, outdoors on an open deck off the lodge. The fishing operation here is top-notch, and diving is offered as well. Packages are weeklong affairs, running Saturday to Saturday.

Blackbird Caye, Turneffe Island Atoll. © **800/815-1304** or 605/578-1304 in the U.S. Fax 605/578-7540. www.tflats.com. 6 units. BZ$2,990–BZ$3,190 (US$1,495–US$1,595) per person per week dive package. BZ$5,190–BZ$6,350 (US$2,595–US$3,175) per person per week fishing package. Rates are based on double occupancy and include all meals, round-trip boat transportation from Belize City, guided daily diving or fishing. Drinks and gear rental are extra. Combination packages are available. AE, MC, V. **Amenities:** Restaurant; bar; full-service dive and tackle shops; tour desk; laundry service. *In room:* A/C, no phone.

Turneffe Island Lodge ⨳⨳   Located on a tiny private caye at the southern tip of the Turneffe Island Atoll, this is probably the swankiest outfit on the outer atolls. It even features a small outdoor oceanfront pool, a rare luxury out here.

You can either stay in one of the well-appointed lodge rooms, or opt for an upgrade to one of their eight private cabanas. One of my favorite features of these cabanas is the private outdoor shower. All rooms come with brightly varnished wood floors, wooden wainscoting and ceilings, and plenty of windows to take advantage of the ample sea breezes. The lodge has some excellent beaches, and several long piers built out into the ocean with thatch-roofed open-air hammock huts built at the end. Both the fishing and dive operations here are excellent.

Little Caye Bokel, Turneffe Island Atoll. ⓒ **800/874-0118** or 713/236-7739 in the U.S. Fax 713/236-7743. www.turneffelodge.com. BZ$3,686 (US$1,843) per person per week dive package. BZ$6,986 (US$3,493) per person per week fishing package. Rates are based on double occupancy and include all meals, round-trip boat transportation from Belize City, and guided daily diving or fishing; drinks and gear rental are extra. Combination packages are available. Rates lower in the off season. AE, MC, V. **Amenities:** Restaurant, bar; small outdoor pool; full-service dive and tackle shops; tour desk; laundry service. *In room:* A/C, no phone.

WHERE TO STAY & DINE ON LIGHTHOUSE REEF ATOLL
EXPENSIVE
Lighthouse Reef Resort 𝒜𝒜𝒜   This should probably be on the very short list for any serious scuba enthusiast. This is the only hotel located in the Lighthouse Reef Atoll, with its own airstrip and easy access to some of the best scuba diving in the world. Fishing is available, but this is a hard-core dedicated dive resort. They even have their own E-6 film developing equipment, so underwater shutterbugs can have nearly instant access to their photographic memories. Accommodations are a mix of individual and duplex cabins and junior suites. All are airy, light, cool, and comfortable. All feature an outdoor deck or covered patio. The resort has an extensive and excellent patch of protected beachfront. The overall atmosphere here is very relaxed and convivial. You just might not wear shoes for an entire week. When you take into account that the rates here include all meals, diving, and round-trip airfare from Belize City, the rates are actually quite reasonable.

Big Northern Caye, Lighthouse Reef Atoll (P.O. Box 1435, Dundee, FL 33838). ⓒ **800/423-3114** or 863/439-6600 in the U.S. www.scuba-dive-belize.com. 11 units. BZ$3,300–BZ$3,924 (US$1,650–US$1,962) per person per week. Rates are based on double occupancy and include all meals, taxes, round-trip air transportation from Belize City, and approximately 17 dives. Drinks and gear rental are extra. Rates lower in the off season. AE, MC, V. **Amenities:** Restaurant; bar; full-service dive shop; tour desk; complimentary kayak use; laundry service. *In room:* A/C, stocked minifridge, no phone.

7

Southern Belize

Southern Belize has only two major towns, **Dangriga** and **Punta Gorda,** and one popular beach village, **Placencia.** This is the least developed region of Belize, and therein lies much of its charm. This is a great place to really get off the beaten track and boldly go where very few fellow travelers have gone before.

Southern Belize is made up of the Stann Creek and Toledo districts. It is home to the **Cockscomb Basin Wildlife Sanctuary,** a major breeding ground and reserve for the New World's largest cat, the jaguar, as well as several other lesser-known and virtually unexplored forest reserves. It is here you'll find Belize's highest mountain, **Victoria Peak,** which stands at 3,675 feet (1,103m).

Offshore, you'll find some of Belize's most beautiful cayes and its most remote atoll, **Glover's Reef.** The cayes and barrier reef down here are as spectacular as that found further north, yet far less developed and crowded. You can literally have an island to yourself down here. Much of the offshore and underwater wonders are protected in reserves, such as the **Southwater Caye Marine Reserve, Glover's Marine Reserve, Sapodilla Cayes Marine Reserve,** and **Laughing Bird Caye National Park.**

For its part, Placencia and the Placencia Peninsula offer what can arguably be called one of the few and finest beaches in Belize. This is the place to come if you want to walk on sand along the water's edge for miles, or plop a towel down in the shade of a coconut palm.

As one of the least developed and colonized regions of Belize, the Southern Zone still maintains ongoing and healthy communities of traditional Mayan and Garífuna peoples. This is one of the few places on the planet where you can comfortably spend a few days in a traditional Mayan or Garífuna village and see how nice it can feel to step away from the 21st century for a bit.

1 Dangriga

72 miles (116km) S of Belize City; 64 miles (103km) SE of Belmopan; 48 miles (77km) N of Placencia

Dangriga, which means "sweet water" in the Garífuna language, was originally called Stann Creek, and you may still hear it referred to as such. The name Stann Creek comes from the Creole version of "Standing Creek," a description of the river's slow-moving waters. As the capital of the Stann Creek District, which is one of the main citrus-growing regions of Belize, Dangriga is a bustling agricultural and fishing community. However, despite its boomtown air, it lacks the seaminess that characterizes Belize City. It's generally safe to walk around Dangriga, even at night, although caution should still be exercised when wandering far from the center of town. The town fronts right on the Caribbean and has several waterfront parks, which are surrounded by simple yet attractive residential neighborhoods.

Southern Belize

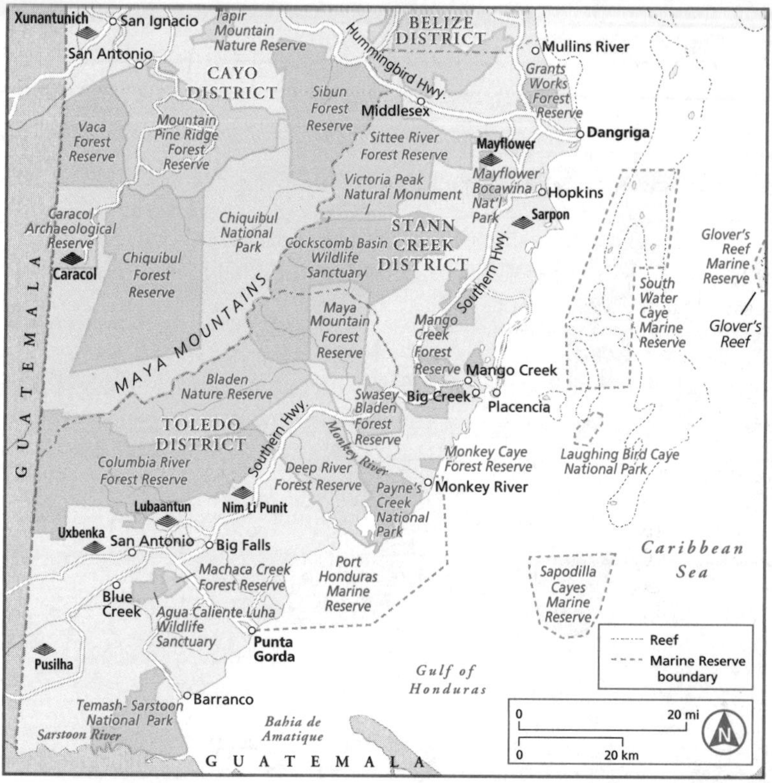
Xunantunich
San Ignacio
Tapir Mountain Nature Reserve
BELIZE DISTRICT
Hummingbird Hwy.
Mullins River
San Antonio
CAYO DISTRICT
Grants Works Forest Reserve
Sibun Forest Reserve
Middlesex
Dangriga
Vaca Forest Reserve
Mountain Pine Ridge Forest Reserve
Sittee River Forest Reserve
Mayflower
Victoria Peak Natural Monument
Mayflower Bocawina Nat'l Park
Hopkins
Caracol Archaeological Reserve
Chiquibul National Park
Sarpon
STANN CREEK DISTRICT
Cockscomb Basin Wildlife Sanctuary
Southern Hwy.
Glover's Reef Marine Reserve
Caracol
Chiquibul Forest Reserve
South Water Caye Marine Reserve
Maya Mountain Forest Reserve
Mango Creek Forest Reserve
Glover's Reef
MAYA MOUNTAINS
Mango Creek
Bladen Nature Reserve
Big Creek
Placencia
Swasey Bladen Forest Reserve
TOLEDO DISTRICT
Monkey River
Monkey Caye Forest Reserve
Laughing Bird Caye National Park
Columbia River Forest Reserve
Deep River Forest Reserve
Payne's Creek National Park
Monkey River
Lubaantun
Nim Li Punit
Uxbenka
San Antonio
Big Falls
Caribbean Sea
Machaca Creek Forest Reserve
Port Honduras Marine Reserve
Sapodilla Cayes Marine Reserve
Blue Creek
Agua Caliente Luha Wildlife Sanctuary
Punta Gorda
Reef
Marine Reserve boundary
Pusilha
Gulf of Honduras
Barranco
Temash- Sarstoon National Park
Sarstoon River
Bahia de Amatique
0
20 mi
0
20 km
N
GUATEMALA
GUATEMALA

Still, Dangriga is of little interest to travelers. There are no good beaches, few good hotels, and the town can feel stifling hot and desolate on most days. Most travelers head further south to either Hopkins Village or Placencia, or out to one of the nearby offshore cayes. In fact, Dangriga is the main maritime transportation hub for trips out to Tobacco Caye, South Water Caye, and Glover's Reef Atoll. (See "What to See & Do," below, for more details.)

Dangriga is the largest city in southern Belize and the seat of the country's Garífuna culture. The Garífunas are a proud and independent people, who have managed to maintain their unique language and culture, which dates to the 16th-century intermingling of free Africans and Carib Indians. The only time Dangriga becomes a major tourist attraction is around Garífuna Settlement Day.

ESSENTIALS

GETTING THERE & DEPARTING

BY PLANE There are numerous flights into and out of little Dangriga Airport (DGA) from Belize City. **Maya Island Air** (**© 226-2435** in Belize City, or 522-2659 in Dangriga; www.mayaairways.com) has 10 flights daily between the Philip S. W. Goldson International Airport and Dangriga. The first flight leaves at 8:15am and the last flight is at 5:10pm. Flight time is 15 minutes; the fare is BZ$89 (US$45) each way. Maya Island Air also has six daily flights between Belize City's Municipal Airport and Dangriga at 8, 10, and 10:30am, and at

The Garífuna

Throughout the 18th century, escaped and shipwrecked slaves inter-married and blended in with the native Carib Indian populations on several islands in the Lesser Antilles, but predominantly on St. Vincent. The West Africans were a mixed lot, including members of the Fon, Yoruba, Ewe, and Nago tribes. Over the years, the West African and indigenous elements blended into a new people, known first as Black Caribs and today as Garífuna or Garinagu. The Garífuna have their own language, traditions, history, and rituals, all of which blend ele-ments of the group's two primary cultural sources. African-style drum-ming with complex rhythmic patterns and call-and-response singing accompany ritual possession ceremonies spoken in a language whose entomological roots are predominantly Arawak.

The Black Caribs were fierce warriors and frequently fought the larger colonial powers to maintain their freedom and independence. In 1797, despite the celebrated leadership of Joseph Chatoyer, the Garífuna were soundly defeated by the British forces, who subse-quently shipped several thousand of the survivors off to exile on the island of Roatan, in then British Honduras. The Garífuna began migrat-ing and eventually settled along the entire coast of what is present-day Honduras, Nicaragua, Guatemala, and Belize.

The Garífuna reached Belize by 1802. Since the British colonial pres-ence was concentrated in the north, the Garífuna chose to settle in the southern parts of Belize, particularly the Stann Creek and Toledo dis-tricts. During the early part of their settlement in Belize, the Garífuna were kept at arm's length by the colonial Baymen, who were still slave owners and feared the influence of this independent free black com-munity. Nevertheless, on November 19, 1832, the Garífuna were offi-cially recognized as members of Belizean society and permitted to participate in the public meetings. For nearly 2 centuries now, the Garí-funa have lived quiet lives of subsistence farming, fishing, and light trading with their neighbors, while steadfastly maintaining their lan-guage, heritage, and traditions.

The principal Garífuna settlements in Belize include Punta Gorda, Seine Bight, Hopkins Village, Barranco, and Dangriga, the community's unofficial capital. Each year on November 19 (and for several days around the 19th), Dangriga comes alive in a riotous celebration of the Garífuna settlement and acceptance in Belize

12:30, 2:30, and 4:30pm. The fare is BZ$61 (US$31) each way. These flights take 30 minutes, because they stop en route to pick up passengers at the interna-tional airport. Maya Island Air flights from Dangriga to Belize City leave at 6:05, 7:25, and 10:50am, and at 12:10, 1:20, 2:30, and 4:50pm. All of these flights stop first at the international airport and continue on to Municipal Airport.

Tropic Air (© 226-2012 in Belize City, or 522-2129 in Dangriga; www.tropicair.com) has six flights daily between Goldson International Airport and Dangriga at 8:15 and 10:20am, and at 12:20, 2:20, 3:20, and 5pm. The fare is

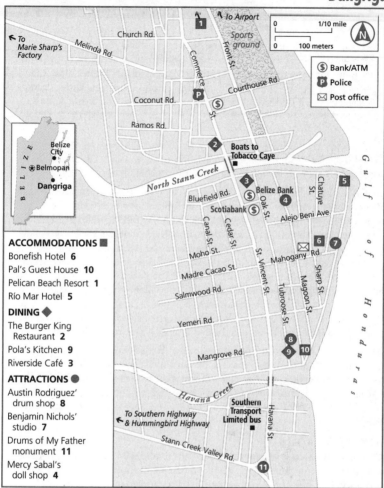

← To
Marie Sharp's
Factory

Church Rd.

Melinda Rd.

Coconut Rd.

Ramos Rd.

North Stann Creek

Bluefield Rd.

Scotiabank

Canal St.

Cedar St.

Moho St.

Madre Cacao St.

Salmwood Rd.

Yemeri Rd.

Mangrove Rd.

Havana Creek

To Southern Highway
& Hummingbird Highway

Stann Creek Valley Rd.

Southern
Transport
Limited bus

Havana St.

Commerce St.

Front St.

Sports
ground

To Airport

Courthouse Rd.

Boats to
Tobacco Caye

Belize Bank

Oak St.

Alejo Beni Ave.

Chatuye St.

St. Vincent St.

Mahogany Rd.

Magoon St.

Sharp St.

Tubroose St.

Belize City
●Belmopan
Dangriga

0   1/10 mile
0   100 meters
N

$ Bank/ATM
P Police
⊠ Post office

Gulf of Honduras

ACCOMMODATIONS ■
Bonefish Hotel **6**
Pal's Guest House **10**
Pelican Beach Resort **1**
Río Mar Hotel **5**

DINING ◆
The Burger King
Restaurant **2**
Pola's Kitchen **9**
Riverside Café **3**

ATTRACTIONS ●
Austin Rodriguez'
drum shop **8**
Benjamin Nichols'
studio **7**
Drums of My Father
monument **11**
Mercy Sabal's
doll shop **4**

BZ$89 (US$45) each way. They also have five daily flights between Municipal Airport and Dangriga leaving at 8:30 and 10:30am, and at 12:30, 2:30, and 4:50pm. The fare is BZ$61 (US$31) each way. Tropic Air flights depart Dangriga for both of Belize City's airports daily at 6:50, 7:45, and 10:25am, and at 12:20, 2:20, and 4:45pm. Flight time runs between 15 and 30 minutes, depending on whether there is an intermediate stop.

Flights to and from Punta Gorda and Placencia on Maya Island Air and Tropic Air stop in Dangriga to pick up and drop off passengers. On both airlines, flights are sometimes added during the high season or suspended during the low season, so check in advance.

BY BUS   Southern Transport Limited, 3 Havana St. (© **207-3937** in Belize City, or 502-2160 in Dangriga), runs buses between Belize City and Dangriga roughly every hour on the hour between 6am and 5pm from the main bus terminal on West Collet Canal Street. The fare is BZ$20 (US$10). The ride takes about 3 hours.

> (*Moments* **Welcome**
>
> As you enter Dangriga you'll come to a traffic circle. Be sure to take a moment to check out the **Drums of My Father** monument here, a larger-than-life bronze casting of three ceremonial *dügü* drums, and the maraca-like shaker or *sísira*. This simple sculpture lets you know right away that you are entering the heartland of Garífuna society and culture.

Tip: Most of the buses take the Hummingbird Highway. A few take the coastal Manatee Road. Unless you are heading to Gales Point, I'd try to take the much more comfortable ride on the Hummingbird Highway.

BY CAR   From Belize City, head west on Cemetery Road, which becomes the Western Highway. Take this all the way to Belmopan, where you will connect with the Hummingbird Highway heading south. Six miles (10km) before Dangriga, the Hummingbird Highway connects with the Southern Highway. Follow the signs into Dangriga; you'll be entering from the south end of town.

Alternatively, you can take the unpaved New Belize or Manatee Road, which turns off the Western Highway just past the Belize Zoo, at around Mile Marker 30. The Manatee Road passes by the small Creole village of Gales Point, and then rejoins the Hummingbird Highway about 8½ miles (17km) outside of Dangriga. This route is shorter as the crow flies, but in worse shape physically, so the going is slower. Either route should take around 2 to 2½ hours from Belize City.

BY BOAT   There are no regularly scheduled boats from Belize City to Dangriga, but aside from flying, water is the most direct means of covering the 36 miles (58km) between the two cities. If you want to come by boat, head to the Marine Terminal or ask around the docks in Belize City. Expect to pay from BZ$200 to BZ$400 (US$100–US$200) for a boat that can carry four to eight passengers.

GETTING AROUND

There are no official car rental agencies, but if you really search, you might be able to find an enterprising local willing to rent you a vehicle. If this is absolutely necessary, your best bet is to have your hotel try and arrange this for you.

For a taxi in Dangriga, call **Neal's Taxi,** 1 St. Vincent St. (© **522-3309**).

Boats to Tobacco Caye leave from the Gumagurugu River or North Stann Creek in front of the River Café, just down from the new bridge. The going rate is around BZ$250 to BZ$275 (US$125–US$138) round-trip for up to eight people, so it's definitely advisable to round up a group before heading out. Alternatively, you can catch a ride with the folks from **Pelican Beach Resort** (© **522-2044**), who run to Tobacco Caye daily and charge BZ$96 (US$48) per person each way.

ORIENTATION

The main street through Dangriga is called St. Vincent Street south of the main bridge over North Stann Creek, and Commerce Street north of it. Most of the town's businesses and attractions lie within a few blocks of this bridge in either direction. The airstrip is on the north end of town, near the Pelican Beach Resort.

FAST FACTS   For the **police,** dial © 522-2022; for the **fire department,** call © 522-2091. The **Dangriga Hospital** (© 522-2078) is located on Courthouse

Road, 4 blocks north and 2 blocks east of the main bridge. The post office (© 522-2035) is in the southern section of town next to the Bonefish Hotel.

Both of the principal banks in town are on St. Vincent Street: **Belize Bank,** 24 St. Vincent St. (© 522-2903), and **Scotiabank,** 10 St. Vincent St. (© 522-2031). If you need some film or developing, try either **Dangriga Photo Plus,** 5 Bluefield Rd. (© 522-2394), or **Gem's Photo,** 77 St. Vincent St. (© 522-3859). For any contact lens or eyeglass problems, head to **Hoy Eye Center,** 18 St. Vincent St. (© 522-0628).

Finally, if your hotel can't or won't do it for you, take your dirty clothes to **Val's Laundry,** 1 Sharp St. (© 502-3324). They charge around BZ$12 (US$6) per load.

WHAT TO SEE & DO

The main activity in Dangriga is a slow walk up and down the main north-south thoroughfare. If you tire of watching the endless procession of people and listening to the colorful mix of English, Creole, and Garífuna, head a block or two over towards the sea and cop a seat in one of the town's oceanfront parks. If you're looking for a more active adventure, you'll have to head out of Dangriga, but your options are plentiful.

If you're staying in Dangriga for any period of time, you may also want to visit any number of the relatively nearby attractions, including Guanacaste National Park, Blue Hole National Park, Caves Branch, Hopkins Village, and Cockscomb Basin Wildlife Sanctuary. For more information on the first three attractions, see chapter 8. For details about the rest, see below.

FISHING   The fishing is excellent out of Dangriga. Most folks head to the flats in search of bonefish, permit, and tarpon. Closer to shore and near the river mouths you can find snook, and beyond the barrier reef lie marlin, sailfish, tuna, wahoo, and dorado. Ask at your hotel, around the docks, or at the Pelican Beach Resort (© **522-2044**). Expect to pay between BZ$600 and BZ$2,400 (US$300–US$1,200) per day for a full day for several anglers aboard a modern sport-fishing boat. Alternatively, you can line up a lower-tech outing around the docks for around BZ$100 to BZ$200 (US$50–US$100) for a half-day.

If You Come to a Fork in the Road, Take Both

Given the unique sights offered by the two possible routes down to Dangriga, you might want to consider taking one route on your way south, and the other on your way back. The **Hummingbird Highway** passes through some of Belize's most picturesque countryside. The road weaves through jungle mountains and crosses clear streams and small rivers. Admire the forest-covered karst hillsides to the west, as you wind your way through mostly uninhabited country. The **Manatee Road** is a red dirt affair, passing through a lot of lowland swamps and mangroves that border Belize's large southern lagoon. Still, this route is not for the faint of heart. In the rainy season it can get quite muddy and slick, while in the dry season, the dirt can form a hard, jarring washboard and dust can be a problem. In some places you'll have to cross single-lane, rail-less wooden plank bridges that give some drivers vertigo, even though they're not very high.

FYI

North Stann Creek is also known as the Gumagurugu River in the local
Garífuna language.

SNORKELING & SCUBA DIVING   Dangriga is the jumping-off point for
some wonderful small cayes situated right on the edge of the barrier reef, as well
as Glover's Reef Atoll. Most of the hotels in town can arrange for a day trip of
snorkeling or scuba diving at Tobacco Caye, South Water Caye, or one of the
cayes comprising Glover's Reef Atoll. Expect to pay from BZ$160 to BZ$240
(US$80–US$120) per person for a full-day snorkel trip out to the reef, including lunch and transportation. Add on an extra BZ$90 to BZ$150
(US$45–US$125) if you plan to scuba dive.

ATTRACTIONS ON THE HUMMINGBIRD HIGHWAY

Located just off the highway in the tiny settlement of Pomona Village is one of
the most important and renowned factories in all of Belize, **Marie Sharp's.** The
factory is small and simple, and depending on the time of year and demand,
they may be making any number of their various hot sauces, jams, and chutneys.
It's best to call in advance to arrange a tour (② **520-2087**). If you're lucky, you'll
get to meet Marie herself. The tour is free, but you'll want to bring some money
to stock up on the sauces.

Tucked a few miles off the highway is **Five Blues Lake National Park** ⚲. The
main feature of this park is a stunning cenote, whose various hues of blue give
the park its name. All around the park are forested lands and distinct karst hill
formations. The park is run by the folks from the local community of Saint Margaret's Village. The park and small village are located on Lagoon Road, just off
the Hummingbird Highway around Mile Marker 32. There are about 3 miles
(5km) of well-marked trails in the park. You can also take a refreshing dip in the
lake, or rent a canoe for a leisurely paddle. Admission is BZ$8 (US$4). Camping is allowed inside the park for BZ$10 (US$5) per person. Some simple
accommodations and restaurants are also available in Saint Margaret's Village.
For more information, check out the park and community's website at **www.5
blueslake.org**.

GALES POINT & THE MANATEES

Gales Point is a small Creole fishing village about 25 miles (40km) north of
Dangriga. It is a peaceful little village where you can get in tune with one of
Belize's traditional cultures and its slower pace of life. The village stretches along
a narrow peninsula that juts into the large brackish **Southern Lagoon,** which is
also called Manatee Lagoon because it's the manatees that inhabit the water of
the lagoon that bring most people to Gales Point in the first place. For BZ$60
to BZ$80 (US$30–US$40), you can hire a small boat to take you out to where
the manatees usually feed. The boats generally will hold up to eight people, so
the more people you can line up, the less it will cost each of you. You can also
ask around in the village about renting a canoe to paddle yourself out to where
the manatees feed. I prefer this option, although be sure to get a lightweight
modern canoe, as the traditional carved tree-trunk dugout canoes are a bear to
paddle. Canoe rentals should run you around BZ$10 (US$5) for a half-day.
Although previously encouraged, swimming with the manatees is no longer
allowed. The contact is potentially dangerous for manatees and humans alike,

and it's best to just enjoy a pleasant sighting of these gentle water mammals. In addition to the manatees, this is a fabulous bird-watching spot, and if you're lucky you might even see a jabiru stork here.

Other possible trips from Gales Point include visits to the beach or some nearby caves and nighttime turtle walks. The beach on either side of the Manatee River is a major nesting site for the hawksbill turtle. The turtles generally lay their eggs from June to August. These tours generally cost between BZ$60 and BZ$100 (US$30–US$50) for the boat and guide.

Gales Point is also home to renowned drum maker **Emett Young,** who also runs a small drumming school. If you're interested in a lesson, which costs about $10 an hour, ask around town for Emett.

Gales Point is one of several villages in Belize to have a community-based ecotourism homestay program. Rooms in local villagers' homes are very basic and often do not have running water or flush toilets. The rates are BZ$10 (US$5) for a single and BZ$15 (US$7.50) for a double. You can also camp in Gales Point at **Metho's Camping** for BZ$6 (US$3) per person. To arrange a homestay in Gales Point, try calling **Deborah Callender** (© 614-5621), who runs the cute little Orchid Café. Alternatively, you can stay at the **Manatee Lodge** (© 220-8040; www.manateelodge.com), a lovely guesthouse at the very end of the peninsula.

To drive here from Dangriga, head out of town to the Hummingbird Highway towards Belize City. At the village of Melinda, you'll see the turnoff for Manatee Road and Gales Point.

To get here by bus from Dangriga, you will have to take a Belize City–bound bus using the Manatee Road. These buses do not always enter the village of Gales Point. Ask in advance; if the bus doesn't enter the village, you will have to hike or hitchhike the final 1½ miles (2.4km) out onto the peninsula. From Belize City, you can take one of the Dangriga-bound buses using the Manatee Road. Again, ask in advance if the bus enters Gales Point village or not.

SHOPPING

As the cultural seat of the Garífuna culture, Dangriga is a great place to pick up, or just admire, local arts and crafts.

If you'd like to have a look at some Garífuna paintings, visit the studio of **Benjamin Nicholas,** 25 Howard St. (© 522-2785). Using a Caribbean naïve style, Nicholas paints scenes of traditional Garífuna village life. You'll find his studio a couple of blocks south of the Gamaragu River and a block east of St. Vincent Street.

If the beat really gets to you, you can buy a handmade wooden drum from **Austin Rodríguez,** 32 Tubroose St. (© 522-2308). Drums vary in size and cost between BZ$75 and BZ$200 (US$38–US$100).

Finally, **Mercy Sabal,** 22 Magoon St. (no phone), has become quite famous for her handcrafted Garífuna dolls. These small dolls are predominantly of female figures in traditional dress, and cost between BZ$30 and B$60 (US$15–US$30).

WHERE TO STAY
MODERATE
Bonefish Hotel Located a block from the water and across the street from a small park, the Bonefish is a good mid-range option right in the heart of Dangriga. The carpeted guest rooms are generally quite spacious. The second-floor

Garífuna Settlement Day

Each year on November 19, Garífuna Settlement Day is celebrated in Dangriga, with Garífunas coming from around Belize and as far away as Guatemala, Honduras, Nicaragua, and New York. The celebration is a riot of street music and colorful parades. There's a grand carnival air to the festivities. Eating, drinking, and dancing go on well into the night. The Garífuna have their own traditional music, which is based on wooden drums and choral singing. The rhythms and songs have strong African roots, and have given birth to a hybrid pop music called Punta Rock, which is probably the country's most popular music and dance form. If you plan to partake in the festivities, be sure to book far in advance, as every hotel room in Dangriga and the nearby towns and villages sells out early. For more information, contact the **National Garífuna Council of Belize** (© 522-3781).

Tip: Garífuna Settlement Day isn't the only opportunity to experience the full color and vitality of traditional Garífuna culture. At the end of the Christmas and New Year season, on the weekend closest to January 6, the local Garífuna community takes to the streets to enjoy the Wanaragua or John Kunnu dancers. Wearing masks, elaborate costumes, colorful headdresses topped with macaw feathers, and vibrating arrangements of shells and vedas, Wanaragua or John Kunnu dance troupes parade through the streets of Dangriga, accompanied by the beat of traditional drummers.

bar and restaurant has a good view of the ocean, and serves good local fare and fresh seafood at reasonable rates. This hotel is owned and run by the same folks who have the Blue Marlin Lodge (p. 177) on South Water Caye, and is a convenient place to stay if you are headed out to Tobacco or South Water Caye.

15 Mahogany St. (P.O. Box 21), Dangriga. © **800/798-1558** in the U.S., or 522-2243. Fax 522-2296. www.bluemarlinlodge.com. 8 units. BZ$120–BZ$180 (US$60–US$90) double. Rates lower in the off season. AE, MC, V. Free parking. **Amenities:** Restaurant; tour desk; laundry service. *In room:* A/C, TV, minifridge, no phone.

Pelican Beach Resort ⊛ This is a comfortable and spacious Caribbean resort and it's certainly the most luxurious option right in Dangriga, although that's not necessarily saying much. The range of prices reflect room location. The most frugal rooms are in a separate building set in from the ocean. The most expensive rooms have second-floor ocean views with wonderful balconies, and I think they're worth the slight splurge. Despite its age, the hotel has been well maintained through the years. There's no real beach here, but there are plenty of palm trees, lounge chairs, and hammocks spread around. There's a small gift shop featuring Garífuna crafts, Belizean books, and popular wildlife photography. The restaurant serves up excellent Belizean and Garífuna meals at reasonable rates. A variety of fishing, diving, and inland tours are available, and Pelican Beach also runs a sister cottage resort out on South Water Caye.

North end (P.O. Box 2), Dangriga. © **522-2044.** Fax 522-2570. www.pelicanbeachbelize.com. 20 units. BZ$160–BZ$200 (US$80–US$100) double. Rates include full breakfast. Rates lower in the off season. AE, MC, V. Free parking. **Amenities:** Restaurant; tour desk; laundry service. *In room:* A/C (in 10 units), TV.

INEXPENSIVE

In addition to the place listed below, the **Río Mar Hotel** (© 522-2201) is a simple and funky budget option with a wonderful location at the mouth of the river, with a popular local restaurant and lively bar.

Pal's Guest House *Value*   This budget hotel is down at the south end of town just off the water, near the mouth of Havana Creek, and is clean and quiet. The rooms with shared bathroom are small and basic, but are otherwise fine. If you have a bit more money to spend, you should opt for one of the second-floor beachfront rooms in the new building, which have air-conditioning and small private balconies overlooking the sea. The owner, Austin Flores, is friendly, knowledgeable, and an active member of the local Garífuna community.

868A Magoon St., Dangriga. © 522-2365. Fax 522-2095. www.palsbelize.com. 19 units (16 with private bathroom). BZ$40 (US$20) double with shared bathroom; BZ$50–BZ$70 (US$25–US$35) double with private bathroom. MC, V. **Amenities:** Tour desk; gift shop; laundry service. *In room:* TV (in 16 units), no phone.

WHERE TO DINE

When you're in Dangriga, be sure to sample some of the local Garífuna cooking. One staple you'll find at many restaurants is a bread made from cassava, also known as yuca. Be sure to hunt down a good bowl of *hudut,* a dish featuring fresh fish cooked in coconut milk, accompanied by pieces of plantain and cassava. If you're lucky, you'll be able to wash everything down with some homemade cashew wine.

Up and down the main street through town—St. Vincent Street and Commerce Street—you'll find numerous very basic restaurants. In addition to the restaurant listed below, **The Burger King Restaurant,** 135 Commerce St. (© 522-2476), which is not affiliated with the Burger King fast-food chain, is a local favorite serving simple Belizean meals heavy on the grease. There are also several very basic Chinese restaurants along the main street.

If you're looking for a bit of a splurge and somewhat slightly more elegant ambience, the restaurant at the **Pelican Beach Resort** (© 522-2044) serves well-prepared local dishes and fresh seafood.

INEXPENSIVE

Pola's Kitchen *Finds* BELIZEAN/GARIFUNA   This is an excellent place to come for traditional Garífuna cooking. You'll find this unassuming restaurant occupying the lower floor of a two-story building, around the corner from Pal's Guest House. The dining room is clean and tiled, and has several ceiling fans as well as air-conditioning. You'll also usually find some Garífuna arts and crafts on display here. Pola lives upstairs and cooks a fresh batch of *hudut* every day. It often goes quickly, so come for lunch if you want to try some. There's also always some stew fish, stew chicken, and stew beef on the menu, as well as specials like cow feet soup. Breakfast is also a treat, with daily freshly baked bread and johnnycakes.

25A Tubroose St., Dangriga. © 522-2675. Main courses BZ$8–BZ$18 (US$4–US$9). No credit cards. Mon–Sat 8am–2pm and 6–9pm.

Riverside Café BELIZEAN   This simple cafe and bar is funky and rather run-down. Still, it's popular with the local boatmen and one of the best places to get travel information in Dangriga. It opens early and serves food throughout the day. You can get a full meal of fried chicken, beans, and rice for BZ$8 (US$4). Breakfasts are hearty and inexpensive. This is the place to ask about rides out to one of the nearby cayes, to set up a tour around the region, and to pick up some brochures from the wall-mounted racks. You'll find the cafe just east of St. Vincent Street on the south side of North Stann Creek.

S. Riverside Dr., Dangriga. ℂ 523-9908. Reservations not accepted. Main courses BZ$3–BZ$10 (US$1.50–US$5). No credit cards. Daily 6am–10pm.

DANGRIGA AFTER DARK

There's not much happening in Dangriga after dark. Your best bets are the bars at either the Bonefish Hotel or Pelican Reef Resort (see "Where to Stay," above).

BEYOND DANGRIGA: OFFSHORE CAYES & GLOVER'S REEF ATOLL

The Tobacco Caye range of mangrove cayes lies just 10 miles (16km) east of Dangriga. A little further south sits South Water Caye. Beyond the barrier reef and further out to sea is Glover's Reef Atoll.

Tobacco Caye 🐟🐟 itself is just 5 acres (2 ha) large, with about five different lodging options set more or less side-by-side. You can walk from one end of the caye to the other in about 3 minutes, and that's at a leisurely pace.

South Water Caye 🐟🐟 is a little bit larger than Tobacco, but you can still walk from one end to the other in about 5 minutes. Nevertheless, the vibe here is slightly more spacious and luxurious than that on Tobacco Caye, although there's not anything approaching real luxury here, either.

To the east of these cayes, and beyond the barrier reef, lies **Glover Reef Atoll** 🐟🐟🐟, a stunning natural coral formation featuring an oval-shaped central lagoon nearly 22 miles (35km) long. Named after the British pirate John Glover, the steep-walled reefs here offer some of the best wall diving anywhere in the Caribbean. The entire atoll is a marine reserve, and in 1996 it was declared a World Heritage Site by the United Nations. Inside the usually calm lagoon, patch reefs are a wonderland for snorkelers.

The largest caye in the area, **Man-O-War Caye** 🐟🐟, is a bird sanctuary and major nesting site for the magnificent frigate, or "man-o-war." A tour to the caye is an impressive sight, with hundreds of these large sea birds roosting on and circling above the tiny caye. As part of their mating ritual, the males inflate a huge red sack on their throats to attract a mate. In addition to the frigates, the island also is home to a large community of brown boobies.

Located just a stone's throw from the south end of South Water Caye, the **Smithsonian Institute of Marine Research** occupies all of the tiny Carrie Bow Caye. Your lodge can make arrangements to visit the caye, meet with resident scientists, and use their beach, which is one of the sandiest in the area.

Finally, fishing for bonefish, permit, and tarpon is excellent throughout this area.

GETTING THERE

Boats to the outlying cayes leave from the south shore of the Gumagurugu River or North Stann Creek in front of the Riverside Café, just down from the bridge. The going rate is from BZ$300 to BZ$400 (US$150–US$200) round-trip for up to eight people, so it's definitely advisable to round up a group before heading out. The ride takes around 30 to 40 minutes to Tobacco Caye, depending on how fast a boat you book. Add on about 20 to 40 minutes and between BZ$100 (US$50) to BZ$200 (US$100) for either South Water Caye or Glover's Reef Atoll. Alternatively, you can catch a ride with the folks from **Pelican Beach Resort** (ℂ 522-2044) who run out to South Water Caye daily and charge BZ$96 (US$48) per person each way.

Tips **Gentle Giants**

From March to June—especially just after the full moons—the waters here are an excellent place to spot and dive with mammoth whale sharks, the largest fish in the sea.

Note: You definitely want to have a reservation before heading out to one of the lodges on these cayes, as there are very limited options and they fill up fast during the high season. Try to arrange your transportation when booking a room.

WHERE TO STAY & DINE ON THE OUTER CAYES

All of the options listed below are self-contained lodges and resorts, meaning you will be taking all of your meals at your hotel. Fishing, diving, and multiday adventure packages are available at all of the places listed below.

In addition to the lodges listed below, **Island Expeditions** (© **800/667-1630,** or 604/452-3212 in the U.S.; www.islandexpeditions.com) and **Slickrock Adventures** (© **800/390-5715,** or 435/259-4225 in the U.S.; www.slickrock.com) run various adventurous multiday kayak and dive tours to small camps and lodges on private isolated cayes of Glover's Reef Atoll.

Blue Marlin Lodge   Taking up much of the northern end of South Water Caye, the Blue Marlin Lodge has probably the most extensive facilities of any of the lodges in this section. The best rooms here are their new wooden cabins set right over the water. These are spacious and air-conditioned, and they're my favorite lodgings in this neck of the woods. While the geodesic dome cabins are unique and comfortable (and also have air-conditioning), they are set in the center of the compound, with no balcony or veranda and somewhat lesser views. The rest of the rooms are housed in a couple of two-story wooden buildings, and while less expensive, I prefer them to the domes.

South Water Caye (P.O. Box 21, Dangriga). © **800/798-1558** in the U.S., or 522-2243 in Belize. Fax 522-2296. www.bluemarlinlodge.com. 17 units. BZ$390 (US$195) double room; BZ$440 (US$220) double cabin. Rates include 3 meals daily and all taxes. AE, MC, V. **Amenities:** Restaurant; tour desk; laundry service. *In room:* No phone.

Glover's Atoll Resort (*Value*)   Located on the private North East Caye, this little island getaway has grown and evolved over the years. Originally a laid-back and rustic retreat on a very isolated caye, it is now actually deserving of its "resort" moniker, although it still retains much of the hostel-like atmosphere and funky charm. Lodging options range from camping to dorm rooms to simple, rustic cabins with private bathrooms and kitchen facilities. My favorites are the new round cabins built on stilts over the ocean. The resort also offers large, semi-permanent tents, or you can pitch your own. And while they do serve meals, a good percentage of the guests here pack in and cook their own food at the resort's communal kitchen. In addition to what you pack in, fresh fish, lobster, and conch can be purchased on the island, as can drinking water and fresh bread. Most visitors here come as part of the resort's weeklong package, which includes transportation. A meal package will run you around $28 per day.

Glover's Reef Atoll (P.O. Box 563, Belize City). © **520-5016** or 614-7177. Fax 223-6087. www.glovers.com.bz. 11 units. BZ$198 (US$99) per week camping; BZ$304 (US$152) per week in dorm room; BZ$416 (US$208) per person per week in a private cabin. Rates include round-trip transportation from Sittee River Village or Dangriga and all taxes. MC, V. **Amenities:** Restaurant; tour desk. *In room:* No phone.

Pelican's Pouch ⭐ Run by the folks at the Pelican Beach Resort in Dangriga, this isolated island getaway is one of the best-run little resorts on these little cayes. The best rooms here are the six individual cabins. Set on raised stilts by the water's edge, these wooden cottages vary in size somewhat, but all are very comfortable and charming. The rooms are housed on the second floor of a converted colonial-era convent. Each of these rooms comes with one double bed and two single beds, and a half-bathroom. A couple of communal showers are located on the ground level. The small price difference makes it very worthwhile to book one of the cabins.

South Water Caye (P.O. Box 2). ℂ 522-2044. Fax 522-2570. www.pelicanbeachbelize.com. 11 units (5 with shared shower). BZ$390 (US$195) double room; BZ$440 (US$220) double cabin. Rates include 3 meals daily and all taxes. AE, MC, V. **Amenities:** Restaurant; tour desk; laundry service. *In room:* No phone.

Reef's End Lodge Occupying the southern tip of Tobacco Caye, this simple lodge offers two distinct rooming options. Most of the rooms here are located on the second floor of a two-story converted house. Each comes with two twin beds and one full bed. They all share a common veranda. The rooms are spartan and are geared towards students, groups, and budget travelers. The two private cabins are a far better bet, and not significantly more expensive. The nicest feature here is the restaurant, which is set on stilts, with a deck and some docks out over the water.

Tobacco Caye (P.O. Box 299, Dangriga). ℂ **522-2419.** Fax 522-2828. www.reefsendlodge.com. 10 units. BZ$260 (US$130) double room; BZ$300 (US$150) double cabin. Rates include 3 meals daily. MC, V. **Amenities:** Restaurant; tour desk; laundry service. *In room:* No phone.

Tobacco Caye Lodge ⭐ 🅥🅐🅛🅤🅔 These six simple wooden cabins are set on raised stilts and overlooking the ocean. Each comes with a small balcony strung with a hammock. The lights and fans are powered by solar energy. There's a simple restaurant serving Belizean cuisine and fresh seafood. Meals are served family style, and most guests sit at one long communal table, sharing tales and getting to know one another. The scuba diving and snorkeling are fabulous. Formerly known as Island Camps, this remains an excellent isolated island lodge, and my favorite lodge on Tobacco Caye.

Tobacco Caye (P.O. Box 213, Dangriga). ℂ 520-5033. www.tclodgebelize.com. 6 units. BZ$180–BZ$240 (US$90–US$120) double. Rates include 3 meals daily. MC, V. **Amenities:** Restaurant; tour desk; laundry service. *In room:* No phone.

EN ROUTE SOUTH: WHERE THE WILD CATS ROAM

Weighing up to 200 pounds (91kg) and measuring more than 6 feet (1.8m) from nose to tip of tail, jaguars are king of the new-world jungle. Nocturnal predators, jaguars hunt peccaries (wild piglike animals), deer, and other small mammals. The **Cockscomb Basin Wildlife Sanctuary** ⭐⭐, established in 1990 as the world's first jaguar reserve, covers nearly 150 square miles (389 sq. km) of rugged forested mountains and has the greatest density of jaguars in the world. It is part of the even larger Cockscomb Basin Forest Reserve, which was created in 1984.

The forests within the preserve are home to other wild cats as well, including pumas, ocelots, and margays, all of which are very elusive, so don't get your hopes of seeing them too high. Few people do, but a good guide may be able to find you some tracks. Other mammals that you might spot if you're lucky include otters, coatimundis, tayra, kinkajous, deer, peccaries, anteaters, and armadillos.

The largest land mammal native to Central America, Baird's tapir, is also resident. Locally known as a "mountain cow," the tapir is the national animal of Belize. A tapir can weigh up to 600 pounds (272kg) and is related to the horse, although its protruding upper lip is more like an elephant's trunk.

Much more easily spotted in the dense vegetation surrounding the preserve's trails are nearly 300 species of birds, including the scarlet macaw, the keel-billed toucan, the king vulture, and the great curassow.

Trails inside the park range from gentle and short to quite arduous and long. Many offer wonderful views of the Cockscomb Mountains and lush forested valleys. There are quite a few waterfalls and swimming holes. During the dry season, you can even climb Victoria Peak, which at 3,675 feet (1,103m) is the country's highest mountain. This trip takes several days and requires a permit and local guide. For more information, contact the **Belize Audubon Society** (© 223-4988; www.belizeaudubon.org).

Caution should be exercised when visiting the preserve. In addition to jaguars, which can be dangerous, there are also poisonous snakes, including the deadly fer-de-lance. Always wear shoes, preferably boots, when hiking the trails here.

The Belize Audubon Society co-manages this park, and even offers a few private cabins and some dormitory sleeping options inside the sanctuary. Rates run between BZ$16 and BZ$36 (US$8–US$18) per person for dormitory-style accommodations, or BZ$107 (US$54) for one of the cabins which can sleep up to six persons. Alternatively, you can stay down near the information center near the highway at the **Tutzil Nah Cottages** (© 520-3044; www.mayacenter.com).

Cockscomb Basin Wildlife Sanctuary is located 6 miles (10km) inland from the Southern Highway, some 20 miles (32km) south of Dangriga. The turnoff and entrance to the sanctuary is at the roadside village of Maya Center. This is where you'll find the sanctuary's information center, and where you'll pay your BZ$10 (US$5) entrance fee. This is also a good place to check out some of the art and craft works at the neighboring shop run by the Maya Center Women's Group, and to hook up with a local guide. I've heard great reports about local guide Greg Sho, who can often be found at Greg's Bar, his other business, located right on the side of the highway before the entrance to Maya Center. Any bus heading south to Placencia and Punta Gorda will drop you off at the entrance. From here you'll have to hike the 6 miles (9.6km) or hire a local taxi for around BZ$30 (US$15) round-trip.

A NEARBY BACK-BUSH NATURE LODGE

Nestled at the foot of the Maya Mountains is an interesting little ecolodge, **Mama Noots Back-A-Bush Jungle Resort** ℛ (©/fax 422-3666; www.mamanoots.bz). With a collection of rustically luxurious rooms, as well as camping and dormitory facilities, the folks at Mama Noots are located in the heart of the newly declared **Mayflower Bocawina National Park.** The park protects the small and barely excavated Mayflower Mayan ruins, as well as vast expanses of tropical forests. There's excellent hiking and bird-watching on miles of trails leaving from the resort. All of the electricity is provided by an inventive mix of solar, hydro, and wind generators. A pure mountain spring provides the water. Multiday packages with transportation provided from Dangriga are the preferred means of visiting this little lodge. Contact them for details.

2 Hopkins Village & Sittee River Village ★★

87 miles (140km) S of Belize City; 79 miles (127km) SE of Belmopan; 33 miles (53km) N of Placencia

Hopkins Village and Sittee River Village are just beginning to get discovered by tourists, and you'd be wise to visit before too long. Hopkins Village is a midsize Garífuna community located on the shore, 15 miles (24km) south of Dangriga. It is a picturesque village with colorfully painted raised clapboard houses. It is also my preferred destination for getting a true taste of and some direct contact with this unique culture. This is a great place to wander around talking with children, fishermen, and elderly folks hanging out in front of their homes. If you stick around long enough, you may be able to learn a bit about traditional Garífuna lifestyles. Fishing is still the main employment of many of the villagers, although tourism is rapidly becoming the main source of employment and income.

Hopkins Village is set on a long curving swath of beach, which in addition to Placencia is one of the few true beaches in the country. This is a long, gently curving swath of white sand beach that is usually quite calm and good for swimming. In recent years, several beach and dive resorts have opened on the stretch of sand south of the village, while in the village itself you'll find a hodge-podge of budget lodgings and simple restaurants. Sittee River Village is a few miles south of Hopkins and a mile or so inland, on the banks of the gently flowing Sittee River. This is a tiny little town, but it does have a hotel or two, as well as a good Internet cafe. Fishermen like the quiet riverside setting and access to both fresh- and saltwater angling.

ESSENTIALS
GETTING THERE & DEPARTING
BY PLANE   The closest airport to Hopkins Village is in Dangriga. See "Dangriga," earlier in this chapter, for flight details. A taxi from Dangriga to Hopkins or Sittee River village should cost BZ$80 to BZ$90 (US$40–US$45) for up to four people.

BY BUS   Southern Transport Limited (© **207-3937** in Belize City) runs three buses daily between Dangriga and Hopkins Village and Sittee River, leaving Dangriga at 7am, 12:15pm, and 5:15pm. The ride takes between 25 and 35 minutes to Hopkins Village, with Sittee River Village just a few miles further on the route. Return buses head back to Dangriga at roughly the same times, although these routes are notoriously fickle and it is always best to ask in the villages for current schedules. The fare is BZ$6 (US$3) each way. The buses heading south from Dangriga continue on to Placencia, and can be caught in either Hopkins or Sittee River if your travels are taking you further south. See "Essentials" in section 1, above, for details on bus travel between Dangriga and Belize City.

BY CAR   From Belize City, head west on Cemetery Road, which becomes the Western Highway. Take this all the way to Belmopan, where you will connect with the Hummingbird Highway heading south. Six miles (10km) before Dangriga, the Hummingbird Highway connects with the Southern Highway. Take the Southern Highway towards Placencia and Punta Gorda. About 8 miles (13km) south of this junction, you'll see signs for the entrance to Hopkins Village. From here, it's 4 miles (6km) on a graded gravel road. A few miles further south on the Southern Highway is the entrance to Sittee River Village; however, you can also enter at Hopkins and head south from there along the coast, as it's really just a small loop.

GETTING AROUND

Hopkins Village itself is very small, and you can easily walk the entire town. If you're staying south of town or in Sittee River Village, or want to explore, a bicycle is the preferred means of transportation. Most of the hotels will either lend you a bike or rent you one for a few dollars per day.

There are no official taxi services, but if you ask around town or at your hotel, you should be able to hire someone for small trips or excursions. There are also a number of freelance guides in the area who have vehicles and may be willing to provide transportation. **Mark** (© **603-9256**) is an unofficial taxi driver and recommended local guide.

ORIENTATION

The access road from the Southern Highway heads right into the heart of Hopkins Village. If you continued straight, you'd be in the Caribbean Sea. The village itself spreads out for a few hundred yards in either direction. Heading south you'll come to the larger resorts listed below. At the turnoff and entrance to Jaguar Reef Resort, the road heads back towards the highway, passing through Sittee River Village. *Note:* It's only a 15- to 20-minute walk from the village to any of the resorts to the south, with the exception of Kanantik, which is further away.

FAST FACTS Both Hopkins and Sittee River villages are tiny and there are no banks or major stores or services. There is a gas station in Hopkins Village, and Internet cafes in both places.

WHAT TO SEE & DO

This is a very isolated and under-developed area. All of the resorts listed below specialize in scuba diving, snorkeling and, to a lesser extent, fishing. All of them also have a long list of tour options to attractions such as Cockscomb Basin Wildlife Sanctuary, Sittee River canoeing, Blue Hole National Park, the Mayflower Mayan ruins, and cultural tours of Dangriga. If you're staying at one of the lodgings in either of the villages, you'll find numerous local operators offering snorkeling, scuba, and fishing outings, as well as all the above-mentioned tours.

SNORKELING & DIVING

Snorkeling and scuba diving are stellar all along Belize's barrier reef. The Tobacco Caye range lies just offshore from Hopkins Village, a simple 30- to 40-minute boat ride away, with numerous snorkeling and dive sites. Moreover, the location makes these dive resorts excellent jumping-off points for trips to Glover's Reef Atoll and even Turneffe and Lighthouse Reef atolls. All of the resorts listed below offer multiday dive packages, which are the way to go for serious divers. The also all offer certification classes and advanced open-water courses. If you're not staying at one of the dedicated dive resorts, your best bet is probably to arrange to dive with them, as their equipment and dive masters are generally top-notch, and the price savings of going with a less active operator just aren't worth it. If you're feeling adventurous, for snorkeling excursions, feel free to ask around the village and head out with a local boat captain or tour guide. The lower cost and cultural richness might just make up for a slow boat, leaky mask, and loose-fitting fins.

FISHING

There's excellent bonefishing in the inland and barrier reef flats in this area. Anglers can also go for tarpon, permit, and snook, or head offshore for bigger game. Experienced guides can help you track any of the above fish, and many are taking their guests out flyfishing for them, just to up the ante. Most of the major lodges and resorts here offer fishing packages and excursions. Well-equipped sport fishing outings cost between BZ$600 and BZ$2,400 (US$300–US$1,200) per day, depending on the size of the boat, number of anglers, and distance traveled. Alternatively you can ask around Hopkins Village to line up a more low-tech outing for around BZ$100 to BZ$200 (US$50–US$100) for a half-day.

SHOPPING

Hopkins Village is a good place to find locally made Garífuna handcrafts. **Rudy Coleman** is a local drum maker, and his drums are excellent. Ask for Rudy around town. If he can't do it himself, he will surely be able to arrange for you to get some lessons on your new drum as well.

It's worth the time to head a little south of town to **Joy Jah's** studio and shop. The folks here specialize in woodcarvings and paintings done on dry coconut husks, mostly in the shape of fish. They also carry a selection of arts and crafts from around Belize. You'll find Joy Jah's (no phone) right on the beach just north of Hamanasi.

WHERE TO STAY

There are a host of lodging options in this area, ranging from simple budget and backpacker hotels in Hopkins Village to upscale dive resorts on the beaches to the south.

VERY EXPENSIVE

Hamanasi ⭐⭐ This new dive and adventure resort offers very comfortable rooms in an intimate setting. Diving is the main focus here, and the hotel has an excellent operation. The beachfront rooms are housed in a couple of ocean-facing two-story buildings, and I definitely recommend the second-floor rooms for the improved view and privacy of your balcony. There are also a series of "treehouses," spacious individual bungalows set on stilts 12 feet (3.6m) high in the midst of the hotel's tiny coastal forest, just a few yards behind the main operation. While these don't have an ocean view, they do offer up a lush sense of tropical isolation. There are wonderful and artistic tile and woodworking touches in all rooms, and most have quite high ceilings. Meals are served either in the main dining room or outdoors on an open-air deck. When I last visited, there were plans to open a rooftop dining area and bar. Hamanasi means "almond" in the local Garífuna language, and you'll see plenty of the namesake *hamans* trees growing around the grounds. Not a true almond, the tree does have an almond-shaped fruit.

Hopkins Village (P.O. Box 265, Dangriga). © 877/552-3483 in the U.S., or 520-7073. Fax 520-7090. www.hamanasi.com. 18 units. BZ$336–BZ$466 (US$168–US$233) double. Rates lower in the off season, slightly higher during peak weeks. MC, V. **Amenities:** Restaurant; bar; outdoor pool; full-service dive operation; tour desk; laundry service. *In room:* A/C, no phone.

Jaguar Reef Lodge ⭐⭐ (Kids) This lively little resort is the largest hotel in the region, offering up the most facilities, lodging options, amenities, and tour options—and it's still growing. The original duplex cabana rooms—rebuilt after a fire—are set in a horseshoe facing the sea. Only a few have good ocean views, but they're still my favorite rooms here. Large and well lit, they feature cool tile floors, high ceilings, Guatemalan bedspreads and decorations, and thatch roofs. There are also the new "colonial" rooms and suites; these are also very well done and comfortable. A few of these come with kitchenettes, televisions with DVD players, and other amenities that make them good for families and longer stays. The second-floor colonial suites have fabulous ocean-facing balconies. A separate little bed-and-breakfast provides the most budget-oriented accommodations here.

In addition to the on-site activities and services, these folks have a private caye, **Coco Plum Island Resort** ★★ (www.cocoplumcay.com), which they use for day trips, but which also has a restaurant and several cabins for overnighting, allowing you to design a combined mainland and outlying caye vacation. They also run the Iguana Day Lodge, a little retreat on the banks of the Sittee River, where you can spend some time bird-watching, lazing in a hammock, or paddling a kayak on the river. If you just want to hang around the lodge, hammocks and Adirondack chairs are set under the shade of palm trees along the lodge's white sand beach, and there's a freshwater pool as well. When I last visited, there were plans to add a spa and even a unique little golf course.

Hopkins Village (P.O. Box 297, Dangriga). © **800/289-5756** in the U.S., or 520-7040. Fax 520-7091. www. jaguarreef.com. 30 units. BZ$240–BZ$320 (US$120–US$160) double; BZ$390 (US$195) cabana. Rates lower in the off season, slightly higher during peak weeks. MC, V. **Amenities:** Restaurant; bar; outdoor pool; full-service dive operation; watersports equipment rental; complimentary bike and kayak use; tour desk; laundry service. In room: A/C, stocked minifridge, hair dryer, safe, no phone.

Kanantik ★★ This is the only "all-inclusive" resort in the area, and it's an interesting option. Except for the purchase of a bottle of wine or some top-shelf liquor, little else doesn't fall within the all-inclusive price you pay, and this includes all your scuba diving and dive equipment or fishing gear. The rooms are all individual hexagonal, thatch-roof cabins, set either right in front of the ocean or slightly set back in flowering gardens. Each cabin is spacious and features zapadillo wood floors, driftwood beds, either one king bed or two queen beds, and fancy stainless steel Italian fixtures. The rooms feature a walk-in closet, and the showers are built of smooth river stones. Meals are served in a large, high-pitched dining room. The owner is Italian, and there's usually an excellent chef on hand serving up a mix of local, Italian, and other international cuisine.

Kanantik is located 18 miles (29km) south of Dangriga, accessed by a graded gravel road that connects with the Southern Highway. They also have their own private airstrip, and charter flights directly to the resort can be arranged. The resort is closed September and October.

South of Hopkins Village (P.O. Box 1482, Belize City). © **800/965-9689** in the U.S., or 520-8048. Fax 520-8089. www.kanantik.com. 25 units. BZ$730 (US$365) per person double occupancy; BZ$1,000 (US$500) per person single occupancy. Rates include all meals, local drinks and soft drinks, taxes, tips, and activities. MC, V. **Amenities:** Restaurant; bar; midsize outdoor pool w/unheated Jacuzzi; full-service dive operation; watersports equipment; complimentary bike and kayak use; tour desk; laundry service. In room: A/C, no phone.

MODERATE

Hopkins Inn (Value) Located right on the beach, near the center of the village, this little hotel offers clean and comfortable individual cabins at an excellent price. The cabins are all tiled, and feature wood-paneled pitched roofs. Each has a small front porch, and most of these face the sea. A simple continental breakfast is served, and a host of restaurants are within easy walking distance. The owners are very friendly and knowledgeable, and can help arrange any number of tours and adventures.

Hopkins Village (P.O. Box 121, Dangriga). ©/fax 523-7013. www.hopkinsinn.com. 4 units. BZ$100–BZ$150 (US$50–US$75) double. Rates include continental breakfast. Rates lower in the off season. No credit cards. **Amenities:** Bike rental; tour desk; laundry service. In room: Minifridge, coffeemaker, no phone.

Mother Nature's Resort   This place is actually located on the other side of the Sittee River from the village. You can drive in a back way, or head to their dock on the river, follow the directions on their sign, and yell "Yoo hoo" or "Hay yo!" Once at the hotel, you'll find simple but comfortable rooms in a large wooden building, and one separate "tree top" cabin. Fishing and diving trips are the staples here, and they have their own little fleet of well-equipped boats, kayaks, and jet skis. The hotel sits on 10 acres (4 ha) of pretty wild land, and has some trails. Camping is also permitted.

Sittee River Village. ✆ 615-2148 or 615-0015. www.mothernaturesresort.com. 5 units. BZ$160–BZ$180 (US$80–US$90) double. MC, V. **Amenities:** Restaurant; tour desk; laundry service. *In room:* No phone.

INEXPENSIVE

In addition to the place listed below, there are literally a score or more of simple guesthouses and small inns. Some are run by a local renting a spare room, others are converted houses. Most inns charge around BZ$16 to BZ$30 (US$8–US$15) per person. Of these, **Yugadah Inn** (✆ **503-7089**) and **Jungle Jeanies** (✆ **523-7047**) are my favorites.

Tipple Tree Beya (Value)   This locale, owned by an English woman who also speaks German, has a laid-back vibe and three rooms in a two-story oceanfront home and one private cabin. This is an excellent option for budget travelers. Located at the far southern end of the village, literally where the pavement ends, Tipple Tree Beya combines the isolated feel of the more expensive beach resorts here, with the convenience and proximity of the in-town options. This place has an excellent stretch of beachfront. There are hammocks spread on a broad shared veranda, and rustic chairs set out on the sand. The cabin has a small kitchen area, equipped with a microwave oven, refrigerator, coffeemaker, and some basic utensils. Camping is permitted for BZ$10 (US$5) per person, with access to a communal shower and bathroom.

Hopkins Village (P.O. Box 206, Dangriga). ✆/fax 520-7006. http://tippletree.net. 5 units (4 with private bathroom). BZ$40 (US$20) double with shared bathroom; BZ$65–BZ$100 (US$33–US$50) double with bathroom. MC, V. **Amenities:** Bike and kayak rental; tour desk; laundry service. *In room:* No phone.

Toucan Sittee (Value)   Set right on the banks of the Sittee River, this is a very simple little hotel with accommodations ranging from a dorm room with a shared bathroom to a duplex cabin facing the river. A couple of the rooms come with kitchenettes for longer stays. The owners are extremely friendly, and an informal family atmosphere reigns here. The bird-watching is excellent and taken seriously.

Sittee River Village. ✆ 523-7039. http://freespace.virgin.net/david.griggs. 5 units (2 with shared bathroom). BZ$16 (US$8) per person dormitory; BZ$60 (US$30) double with shared bathroom; BZ$90–BZ$120 (US$45–US$60) double with private bathroom. MC, V. **Amenities:** Restaurant; tour desk; laundry service. *In room:* Minifridge, no phone.

WHERE TO DINE

Even if you're staying at one of the large resorts around here, it's worth heading into town to try a meal at one of the simple, local-run restaurants on the main street. Of these, both **Iris's Restaurant** and **Innies Restaurant** are perennial favorites. Both serve excellent fresh fish and seafood, and will usually have some *hudut* and other Garífuna dishes on hand. Both are very basic, inexpensive, and somewhat funky in decor and vibe.

HOPKINS VILLAGE AFTER DARK

Aside from the various resort hotels, there is very little in the way of nightlife here—unless you can line up a night dive. Most of the resorts, however, rotate hiring local bands and dance troupes to entertain their guests. It's worth combining a dinner at one of these places with the nightly show. The liveliest bar on Hopkins Village's main road is **The Watering Hole,** which even has a pool table.

3 Placencia (★/★

150 miles (242km) S of Belize City; 100 miles (161km) SE of Belmopan; 55 miles (89km) NE of Punta Gorda

Located at the southern tip of a long, narrow peninsula that is separated from the mainland by a similarly narrow lagoon, Placencia is Belize's premiere beach destination. With nearly 16 miles (26km) of white sand fronting a calm turquoise sea and backed by palm trees, Placencia attracts everyone from hippy backpackers to avid naturalists to hard-core divers to upscale snowbirds. The whole peninsula has been booming in recent years, and there are actually several sections of it being developed, including Maya Beach on the northern end of the peninsula and Seine Bight Village in the middle.

Placencia itself is a tiny Creole village of colorful clapboard houses mostly built on stilts. Once you settle into the slow pace and relaxed atmosphere, it's hard to move on. Placencia is *the* definition of laid-back. For years, the village's principal thoroughfare was a sidewalk, although the recent construction and development boom have made the main road through town (called "the Back Road") actually busy most days. Once listed in the *Guinness Book of World Records* as the narrowest street in the world, the sidewalk still runs through the heart of the village parallel to the sea.

On October 8, 2001, Placencia was devastated by Hurricane Iris. The eye of this Category Four storm passed right over the tiny village of Monkey River, just south of Placencia. The destruction was massive. Nonetheless, almost everything has been either rebuilt, or leveled and cleaned, and it's almost hard to tell the hurricane actually passed through.

ESSENTIALS
GETTING THERE

BY PLANE   There are numerous flights into and out of Placencia's little airport (PLJ). **Maya Island Air** (© 226-2435 in Belize City, or 523-3475 in Placencia; www.mayaairways.com) has 10 flights daily between the Goldson International Airport in Belize City and Placencia. The first flight leaves at 8:15am and the last flight is at 5:10pm. Flight time is 35 minutes, with a brief stop in Dangriga; the fare is BZ$140 (US$70) each way. They also have six daily flights between the Belize City's Municipal Airport and Placencia at 8, 10, and 10:30am, and at 12:30, 2:30, and 4:30pm. The fare is BZ$118 (US$59) each way. These flights take 50 minutes, because they stop en route to pick up and let off passengers at the international airport and in Dangriga. Maya Island Air flights from Placencia to Belize City leave at 5:45, 7:05, 10:30, and 11:50am, and at 1, 2:10, 2:45, and 4:30pm. Most of these flights stop first in Dangriga, and then at the international airport, before continuing on to Municipal Airport.

Tropic Air (© 226-2012 in Belize City, or 523-3410 in Placencia; www.tropic air.com) has six flights daily between Goldson International Airport and Placencia at 8:15 and 10:20am, and at 12:20, 2:20, 3:20, and 5pm. The fare is BZ$140

(US$70) each way. They also have five daily flights between Municipal Airport and Placencia leaving at 8:30 and 10:30am and at 12:30, 2:30, and 4:50pm. The fare is BZ$118 (US$59) each way. Tropic Air flights depart Placencia for Belize City's airports daily at 6:30, 7:25, and 10:05am, and at noon, 2, 4, and 4:25pm.

Flights to and from Punta Gorda on Maya Island Air and Tropic Air stop in Placencia to pick up and drop off passengers. On both airlines, flights are sometimes added during the high season or suspended during the low season, so check in advance. Flight time runs between 25 and 50 minutes, depending on whether there is an intermediate stop or two.

BY BUS Southern Transport Limited (© 207-3937 in Belize City) has nearly hourly service to Dangriga. Buses leave Dangriga for Placencia daily at 12:15, 3:30 and 5:15pm. The fare is BZ$10 (US$5).

Buses leave Placencia for Dangriga, with onward connection to Belmopan, San Ignacio, and Belize City, daily at 5:30 and 6am, and at 1:30pm. If you're heading south, you'll want to catch the *Hokie Pokie* ferry that leaves from Placencia for Independence Village daily at 6:45 and 10am, and at 4pm. This short ferry cuts a lot of miles off the road trip, and will let you connect with the regular southbound buses that pass through Independence Village. Fare for the ferry is BZ$10 (US$5); the ride takes 30 minutes. It will cost another BZ$10 (US$5) for the bus on to Punta Gorda. The return ferry from Independence Creek leaves daily at 6:30 and 8am, and at 2:30 and 4:30pm.

BY CAR From Belize City, head west on Cemetery Road, which becomes the Western Highway. Take this all the way to Belmopan, where you will connect with the Hummingbird Highway heading south. Six miles (10km) before Dangriga, the Hummingbird Highway connects with the Southern Highway. Take the Southern Highway towards Placencia and Punta Gorda. After 23 miles (35km) on the Southern Highway, turn left onto the road to Riversdale and Placencia. From this turnoff, it's another 20 miles (32km) to Placencia. The drive from Belize City should take around 3 hours.

When I last visited, the road was still a hard-packed gravel road, but it is slated to be paved in 2005. Given the amount of development going on here, I expect this to actually happen. Currently, the road is paved from the airstrip into the center of the village.

GETTING AROUND
Placencia Village itself is tiny, and you can walk the entire length of the sidewalk, which covers most of the village, in about 10 to 15 minutes. If you need a taxi, call **Ben's Taxi** (© 523-3367), **Evan's Taxi** (© 606-7386), or **Kingfisher Taxi** (© 601-1903). Fares within the village run around BZ$3 to BZ$5 (US$1.50–US$2.50) per person. A trip from the airstrip to the village costs BZ$10 (US$5) for one person, or BZ$5 (US$2.50) per person for two or more.

If you want to explore more, a scooter is a good way to get around. Several hotels and operators in the area rent scooters. Rates run around BZ$40 (US$20) for a half-day and BZ$75 (US$38) for a full day.

If you want a little more exercise, a bicycle is a decent option. The terrain is flat, although it can get hot and dusty on the main road, and there aren't really any trails or off-road options. Once the road is paved, a bicycle will be an excellent way to get up the peninsula to find some deserted stretch of beach or visit Seine Bight. Many hotels have bikes either free for the guests or for rent. Several shops around town also rent out bicycles. A relatively modern bike in good shape should cost between BZ$15 and BZ$24 (US$7.50–US$12) per day.

Placencia

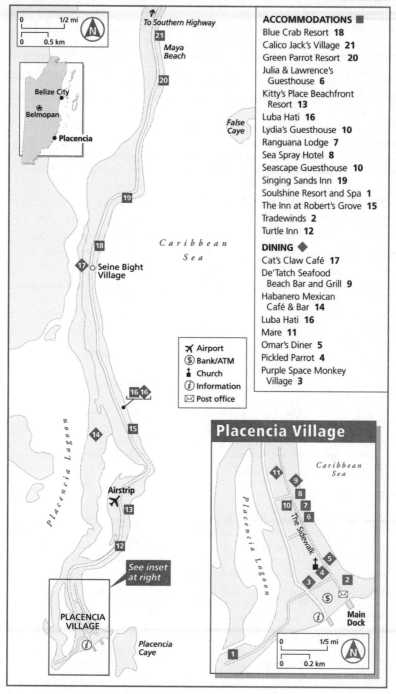

ACCOMMODATIONS ■

Blue Crab Resort **18**
Calico Jack's Village **21**
Green Parrot Resort **20**
Julia & Lawrence's Guesthouse **6**
Kitty's Place Beachfront Resort **13**
Luba Hati **16**
Lydia's Guesthouse **10**
Ranguana Lodge **7**
Sea Spray Hotel **8**
Seascape Guesthouse **10**
Singing Sands Inn **19**
Soulshine Resort and Spa **1**
The Inn at Robert's Grove **15**
Tradewinds **2**
Turtle Inn **12**

DINING ◆

Cat's Claw Café **17**
De'Tatch Seafood Beach Bar and Grill **9**
Habanero Mexican Café & Bar **14**
Luba Hati **16**
Mare **11**
Omar's Diner **5**
Pickled Parrot **4**
Purple Space Monkey Village **3**

✈ Airport
$ Bank/ATM
✝ Church
ⓘ Information
✉ Post office

To Southern Highway

Maya Beach

False Caye

Caribbean Sea

Belize City
Belmopan
Placencia

Seine Bight Village

Placencia Lagoon

Airstrip

See inset at right

PLACENCIA VILLAGE

Placencia Caye

Placencia Village

Caribbean Sea

Placencia Lagoon

The Sidewalk

Main Dock

ORIENTATION

For most of the peninsula there is only one road. As the road reaches the end of the peninsula and the village of Placencia, it basically dead-ends at the Shell station and some boat docks. Just before this, a dirt spur turns right just beyond the soccer field and heads for a few hundred yards towards the lagoon. Once you've arrived, your main thoroughfare will hopefully be the beach and the sidewalk, both of which run parallel to each other starting near the docks and heading north.

Hotels and resorts are spread all along the length of the Placencia peninsula. To make it easier to understand where a hotel or resort is, the peninsula is broken up into three broad sections: Maya Beach, Seine Bight, and Placencia Village. Maya Beach is the northernmost section of the peninsula, and the hotels and resorts here are quite spread out, with few other services or businesses. More or less anchoring the center of the peninsula is the tiny Garífuna village of Seine Bight. Just to the north and south of Seine Bight village are several other isolated resorts. Down at the southern end of the peninsula is Placencia Village itself.

The very helpful **Placencia Information Center** (© **523-4045;** www. placencia.com) is located at the end of the road, by the Shell Gas Station, just before the pier.

FAST FACTS   For the local **police,** dial © 523-3129; you can also reach the newly formed **tourist police** at © 604-0275. If you need any medical attention, the **Placencia Medical Center** (© 523-3326) is located behind the school in the center of the village.

There's a **Scotiabank** (© 523-3277) on the main road near the center of the village, as well as an **Atlantic Bank** (© 523-3431). Scotiabank has an ATM that should accept international cards. There's a **pharmacy** attached to Wallen's Market (© 523-3128), in the center of the village. The **post office** is located above the Fishermen's Co-op, near the start of the sidewalk.

There are a couple of gas stations in Placencia. You'll find the Shell station where the road hits the end of the peninsula in the heart of the village. There's also a Texaco station at the Inn at Robert's Grove Marina.

If you need to use the Internet, head to the **Purple Space Monkey** (© 523-4094) or **Placencia Office Supply** (© 523-3433). Both are on the main road and have high-speed connections. Rates run around BZ$8 to BZ$10 (US$4–US$5) per hour.

FUN ON & OFF THE BEACH

Placencia is the quintessential laid-back beach town. You just can't help slowing down and relaxing. Sit back, sip a seaweed shake, and forget your cares. Nobody ever seems to get up early (except maybe the fishermen), and most people spend their days camped in the sand reading books and eating seafood. The beach, although narrow in places, is arguably the best in Belize. You can walk for miles and see hardly a soul. Still, if you need more activity and adventure, there are a host of options.

WATERSPORTS EXCURSIONS

On these trips, be sure to bring plenty of sunscreen, a broad-rimmed hat, and a T-shirt to cover your back.

SNORKELING & SCUBA DIVING   There's often decent snorkeling right off the beach, especially if you head north a mile or so. The water's clear and you'll see plenty of fish and bottom life in the seagrass and along the sand bottom.

Seaweed Shake

It sounds weird at first, and it may not look all that inviting, but don't miss the chance to sip a "seaweed shake" while you're here. The basic building block of this unique concoction is a tea made from locally harvested seaweed. This is then combined in a blender with both condensed and evaporated milk, cinnamon, nutmeg, vanilla, and some ice. The drink is surprisingly refreshing and tasty. What's more, the folks here in Placencia claim that not only is it a proven aphrodisiac, but that it can also cure everything from anemia to tuberculosis.

One of the more popular snorkel excursions is to the nearby **Laughingbird Caye** (www.laughingbird.org). Located just a few miles offshore from Placencia, Laughingbird Caye is a national park. It's a tiny little island measuring roughly 35 feet by 350 feet (11m by 105m). There's good snorkeling and swimming offshore, and a host of tour operators take folks here, and then serve a picnic lunch on the beach.

However, if you're serious about diving or snorkeling, you'll want to get out to the **barrier reef** and its dozens of little offshore cayes. It's between 10 and 25 miles (16–40km) out to the reef here, making it a relatively quick and easy boat ride. Diving here is as spectacular as at other more popular dive destinations in Belize, and you'll often have far fewer fellow divers around.

The offshore **Gladden Spit** ✸✸✸ site is a world-renowned spot to dive with massive whale sharks. Whale shark sightings are fairly common here from March to May, and to a lesser extent during the months of August through October and December and January.

Most of the larger resorts have their own dive operations, and there's a handful of independent operators in the village servicing folks at the rest of the hotels. If you're not staying at a hotel with a dedicated dive operation, check in with the folks at **Natural Mystic Dive Shop** (© 523-3278) or **Seahorse Dive Shop** ✸ (© 523-3166; www.belizescuba.com).

A snorkeling trip should cost between BZ$50 and BZ$120 (US$25–US$60), depending on the distance traveled and whether or not lunch is included. Rates for scuba diving run between BZ$110 and BZ$300 (US$55–US$150) for a two-tank dive, also depending upon the length of the journey to the dive site and whether or not lunch is included. Equipment rental should cost from BZ$12 to BZ$30 (US$6–US$15) for a snorkeler, and BZ$30 to BZ$50 (US$15–US$25) for a scuba diver.

FISHING   Fishing around here is some of the best in Belize. There's excellent bonefishing in flats in this area. Anglers can also go for tarpon, permit, and snook, or head offshore for bigger game, including grouper, yellowfin tuna, king mackerel, wahoo, mahimahi, and the occasional sail or marlin. Experienced guides can help you track any of the above fish, and many are taking their guests out fly-fishing for them as well. Most of the big lodges and resorts here offer fishing packages and excursions. Well-equipped sport-fishing outings run between BZ$1,200 and BZ$2,400 (US$600–US$1,200) per day, depending on the size of the boat, number of anglers, and distance traveled. However, you can hire a smaller open-air skiff perfectly suited for fly-casting for bonefish, permit, or tarpon for between BZ$400 and BZ$600 (US$200–US$300) per day.

Tips BYO

While most hotels and all of the dive shops in town have snorkeling and diving gear for rent, you might consider bringing your own. If nothing else, bring your own mask and snorkel. Fins are a lesser concern, as most operators should have fins to fit your feet. If you plan on going out snorkeling or diving more than a few times, the investment will more than pay for itself.

The folks at **Kingfisher Adventures** ⭐ (© 523-3323; www.tarponcaye.com) are some of the more reputable fishing guides. They even have a small fishing lodge on the remote Tarpon Caye. You can also try **Southern Guides** (© 523-3433; www.southernguides.com), another longstanding local operation with well-regarded guides.

KAYAKING   Several hotels and tour operators in town rent out sea kayaks. The waters just off the beach are usually calm and perfect for kayaking. However, the lagoon is probably a better choice, offering up more interesting mangrove terrain and excellent bird-watching opportunities.

Rates for kayak rental run around BZ$10 to BZ$20 (US$5–US$10) per hour, or BZ$60 to BZ$80 (US$30–US$40) for a full day. A guided tour of the mangroves or a combined snorkeling and kayak tour offshore should cost between BZ$80 and BZ$140 (US$40–US$70) per person.

SAILING   The crystal-clear waters, calm seas, and isolated islands surrounding Placencia make this an excellent place to go out for a sail. Your options range from crewed yachts and bareboat charters for multiday adventures to day cruises and sunset sails.

The Moorings (© **888/952-8401** in the U.S. and Canada, or 523-3351; www.moorings.com) and **TMM** (© **800/633-0155** in the U.S., or 226-3026; www.sailtmm.com) are two large-scale charter companies with operations in Placencia. Options include monohulls, catamarans, and trimarans of varying sizes. Given the shallow draft, increased interior space, and reduced drag, a multihull is your best bet. All of the boats are well equipped and seaworthy. Rates for a week-long charter run between BZ$3,700 and BZ$13,000 (US$1,850–US$6,500), depending on the size of the boat.

A day cruise, including lunch, drinks, and snorkeling gear, should cost between BZ$200 and BZ$300 (US$100–US$150) per person. Most hotels and tour operators around town can hook you up with a day sail or sunset cruise, or you can simply head to the docks, or check in with the folks at **Kingfisher Adventures** (© 523-3323; www.tarponcaye.com).

GUIDED DAY TRIPS

While the ocean and outlying cayes are the focus of most activities and tours in Placencia, there are a host of other options. The most popular of these include tours to Cockscomb Basin Wildlife Sanctuary (see "Dangriga," earlier in this chapter), the Mayan ruins of Lubaatun and Nim Li Punit (see "Punta Gorda & the Toledo District," later in this chapter) and up the Monkey River. Day trips can run between BZ$90 and BZ$200 (US$45–US$100) per person, depending upon the distance traveled and the number of activities offered or sites visited. Almost every tour agency in town offers these trips, or ask at your hotel for a recommended guide or operator.

MONKEY RIVER ⚐ Perhaps the most popular "inland" trip offered out of Placencia is up the Monkey River, and most of this is actually on the water, anyway. Located about a half-hour boat ride down the coast and through the mangroves, the Monkey River area is rich in wildlife. If you're lucky, you might spot a manatee on your way down. Once traveling up the Monkey River, you should keep your eyes peeled for crocodiles, green iguana, wild deer, howler monkeys, and the occasional boa constrictor. In addition, you're likely to see scores of bird species. These tours can be done entirely in a motor launch, or may allow you to kayak on the Monkey River portion; I recommend the latter. Most tours include lunch in the quaint little Creole fishing village of Monkey River itself, as well as a short hike through a forest trail. Monkey River trips cost between BZ$80 and BZ$120 (US$40–US$60) per person.

ULTRALIGHT One of the newest tour options available in Placencia, the folks at **Belize Ultralight Flying Adventure** (✆ 523-3279; firstbufa@hotmail. com) offer ultralight flights and lessons on a unique ultralight craft that can land on either sand or sea. An introductory flight, lasting around 2 hours, costs BZ$100 (US$50). You can find these folks on the docks on the lagoon side, near the Jungle Juice restaurant.

SPAS & BODYWORK

If you're looking for a little pampering while in Placencia, there are several options. Most of the big resorts, like Turtle Inn and The Inn at Robert's Grove, have their own spas and spa services, which you may be able to book even if you're not a guest there. Alternatively, there are a couple of day spas right in the village. The **Secret Garden Day Spa** (✆ 523-3420) is located behind Wallen's Market near the center of the village, while **Soulshine Resort & Spa** (✆ 523-3347; www.soulshine.com) is out on the southwestern tip of the peninsula. An hour-long massage should cost you between BZ$90 and BZ$140 (US$45–US$70).

If you want to have an acupuncture treatment, head to the **Acupuncture Center** (✆ 523-3172), which is also near Wallen's Market. These folks also offer massage and regular yoga classes.

SHOPPING

There is no shortage of simple souvenir shops in Placencia. Located just off the sidewalk near the center of the village, the **Beach Bazaar** ⚐ (✆ 523-3113) is the best of the bunch. They've got all the traditional trinkets and souvenirs, as well as some higher-end ceramic, wood, and metal artworks.

If you're looking for some finer art, stop in at **Art 'N' Soul** (✆ 603-0398), which is on the sidewalk about 300 feet (90m) north of the pier, and features paintings and prints by local artists. While further north, in Seine Bight, you should definitely stop in at **Lola's Art Gallery** ⚐ (✆ 603-0398), which features the colorful acrylic paintings of owner Lola Delgado. These paintings come in a wide range of sizes and prices.

WHERE TO STAY

There is a host of options in and around Placencia. In general, the budget hotels and guesthouses are located in the village proper, either just off the sidewalk or around the soccer field. As you head north to the broader and more isolated beaches, prices tend to rise.

Moments   **Get Your Bib Out**

Lobster season opens each year on June 15, and Placencia pulls out all the stops to celebrate the culinary possibilities of this underwater arachnid. In addition to concerts, games, and sidewalk booths hawking all sorts of goods and treats, you'll be able to sample everything from lobster fritters to lobster quiche to lobster bisque and beyond. If it can be made with lobster, you'll probably find it here. The Placencia Lobster Festival is held in late June each year; for more information and exact dates, contact the **Placencia Information Center** (© **523-4045;** www.placencia.com).

VERY EXPENSIVE

The Inn at Robert's Grove ★★★ *Kids*   One of the original luxury resorts on the Placencia peninsula, this place has aged well, expanding and upgrading regularly along the way. All of the rooms are roomy, comfortable, and come with a host of modern amenities. Rustic red tile floors, Guatemalan textiles, and Mexican ceramic accents abound. The standard rooms come with either one king bed or two twin beds, as well as a fold-down futon couch. All come with a private balcony, hung with a hammock. A pair of ceiling fans means you can opt to forgo the air-conditioning. I'd try to land a second-floor room, as these feature higher ceilings and better views. The suites come with fully equipped kitchenettes, a large living room, and a large balcony. There are six—count them—six rooftop Jacuzzis spread around the resort. These are particularly inviting for late-night stargazing and soaking.

Truly a full-service resort, the Inn at Robert's Grove features two restaurants, two pools, an in-house spa, professional dive and fishing operations, a tennis court, and host of tour and activity options. Guests enjoy unlimited free use of the hotel's sea kayaks, windsurfers, Hobie Cat sailboats, tennis court, and bicycles, as well as free airport transfers. The hotel also owns and manages two small private islands, Ranagua Caye and Robert's Caye. In addition to the extensive list of tours and activities offered, guests at the Inn have the option of taking a day trip to these tiny offshore cayes, or staying a night or two on one of them in a simple, yet comfortable cabin.

Placencia, on the beach north of the airstrip. © **800/565-9757** in the U.S., or 523-3565 in Belize. Fax 523-3567. www.robertsgrove.com. 32 units. BZ$358–BZ$398 (US$179–US$199) double; BZ$500–BZ$750 (US$250–US$375) suite. Rates lower in the off season, higher during peak weeks. AE, MC, V. **Amenities:** 2 restaurants; 3 bars; lounge; 2 outdoor 50-ft. (15m) lap pools; lit outdoor tennis court; full-service dive shop; exercise room; small spa; complimentary watersports equipment and bike use; tour desk; limited room service (7am–9pm); babysitting; laundry service; all rooms nonsmoking. *In room:* A/C, TV, minifridge, hair dryer, safe.

Luba Hati ★★   This intimate beachfront hotel was recently taken over by a couple of American expatriates, who are in the process of remodeling and upgrading the entire place. There are seven rooms in the horseshoe-shaped main building. All have a private balcony or patio facing the sea, feature cool terracotta tile floors, and are decorated with an interesting mix of local, Guatemalan, and African artworks and crafts. I prefer those on the second floor, particularly those on the ends closest to the ocean. On one of these ends you'll find the two-bedroom, two-bathroom suite, with a full kitchen and private Jacuzzi. On the other end, the "Luna" room is hands-down the best of the standard rooms. Off the main building, there are four individual beachfront casitas. These are large and comfortable private cabins, with a king bed, kitchenette, living room, air conditioning, and comfortable oceanview porch. There's a postage stamp–size pool down near the ocean, as well as a poolside bar. Guests can use the hotel's sea kayaks and bicycles for free. The restaurant here is one of the most creative in Placencia, and it features a trendy martini bar to boot (see complete review in "Where to Dine," below).

Placencia, on the beach north of the airstrip. © 523-3402. Fax 523-3403. www.lubahati.com. 13 units. BZ$340 (US$170) double; BZ$400 (US$200) casita; BZ$1,000 (US$500) suite. Rates include continental breakfast. Rates lower in the off season, higher during peak weeks. AE, MC, V. **Amenities:** Restaurant; 2 bars; small outdoor pool; watersports equipment rental; complimentary bike and kayak use; tour desk; limited room service (7am–9pm); babysitting; laundry service; nonsmoking rooms. *In room:* Safe, no phone.

Soulshine Resort & Spa ⭐

This interesting little resort and spa is located on a tiny island set across a narrow canal on the very tip of the Placencia peninsula, fronting the lagoon. The individual wooden bungalows are all quite large, with high thatch roofs and private little porches facing the water. The rooms come with a host of amenities, and a couple of soft terry cloth robes to let you know you're at a spa, although this is no Canyon Ranch. And while they offer a wide range of treatments and therapies, the spa facilities are quite limited, in fact. Still, the restaurant serves up fresh and healthy fare, and pampering spa packages are offered. Overall, there is a nice sense of isolation and tranquillity here, especially on the small pier jutting out into the lagoon and strung with a couple of hammocks. There is also a handful of open-air thatch-roofed palapas spread around the ground, also hung with hammocks for relaxing your days away. This place is about a 5-minute walk from the center of Placencia Village and the beach.

Placencia Village, on the southwestern tip of the peninsula, beyond the soccer field. © 523-3347. Fax 523-3369. www.soulshine.com. 7 units. BZ$310 (US$155) double. Rates include full breakfast and airport transfers. MC, V. **Amenities:** Restaurant; bar; outdoor pool and Jacuzzi; small spa and exercise room; tour desk; laundry service. *In room:* A/C, minifridge, coffeemaker, hair dryer, no phone.

Turtle Inn ⭐⭐⭐ (Finds)

This place gets my vote for having the most luxurious and decadent rooms in all of Belize. You get your choice of a one- or two-bedroom private villa here. Either way you go, you're going to have plenty of space, including a large living room and a spacious bathroom that lets out on to a private interior rock garden, with its own open-air shower whose fixture is a piece of bamboo. There's tons of beautiful woodwork and craftsmanship, and a heavy dose of Asian decor and furnishings. All of the villas are set on the sand just steps from the beach, but not all have ocean views, hence the price variations. The Francis Ford Coppola Pavilion is a two-bedroom unit set a little off the main resort, right in front of the ocean, with its own pool and a working kitchen, wine cellar, and a steam bath/shower in each of the two bathrooms. There's an elegant kidney-shaped pool set just off the sand and sea in the center of the resort. The resort's restaurant, Mare (p. 196), serves excellent Italian and international fare. A whole host of tour options are offered, and when I last visited there were plans to add an extensive spa facility with a wide range of treatment options.

Placencia Village, on the beach north of the center of the village. © 800/746-3743 in the U.S., or 523-3244. Fax 523-3245. www.turtleinn.com. 19 units. BZ$500–BZ$600 (US$250–US$300) 1-bedroom double; BZ$750–BZ$950 (US$375–US$475) 2-bedroom double; BZ$2,400 (US$1,200) Pavilion House. Rates include continental breakfast. Rates lower in the off season, higher during peak weeks. AE, MC, V. **Amenities:** 2 restaurants; 2 bars; outdoor pool; full-service dive shop; watersports equipment rental; complimentary bikes and kayaks; concierge; tour desk; limited room service (6am–9pm); babysitting; laundry service. *In room:* Stocked minibar, coffeemaker, hair dryer, safe.

EXPENSIVE

In addition to the places listed below, the **Green Parrot Resort** (© 523-2488; www.greenparrot-belize.com) and **Calico Jack's Village** (© 520-8103; www. vacationsbelize.com) are two more good options on the northern Maya Beach end of the peninsula.

Kitty's Place Beachfront Resort ⭐   This collection of beach cabañas and colonial-styled clapboard buildings just north of Placencia proper has been one of the most popular hotels in this area for quite some time. The whole property has a resort feel without the hype. Accommodations range from cement-floor garden rooms with shared bathrooms to spacious beach cabañas with high ceilings, Guatemalan bedspreads, full bathtubs, and private porches with hammocks. The folks here also manage nearly a dozen private houses for weekly and long-term rentals. Some of these are actually quite economical.

There's a little keyhole-shaped pool on the beach, and the open-air Sand Bar next to it. The restaurant is housed on the second floor of the original building here, and still enjoys an excellent reputation for serving up fresh seafood and local and international fare. There's a wealth of activities and tours available, including scuba diving, sea kayaking, and bike rentals, as well as trips to Mayan ruins and the Cockscomb Basin Wildlife Sanctuary. They even run overnight kayaking trips to their own private island, French Louis Caye.

Placencia Village, on the beach north of the center of the village. © 523-3227. www.kittysplace.com. 11 units (2 with shared bathroom). BZ$80–BZ$120 (US$40–US$60) double with shared bathroom; BZ$270–BZ$350 (US$135–US$175) double with private bathroom. Rates lower in the off season. AE, DISC, MC, V. **Amenities:** Restaurant; outdoor pool; watersports equipment rental; bike rental; tour desk; laundry service. *In room:* A/C, minifridge, coffeemaker, no phone.

Singing Sands Inn ⭐   This small hotel has the lushest gardens and grounds in the area. The six individual thatch-roofed wooden cabins are simple affairs with either a queen bed or a double bed, as well as a separate twin bed or bunk beds. They are set in a row perpendicular to the beach, with cabin nos. 1 and 2 closest to the ocean. You'll still get something of an ocean view from cabin nos. 3 and 4, while nos. 5 and 6 are set amidst the flowers and foliage. Each has a small porch with a couple of chairs for lounging in. In addition to the cabins there are a couple of larger, fully equipped apartments with kitchenettes. There's an inviting outdoor pool and a large open-air deck area facing the ocean, where meals and drinks are served, as well as a covered dining area in case it's raining. Guests have free use of sea kayaks, and there's a long dock built out into the sea with an inviting shaded palapa at the end of it. Singing Sands Inn is located on the northern end of the peninsula, on a quiet section of Maya Beach.

Maya Beach. ©/fax 523-2243 or 523-8017. www.singingsands.com. 8 units. BZ$200–BZ$240 (US$100–US$120) double. Rate includes continental breakfast. Rates lower in the off season. AE, DISC, MC, V. **Amenities:** Restaurant; outdoor pool; watersports equipment rental; tour desk; laundry service. *In room:* Minifridge, no phone.

MODERATE

Blue Crab Resort ⭐   There's a wonderfully relaxed and laid-back atmosphere at this small beachfront hotel north of Seine Bight village. The rooms are all simple and clean, and housed in several separate wooden buildings set on stilts a few feet above the sand. The newer air-conditioned rooms are all located in a four-plex building. I'd definitely try to get one that faces the beach. The two older individual cabanas are actually closer to the water, but are a bit smaller and lack air-conditioning. Of these, cabana no. 1 is your best bet, as it's closest to the sea and gets good cross-ventilation. The tiny restaurant here is locally famous for its cuisine, as the owner was born in Taiwan, and he serves up an enticing mix of Asian, international, and local fare. The hotel has quite a bit of land, extending from the ocean all the way to the lagoon, and as yet few neighbors.

Seine Bight, on the beach north of the village. ℂ 523-3544. Fax 523-3543. www.bluecrabbeach.com. 6 units. BZ$170–US$190 (US$85–US$95) double. Rates include airport transfers. Rates lower in the off season. MC, V. **Amenities:** Restaurant; tour desk. *In room:* No phone.

Ranguana Lodge *Value*   The five individual cabins at this small family-run hotel are all clean and cozy. In the two older cabins, nearly everything is made of hardwood—walls, floors, ceilings, even the louvered windows. These rooms feature a full kitchenette. The three oceanfront cabins are the newest, and while they are right in front of the sea and have air-conditioning, they are a little smaller and have a little less character. All of the cabins are just steps from the ocean, and all come with a private balcony or porch area. All are painted a blinding pure white, with a different primary or Day-Glo color used for trim.

Placencia Village, on the beach in the center of the village. ℂ/fax 523-3112. www.ranguanabelize.com. 5 units. BZ$130–US$144 (US$65–US$72) double. AE, MC, V. **Amenities:** Tour desk. *In room:* Minifridge, coffeemaker, no phone.

INEXPENSIVE

If the places listed below are full, you can simply walk around the village and see what's available, or head to either **Julia & Lawrence's Guesthouse** (ℂ 523-3478) or **Seascape Guesthouse** (ℂ 523-4078), both located just off the sidewalk towards the center of the village.

Lydia's Guesthouse *Value*   This is one of the longest-running and most popular budget options in Placencia, and it's fitting that this classic two-story converted home survived Hurricane Iris. The rooms are simple and clean, although a few can be a bit cramped. The shared bathrooms and showers are kept immaculate, and guests have free use of the kitchen that takes up the ground floor of the amiable Lydia Villanueva's private home next door. You'll find a convivial hostel-like atmosphere and travelers from around the world here. There's even a good ocean view from the shared balcony on the second floor, a real steal in this price range. Lydia also rents various houses for longer stays.

Placencia Village, towards the northern end of the sidewalk. ℂ 523-3117. Fax 523-3354. lydias@btl.net. 8 units, all with shared bathroom. BZ$43 (US$22) double. Rates slightly lower in the off season. MC, V. *In room:* No phone.

Sea Spray Hotel   Rooms and prices vary substantially in this perennial budget and backpacker favorite. The "economy" rooms are a bit cramped and dark. Most rooms are in a two-story building built perpendicular to the sea. The four deluxe rooms are in a separate two-story building fronting the sea, and these come with televisions and kitchenettes, as well as comfortable private oceanview balconies. There's also a separate fully equipped beachfront cabana, although I think the deluxe rooms are a better and more comfortable choice. The attached De'Tatch Seafood Beach Bar & Grill serves hearty local fare at very reasonable prices, and also has an Internet cafe. As at Lydia's (above), there's a convivial hostel-like atmosphere here.

Placencia Village, on the beach towards the middle of the sidewalk. ℂ 523-3148. Fax 523-3364. www.seasprayhotel.com. 21 units. BZ$50–BZ$120 (US$25–US$60) double. AE, DISC, MC, V. **Amenities:** Restaurant; tour desk; laundry service. *In room:* Minifridge, no phone.

Tradewinds *Finds*   Set right on the ocean's edge towards the southern end of the village, the eight individual cabins here are just a few feet from the water. All are comfortable, roomy, and come with a very inviting porch, hung with a hammock overlooking the waves, where I predict you'll spend most of your time here. The less expensive rooms here are set a bit further back from the sea in a simple triplex building, although each comes with its own little veranda. Everything is painted in lively pastels, and there's a friendly family-like vibe to the whole operation.

Placencia Village, on the beach, south end of the village. *C* 523-3122. Fax 523-3201. www.placencia.com. 11 units. BZ$60–US$120 (US$30–US$60) double. Rates slightly lower in the off season, higher during peak weeks. MC, V. *In room:* Minifridge, coffeemaker, no phone.

WHERE TO DINE

In addition to the places mentioned below, the restaurants at **Kitty's Place** (p. 194) and the **Inn at Robert's Grove** (p. 192) are both consistently excellent. Be sure to stop in at **Tutti Frutti Ice Cream Shop** and **Daisy's Ice Cream Parlour**, two dueling and equally delicious ice cream shops. Tutti Frutti is on the main road near the gas station and docks and tends towards more Italian-style offerings, while Daisy's is off the northern end of the sidewalk and offers traditional homemade ice cream as well as various baked goods and full meals.

There are also several grocery stores in the village, in case you want to put together a picnic lunch.

EXPENSIVE

Luba Hati *Finds* FUSION   The restaurant at this boutique hotel serves the most inventive and adventurous fair in Placencia. Using local and regional ingredients as much as possible, they've created a wonderful menu that ranges far and wide. Start with a bowl of chilled cantaloupe, mint and yogurt soup, or a not-so-traditional El Salvadoran *pupusa* (cornmeal tortilla) topped with an olive and eggplant tapenade. If the season's right, have some local lobster in a basil butter sauce served with *calaloo,* a local stew. For dessert, the Kahlúa flan and Mexican chocolate cake are both excellent. Service is attentive and unpretentious. They have a small yet well-varied wine list, as well as a trendy little "martini" bar. I personally recommend their signature margarita, which is blended with hibiscus flowers and a splash of fresh orange juice.

At Luba Hati hotel, north of the airstrip. *C* 523-3402. www.lubahati.com. Reservations recommended. Main courses BZ$30–BZ$42 (US$15–US$21). AE, MC, V. Daily 11am–2pm and 6–9pm.

Mare   ITALIAN/SEAFOOD   This is the most elegant restaurant in the Placencia region. The lighting at night is subdued in this open-air deck area. Tables and chairs are made of heavy teak, and adorned with candles and fresh flowers. The restaurant looks out over the hotel's pool and on to the sea, and the setting is also wonderful during the day for lunch. The kitchen serves up expertly prepared Italian cuisine and fresh seafood. I like to start things off with the *insalata de pesce,* which features fresh red snapper smoked on the premises. In addition to nightly specials, there are delicious thin-crust wood-oven pizzas, a selection of pastas, and several hearty main dishes. Whole freshly caught fish are roasted in the wood oven, as are lobster tails in season. Most of the herbs and vegetables served are grown right here at the hotel's organic garden. The wine list features a range of fine wines from Francis Ford Coppola's own vineyard.

At Turtle Inn, on the beach north of the center of the village. *C* 523-3244. www.turtleinn.com. Reservations recommended. Main courses BZ$26–BZ$55 (US$14–US$23). AE, MC, V. Daily 11am–3pm and 6:30–9pm.

Moments   **A Special Evening**

If you're in the mood for dinner and a show, try the **Cat's Claw Café** ✿ ((✆) **603-0398**) at Lola's Art Gallery in Seine Bight. The food and entertainment are pure Garífuna. You'll get a traditional Garífuna meal, with cassava bread and plenty of trimmings, as well as a performance of Garífuna dancing and song. Reservations are definitely recommended. Depending on the size of your party, the price ranges from BZ$60 to BZ$90 (US$30–US$45) per person.

MODERATE

De'Tatch Seafood Beach Bar & Grill ✿ BELIZEAN/SEAFOOD   This funky open-air beachfront joint is one of the most popular spots in town. Traditional Belizean breakfasts here are hearty and inexpensive. You can get excellent seafood or shrimp burritos or tacos for lunch or dinner. There's an Internet cafe off to one side, and the sea is just steps away. The newest addition here is a second-floor open-air deck, which is especially nice on starry nights.

Placencia Village, on the ocean just off the Sea Spray Hotel towards the center of the village. (✆) **523-4011.** Reservations not accepted. Breakfast and lunch main courses BZ$6–BZ$16 (US$3–US$8); dinner main courses BZ$12–BZ$32 (US$6–US$16); lobster BZ$32–BZ$45 (US$16–US$23). MC, V. Thurs–Tues 7am–10pm.

Habanero Mexican Café & Bar ✿ MEXICAN   Set on the lagoon side of the peninsula beside the marina at Robert's Grove, this new restaurant serves up a mix of Tex-Mex and traditional Mexican fare. When the bugs aren't biting, you'll want to grab a table outdoors on the deck overlooking the water. This is also a great spot to catch the sunset. When the bugs are biting, you can seek refuge in the screened-in main dining room. My favorite dishes here are the garlic shrimp tacos and the spicy fish chimichanga. For those looking for a fiesta, you can order sangria and margaritas by the pitcher.

At the marina across from the Inn at Robert's Grovel, north of the airstrip. (✆) **523-3665.** Main courses BZ$16–BZ$28 (US$8–US$14). AE, MC, V. Daily noon–10pm.

Pickled Parrot ✿ INTERNATIONAL   This popular place serves three hearty meals daily, with a menu ranging from fresh seafood and local cuisine to pizzas, burgers, and burritos. There's a relaxed informal atmosphere at this open-air sand-floored restaurant, and the bar can even get rowdy at times, especially after folks have downed a few rounds of "Parrot Piss," the bar's signature mixed drink. Dinner specials range from rum-glazed chicken to lobster curry. This is also a great spot for breakfast, and I particularly like their hearty breakfast burrito.

Placencia Village. (✆) **604-0278.** www.pickledparrotbelize.com. Reservations not accepted. Breakfast and lunch main courses BZ$6–BZ$12 (US$3–US$6); dinner main courses BZ$16–BZ$26 (US$8–US$13); lobster BZ$35–BZ$45 (US$18–US$23). V. Mon–Sat 8am–10pm; Sun 5–10pm.

Purple Space Monkey Village ✿ *Kids* *Finds* INTERNATIONAL   Housed in a massive open-air thatch roof structure that had to be rebuilt after Hurricane Iris, this is a central meeting place for world travelers, expatriates, and locals alike. The heavy wooden tables are painted purple, and the chairs are a rainbow of complementary colors. The food is well prepared, abundant, and reasonably priced. I like to start the day with their fryjacks stuffed with eggs and cheese (BZ$8/US$4). The lunch menu tends towards burgers, sandwiches, and burritos,

---

(*Moments* **Place Your Bet**

Whether or not you're the gambling type, you'll want to wager a few bucks on a **chicken drop.** This very loose variation on roulette involves wagering on a number written on a wooden board. Above the board is a wire cage. Once all the bets are in, a chicken is placed in the cage, and the number where the chicken's poop lands wins the pot. The "lucky" winner, however, usually must clean up the board before collecting. Several bars in Placencia, and around the country, feature chicken drops. Kitty's Place (p. 194) was one of the first in the area to host a chicken drop, and is still one of the liveliest.

---

whereas their dinner menu gets more creative and extensive. Specialties here include Caribbean pork tenderloin and lime-butter shrimp. They even have a children's menu, which is a rarity anywhere in Belize, much less little old Placencia, and there's a popular Internet cafe here as well.

Placencia Village, in front of the soccer field. ℂ **523-4094.** www.purplespacemonkey.com. Breakfast and lunch main courses BZ$6–BZ$12 (US$3–US$6); dinner main courses BZ$16–BZ$26 (US$8–US$13); lobster BZ$35–BZ$45 (US$18–US$23). MC, V. Daily 7am–2pm and 5:30–10pm.

INEXPENSIVE

Omar's Diner *Value* BELIZEAN/MEXICAN There's no assembly-line production, Styrofoam wrappings, or chainlike efficiency here. In fact, the speed of service sometimes doesn't live up to the name. Still, this simple restaurant serves up hearty and tasty local fare at great prices. Located just off the sidewalk in the center of the village, the dining room is screened-in. If there's no free table, you might be able to take a seat with another fellow traveler, or at one of the large communal tables.

Placencia Village, off the sidewalk in the center of the village. ℂ **523-4094.** Breakfast and lunch main courses BZ$5–BZ$15 (US$2.50–US$7.50); dinner main courses BZ$10–BZ$22 (US$5–US$11); lobster BZ$30–BZ$40 (US$15–US$20). MC, V. Daily 7am–2pm and 5:30–10pm.

PLACENCIA AFTER DARK

Placencia is a quiet and remote beach destination. There are a few bars in the village, and some of the larger resort hotels have lively nightlife scenes. Still, my favorite late-night activity here is taking a stroll on the beach and stargazing.

One of my favorite bars in town is **Sugar Reef Lounge** (ℂ **523-3289**), located on Sunset Drive, the road that heads out behind the soccer field. It seems like practically the entire village shows up for their Wednesday night karaoke party.

---

4 Punta Gorda & the Toledo District

205 miles (330km) S of Belize City; 100 miles (161km) S of Dangriga

Punta Gorda, or simply "P.G.," is Belize's southernmost town. It's the end of the road, and feels a bit like the end of the world. P.G. is a quiet place with clean paved streets, few cars, lush vegetation, and a very slow pace. Although it is right on the Caribbean, there is no beach to speak of, and the water just off town is rather murky and uninviting. However, there are several wonderful offshore cayes within easy reach that have excellent beaches and serve as bases for equally

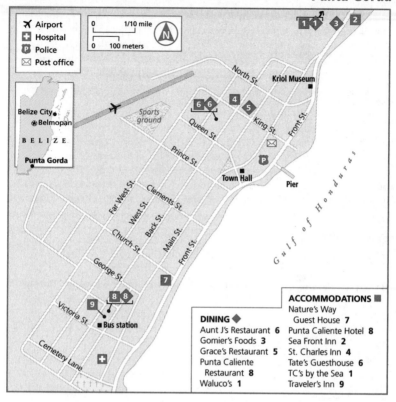

Legend:
- ✈ Airport
- ✚ Hospital
- P Police
- ✉ Post office

0 — 1/10 mile
0 — 100 meters

Belize City
⊛ Belmopan
B E L I Z E
Punta Gorda

North St.
Kriol Museum
Sports ground
Queen St.
King St.
Front St.
Prince St.
Town Hall
Pier
Far West St.
Clements St.
West St.
Back St.
Church St.
Main St.
Front St.
George St.
Victoria St.
■ Bus station
Cemetery Lane

Gulf of Honduras

DINING ◆
Aunt J's Restaurant **6**
Gomier's Foods **3**
Grace's Restaurant **5**
Punta Caliente Restaurant **8**
Waluco's **1**

ACCOMMODATIONS ■
Nature's Way Guest House **7**
Punta Caliente Hotel **8**
Sea Front Inn **2**
St. Charles Inn **4**
Tate's Guesthouse **6**
TC's by the Sea **1**
Traveler's Inn **9**

excellent snorkeling, scuba diving, and fishing. Inland from P.G., the surrounding scenery is as verdant as you'll find anywhere in Belize (due to nearly 200 in. of rain a year). The surrounding Toledo District is home to several Mayan ruins and numerous villages that are still peopled by Kekchi and Mopan Maya Indians, who have been migrating here from Guatemala over the last century.

Settled by Garífunas in 1823, Punta Gorda was only accessible by boat for decades, and even though the Southern Highway is now paved and easily connects the town with points north, there's still a sense of this being a distant frontier. As the administrative center for the Toledo District, Punta Gorda has an active market and bus services to the many surrounding Mayan villages, although connections are not very frequent. Most travelers do little more than pass through Punta Gorda on their way to or from Guatemala by way of the Puerto Barrios ferry. However, there is plenty to keep the adventurous traveler busy for several days, including fishing, scuba diving, rainforest hiking, and bird-watching.

ESSENTIALS
GETTING THERE & DEPARTING
BY PLANE   There are several daily flights into and out of Punta Gorda's little airport (PND). **Maya Island Air** (© **226-2435** in Belize City, or 722-2856 in Punta Gorda; www.mayaairways.com) has five flights daily between Belize City and Punta Gorda. The flights leave the Municipal Airport at 8 and 10am, and

at 12:30, 2:30, and 4:30pm. These flights stop 15 minutes later at the Goldson International Airport to pick up passengers. The fare is BZ$152 (US$76) each way from Municipal Airport, and BZ$177 (US$89) each way from the international airport. When you're ready to leave, Maya Island Air flights from Punta Gorda to Belize City depart at 6:45, 10, and 11:30am, and at 1:50 and 4pm. Most of these flights stop first in Placencia and Dangriga, and then at the international airport, before continuing on to Municipal Airport.

Tropic Air (© **226-2012** in Belize City, or 722-2008 in Punta Gorda; www.tropicair.com) has five daily flights from Municipal Airport to Punta Gorda at 8:15 and 10:20am, and at 12:20, 2:20, and 5pm. These flights stop 15 minutes later at Goldson International Airport to pick up passengers. The fare is BZ$152 (US$76) each way from the Municipal Airport, and BZ$177 (US$89) each way from the international airport. Tropic Air flights depart Punta Gorda for Belize City's airports daily at 7, 9:40, and 11:45am, and at 1:35 and 4pm.

Flight times run between 55 minutes and 1 hour and 20 minutes depending on the number of stops, since most flights to and from Punta Gorda on Maya Island Air and Tropic Air stop in Placencia and Dangriga to pick up and drop off passengers. On both airlines, flights are sometimes added during the high season or suspended during the low season, so check in advance.

BY BUS   Southern Transport Limited (© **207-3937** in Belize City, or 702-2165 in Punta Gorda) buses leave Belize City for Punta Gorda roughly every hour from the main terminal on West Collett Canal. The trip takes between 6 and 7 hours. In some cases, you may have to change buses in Belmopan or Dangriga. The one-way fare is BZ$22 (US$11).

BY CAR   It is a long way to Punta Gorda. However, the Southern Highway, which starts just outside of Dangriga, has been paved the entire 100 miles (161km) to Punta Gorda, where it ends. Coming from Belize City, head first to Belmopan and turn south on the Hummingbird Highway. Just before Dangriga, the Hummingbird Highway connects with the Southern Highway, which takes you all the way to Punta Gorda. Alternatively, you can take the Manatee Road turnoff just past the Belize Zoo, although the Manatee Road is a washboard dirt and gravel road for most of its length. See "By Car" in "Essentials" in section 1, earlier in this chapter, for more information. It should take between 4 to 5 hours to drive between Belize City and Punta Gorda.

BY BOAT   Several boats run daily between Punta Gorda and Puerto Barrios, Guatemala. If there's enough demand, the boats may stop in Livingston, Guatemala as well. Expect to pay between BZ$20 and BZ$30 (US$10–US$15) per person. The boats leave from the main pier in Punta Gorda. **Requena's Charter Service,** 12 Front St. (© **722-2070;** watertaxi@btl.net), is one of the more dependable operators. When the seas are calm, the crossing takes about 1 hour. Departures for Guatemala tend to leave between 8:30 and 9am, although there are often afternoon departures as well. The boats tend to return from Puerto Barrios between 2 and 4pm. You'll have to pay the BZ$28 (US$14) in exit taxes. *Note:* When coming and going, be sure to get your passport stamped at the immigration office just up from the dock.

GETTING AROUND
Punta Gorda is a very small and compact town, and you should be able to get around primarily on foot. If you're just too hot or tired, or you're heading further afield, call **Galvez's Taxi Travel & Tour Service** (© 722-2402) or the **Roots & Herbs Taxi Service** (© 722-2834).

Another option for getting around is to rent a bike. For bike rentals, head down to **Aba Iseni** (© 606-6650). Aba Iseni means "one love" in the Garífuna language, and the shop is run by a personable Garífuna man who goes by the name of Fubu. He rents bikes by the day for BZ$25 (US$13), or BZ$15 (US$7.50) for a half-day. The shop is located on North Street; it's open Monday through Saturday from 8:30am to 12:30pm and 3 to 8:30pm, and Sunday from 11am to 5pm. **The Lodge At Big Falls** (p. 206) also rents good quality mountain bikes for around BZ$40 (US$20) per day.

ORIENTATION

Punta Gorda is a small coastal town, and the road into town runs right along the water before angling a bit inland. There's a tiny triangular park at the center of the town. On one side is the Civic Center, or Town Hall. On one corner is a cute little clock tower, and the Belize Bank anchors another corner. Still, much of the town's activity is water-based, and many of the most important businesses, hotels, restaurants, and government offices are located on Front Street, which runs along the waterfront. The town's main pier is off the center of Front Street. On the western edge of town, only 6 blocks from the water, is P.G.'s airstrip.

There are two well-staffed and helpful information centers in Punta Gorda. **The Belize Tourist Board** (© 722-2531) has an office on Front Street about a block south of the main pier, and the private **Toledo Visitor's Information Center** (© 722-2470) is also on Front Street, next to the main pier. The latter is run by the folks at Dem Dats Doin and is the main office for the Mayan Village Homestay program (see "What to See & Do," below).

FAST FACTS   For the local **police,** dial © 722-2022, and for the **fire department,** call © 722-2032. If you need medical attention, go to the **Punta Gorda Hospital** on Main Street, towards the southern end of town (© 722-2026). The **post office** (© 722-2087) is on Front Street across from the main pier.

Belize Bank, 30 Main St. (© 722-2324), can hopefully handle most of your banking needs; alternatively, you could try **Casa de Cambio GC,** 21 Main St. (© 722-0168), a money-exchange operation.

There's a **Texaco** gas station (© 722-2926) out towards the northern end of Front Street. Finally, if your hotel can't or won't do it for you, take your dirty clothes to **Punta Gorda Laundry Services,** 2 Prince St. (© 702-2273), which charges around BZ$10 (US$5) per load.

WHAT TO SEE & DO

There's very little in the way of attractions right in town. A stroll through Punta Gorda is the best way to enjoy the Caribbean atmosphere. One interesting stop for those interested in local culture is the **Kriol Museum,** 6 Front St. (© 702-2140), which is the converted front portion of local singer Leila Vernon's home. The "museum" features displays and items illustrating various aspects of daily life for the local Creole people, as well information about their history, customs, and culture. Donations are encouraged.

If you get a little antsy at such a slow pace, there are plenty of cultural wonders and natural adventures within easy reach of Punta Gorda. There are a host of tour operators and guides in P.G. Your hotel and the two information centers listed in "Essentials" above can probably hook you up with a good guide or adventure operator. Alternatively, you can check in with the folks at **Tide Tours** ✦ (© 722-2129; www.tidetours.org), a local ecotourism initiative that integrates environmentally and socially aware practices with their wide range of tour and adventure options.

REACHING THESE ATTRACTIONS   The villages and attractions (such as Nim Li Punit) discussed below, located along the highway, have regular bus service every day. Buses to and from the other villages and attractions generally run on Monday, Wednesday, Friday, and Saturday. Buses leave for the villages from Punta Gorda between 11:30am and noon, depending upon which village or destination you are traveling to. These buses all leave from the market area in front of the Civic Center along Queen Street.

The time of departure from the villages to P.G. varies but is usually early in the morning, sometimes before dawn. There's usually only one bus per day, but some villages have two daily buses. Ask in P.G., or in the actual village, as schedules are subject to change. Fares run around BZ$2 to BZ$4 (US$1–US$2) per person each way.

Another alternative is to hire a taxi or go on an organized trip. Ask at your hotel or one of the information centers and you should be able to set up a trip. You can usually hire a car and driver/guide for BZ$200 to BZ$300 (US$100–US$150) per day. This price will usually cover a group of four.

The truly adventurous might want to tour this area by mountain bike. You can reach most of the above sites and villages in an athletic couple of hours of riding. Leave early to avoid the oppressive midday heat, and expect slow going and lots of mud in the rainy season.

MAYAN RUINS

None of the southern ruins are as spectacular or actively restored as the more famous sites in northern and western Belize. Still, the ancient Maya did have substantial cities and trading posts all up and down the Belizean coast and several impressive reminders can be found near Punta Gorda. Travelers interested in the ongoing Mayan tradition will find themselves in a region of numerous small Kekchi and Mopan Maya villages, many of which have taken tentative steps to enter the tourism industry with homestay programs or basic guesthouses.

LUBAANTUN ✦   The largest of the nearby Mayan ruins is **Lubaantun.** The name, which means "Place of the Fallen Stones" in Yucatec Maya, was given to the site in 1924 and it was descriptive of the state of the buildings at that time. This Late Classic Maya ruin is unusual in that the structures were built using a technique of cut-and-fitted limestone blocks rather than the usual rock and mortar construction technique used elsewhere by the Mayans. Set on a high ridge, the site features five plazas and three ball courts. The highest temple here rises just 50 feet (15m) or so, but this is enough to afford an excellent view over the surrounding forest and, on a clear day, the Caribbean Sea. Although largely unexcavated, the ancient city's center has been well cleared, and the surviving architecture and urban outline give a good sense of the former glory of this Mayan ceremonial center.

Lubaantun is perhaps most famous as the site where a crystal skull was allegedly discovered by a young Canadian woman in 1926. There's much debate as to the origin and age of the skull, which some say was planted as a surprise present for Anna Mitchell-Hedges, who just happened to discover the carved skull on her 17th birthday while accompanying her father, who just happened to be leading the archaeological expedition. Others claim that the skull was actually purchased in London by Mitchell-Hedges years after the expedition. There are also claims that the crystal skull is the work of extraterrestrials, and that it has shown remarkable healing powers. The skull is currently kept in a vault in Canada.

Lubaantun is located about 20 miles (32km) northwest from Punta Gorda, about a mile (1.6km) from the village of San Pedro Columbia, where you must park your vehicle. From here, it is a 20-minute walk to the ruins.

NIM LI PUNIT ✦   Nim Li Punit, meaning "Big Hat" in Kekchi Mayan, features 25 stelae, including the largest Maya carved stele in Belize, measuring almost 30 feet (9m) tall. This stele bears the depiction of a local ruler wearing a large broad diadem, or "big hat," hence the name of the site. Only discovered in 1976, Nim Li Punit is a relatively small site, with four compact plazas and one ball court. One of the plazas served as an astronomical observation area, with a platform and stone markings indicating the point where the sun rises on the equinoxes. Very little excavation or restoration has been undertaken. Nonetheless, the eight carved stelae, and in particular, stele 14, make this a worthwhile stop. The best-preserved stelae, including stele 14, are currently housed at the visitor's center at the entrance to the site.

Nim Li Punit is located about 2 miles (3km) off the Southern Highway, near the village of Indian Creek, 25 miles (40km) north of Punta Gorda. A dirt road leads from the highway to a parking area near the visitor's center. Admission is BZ$10 (US$5).

Other minor ruins in the area include **Uxbenka** near Santa Cruz and **Pusilha** near Aguacate.

PLACES FOR A DIP

Mayan culture, past and present, may be the main attraction of Punta Gorda, but it also boasts plenty of natural attractions. In the forested hills south of San Antonio is one of the most beautiful swimming holes in all of Belize. Flowing out of a cave in a limestone mountain, the aptly named **Blue Creek** is a cool stream with striking deep turquoise water. Lush rainforest shades the creek, creating an idyllic place to spend an afternoon. You can cool off by swimming up into the mouth of the cave from which the stream flows. Blue Creek is also known locally as Ho Keb Ha, which means "the place where the water flows from." During the dry season, you can actually hike about 5 miles (8km) through the cave to an aboveground exit. The village of Blue Creek is reached from a turnoff about 1½ miles (2.4km) east of San Antonio. From here it's another 2½ miles (4km) south on a rough dirt road. The creek runs right through the little village, but the best swimming holes and the cave source of the creek are about a 10- to 15-minute hike upstream.

Just off the Southern Highway, near the village of Big Falls, there is a natural **hot spring** that's billed as the only such hot spring in Belize. You can have a refreshing swim in the river at the falls and then warm your muscles in the hot spring. This is a popular spot for locals on weekends.

There are also some attractive small waterfalls near the village of San Antonio, with inviting pools for a refreshing dip.

WATERSPORTS

The fishing, scuba diving, and snorkeling to be had off of Punta Gorda is world class. Kayaking on the ocean or up the Moho River is also excellent. See above for information about finding a good guide or adventure operator.

A BOTANICAL GARDEN

In addition to running the Toledo Visitor's Information Center, the folks at **Dem Dats Doin,** Front Street, beside the main pier (℗ 722-2470), manage the **Toledo Botanical Arboretum** ✦, a sustainable farm and botanical gardens project. In

---

⟨ Moments Deer Dance

The Mopan Mayan village of San Antonio is the site of the Deer Dance, a 9-day traditional Mayan cultural celebration, which takes place in late August and early September. Although this traditional cultural ceremony coincides with a Catholic religious holiday, the Feast of San Luis, its roots are traditional and Mayan.

---

addition to a broad variety of ornamental flowers and orchids, tropical palms and bromeliads, they grow over 50 varieties of tropical fruit, and something is always ripe for a just-picked treat. The Toledo Botanical Arboretum is within walking distance of the Kekchi Maya village of San Pedro Columbia and Lubaantun ruins. A 2-hour guided tour of the facility costs around BZ$10 (US$5). Visits and transportation should be arranged in advance with the folks at Dem Dats Doin.

STAYING IN A MAYAN VILLAGE

Many people who make it as far as Punta Gorda are interested in learning more about Mayan village life. Though the ruins were abandoned centuries ago, Maya Indians still live in this region. The villages of the Toledo District are populated by two main groups of Maya Indians, the Kekchi and the Mopan, who have different languages and agricultural practices. The Mopan are upland farmers, while the Kekchi farm the lowlands. Both groups are thought to have migrated into southern Belize from Guatemala less than 100 years ago. Four decades of political violence and genocide in neighboring Guatemala has bolstered this migration.

San Antonio, the largest Mopan Maya village, is in a beautiful setting on top of a hill, with an old stone church in the center of the village. Steep streets wind through the village, and there are both clapboard houses and traditional Mayan thatched huts. In addition to the Deer Dance, San Antonio is also known for its annual festival on June 13th in honor of the village's patron saint. The festival includes masked dances and other Mayan rites mixed with more traditional Catholic themes and celebrations.

Beyond San Antonio there is a host of even smaller and more remote traditional Mayan villages. Two programs are actively working to allow tourists a chance to experience life in a traditional Mayan village, while providing the Maya with an ecologically friendly means of income. The two programs take a somewhat different approach. One has constructed separate, basic guesthouses in the villages for the tourists, while the other arranges direct homestays with the actual villagers. The former claims to offer a much more predictable and sanitary experience and to spread the income around more equitably, while the latter claims to be entirely run by local Maya, with all the income going directly to the local families.

The **Toledo Ecotourism Association** (**TEA; ⓒ 722-2096;** ttea@btl.net) operates 10 guesthouses in different villages around the region, including one in the Garífuna village of Barranco. Rates at the guesthouses are BZ$19 (US$9.50) per person per night and meals are an additional BZ$22 (US$11) per person per day. The guesthouses are all maintained by the TEA, and come with fresh sheets, foam mattresses, mosquito nets, indoor showers, and ventilated pit latrine outhouses. You can also arrange guided hikes through the forest; visits to ruins, waterfalls, and caves; and traditional music, dancing, and storytelling performances for around BZ$7 (US$3.50) per hour. TEA has an office on the northern end of Main Street.

Alternatively, **The Toledo Host Family Network,** which can be reached through the Toledo Visitors Information Center on Front Street (© 722-2470), provides accommodations directly with families in the Mayan villages. There's a BZ$10 (US$5) registration fee for any stay, and then accommodations cost BZ$10 (US$5) per person per night and meals BZ$6 (US$3) per person per day. These fees are paid directly to your host family. Accommodations during a homestay can range from a hammock to a simple bed, and almost all families have some sort of bathroom or latrine. Currently, the villages involved in the homestay program include Laguna, Na Luum Ca, and San Pedro Columbia.

In both programs you can expect plenty of close contact with the local villagers. You will also to be eating what the locals eat, which in most cases means plenty of beans and tortillas, as well as the occasional chicken soup or meat dish. One of the highlights for many guests is participating in the cooking chores, and learning the simple art of tortilla making.

STAYING WITH A GARIFUNA FAMILY

Those seeking a unique Caribbean cultural experience can look into staying with a local Garífuna family. Just 11 miles (18km) south of Punta Gorda lies the small Garífuna village of Barranco. With a little over 100 residents, Barranco is a quintessential quiet Garífuna village. Although the road to Barranco is usually passable during the dry season, it's best to get there by boat. Ask around at the Punta Gorda pier if there's any regular ferry service. If not, you should be able to hire a ride for about BZ$80 (US$40) per boat.

The **Toledo Ecotourism Association** (© 722-2096; ttea@btl.net) can either arrange a stay in Barranco, as part of their Mayan village guesthouse program (see above), or they can set you up with a home visit and meal with a Punta Gorda Garífuna family. For around BZ$20 (US$10) per person, you and a couple of friends can spend the morning or afternoon with a Garífuna family, help in the purchasing and preparation of the meal, and then dine with your hosts.

SHOPPING

Wednesday and Saturday are market days around the small market square in front of the Civic Center and along the waterfront. This is a great time and place to find local and Guatemalan handcrafts, as well as fresh fruit and produce. If the outdoor market isn't happening, you can find most of the same items at either the **Southern Frontier Giftshop,** 41 Front St. (© 722-2870), or the **Fajina Craft Center** 𝕗 on Front Street next to the post office (© 722-2470), which is a cooperative of Mayan women from the area.

WHERE TO STAY

In addition to the places listed below, **Belize Lodge & Excursions** (© 223-6324; www.belizelodge.com) has a nice little nature lodge near the village of Indian Creek, as well as a more rustic jungle camp site about 5 miles (8km) south of this. They are also planning to open a small lodge on Moho Caye sometime in 2005. Near the village of Blue Creek, **International Zoological Expeditions** (© 800/548-5843 in the U.S.; www.ize2belize.com) has a research station and rustic lodge where they offer educational and adventure travel tours and packages.

VERY EXPENSIVE

El Pescador South 𝕗𝕗   This is a sister lodge to El Pescador (p. 142) on Ambergris Caye. This place is geared towards fishermen, and fly-fishing for world-class permit is the principle game, although tarpon, bonefish, and snook can also be tackled. The accommodations are 12 large and luxurious individual bungalows, set on a high hillside of rich forest above the Río Grande. The bungalows feature cool red tile floors, high-pitched ceilings, two queen-size beds with colorful Guatemalan bedspreads, and a large veranda with an excellent view and inviting hammock. There are large and ample windows that let in plenty of light and cross-ventilation if you decide to opt out of the air-conditioning. Meals are served family-style in the main dining room, and the large main lodge also has a bar and lounge area with a pool table, as well as a full-service and well-equipped tackle shop. The kidney-shaped pool has a broad and inviting deck area around it, and it's set on one of the highest points on the property, giving it excellent views all around. A tramway connects the lodge to the river below, where its fleet of fishing boats are docked. A meal package here runs BZ$110 (US$55) per person per day.

P.O. Box 135, Punta Gorda. © 800/242-2017 in the U.S., or 722-0050. Fax 722-0051. www.elpescadorpg. com. 12 units. BZ$360 (US$180) double. Rates lower in the off season. **Amenities:** Restaurant; bar; lounge; outdoor pool; tour desk; laundry service. *In room:* A/C, no phone.

EXPENSIVE

The Lodge At Big Falls ⋆   This comfortable nature lodge is set on the banks of the Río Grande, just outside the village of Big Falls. The six individual cabins all overlook the river and feature high thatched ceilings, large windows providing plenty of cross-ventilation, and cool rustic tile floors. Each comes with a large covered veranda equipped with a hammock for lazing away and watching the river flow. Although there's electricity here, at night the light is provided by kerosene lanterns. A host of tour options are available, and the lodge caters to ecotourists and those looking to explore the nearby Mayan ruins and villages. Meals are a well-prepared mix of local and international cuisine, and a meal package runs around BZ$80 (US$40) per person per day.

Near the village of Big Falls, 18 miles (29km) north of Punta Gorda (P.O. Box 103, Punta Gorda). ©/fax 722-2878. www.thelodgeatbigfalls.com. 6 units. BZ$270 (US$135) double. Rates lower in the off season. MC, V. **Amenities:** Restaurant; bar; tour desk; gift shop; laundry service. *In room:* No phone.

MODERATE

Located just off the Z-Line bus terminal, the **Traveler's Inn,** José María Núñez Street (© 702-2568), is a comfortable mid-range option, although it lacks any sense of local character, and I personally would opt to stay closer to the center of town and the water.

Sea Front Inn ⋆   This is hands-down the most upscale and comfortable option in P.G. proper. As the name implies, the hotel is located right in front of the Caribbean Sea, a few blocks north of the docks. The hotel itself is a large, four-story building with a row of high-pitched gables and expansive seaview windows, balconies, and verandas. The architecture almost seems like it should be set on the Hamptons or Martha's Vineyard. The furnishings and decor are quite simple, and in fact border on spartan, but the rooms are spacious and everything is kept immaculate. The hallways and common areas feature interesting hand-painted murals of local characters, flora, and fauna. The third-floor restaurant offers fabulous views of the ocean. A wide range of tour and activity options is available.

Fully furnished apartments are also available by the week or month.

Front St. (P.O. Box 20), Punta Gorda. © 722-2300. Fax 722-2682. www.seafrontinn.com. 11 units. BZ$120–BZ$150 (US$60–US$75) double. MC, V (4.5% surcharge). **Amenities:** Restaurant; bar; tour desk. *In room:* A/C, TV, no phone.

INEXPENSIVE

Punta Gorda has a host of budget lodgings. In addition to the places listed below, you could check out the **Punta Caliente Hotel,** 108 José María Núñez St. (© 722-2561); the **St. Charles Inn,** 23 King St. (© 722-2149); or **Tate's Guesthouse,** 34 José María Núñez St. (© 722-2196).

Nature's Way Guest House *Value*   Located 3 blocks south of the central park and across the street from the water, Nature's Way is a longtime favorite of budget travelers in Punta Gorda. There are a variety of room, bathroom, and bed configurations, and everything is quite basic. Still, even though most rooms do not have private bathrooms, everything is kept tidy, and the shared bathrooms are large and clean. The guesthouse is operated by an American named William "Chet" Schmidt, who moved down here more than 25 years ago to promote sustainable agricultural and tourism practices. Chet is a wealth of information about the area and helped start the TEA Mayan guesthouse program.

65 Front St., Punta Gorda. ©/fax 702-2119. 12 units (2 with private bathroom). BZ$26–BZ$36 (US$13–US$18) double. MC, V. **Amenities:** Restaurant; bar; tour desk. *In room:* No phone.

TC's By the Sea *Value*   Located a little over a mile north of town, and right on the water, this humble little hotel provides good value in a quiet and relaxing atmosphere. The accommodations are simple but well kept. Several of the rooms have waterbeds, although more traditional and firmer mattresses are also available. If you're looking for a break from your steady diet of seafood, the open-air restaurant here actually specializes in steaks, ribs, and barbecue chicken. The hotel provides complimentary transfers to the airstrip or bus terminal, but if you're going regularly into town, you'll have to hoof it or take a taxi.

Cattle Landing (P.O. Box 155), Punta Gorda. ©/fax 722-2963. www.belizebythesea.com. 7 units. BZ$58 (US$29) double with shared bathroom; BZ$90–BZ$140 (US$45–US$70) double with private bathroom. Rates include continental breakfast. **Amenities:** Restaurant; bar; tour desk. *In room:* TV, no phone.

WHERE TO DINE

Dining options are far from extensive in Punta Gorda. In addition to the restaurants listed below, check out the restaurant at the **Hotel Punta Caliente,** 108 José María Núñez St. (© 722-2561), for authentic Garífuna cooking; and for casual local dining, **Aunt J's Restaurant,** on Main Street across from the central park (© 722-2756), and **Grace's Restaurant,** at the corner of Main and King sts. (© 702-2414).

For a cool treat on a hot day, head to **Vicky's Ice Cream Parlour,** 57 Main St. (© 722-2572).

Gomier's Foods *Finds* BELIZEAN/VEGETARIAN   This should definitely be the first stop for any vegetarian or health-food nut. While the menu at this place features plenty of traditional locally prepared food and dishes, this is the only place in P.G. to find stir-fried tofu and a wide range of vegetarian entrees. Most of the herbs and vegetables are organically grown by the owner Gomier himself.

At the corner of Vernon and Front sts. © 722-2929. Main courses BZ$8–BZ$18 (US$4–US$9). No credit cards. Mon–Fri 8am–5pm.

Waluco's BELIZEAN/INTERNATIONAL   This relatively new place has quickly become a local favorite. Set overlooking the water north of town, this simple open-air joint serves hearty Belizean and international fare. Their Sunday afternoon barbecues are the best bargain and best time to be had in town. You also can't go wrong with any of the fresh fish or conch dishes. When you finish eating, be sure to walk to the end of their pier with a fresh cold drink and sit for a while with the water lapping beneath your feet. This is why you came to Belize, isn't it?

1 mile (1.6km) north of town, on the waterfront. ⒞ **722-0196.** Reservations not accepted. Main courses BZ$8–BZ$24 (US$4–US$12). MC, V. Tues–Sun 8am–5pm.

PUNTA GORDA AFTER DARK

While they often show sporting events at the **PG Sports Bar,** this is really an all-purpose nightspot with occasional live bands, DJs, and karaoke nights. It's located on Main Street at the southern edge of the little central park. A little further north at 11 Main Middle St., there's usually a mellow reggae scene happening at **Earth Runnings,** and folks have been heading out north of town to **Waluco's,** where there are occasionally live music jam sessions, a local Punta Rock band, or a Garífuna drumming outfit

8

The Cayo District & Western Belize

The western region of Belize, from the capital city of Belmopan to the Guatemalan border, is a land of rolling hills, dense jungles, abundant waterfalls, clear rivers, extensive caves, and numerous Mayan ruins. This area was the heart of the Belizean Mayan world, with the major ruins of **Caracol, Xunanatunich,** and **El Pilar,** as well as lesser sites like **Cahal Pech.** At the height of the Classic Mayan period, there were more residents in this area than in all of modern Belize.

Today, the area around Belmopan and extending throughout the Cayo District is the heart of Belize's ecotourism industry. There are a host of national parks and protected areas, including the **Guanacaste** and **Blue Hole National Parks,** the **Mountain Pine Ridge Forest Reserve,** and the **Chiquibil National Park.** The pine forests and rainforests here are great for hiking and bird-watching; the rivers are excellent for canoeing, kayaking, and inner tubing; and the dirt roads are perfect for horseback riding and mountain biking.

The cave systems of the Cayo District were sacred to the ancient Maya, and many of them are open for exploration by budding and experienced spelunkers alike. Some of the more popular underground attractions include **Actun Tunichil Muknal, Barton Creek Cave, Chechem Ha, Crystal Cave,** and the **Río Frío Cave.** Of particular interest is the **Caves Branch River,** which provides the unique opportunity to float on an inner tube, kayak, or canoe through a series of caves.

The Western Highway runs through the heart of the Cayo District all the way to the Guatemalan border, and serves as the gateway to side trips into Guatemala's Petén Province and the majestic Mayan ruins of **Tikal** (see chapter 9).

1 Belmopan

52 miles (84km) W of Belize City; 20 miles (32km) E of San Ignacio; 100 miles (161km) NW of Placencia

After Hurricane Hattie devastated Belize City in 1961, government officials figured enough was enough and decided to move the country's capital safely inland. Belmopan is an example of what happens when you build it and no one comes. Conceived as a model city that would become the dynamic center of a growing Belize, Belmopan is actually a sleepy place set 2 miles (3km) in from the Western Highway.

Belmopan is a planned city designed and built from scratch in the jungle at the geographical center of the country. Unfortunately, the planners who designed it didn't count on the people's resistance to moving here. A host of government buildings, including the National Assembly, are laid out according to a master plan, surrounded by residential areas, with everything connected by a ring road. Still, Belmopan has yet to see any substantial growth in its current population of only 7,000 or so. In fact, many government workers make the daily commute from Belize City, as it's an easy shot on a well-paved road.

Most visitors avoid Belmopan entirely, but if you are traveling around by bus, you will at least pass through it. If you get into town late at night, don't despair—you can easily spend the night and make an early onward connection in the morning. Belmopan also makes a convenient base for visits to the nearby **Guanacaste** and **Blue Hole National Parks,** as well as the **Caves Branch River** and its network of hollowed-out limestone caves. There are also several very comfortable and interesting nature lodges in close proximity to Belmopan.

ESSENTIALS
GETTING THERE & DEPARTING
BY PLANE   Belmopan has a small airport (BCV), and **Maya Island Air** (© 226-2435 in Belize City; www.mayaairways.com) has regularly scheduled flights to Belmopan from Belize City. Fares average BZ$140 to BZ$180 (US$70–US$90) each way. The flight from Belize City is just 15 minutes, although there is really little reason to fly in to Belmopan, as it's such a short and easy drive from Belize City.

BY BUS   Belmopan has very frequent bus service from Belize City. Nearly all buses heading west and south from Belize City stop in Belmopan. **Novelo's Bus Line** (© 207-2025 in Belize City, 822-0528 in Belmopan) buses to Belmopan leave roughly every half-hour from the main bus station on West Collet Canal Street between 5am and 7pm. Return buses to Belize City leave the main bus station in Belmopan about every half-hour between 5am and 6:15pm. The fare each way is BZ$7 (US$3.50). The trip takes 1½ hours. From Belmopan, there are also frequent onward connections to Dangriga, Placencia, Punta Gorda, and other points south, as well as to San Ignacio, Benque Viejo, and the Guatemalan border.

BY CAR   From Belize City, take Cemetery Road to the Western Highway. At Mile 50 you'll see the well-marked turn off for the Hummingbird Highway and Belmopan. Turn left here and follow signs to Belmopan, about 2 miles (3km) beyond the turnoff. It should take about 1 hour to drive from Belize City to Belmopan.

GETTING AROUND
Belmopan is an extremely compact little city. You can easily walk to most places around the central hub. If you need a taxi, call **Blades Taxi Service** (© 822-2468) or **Elvis Taxi Service** (© 802-3732). A taxi ride anywhere in town should cost around BZ$5 (US$2.50).

ORIENTATION
Belmopan is a planned city with a ring road and wide, mostly deserted streets, located just off the Hummingbird (Southern) Highway, 2 miles (3km) south of the Western Highway. The Novelo's bus station and small central market area are the heart of the town, and you will hit them soon after heading in off the highway. Within a 2-block radius, you'll find a couple of banks, two gas stations, and a few small strip malls. At the center of the city's radius, just off the market and bus station, is Independence Plaza, which houses the post office and Prime Minister's office. Sidewalks cut through Independence Plaza in various directions, making most of downtown Belmopan easily accessible by foot.

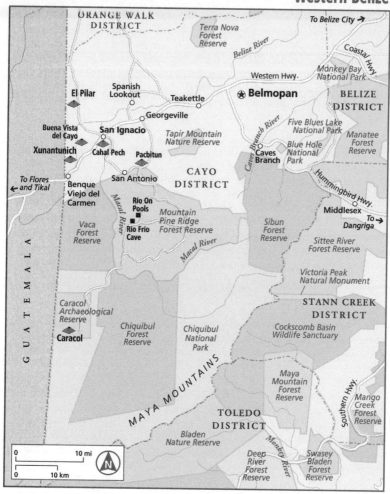

FAST FACTS Both of the principal banks in town, **Scotiabank,** Ring Road (✆ 822-1414), and **Belize Bank,** 60 Market Sq. (✆ 822-2303), are located close to the central market and bus station.

For the **police,** dial ✆ 822-2222; for the **fire department,** dial ✆ 822-2311. The **Belmopan Hospital** (✆ 822-2264) is located on Constitution Drive, a block north of its intersection with the North Ring Road.

The **Market Square Drug Store** (✆ 822-0045) is a well-stocked pharmacy located just off the Market Square. If you need film or developing, head to **Belicolor** on Market Square (✆ 822-0527).

WHAT TO SEE & DO

Perhaps the biggest attraction close to Belmopan is the **Belize Zoo,** Western Highway, Mile Marker 29 (✆ **220-8004;** www.belizezoo.org). For more information on visiting the zoo, see p. 96.

Although many finds have been left on-site, or transferred to the new Museum of Belize in Belize City (p. 94), a broad selection of Mayan artifacts found at sites around the country are stored in the basement of the **Archaeology Department** (© 822-2106) of the University of Belize here in Belmopan. It is located on the ground floor of the building at the far side of the quadrangle that is adjacent to the bus-depot market. While it is no longer regularly open to the public, if you call in advance, you may be able to arrange a tour of their collection.

THE UNDERWORLD

The ancient Maya believed that caves were a mystical portal between the world of the living and the underworld of spirits and the dead. From their earliest days, there is evidence that the Mayans made extensive use of caves for ritual purposes, as well as for more mundane and rudimentary things as keeping dry, storing grains, and gathering water. They called this mystical realm **Xibalba.**

Belize is literally riddled with caves. In almost every explored cave to date, some evidence of use by the Mayans has been uncovered. Fire pits, campsites, burial mounds, and ritual altars have all been found. Numerous pieces of pottery and abundant bones and artifacts have also been encountered. Belize offers many unique and easily accessible opportunities to explore this fascinating world, on foot, by kayak or canoe, or by floating on an inner tube. Don't miss it.

Caves Branch ✦✦✦

The Caves Branch River is a gently flowing body of water coming down off the Mountain Pine Ridge. It really should be called a creek in most places. However, what makes the Caves Branch River unique is the fact that it flows in and out of a series of long limestone caves that are easily navigable on inner tubes and in kayaks.

There are two major entry points along the river for visits to the Caves Branch caves: One is at **Ian Anderson's Caves Branch** jungle lodge (p. 217), and the other is just above **Jaguar Paw,** a luxury hotel built on the banks of the river (p. 217). In general terms, travelers looking for more adventurous and gritty trips into the caves should head to Ian Anderson's place; those seeking a more luxurious excursion into the underworld should head to Jaguar Paw. If you want something in between, try one of the numerous tour operators (in Belmopan, Belize City, San Ignacio, and even the cayes) that offer day trips to the Caves Branch region. For anyone looking for some serious cave adventures and explorations, both of the aforementioned lodges offer a host of guided tours to much less commonly explored caves, including the fabulous **Crystal Cave** ✦✦✦, located just off the Jaguar Paw grounds.

By far, most visitors go either directly through Jaguar Paw or use the same section of the river. There's a government-operated parking area (BZ$4/US$2) about a half-mile downriver from Jaguar Paw and a host of operators running the tubing tour from here. Either way, you will have to hike upstream to a put-in. Depending on the tour you choose and the amount of hiking you want to do, you will eventually climb into your inner tube and begin a slow float through anywhere from one to four caves. You will be equipped with a headlamp, and little else. If your group is small enough, I recommend you coordinate and all shut off your headlamps for a period of time. It's quite a spooky sensation to be floating in total darkness, wondering where the walls and ceilings are and whether or not you'll ever emerge into daylight again.

Most of the caves here contain Mayan pottery and artifacts, although you won't see them on most tube trips, unless your guide stops for a short hike.

Cave tubing tours cost between BZ$80 and BZ$190 (US$40–US$95), depending on the length of the tour. The most inexpensive way to go is to drive yourself to the government parking area below Jaguar Paw and hire one of the local guides there for around BZ$30 to BZ$50 (US$15–US$25). However, you'll generally get better guides, better service, and better equipment if you go with one of the more established operators.

Actun Tunichil Muknal 🐾🐾

Actun Tunichil Muknal means "Cave of the Crystal Sepulchre," and the site was featured in the 1993 National Geographic Explorer film *Journey Through the Underworld*. This is one of the most adventurous and rewarding caves you can visit in Belize. The trip involves a 45-minute hike through dense forest to the entrance of the cave. A midsize stream flows out of the beautiful entrance. From here you wade, crawl, and scramble, often up to your waist in water. There are some tight squeezes. Inside, you'll come to several ceremonial and sacrificial chambers. Fourteen skeletons and burial sites have been found inside here, as well as numerous pieces of pottery and ceramic shards. There are even two rare slate stelae, believed to have been used by Mayan religious and political leaders for ritual bloodletting ceremonies. Many of the skulls, skeletons, and pieces of pottery have been encased in calcium creating an eerie effect, while others are very well

---

Tips For the Most Enjoyable Experience

Caves Branch is a very popular tourist attraction, and it can get crowded at times, especially around the last three caves closest to Jaguar Paw and the public entrance. When the cruise-ship groups are in the caves, it's downright overcrowded. Whatever tour operator you use, try to be sure to time it so that you avoid other large groups if possible. I also highly recommend hiking the extra 15 minutes or so upstream to get to the fourth cave. However, wear plenty of insect repellent, as the mosquitoes can be fierce here (only on the hike—once you're in the caves there are none).

---

maintained, making it hard to imagine that they are over a thousand years old. Moreover, given its remote location and relatively recent discovery, Actun Tunichil Muknal has been spared much of the serious looting that has plagued many other Mayan cave sites. Only licensed guides can take visitors into this cave. Most hotels and tour agencies in the Cayo District can arrange these tours.

Note: You will get wet on this trip. Make sure your guide has a dry bag for your camera, and be sure to pack a change of clothing for when you get back to your transportation.

NATIONAL PARKS

Guanacaste National Park (★), a 50-acre (20 ha) park located where the Hummingbird Highway turns off of the Western Highway, about 2 miles (3km) north of Belmopan, is an excellent introduction to tropical forests. The park is named for a huge old guanacaste (or tubroos) tree that is found within the park. Guanacaste trees were traditionally preferred for building dugout canoes, but this particular tree, which is about 100 years old, was spared the boat-builders' ax because it has a crooked and divided trunk that makes it unacceptable for canoe building. More than 35 species of epiphytes (plants that grow on other plants), including orchids, bromeliads, ferns, mosses, lichens, and philodendrons, cover its trunk and branches.

There are nearly 2 miles (3km) of well-marked and well-maintained trails in the park, with several benches for sitting and observing wildlife. The park is bordered on the west by Roaring Creek and on the north by the Belize River. Among the animals you might see are more than 120 species of birds, large iguanas, armadillos, kinkajous, deer, agoutis (large rodents that are a favorite game meat in Belize), and jaguarundis (small jungle cats). Bring along a bathing suit, in case you want to take a refreshing dip in the Belize River.

The park is open daily from 8am to 4:30pm; admission is BZ$5 (US$2.50). A self-guided trail map and a brochure about the park are available at the small visitor's center. And if the park ranger is available, he'll usually throw in a brief guided tour for free.

The Maya Mountains are primarily limestone and laced with caves, which is why this region of Belize is also known as Cave's Branch. About 12 miles (19km) south of Belmopan on the Hummingbird Highway, you'll find **Blue Hole National Park** (★). The first signs you see of the park will be the parking area, visitor center, and trail entrance to **St. Herman's Cave.** It's less than a half-mile hike from the road to one of the largest and most easily accessible caves in Belize. You'll need a good flashlight and sturdy shoes to explore this undeveloped half-mile-long (.8km) cave.

A little further on down the Hummingbird Highway you'll come to a second entrance to **Blue Hole National Park.** The park gets its name from a crystal-clear pool, or *cenote,* formed in a collapsed cavern. A short well-marked trail leads to the main attraction here. Dense jungle surrounds a small natural pool of deep turquoise. A limestone cliff rises up from the edge of the pool on two sides. The water flows for only about 100 feet (30m) on the surface before disappearing into a cave and flowing on underground to the Sibun River. This is a great place for a quick dip on a hot day because the water is refreshingly cool and clear. It can get crowded here on weekends, but early in the morning during the week, you may have the place almost to yourself. You can clearly see fish swimming around the edges of the Blue Hole. A 1.5-mile (2.4km) trail connects the Blue Hole pool with St. Herman's Cave. This trail passes through lush and beautiful primary and secondary tropical forests that are rich in flora and fauna. Over 200 species of birds have been recorded here. Be sure to wear plenty of insect repellent or long-sleeved clothing, as the mosquitoes can be fierce here. *Tip:* If you're only interested in the pool, be sure to continue on the Hummingbird Highway, and don't park at the St. Herman's Cave entrance.

With a guide hired at the park entrance, you can also explore the **Crystalline Cave** here. This cave system goes on for miles and features beautiful geological structures and formations, Mayan relics, and some calcified skeletons. The park is open daily from 8am to 4pm, and admission is BZ$8 (US$4). You'll have to pay an additional BZ$20 (US$10) for a 1½- to 2-hour guided tour of the Crystalline Cave.

A PRIVATE PARK & EDUCATIONAL CENTER

Located just inland from Mile Marker 31 on the Western Highway is **Monkey Bay Wildlife Sanctuary** (© 820-3032; www.monkeybaybelize.org), a private reserve and environmental education center comprised of some 1,070 acres (428 ha) of varied natural habitat. There's a visitor center, and a range of tours is offered. This place specializes in hosting student groups, but anyone can visit for the day, or even stay in accommodations that range from somewhat plush private rooms to a dormitory-style bunkhouse to camping. In all cases, be forewarned: The showers are cold water only, and the bathrooms are outdoor latrines. Tours include guided hikes, bird-watching expeditions, cave explorations, and canoe outings on the Sibun River. With the recent declaration of the neighboring 2,250-acre (900 ha) **Monkey Bay Nature Reserve,** this has become a considerably large protected area, with over 250 recorded bird species.

While walk-ins can often be accommodated, it's best to contact them in advance before coming for any tour or stay. Rates run around BZ$10 (US$5) per person for camping; BZ$15 (US$7.50) per person for a dorm bunk; and from BZ$30 to BZ$40 (US$15–US$20) for a double room. Meals cost between BZ$8 and BZ$12 (US$4–US$6). A guided 3-hour paddle on the Sibun River costs BZ$50 (US$25) per person.

⬭ Tips Worth the Search

Located a little further south along the Hummingbird Highway is **Five Blues Lake National Park** (www.5blueslake.org), which features a similar, albeit larger *cenote.* This park is much less visited than Blue Hole National Park. For more information, see chapter 7.

WHERE TO STAY
IN BELMOPAN

In addition to the places listed below, the **Belmopan Hotel** (© 822-2327) is located right across from the bus station. This place is quite convenient, and even has a swimming pool. Still, it often feels rather run-down and neglected.

Moderate

Bullfrog Inn   This is the most modern and comfortable hotel in Belmopan. Rooms are spacious, and come with one king bed or two queen beds, air-conditioning, and cable television. Most rooms have a small private balcony with a wrought iron railing overlooking a small patch of grass and the ring road. This place is justifiably popular with business travelers, as it's really the only game in town. The restaurant here is one of the more dependable in town, and the bar can actually get hopping.

25 Half Moon Ave. (P.O. Box 28), Belmopan. © 822-3425. Fax 822-3155. www.bullfroginn.com. 25 units. BZ$150 (US$75) double. MC, V. **Amenities:** Restaurant; bar; tour desk; laundry service. *In room:* A/C, TV.

Inexpensive

El Rey Inn   If you looking for a clean, inexpensive place to spend the night, try this small hotel located in a residential neighborhood just off the north ring road. The rooms are fairly basic, but the rates are some of the best in Belmopan. This little hotel has a simple restaurant serving reasonably priced meals, and a host of tours can be arranged. El Rey Inn is about a 10-minute hike or a short taxi ride from the bus station.

23 Moho St., Belmopan. © 882-3438. Fax 882-2682. hibiscus@btl.net. 12 units. BZ$50 (US$25) double. MC, V. **Amenities:** Restaurant; tour desk; laundry service. *In room:* No phone.

NEAR BELMOPAN

While Belmopan itself is of very little interest to most travelers, several of the country's best and most interesting nature lodges are located within close proximity to the capitol city. All of the places below have their unique charms.

Banana Bank Lodge 🐾 *Kids*   Owners John and Carolyn Carr moved to Belize from the United States over 25 years ago. Carolyn is an artist and John is a cowboy from Montana. Together, they operate one of the oldest cattle ranches in Belize and one of the original ecolodges in the country. There are a variety of options, from two-bedroom cabañas that are well suited to families to lodge rooms to the new Chateau Brio suites, which are the most luxurious rooms here. Three of these suites have full kitchenettes. I find some of the furnishings and decor touches a bit too provincial and quaint for my taste, but this is often offset by beautiful stained glass pieces and interesting architectural touches. All of the rooms here are nonsmoking.

The lodge is set on a high hill above the Belize River. There's a pool for lazing around or cooling off on hot days. Horseback riding is the most popular attraction here, but canoeing, visits to Maya ruins, and other day and overnight trips can all be arranged at additional cost. On the grounds, you can visit Carolyn's studio and get close to the Carrs' pet jaguar, Tika. Cruise-ship passengers come here frequently for day trips, and it can get a little crowded and hectic when they are around. The turnoff for Banana Bank Lodge is at Mile 47 on the Western Highway, just before the turnoff for Belmopan. From here, it is about 1¼ miles (2km) to a parking area across the Belize River from the ranch. Here, you'll have to clang the gong or scream really loudly for a quick boat ride across the river.

Western Hwy., Mile Marker 4½ (P.O. Box 48, Belmopan). ℂ 820-2020. Fax 820-2026. www.banana bank.com. 14 units. BZ$160–BZ$300 (US$80–US$150) double. AE, MC, V. **Amenities:** Restaurant; bar; outdoor pool; tour desk; laundry service; nonsmoking rooms. *In room:* A/C, no phone.

Ian Anderson's Cave Branch ⍟   Originally a rustic camp for hard-core adventure travelers, this place has expanded, and while maybe they haven't softened excessively, they've certainly added some comfortable accommodations. Set on the banks of the Caves Branch River amidst dense forest, this collection of individual cabins, suites, bunkhouses, and camping sites still is geared predominantly to adventure seekers and backpackers.

By far the most luxurious options here are the jungle suites and bungalows, and these are in fact quite comfortable. The latter feature red tile floors, large verandas, and a beautiful shower with a large screened window opening up to the forest. Folks choosing to camp or stay in the jungle cabañas or bunkhouse share common bathroom and shower areas. These open-air showers are quite fun, as the showerheads are just old buckets with nail holes perforating them. When I last visited, they were building three new "treehouse" rooms, overlooking the river. A wide range of cave explorations, hiking, mountain biking, and kayaking tours are offered here, including overnight tours and jungle treks. Meals are served buffet style, and a meal plan here costs BZ$82 (US$41).

Hummingbird Hwy., Mile Marker 41½ (P.O. Box 356, Belmopan). ℂ 822-2800. www.cavesbranch.com. 16 units. BZ$10 (US$5) per person camping; BZ$30 (US$15) per person bunkhouse; BZ$156 (US$78) double cabaña; BZ$216–BZ$256 (US$108–US$128) double suite or bungalow. No credit cards. **Amenities:** Restaurant; bar; tour desk; laundry service; nonsmoking rooms. *In room:* No phone.

Jaguar Paw ⍟⍟   With bold architectural and decor touches, and a prime location amidst dense forests at the heart of the Caves Branch river and cave network, Jaguar Paw is one of the most unique nature lodges in Belize. The 16 rooms here are housed in a series of fourplex buildings spread through the lush grounds. While each room is identical in size, they are radically different in decor, each sporting a unique motif. My favorites include the Africa, Aboriginal, and Shell rooms. Honeymooners or couples looking for some "jungle fever" should request the Bordello room. All of the rooms are plenty spacious and have a small front porch area. The restaurant here is excellent.

This hotel's greatest attraction is its location on the banks of the Caves Branch River, from where the popular cave tubing trips leave, and just a 5-minute walk from the entrance to the very impressive Crystal Cave. Since most of the cruise ships use Jaguar Paw for their cave tubing excursions, guests here can usually avoid the crowds by coordinating with the hotel and going before or after the masses hit the river. The owners here were instrumental in the exploration of the surrounding cave system, and their dedication to the exploration and preservation is very apparent.

Western Hwy., Mile Marker 37 (P.O. Box 1832, Belmopan). ℂ 888/775-8645 in the U.S., or 820-2023. Fax 820-2024. www.jaguarpaw.com. 16 units. BZ$340 (US$170) double. Rates lower in the off season. AE, MC, V. **Amenities:** Restaurant; bar; outdoor pool; tour desk; laundry service. *In room:* A/C, no phone.

Pook's Hill ⍟ *Finds*   This isolated little nature resort is set on the grounds of a small Mayan ruins in the midst of a lush forest and a 300-acre (120 ha) private reserve. The individual thatch roof cabins are set on a hillside just off the small Mayan plaza, and are named after local fauna. Those highest up the hill have the best views of the surrounding forest, but they're a little bit smaller and slightly less luxurious than the newer units a little lower down. My favorite cabin is Kinkajoo, which is tiled with river stones. The two newest cabins are below the main lodge and across a small creek, and are built on raised stilts, 12 feet (3.6m) above the ground. These two cabins have large decks and are great for bird-watching.

A host of activities and tours are offered, including horseback riding, mountain biking, cave tubing, and guided hikes and bird-watching tours. Pook's Hill is about a 2-hour hike from the Actun Tunichil Muknal cave, and day trips are offered here. Meals are served in a screened-in common dining area. Above the dining area is the open-air lounge and bar, which is lit by kerosene lanterns at night, and buzzing with hummingbirds during the day. A meal plan here costs BZ$72 (US$34) per person per day.

Western Hwy., Mile Marker 52½ (P.O. Box 14, Belmopan). ©/fax **820-2017**. www.pookshillbelize.com. 11 units. BZ$296 (US$148) double. Rates lower in the off season. MC, V (5% surcharge). Turn south off Western Hwy. at Mile Marker 52½ at Teakettle Village. Follow signs on the dirt roads 6 miles (10km) until you reach the lodge. **Amenities:** Restaurant; bar; tour desk; laundry service. *In room:* No phone.

WHERE TO DINE

The restaurant at the **Bullfrog Inn** (© 822-3425), which serves a mix of local and international cuisine, is probably the best restaurant in Belmopan proper. Budget travelers and those looking for some local flavor should probably grab food from the various vendors and stalls at the central market. If you fear for your tender stomach or aren't impressed with the hygienic standards around the market, head to **Caladium Restaurant** (© 822-2754), just across from the market.

However, your best options lie just outside of the city, about 16 miles (26km) east along the Western Highway at Mile Marker 32, where you'll find three popular roadside restaurants and bars: **Cheers** (© 614-9311), **Amigos** (© 820-2014), and **J. B. Watering Hole** (© 820-2071). Of these, J. B.'s is the most famous, as it was reportedly Harrison Ford's favorite haunt during the filming of *The Mosquito Coast.* However, J. B.'s changed hands several times in recent years, and locals insist that Amigos is currently the best.

BELMOPAN AFTER DARK

There's really very little in the way of nightlife in and around Belmopan. The **Bullfrog Inn,** 25 Half Moon Ave., is probably the city's most reliable and popular watering hole. The restaurants out on the Western Highway mentioned above are actually your best bet for an evening out.

2 San Ignacio ★★

72 miles (116km) W of Belize City; 20 miles (32km) W of Belmopan; 9 miles (14km) E of the Guatemalan border

In the foothills of the mountains close to the Guatemalan border lie the twin towns of Santa Elena and San Ignacio on either side of the beautiful Macal River (good for a swim). For all intents and purposes, San Ignacio is the more important town, both in general terms and particularly for travelers. Just north of town, the Macal and Mopan rivers converge to form the Belize River. San Ignacio is the business and administrative center for the Cayo District, a region of cattle ranches and dense forests, of clear rivers and Mayan ruins. It is also the second largest metropolitan center in the country. Still, you won't find any urban blight here. If you've come from Guatemala, you'll sense immediately that you are now in a Caribbean country. If you've come up from the coast, you might be surprised by how cool it can get up here in the mountains. The Cayo District and the cayes are worlds apart. While the cayes cater to those looking

ACCOMMODATIONS

Hi-Et **7**
Martha's Guest House **8**
Midas Tropical Resort **1**
New Balmoral Hotel **10**
Plaza Hotel **12**
San Ignacio Resort Hotel **13**
Tropicool **4**

DINING

Café Sol **2**
Erva's **6**
Eva's Restaurant & Bar **5**
Hannah's **11**
Martha's Restaurant
  & Pizza House **8**
Maxim's Chinese
  Restaurant **9**
Running W Steak House
  & Restaurant **13**
Serendib Restaurant **3**

for fun in the sun, Cayo caters to those interested in nature and classic Mayan ruins. This area makes a good first stop in Belize; you can get in a lot of activity before heading to the beach to relax.

ESSENTIALS
GETTING THERE & DEPARTING

BY PLANE **Maya Island Air** (✆ **226-2435;** www.mayaairways.com) has three daily flights between both Belize City airports and the airstrip in San Ignacio (SQS). These flights leave Belize City Municipal Airport at 8:15am and 1:30 and 4:45pm, stopping 10 minutes later at the Philip S.W. Goldson International Airport to pick up additional passengers. Flights return to Belize City at 9am, 2:15pm, and 5:30pm. Flight duration is 45 minutes from the municipal airport and 30 minutes from the international airport. Fare is BZ$152 (US$76) from the municipal airport, and BZ$177 (US$89) from the international airport.

You can make connections to the San Ignacio flights from most other major destinations in Belize.

BY BUS San Ignacio has very frequent bus service from Belize City. **Novelo's Bus Line** (✆ **207-2025** in Belize City, 824-3360 in San Ignacio) buses to San Ignacio leave roughly every half-hour from the main bus station on West Collet Canal Street between 5am and 7pm. Return buses to Belize City leave the main bus station in San Ignacio roughly every half-hour between 4am and 5pm. The

For Short

The name "Cayo" is used to refer to both the Cayo District as well as to the city of San Ignacio.

fare is BZ$2.50 (US$5). The trip takes 2½ hours. Most of the western-bound buses continue on beyond San Ignacio to Benque Viejo and the Guatemalan border.

BY CAR   Take the Western Highway from Belize City. It's a straight shot all the way to San Ignacio. Be careful about the numerous speed bumps spread out along the highway. You'll come to the small town of Santa Elena first. Across the Macal River lies San Ignacio. When I last visited, the Hawksworth Bridge had been dedicated for traffic heading east out of San Ignacio towards Santa Elena. If you're heading to San Ignacio and points west, a well marked detour will lead you through the town of Santa Elena to a semi-permanent Balley bridge that enters San Ignacio towards the north end of town.

GETTING AROUND

The downtown center of San Ignacio is quite compact and easily navigated by foot. If you want to visit any of the major attractions listed below, you'll probably have to find transportation. Frequent buses (see above) will take you to the entrances to most of the hotels listed below on Benque Viejo Road, as well as within walking distance of the Xunantunich ruins. Infrequent buses (ask around town or at the Novelo's bus station; (824-3360) do service the Mountain Pine Ridge area. However, if you don't have your own vehicle, you will probably need to take some taxis or go on organized tours.

As in the rest of Belize, roads are minimal and almost everything can be found on or just off the Western Highway, or the road through Mountain Pine Ridge. Numerous buses ply the main road between Belmopan and San Ignacio, continuing on to the border town of Benque Viejo del Carmen. If you want to drive yourself, particularly anywhere off the main highway, a four-wheel-drive vehicle is recommended.

You can rent a car from **Cayo Rentals** ((824-2222) in San Ignacio. A small four-wheel-drive vehicle here should run you around US$75 per day

If you need a cab, call the **Cayo Taxi Association** ((824-2196) or **San Ignacio Taxi Stand** ((824-2155). Taxi fares around the Cayo District should run you as follows: BZ$5 (US$2.50) around town; BZ$15 (US$7.50) between San Ignacio and Bullet Tree Falls; BZ$50 (US$25) between San Ignacio and Chaa Creek or duPlooy's. Collective taxis run regularly between downtown San Ignacio and the border at Benque Viejo; the fare is BZ$5 (US$2.50) per person.

ORIENTATION

San Ignacio is on the banks of the Macal River, on the western side of an old metal bridge across from its sister city of Santa Elena. Across the single-lane Hawksworth Bridge is a traffic circle and Shell gas station. Downtown San Ignacio is to the north on Burns Avenue, and the San Ignacio Hotel is located south up a steep hill on Buena Vista Road. Most of the hotels and restaurants in town are on or within a block of Burns Avenue. The road to Benque Viejo del Carmen, Xunantunich ruins, and the Guatemalan border branches off Buena Vista Road. This is actually a continuation of the Western Highway.

If you can't find the information you need on the walls of Eva's Restaurant on Burns Avenue, ask **Bob Jones** behind the counter. He can help you arrange tours and accommodations, and will put you in touch with fellow travelers with similar interests and budgets.

FAST FACTS   There are several banks located right in the heart of downtown San Ignacio: **Atlantic Bank,** at Burns Avenue and Columbus Park (© 824-2347); **Scotiabank,** at Burns Avenue and Riverside Street (© 824-4190); and **Belize Bank,** 16 Burns Ave. (© 824-2031).

To reach the **police,** dial © **824-2022;** for the **fire department,** dial © **824-2095.** The **San Ignacio Hospital** is located on Simpson Street, on the western side of town (© **824-2066**). The **post office** (© 824-2049) is located on Hudson Street, near the corner of Waight's Avenue. There's even an office of **DHL** on Benque Viejo Road (© **824-2222**).

For film or developing, head to **Belicolor Photo Service** on Hudson Street (© 824-3549). If you need eyeglass repair or help, head to the **Hoy Eye Center,** 4 Far West St. (© **824-4101**). The succinctly named **The Pharmacy** (© 824-2510) is located on West Street. If you need laundry done and your hotel doesn't offer the service or charges too much, you can drop off your dirty clothes at **Martha's Guesthouse,** 10 West St. (© **824-3647**) for same-day service at about BZ$10 (US$5) per load.

If you need to log on, head to **Eva's Restaurant,** 22 Burns Ave. (© **804-2267**); or the **Green Dragon,** 8 Hudson St. (© 824-4782). Both offer high-speed Internet connections. Eva's is one of the most popular restaurants and meeting places in town, while the Green Dragon has an organic market and interesting little bookstore.

WHAT TO SEE & DO

The Cayo District is Belize's prime inland tourist destination. There's a lot to see and do in this area, from visiting Mayan ruins and caves to a broad range of adventure activities. In addition to the tours, activities, and attractions listed below, all of the listings in the Mountain Pine Ridge section (later in this chapter), and in the Belmopan section (earlier in this chapter) are easily accessible from San Ignacio.

Some of the tours, activities, and attractions listed below can be done on your own, but others will require a guide or adventure tour operator. Most hotels in the area either have their own tour operations or can arrange to hook you up with a reputable local operator. In addition, there are several long-standing tour agencies based in San Ignacio. Some of the best of these include **Belize Eco Tours** (© 824-4290; www.belize-ecotours.com), **Cayo Adventure Tours** (© 824-3246; www.cayoadventure.com), **Mayawalk Tours** (© 824-3070; www.mayawalk.com), and **Yute Expeditions** (© 824-2076; www.inland belize.com). All of these companies offer virtually all of the options listed in this chapter and more, including multiday tours, treks, and adventures. In addition, serious bird-watchers might want to give a call to **Birds Without Borders** (© 824-4416).

MAYAN RUINS

The Cayo District is in the heart of the Mayan highlands, with several major ruins and cave systems used by the ancient residents of this region. The most impressive are **Xunantunich** (on Benque Viejo Rd.), **El Pilar** (near Bullet Tree Falls Village), and **Caracol** (deep in the Mountain Pine Ridge area; see "Mountain Pine Ridge & Caracol," later in this chapter), but true Maya-philes can keep busy visiting a host of sites in this area. Close by, in Guatemala, lies **Tikal** ✿✿✿, perhaps one of the best excavated and most impressive Mayan cities in Mesoamerica. See chapter 9 for complete coverage.

CAHAL PECH ✿   High on a hill to the southwest of downtown San Ignacio are the Mayan ruins of **Cahal Pech.** Although compact, there are actually seven plazas here, as well as numerous residences, temples, and a couple of ball courts. Formerly the home of Mayan royals, this site has received some meticulous restoration. The restoration created a bit of controversy in town because parts of the ruins were restored to an approximation of the way they were supposed to have looked when they were first built, which is a bit more polished and modern-looking than most people like their ruins. However, the setting is beautiful, with tall old trees shading the site's main plaza and pyramid. *Tip:* Be sure to climb the small B4 pyramid, on your left near the entrance to the site. Though diminutive, it offers excellent views to the Macal River.

The name Cahal Pech means the "Place of the Family of Pech" ("Pech" means tick in Mayan). The name was given to the site in the 1950s when there were quite a few ticks in the area. The ruins date back to between 650 and 900, though there are indications that the site was used prior to this time as well.

At the entrance, there's a small museum that displays a collection of artifacts recovered from the site and provides insight into the Cahal Pech social structure. It also has a small model of the old city, as well as a skeleton recovered from one of the graves here.

Admission to the museum and ruins is BZ$10 (US$5), and the site is open daily from 8am to 5pm. Be sure to ask for a copy of the very informative guide to the site. To reach Cahal Pech, walk or drive up toward the San Ignacio Resort Hotel (p. 227), continuing on around the curve for a few hundred yards until you pass the soccer field. Turn left here and climb the hill towards the ruins. The entrance to the ruins is beyond a large thatched building that houses the Cahal Pech disco. It's about a 20-minute walk.

XUNANTUNICH ✿✿   Although you may have trouble pronouncing it (say "soo-nahn-too-*neetch*"), Xunantunich is an impressive, well excavated, and easily accessible Mayan site. The name translates as "maiden of the rocks." The main pyramid here, El Castillo, rises to 127 feet (38m) and is clearly visible from the Western Highway as you approach. It's a steep climb, but the view from the top is amazing—don't miss it. You'll be able to make out the twin border towns of Benque Viejo, Belize, and Melchor de Menchos, Guatemala. On the east side of the pyramid, near the top, is a remarkably well-preserved stucco frieze.

Down below in the temple forecourt, archaeologists found three magnificent stelae portraying rulers of the region. These have been moved to the protection of the small, on-site museum, yet the years and ravages of weather have made most of the carvings difficult to decipher. Xunantunich was a thriving Mayan city about the same time as Altun Ha, in the Classic Period, about 600 to 900.

The visitor center at the entrance contains a beautiful scale model of the old city, as well as a replica of the original frieze. Open daily from 8am to 4pm, the site charges an admission of BZ$10 (US$5). Xunantunich is located 6½ miles past San Ignacio on the road to Benque Viejo. To reach the ruins, you must cross the Mopan River aboard a tiny hand-cranked car-ferry in the village of San José Succotz. You may be able to watch colorfully dressed women washing clothes in the river as you are cranked across by the ferryman. After crossing the river, it is a short, but dusty and vigorous, uphill walk to the ruins. If you've got your own

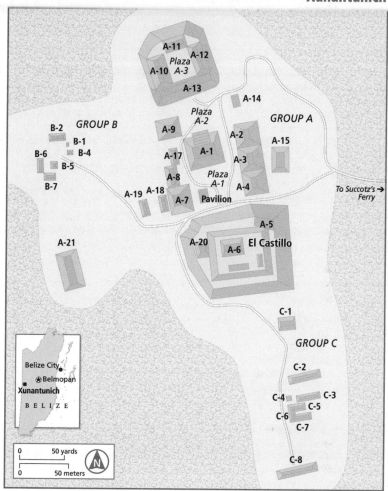

vehicle, you can take it across on the ferry and drive right to the ruins. To get here by bus, take any bus bound for Benque Viejo and get off in San José Succotz.

CHECHEM HA This ancient Mayan burial cave was discovered by accident when a local hunter, Antonio Morales, went chasing after his errant dog. When the cave was explored, a cache of Mayan artifacts, including many large, fully preserved pots, was discovered within the cave. Archaeologists estimate the relics could have been placed here over 2,000 years ago. This cave is one of only two in the area with an elaborate altar used for ceremonial purposes by the religious and ruling classes. Chechem Hah, which means "Cave of Poisonwood Water," is privately owned by the Morales family, and admission is only allowed with a pre-arranged guided tour.

Chechem Ha is located 10 miles (16km) south of Benque Viejo, on a dirt road that is recommended only for four-wheel-drive vehicles. Ideally, you should make a reservation in advance, although it's often hard to contact and confirm with the Morales family; their phone number is (📞 **820-4063.** If you receive no response, you can usually drive out to the entrance any morning and arrange the tour directly with the Morales family beforehand. The cost of a 45-minute tour is BZ$50 (US$25) for up to three people. You can also visit Chechem Ha on an organized tour with one of the local agencies working with the Morales family. Almost every hotel and tour agency in the area can arrange this for you, although they tend to charge a little bit more for their efforts.

A short hike from the entrance, the Chechem Ha Falls make a refreshing spot to wash and cool off after clambering around inside the caves. Also close to Chechem Ha is **Vaca Falls,** a beautiful and remote waterfall that's often combined with a visit to the cave, or a destination in itself.

RIVER TOURS

For much of Belize's history, the rivers were the main highways. The Mayans used them for trading, and British loggers used them to move mahogany and logwood. If you're interested, you can explore the Cayo District's two rivers—the Macal and Mopan—by canoe, kayak, and inner tube. Throughout most of the year, the waters in these rivers are easily navigable both up- and downstream. However, during the rainy season, things can change drastically—and fast. I've heard of a few flash floods, and even one story of water nearly reaching the road on the Hawksworth Bridge.

Still, for the most part, trips are leisurely, with plenty of places to stop for a quick swim or land excursion. During the rainy season (July–Sept), white-water kayaking is available, although it's not very consistent. Inflatable kayaks are a much more common and dependable option, not requiring nearly as much technical proficiency or water.

Most tours put in upstream on the Macal River somewhere around Chaa Creek (p. 231) or duPlooy's (p. 232) and then float leisurely downstream. The trip can take anywhere from 1 to 3 hours, depending on how much time you spend paddling, floating, or stopping to hike or swim. Both of these hotels offer this service, as well as a host of operators in San Ignacio. For its part, the Mopan River is more easily accessible in many ways, since Benque Viejo Road borders it in many places. The Mopan is well suited for inflatable kayaks and inner tubes.

In addition to most of the tour operators listed above, you can contact **Toni's River Adventures** (📞 824-3292) or **David's Adventure Tours** (📞 824-3674). If you want to go inner tubing, contact the folks at the **Trek Stop** (📞 823-2265).

Both of Cayo's principal rivers are great for swimming. On the Macal River you can join the locals right in town where the river is treated as a free laundry, car wash, horse and dog wash, and swimming hole. However, you'll do better to head upstream. The further upstream you head, the more isolated and clear the swimming holes become.

Another alternative is to head downriver about 1½ miles (2.4km) to a spot called **Branch Mouth,** where the different-colored waters of the Macal and Mopan rivers converge. Branch Mouth is a favorite picnic spot, with shady old trees clinging to the riverbanks. There's even a rope swing from one of the trees. The road is dusty, so you'll be especially happy to go for a swim here. Further upstream, on both the Macal and Mopan rivers, are numerous swimming holes.

OTHER ADVENTURE ACTIVITIES & NATURAL WONDERS

BELIZE BOTANIC GARDENS 🌸🌸   Located next to duPlooy's (p. 232) and run by the same family, the Belize Botanic Gardens (📞 **824-3101;**

River Race

While it's still possible to navigate the Belize River all the way to Belize City—the Macal and Mopan rivers join and become the Belize River—this is not generally something tourists get to do. Still, each year in early March, scores of three-person canoe teams undertake the long 180-mile (290km) paddle from San Ignacio to Belize City in the **Ruta Maya Belize River Challenge.** Teams gather in San Ignacio below the Hawksworth Bridge on March 5 and thousands of people line the banks of the river for the start. The finish line, fittingly enough, is the Swing Bridge in Belize City. It takes between 3 and 4 days to complete the course, with the teams scheduled to arrive in Belize City on or around Baron Bliss Day, on March 9.

www.belizebotanic.org) is a sprawling collection of local and imported tropical fauna. They have an excellent mix of fruit trees, palms, bromeliads, and bamboos, all well laid out whether or not you are taking a self-guided or guided tour. The orchid house is not to be missed, with its beautiful collection of orchids and sculpted waterfall wall. The gardens are open daily from 7am to 5pm. Admission is BZ$5 (US$2.50). Guided tours cost BZ$15 (US$7.50) per person, including the entrance fee. You can also buy a helpful self-guided tour booklet for BZ$15 (US$7.50), and even take a leisurely horse and buggy ride through the lovely gardens for BZ$20 (US$10) per person.

BARTON CREEK CAVE ⋒   This is one of the less strenuous and demanding caves to explore. The trip is conducted by canoe, and while there are a few tight squeezes and areas with low ceilings, in general you won't get as wet (you'll stay dry, in fact) or claustrophobic here as you will at many of the other caves in Belize. Barton Creek itself is navigable for nearly a mile inside the cave. Along the way, by the light of headlamps and strong flashlights, you'll see wonderful natural formations, a large gallery, and numerous Mayan artifacts, including several skeletons, believed to be the remains of ritual sacrifices. A skull sits prominently atop a natural bridge, but it actually seems likely that a local tour operator moved that skull there to heighten the dramatic effect. You can climb along the dry edges of the cave in certain parts.

There's a BZ$10 (US$5) fee to visit the site, but that doesn't include the canoe trip or transportation. Tours out of San Ignacio average around BZ$50 to BZ$70 (US$25–US$35) per person, not including the entrance fee. Barton Creek Cave is located just off the Pine Ridge Road, about 4 miles (6km) from the Western Highway. Visits to Barton Creek Cave are often combined with a stop at the Green Hills Butterfly Ranch (see "Mountain Pine Ridge & Caracol," later in this chapter).

HORSEBACK RIDING   If you enjoy horseback riding, there's some wonderful terrain in this area. Rides can be combined with visits to jungle waterfalls and swimming holes, as well as nearby Mayan ruins. **Easy Rider** (© 824-3734; easyrider@btl.net) offers jungle, valley, and ruins trips for around BZ$80 (US$40) per person per day, or BZ$50 (US$25) for a half-day. Call them for free pickup in San Ignacio.

Alternatively, you can contact the folks at **Mountain Equestrian Trails** (© 820-4041; www.metbelize.com), who have one of the better stables and horse riding operations in the Cayo District. Also, keep in mind that most lodges in the area offer horseback riding, so ask at your hotel or lodge first.

IX CHEL FARM & THE PANTI RAINFOREST MEDICINE TRAIL ⚔

Ix Chel is the Mayan goddess of healing. Located directly between the Chaa Creek and the Macal River Jungle Camp, Ix Chel Farm was a pioneering tropical plant research center operated by Drs. Rosita Arvigo and Greg Shropshire. Rosita studied traditional herbal medicine with Don Elijio Panti, a local Mayan medicine man and a folk hero in Belize. Panti died in February 1996 at the estimated age of 104. Here on the farm, they built a trail through the forest to share with visitors the fascinating medicinal values of many of the tropical forest's plants. At the end, there is a full-scale replica of Don Panti's thatch-and-bamboo-hut clinic.

There's a small gift shop at the farm that features local crafts, T-shirts, and several relevant books, including Arvigo's *Sastun: My Apprenticeship with a Mayan Healer*. You'll also find Ix Chel's line of herbal concentrates, salves, and teas called Rainforest Remedies.

Visits to Ix Chel Farm and the Medicine Trail, along with a tour of Chaa Creek's Natural History Museum and their Blue Morpho Butterfly Breeding project, cost BZ$16 (US$8). You can easily spend 3 hours visiting all three attractions. Call ⓒ 824-2037 for reservations.

MOUNTAIN BIKING   If your preferred activity is mountain biking, you can go on an organized tour or rent bikes in San Ignacio. From San Ignacio, a great ride is out to El Pilar ruins. You can also ride out to Xunantunich; however, that ride is mostly on the main highway. Mountain bike rentals should cost around BZ$5 (US$2.50) per hour, or BZ$30 to BZ$50 (US$15–US$25) per day. **Tropicool,** 30A Burns Ave. (ⓒ 824-3052), is a good place to rent a bike.

Be careful, the hills here are steep, and the heat and humidity can be overwhelming. Take (and drink) lots of water, and try to avoid pedaling during the middle of the day.

A SPA   If you want some serious pampering, or a soothing massage after some hard-core adventure, head to the **Spa at Chaa Creek** ⚔⚔ (ⓒ 824-2037; www.chaacreek.com). A wide range of treatments are offered, including a hydrating manicure (BZ$56/US$28), a full body polish (BZ$130/US$65), and a 90-minute aromatherapy massage (BZ$210/US$105). Multiday spa packages are also available. The spa itself is quite lovely, set on a high hill above the Chaa Creek hotel (p. 231), and the equipment and facilities are top-notch.

TROPICAL WINGS NATURE CENTER ⚔   Located just off the main road at Mile Marker 71½ near the village of San José Succotz is this small attraction. You'll find an enclosed butterfly garden with scores of brightly colored and varied species flitting about. There's also a butterfly breeding center, as well as an open-air medicinal plant nature trail. Hummingbird feeders ensure that you'll be buzzed by these frenetic flighty creatures. This place is open daily from 9am to 5pm; admission is BZ$5 (US$2.50). Call ⓒ 823-2265 for more information.

SHOPPING

Probably the best stocked gift shop in this region, if not the whole country, can be found at **Caesar's Place** (ⓒ 824-2341; www.belizegifts.com) about 7 miles (11km) east of San Ignacio. These folks have a smaller show room right in San Ignacio called the **Black Rock Gift Shop** on Burns Avenue (ⓒ 824-3770). However, I find the prices at both their outlets quite high, and similar goods can be found much less expensively at other shops. A good alternative in town is **Arts & Crafts Of Central America,** 24 Burns Ave. (ⓒ 824-2253).

Throughout Belize, and especially in Cayo, you will see slate carvings of Mayan hieroglyphs. If you're in the area, it's worth a visit to one of the sources, the **Garcia Sisters.** This family of artisans runs an interesting little museum-cum-craft shop. It's located outside of San Antonio village on the road to Mountain Pine Ridge (see "Mountain Pine Ridge & Caracol," later in this chapter, for more information).

WHERE TO STAY
EXPENSIVE
San Ignacio Resort Hotel ⟨R⟩   This small full-service resort is easily the most comfortable and luxurious option right in town. The San Ignacio Hotel is located a couple hundred yards up the steep hill, past the police station, at the west end of the bridge into town. Set on a high ridge above the Macal River, it has magnificent views of the lazy river below and surrounding forests. The rooms are all spacious, modern, and well kept. The best rooms come with a private balcony, so be sure to request one.

The hotel has a swimming pool, basketball court, and convention and conference facilities. There are jungle trails, a small iguana farm, a riverside beach and swimming hole, and a medicinal trail. A host of guided hikes and tours are offered, both on the grounds and further afield. There's also a modest gift shop and a good restaurant and bar with great views from its terrace. The newest addition here is a small casino, which is equally popular with locals and guests.

18 Buena Vista St. (P.O. Box 33), San Ignacio, Cayo. ⓒ **800/448-2627** in the U.S., or 824-2034. Fax 824-2134. www.sanignaciobelize.com. 24 units. BZ$220 double (US$110) double. Rates slightly lower in the off season. AE, MC, V. **Amenities:** 2 restaurants; bar; lounge; midsize outdoor pool; tour desk; laundry service. *In room:* A/C, TV.

MODERATE
Cahal Pech Village Resort ⟨R⟩ ⟨Value⟩   Set on a hillside on the outskirts of town, this hotel has a spectacular view of San Ignacio and is a stone's throw away from the Cahal Pech ruins. Accommodations can be had either in the main building or in one of the 14 thatch roof individual bungalows. All are clean, spacious, and well maintained, and feature carved Mayan wall hangings and colorful Guatemalan bedspreads. The rooms are a bit newer, have larger bathrooms, and come with air-conditioning. They also are higher up, and thus have better views from their private balconies—particularly the rooms on the third floor. On the other hand, the bungalows give a wonderful sense of privacy, and are set amidst well-tended gardens on the hillside below the main building. There's a large, open-air restaurant on the second floor of the main building, where guests gather for meals and to trade travel tales. The hotel is located just next to the Cahal Pech disco, however, and this can be a bit of a problem if you want an early night's sleep on the weekend.

Cahal Pech Hill, San Ignacio, Cayo District. ⓒ **824-3740.** Fax 824-2225. www.cahalpech.com. 35 units. BZ$100 (US$50) double bungalow; BZ$120 (US$60) double room. MC, V. **Amenities:** Restaurant; bar; lounge; mountain bike rental; tour desk; laundry service. *In room:* TV, no phone.

INEXPENSIVE
San Ignacio is a very popular budget travel destination, and there are a host of good options in town. During the high season, reservations are recommended for the more popular places. At other times, backpackers might prefer to arrive in town early enough to visit a few places, and see which place gives the best bang for the buck. In addition to the places listed below, **Tropicool,** 30A Burns Ave. (ⓒ **824-3052**), consistently gets good marks. Those looking for accommodations with the trappings of a business-class hotel but at budget prices could

check out either the **New Balmoral Hotel,** 17 Burns Ave. (© **824-2024**), or the **Plaza Hotel,** 4A Burns Ave. (© **824-3332**). While these are clean and comfortable options, they lack any sense of style or individuality.

Cosmos Camping (© **824-2116**) is a campground on the road leading out toward Branch Mouth and Las Casitas, where you can pitch your tent for BZ$8 (US$4) per day. There are showers and communal bathrooms that are kept clean, and the river is just across a field. This place is about a 15-minute hike from downtown San Ignacio, doable for a backpacker. They've even added some simple cabins here as well. Still, I prefer the camping options further outside of town, including Clarissa Falls Cottages and the Trek Stop, or Midas Tropical Resort, which is on the same road before Cosmos. See below for more information on all of these options.

Hi-Et Beyond the obvious but playful name, this hotel has a funky, run-down charm. The Hi-Et is family-run, clean, and secure. The three-story wooden building housing this place is located on a corner In the heart of the town, and features a wraparound veranda and some interesting gingerbread trim work. There's a room set in a dormer jutting through the roof and constituting the third-floor here. While this room is pretty small, it's also quite private and charming. This is one of the best of the bottom-of-the-budget hotels in San Ignacio, and it's often full.

12 West St., San Ignacio, Cayo District. © 824-2828. 5 units (all with shared bathroom). BZ$16 (US$8) double. MC, V. **Amenities:** Laundry service. *In room:* No phone.

Martha's Guest House This small guesthouse is located in the heart of San Ignacio, above a popular little restaurant. The vibe here is somewhere between that of a homestay and a youth hostel. All of the rooms are spacious and immaculate. The more expensive rooms have their own bathrooms and cable televisions, although there are a couple of common lounge areas, where guests in the budget rooms can hang out and watch TV as well. The fourth-floor suite is quite large, and features a similarly large balcony with wonderful views of the town. It also comes with its own kitchenette, making it a good option for families.

10 West St. (P.O. Box 140), San Ignacio, Cayo District. © 824-3647. Fax 824-2732. www.marthasbelize.com. 11 units (5 with private bathroom). BZ$60 (US$30) double with shared bathroom; BZ$90 (US$45) double with private bathroom; BZ$130 (US$65) suite. AE, MC, V. **Amenities:** Restaurant; bar; 2 lounges; tour desk; laundry service. *In room:* No phone.

Midas Tropical Resort *(Value)* Though Midas is just a short walk from downtown San Ignacio, it feels a world away. The rooms are an excellent value when stacked up against other in-town options. The round Mayan-style cottages have thatch roofs and screen walls and there are also some wood cabins on raised stilts with corrugated roofs. All are comfortable, clean, and spacious, with ceiling fans and plenty of screened windows for ventilation. The wooden cabins come with their own private veranda, which I like. The hotel has ample grounds with plenty of shady trees. Camping here will run you BZ$8 (US$4) per person. The Macal River is only a stroll away down a grassy lane, and you can spend the day lounging on the little beach on the riverbank. The restaurant here serves good Belizean and international cuisine at excellent prices. To reach Midas, walk north out of town on Savannah Street, which is 1 block east of Burns Avenue. The hotel is only about half a mile (.8km) from the center of town.

Branch Mouth Rd., San Ignacio, Cayo District. © 824-3172. Fax 824-3845. www.midasbelize.com. 13 units. BZ$68 (US$34) double. Rates lower in the off season. MC, V. **Amenities:** Restaurant; tour desk; laundry service. *In room:* No phone.

WHERE TO DINE
MODERATE

Running W Steak House & Restaurant ★★ STEAKHOUSE/BELIZEAN

This restaurant is located in the San Ignacio Resort Hotel and is affiliated with Belize's largest beef and cattle operation, its namesake. Try the Mayan Steak, marinated strips of tenderloin grilled and served with fresh tortillas. If you want something more traditional, order the 16-ounce Porterhouse. There are also fish and chicken dishes, as well as some Belizean standards. The dining room is large and comfortable, with plenty of varnished wood. A few wrought iron tables line an outdoor patio and make a great place to have lunch with a jungle view, or dinner under the stars.

18 Buena Vista St., in the San Ignacio Resort Hotel. (✆ 824-2034. Reservations recommended. Main courses BZ$14–BZ$44 (US$7–US$22). AE, MC, V. Daily 7am–11pm.

INEXPENSIVE

In addition to the places listed below, **Hannah's,** 5 Burns Ave. (✆ **824-3014**), is another excellent place, serving Belizean, Indian, and Thai cuisine.

Café Sol ★ Finds INTERNATIONAL/VEGETARIAN

This simple, downtown restaurant and coffeehouse features an eclectic menu ranging from a Thai noodle salad to jerk chicken to soy burgers. You can also get burritos and quesadillas, and a range of pasta dishes. Be sure to check the chalkboard for the daily specials. I like the few tables on the front porch, although most of these are just plastic lawn furniture. If you want a sturdier wooden table—painted in bright primary colors—head inside, where you'll also find a small Internet cafe and a helpful corkboard with a variety of tour and hotel brochures and information. This is a great place for everything from breakfast to a coffee break to a filling meal.

Far West St. (✆ 824-4853. Main courses BZ$9–BZ$16 (US$4.50–US$8). MC, V. Tues–Sat 7am–2:30pm and 6:30–9pm; Sun 7am–2:30pm.

Erva's BELIZEAN/MEXICAN

There are scores of places in San Ignacio serving local cuisine, but this place is a local favorite. Erva is an excellent cook and congenial hostess. In addition to traditional Belizean and Mexican standards, you can get pizza and some seafood dishes here. Still, it's the stew chicken and rice and beans that brings folks in the door, and keeps them (and me) coming back for more. Erva's is located on the ground floor of the Pacz Hotel.

4 Far West St. (✆ 824-2821. Main courses BZ$6–BZ$16 (US$3–US$8). MC, V. Daily 7am–10pm.

Eva's Restaurant & Bar Finds BELIZEAN/INTERNATIONAL

Above and beyond dishing up good economical meals, Eva's serves as San Ignacio's central meeting place and unofficial tourist bureau. Hotel and tour advertisements cover the walls here, and brochures are abundant. Owner Bob Jones is a wealth of information about the area, in case what you're looking for is not listed. If you want to get a group of people together to rent a taxi or canoe or to defray the costs of a tour, let Bob know—he'll try to put you in touch with other like-minded folks. The social scene is the main draw here, but you can get hearty servings of well-prepared Belizean and Mexican standards.

22 Burns Ave. (✆ 804-2267. www.evasonline.com. BZ$6–BZ$14 (US$3–US$7). MC, V. Daily 7am–midnight.

Martha's Restaurant & Pizza House BELIZEAN/PIZZA

The restaurant at this popular budget hotel is equally popular. The homemade pizzas are excellent. You have your choice of a variety of toppings, and you can build your own pizza. You can also get everything from burgers to burritos to vegetarian entrees, as well as local Mayan specialties, like chaya tamales, made from cornmeal and a locally grown green. This is a great place for breakfast, including the typical Belizean breakfast of fry jacks, eggs, and beans, as well as excellent huevos rancheros and strong coffee. Try to grab one of the outdoor tables, and be sure to thank Martha herself.

10 West St. ⓒ 824-3647. Main courses BZ$22–BZ$40 (US$11–US$20). MC, V. Daily 7am–10pm.

Maxim's Chinese Restaurant CHINESE   This is probably your best bet for Chinese food in San Ignacio. The menu is heavy on chop suey, chow mein, and fried rice. However you can get spicier dishes like Kung Pao chicken and assorted curries. There's also a host of vegetarian dishes, and takeout is available.

23 Far West St. ⓒ 824-2283. Main courses BZ$6–BZ$20 (US$3–US$10). MC, V. Daily 10am–midnight.

Serendib Restaurant ⭐ BELIZEAN/SRI LANKAN/CHINESE   This pleasant little restaurant is an unexpected and eclectic surprise in the tiny town of San Ignacio. Owner Hantley Pieris is from Sri Lanka and came to Belize years ago with the British army. He now runs a restaurant serving excellent curries in the style of his native country. You can get beef or chicken curry with yellow or fried rice and potato salad. In addition, there are sandwiches, burgers, chow mein, and fried fish on the menu. Breakfasts are also excellent, and on hot days, this is a great place to get an afternoon ice cream treat or cold coffee drink.

27 Burns Ave. ⓒ 824-2302. BZ$6–BZ$22 (US$3–US$11). MC, V. Mon–Sat 8am–3pm and 6–11pm.

SAN IGNACIO AFTER DARK

San Ignacio is a pretty sleepy town. Most travelers chose to spend quiet evenings at **Eva's Restaurant** (see "Where to Dine," above), trading tales and planning adventures with new friends. There are several bars around the downtown area. Most nights, but especially on weekends, the most happening spot in town can be found up the hill at **Cahal Pech Tavern** (ⓒ 824-3380). This place burned down a couple years ago, but has arisen from the ashes and is once again rocking the town and Mayan spirits to a loud mix of reggae, soca, and Punta Rock. Alternatively, you can find out if there's live music at **Caesar's Place** (ⓒ 824-2341), which is the home turf of the Mango Jam band, a local jazz outfit. Caesar's is located out on the Western Highway, about 7 miles (11km) east of San Ignacio.

If you're the gambling type, you'll want to head to the **Princess Casino** (ⓒ 824-4099), located at the San Ignacio Resort Hotel, 18 Buena Vista St.

NEARBY LODGES & RETREATS
ON THE ROAD TO BENQUE VIEJO & THE GUATEMALAN BORDER

While San Ignacio is the regional hub and does make a good base for side trips, the real attractions here are up the rivers and in the forests. Within a few miles of San Ignacio are a host of lodges set somewhat off the beaten path, where you can canoe down clear rivers past 4-foot (1.2m) iguanas sunning themselves on the rocks, ride horses to Mayan ruins, hike jungle trails, and spot scores of beautiful birds and, occasionally, other wild animals. Out on the road to Caracol and Mountain Pine Ridge, there are more of these lodges. Except for the true budget traveler, I highly recommend that you stay at one of the lodges listed below while you're in the area. A few of the lodges can be reached by public bus from San Ignacio, though you may have up to a 20-minute walk after getting off the bus, so consider taking a taxi or arranging pickup in town. All the lodges offer a wide range of active adventures and tours to all the principal sites in the area.

Very Expensive

In addition to the places listed below, **Ek' Tun** ⚜⚜ (℗ **820-3002;** www.ektun belize.com) is a unique, isolated, and gorgeous retreat with just two individual cottages set on the banks of the Macal River that can only be reached by boat.

Mopan River Resort ⚜⚜   This lovely and interesting resort is set right on the banks of the Mopan River just across from the border town of Benque Viejo. In fact, you must reach the resort by crossing the river in the resort's little diesel-powered ferry. The resort is run as a super-all inclusive, meaning aside from a very limited number of entrance and border crossing fees (if you go to Tikal), you should have virtually no out-of-pocket expenses beyond the hotel rates, which include all food, drinks, tips, and taxes, as well as a full menu of tours and activities, and transfers to and from the international airport.

The 12 individual bungalows are spread along the hotel's lush property lining the banks of the river, so all have a view of the flowing water. The bungalows are quite spacious, with high-pitched thatch roofs, varnished wood floors and walls, and plenty of dresser and closet space. I find the bathrooms just a tad small and not quite up to the luxurious standards set throughout the rest of the operation. Quite a few of the units come with two twin beds, so if you want a true king-size bed, be sure to specify. Three of the units are suites, and in addition to being larger, they come with a kitchenette and comfortable sitting area.

Given all that is included in the package prices, the rates are actually quite reasonable. Still, this is not the place for independent and spontaneous travelers. Tours are scheduled on a rotating basis, with the rotation repeating every 6 days or so. So, if you absolutely must visit Tikal, make sure it's on the rotation during your stay. Dinners are usually served buffet-style. Breakfasts are a la carte, and lunches are often packed lunches served during the day's tour or activity. Overall, the food is quite well done and varied. A minimum stay of 3 nights is required. The resort is closed July through October.

Riverside North, Benque Viejo del Carmen, Cayo District. ℗ **823-2047.** Fax 823-3272. www.mopanriver resort.com. 12 units. BZ$1,340–BZ$1,508 (US$670–US$754) per person for a 3-night package, double occupancy. Rates are all-inclusive. DISC, MC, V. **Amenities:** Restaurant; bar; lounge; outdoor pool; tour desk; laundry service; nonsmoking rooms. *In room:* A/C, TV, stocked minibar, coffeemaker, hair dryer, safe, no phone.

Chaa Creek ⚜⚜⚜ *(Finds)*   This is definitely the premier lodging choice in this neck of the woods, and one of the nicest hotels in the country. Much loving care has gone into creating the beautiful grounds and cottages here. Located on a high, steep bank over the Macal River, this is one of the oldest of the original jungle lodges in the Cayo District, and it's only improved with age. All of the thatched-roof cottages are artistically decorated with local and Guatemalan textiles and handcrafts. Each comes with a quiet porch or balcony area set amid the flowering gardens. The choicest rooms here are the treetop suites, which are quite large, and feature a king bed, a sunken living-room area, and a wraparound deck fitted with a sunken Jacuzzi. Of the standard rooms, nos. 1 and 2 are my favorites.

The newest addition at Chaa Creek is a lovely little full-service spa. They also have an informative little natural history museum, as well as a Blue Morpho butterfly breeding project. The guides here are well trained and knowledgeable. Chaa Creek has also taken over the former Panti Medicine trail and the neighboring Ixchel Farm, which you can explore with a guide or with a self-guided trail map. There are canoes and mountain bikes available, and horseback rides can always be arranged. Over 250 bird species have been spotted within a 5-mile (8km) radius of the lodge. Mick and Lucy Fleming, who originally began farming this land in 1977, are the engaging hosts here, and much of the food served

---

Moments **Los Finados**

On November 2, the residents of Benque Viejo del Carmen celebrate **Los Finados,** a local version of El Día de los Muertos (The Day of the Dead), or All Souls' Day. Families visit the local cemetery, where graves are spruced up and adorned with flowers and votive candles. Many families set up a makeshift altar for their dead at home or on the front lawn. *Bollos* are prepared of cornmeal dough stuffed with chicken and a local purple bean, the *ixpelon.* Local children make jack-o-lanterns out of hollowed-out squash or even grapefruit. At night the cemetery is alight with the flicker from hundreds of candles.

---

in the lovely screened-in dining room is organically grown on the hotel's own farm. There's also a separate open-air bar and lounge area, where guests congregate most evenings before and after diner.

To reach Chaa Creek, drive 5 miles (8km) west from San Ignacio and watch for the sign on your left. It's another couple of miles down a rough dirt road from the main highway.

Off the road to Benque Viejo (P.O. Box 53, San Ignacio), Cayo District. © 824-2037. Fax 824-2501. www. chaacreek.com. 23 units. BZ$370 (US$185) double; BZ$430–BZ$560 (US$215–US$280) suite. AE, MC, V. **Amenities:** Restaurant; bar; lounge; small, well-equipped spa; bike rental; tour desk; laundry service; non-smoking rooms. *In room:* No phone.

Expensive

duPlooy's 🔍   This family-run lodge is situated overlooking the Macal River, with jungle-covered limestone cliffs opposite. Jungle covers the surrounding hills. DuPlooy's has everything from clean budget rooms with shared bathrooms to luxurious new bungalows and a two-story casita with a large Jacuzzi and wraparound balcony. This, combined with the stunning location and personalized attention, make duPlooy's one of Cayo's most popular jungle lodges. My favorite rooms here are the three spacious bungalows, which come with king-size bed, futon couch, and large wooden veranda. The older lodge rooms are housed in three stone-and-stucco buildings with tile roofs, and have aged well. Each has two queen beds and a screened porch area. The Pink House is a seven-room, two-bathroom ranch house, well suited to families or budget travelers.

The open-air bar features a spacious deck overlooking the river. And one of the nicest features here is an elevated walkway running at the level of the forest canopy, which connects much of the complex and also juts out into the forest, offering up wonderful opportunities for bird-watching. The newest addition is the neighboring **Belize Botanic Gardens** 🔍🔍, which provides even greater bird-watching opportunities, in addition to all of the tropical flora. There's a beach on the river, as well as several trails through the forest. Horses and canoes are available for rent.

To get here, head out of town on the road to Benque Viejo; the turnoff for duPlooy's is the same as that for Chaa Creek, and it is well marked. DuPlooy's is a bit farther on the same dirt road, but be sure to take the right fork and follow the signs.

Off the road to Benque Viejo (P.O. Box 180, San Ignacio), Cayo District. © 824-3101. Fax 824-3301. www. duplooys.com. 20 units (7 with shared bathroom). BZ$120 (US$60) double with shared bathroom; BZ$260–BZ$360 (US$130–US$180) double; BZ$500 (US$250) double casita. AE, MC, V. **Amenities:** Restaurant; bar; lounge; bike rental; tour desk; laundry service. *In room:* No phone.

Moderate

Black Rock Jungle River Lodge ✿

So, you *really* want to get away from it all? Well, this is the place. To reach Black Rock, you travel 6 miles (10km) down a dirt road and a mile (1.6km) alongside the Macal River. The setting, and this specific section of the Macal River, is one of the nicest in the area. Swimming and inner tubing on the river from the lodge are excellent. The deluxe cabanas are truly beautiful, with stone floors, two queen beds, plenty of large screened windows, and views of the valley and river below. The standard cabanas and shared bathroom units are quite comfortable and beautifully situated as well. Meals are served family style in the large open-air dining room and main lodge area. Three meals a day will run you BZ$72 (US$36) per person, per day. This lodge is owned by the same folks who run Caesar's Place at Mile Marker 60 on the Western Highway; you can just get yourself dropped off there before continuing on to Black Rock. If you're driving, take the turnoff for Chaa Creek and duPlooy's, and continue on beyond duPlooy's.

Off the road to Benque Viejo (P.O. Box 48, San Ignacio), Cayo District. © 824-2341. Fax 824-3449. www.black rocklodge.com. 13 units (2 with shared bathroom). BZ$100 (US$50) double with shared bathroom; BZ$190–BZ$290 (US$95–US$145) double. AE, MC, V. **Amenities:** Restaurant; tour desk; laundry service. *In room:* No phone.

Log Cab-Inns

These unique, and seemingly out-of-place, log cabin bungalows are located about a mile from San Ignacio on the road to Benque Viejo and Xunantunich. The cabins are all clean and spacious, with two double beds, a plywood table, plastic chairs, and a small black-and-white television. The cabins are separated by neat cement paths through the former cattle land that is planted with a wealth of fruit trees and tropical flowers. There's a small screened-in dining room, bar, lounge, and gift shop. The newest addition here is a midsize kidney-shaped pool. The local family who runs these cabins is very friendly; they will help arrange a variety of tours and will usually provide complimentary rides into and from town.

Benque Viejo Rd., Mile Marker 68, Cayo District. © 824-3367. Fax 824-2289. www.logcabinns-belize.com. 9 units. BZ$130 (US$65) double. MC, V. **Amenities:** Restaurant; outdoor pool; tour desk; laundry service. *In room:* Coffeemaker, no phone.

Macal River Jungle Camp (Finds)

Run by the folks at Chaa Creek Cottages, this deluxe campsite is a great choice for those who want to be close to nature, but like to have a few frills and easy accessibility. These 10 spacious units are all set on raised platforms among the forest trees. Each comes with between two to four single beds, as well as a couple of kerosene lanterns. There's a small sitting area or front porch, with an oil lamp and a couple of chairs. Meals are served in a central open thatched roof structure, which also has some hammocks for hanging out. The communal bath and shower areas are clean and well maintained. The river is down a short path from the campsite, and Ix Chel Farm and Chaa Creek are nearby. Guests at the tent camp can rent canoes, head over for meals a la carte, or sign up for any tours offered at Chaa Creek. Overall, this is a pretty plush camping experience, but you may be asked to help wash your own dishes.

Off the road to Benque Viejo (P.O. Box 53, San Ignacio), Cayo District. © 824-2037. Fax 824-2501. www. belizecamp.com. 10 tents. BZ$110 (US$55) per person. Rates include breakfast and dinner. Rates slightly lower during the off season. AE, MC, V. **Amenities:** Restaurant; tour desk; laundry service. *In room:* No phone.

Inexpensive

Clarissa Falls Resort (Value)

Clarissa Falls, which are really more rapids than waterfalls, and the jade-green waters of the Mopan River are the backdrop for this, one of my favorite budget lodgings in Cayo. Situated on an 800-acre (320 ha) working cattle ranch, there's a range of accommodations from one deluxe suite to a series of individual cabins to a dormitory-style bunkhouse. The individual cabins here are fairly basic, with cement floors, bamboo walls, simple beds, and little else. However, the spartan decor is more than compensated for by the beautiful surroundings of hilly pastures and river. The suite is quite nicely done and features a full kitchen and dining area. There's also a camping area here that even has a hookup for an RV.

Owner Chena Galvez is extremely personable. An open-air restaurant serving excellent Belizean and Mexican cuisine for very reasonable prices sits atop a small Mayan ruin. Boats and inner tubes can be rented and horseback riding is available. If you'd like to just visit for the day, you can swim in the river and picnic for BZ$2 (US$1), which is a very popular activity on weekends (if you crave peace and tranquillity, visit on a weekday). Clarissa Falls Resort is about a mile (1.6km) down a dirt road, off the highway about 4 miles (6km) west of San Ignacio. The bus to Benque Viejo will drop you at the turnoff.

Benque Viejo Rd., Mile Marker 70½ (P.O. Box 44, San Ignacio), Cayo District. ©/fax 824-3916. 12 units (11 with private bathroom). BZ$30 (US$15) per person in bunkhouse; BZ$80 (US$40) double; BZ$350 (US$175) suite; BZ$15 (US$7.50) per person to camp. MC, V. **Amenities:** Restaurant; tour desk; laundry service. *In room:* No phone.

The Trek Stop   This rustic little outpost is geared towards backpackers and adventure travelers. There are some simple cabins, as well as semi-permanent tents, and campsites. The wooden cabins are quite small, but they do come with a private little front porch, where you can sit and read a book. Guests can either eat at the little restaurant here, or cook their own food in the communal kitchen. A wide range of tours and activities is offered, and inner tubing on the Mopan River is one of their specialties. This place is very close to the ferry over to Xunantunich. The Trek Stop is located next to the Tropical Wings Nature Center, just off the main road about 6 miles (10km) west of San Ignacio.

Benque Viejo Rd., Mile Marker 71½. San José Succotz, Cayo District. © 823-2265. www.thetrekstop.com. 6 units (all with shared bathroom). BZ$40 (US$20) double cabin; BZ$28 (US$14) double tent; BZ$10 (US$5) per person camping. MC, V. **Amenities:** Restaurant; mountain bike rental; tour desk; laundry service. *In room:* No phone.

ON THE ROAD TO BULLET TREE FALLS

El Pilar 🐾🐾 (© 824-3612; www.marc.ucsb.edu/elpilar) was discovered in the 1970s, but real excavation and exploration didn't begin for another 20 years, and in fact it's barely begun. The site sits on a high hill some 900 feet (270m) above the Mopan River and is one of the largest Mayan settlements in Belize. Some say it even rivals Caracol. This ancient ceremonial city featured over 25 known plazas and covered some 100 acres (40 ha), straddling the Belize and Guatemala border. The site is quite large, but most visitors concentrate on Xaman Pilar (North Pilar) and Nohol Pilar (South Pilar). Pilar Poniente (West Pilar) is in Guatemala, a little less than a mile away. There are several well-marked and well-maintained trails through the site. While you can explore El Pilar by yourself—you can even download a very informative trail map from the above website—I still recommend hiring a local guide. Plan on spending at least 3 hours here, and realize you could easily spend a full day or two exploring this site. The sunsets from Plaza Ixim looking west to Pilar Poniente and the forested hills of Guatemala are spectacular.

El Pilar is located about 12 miles (19km) north of San Ignacio, past the village of Bullet Tree Falls. In addition to driving your own vehicle, several tour agencies in San Ignacio offer horseback or mountain bike tours out to El Pilar.

A Place to Stay in Bullet Tree Falls

In addition to the place listed below, I've gotten good reports about the new **Cohune Palms River Cabanas** (© 609-2738; www.cohunepalms.com), which has some simple cabins on the banks of the Mopan River.

Parrot's Nest   Located 3 miles (5km) outside of San Ignacio and operated by Fred Prost, who once ran the popular Seaside Guest House in Belize City, the Parrot's Nest features a couple of the most unique rooms in the Cayo District. Set on a 5-acre (2 ha) tropical plant farm on the banks of the Mopan River, this simple lodge consists of a few rustic wooden cabins. Two of these are set high on stilts, amongst the branches of a huge guanacaste tree. Only one of the units has a private bathroom, but the shared showers and toilets are kept immaculate. A host of tours and activities can be arranged. You can also just take an inner tube right from the lodge and spend some time floating on the river.

To get here, take Waight's Avenue west out of the center of San Ignacio. This turns into Bullet Tree Falls Road. If you arrange it in advance, the owners will often provide pickup, or a taxi should cost you around BZ$16 (US$8).

Bullet Tree Falls (P.O. Box 198, San Ignacio), Cayo District. © **820-4058**. www.parrot-nest.com. 6 units (5 with shared bathroom). BZ$80–BZ$100 (US$40–US$50) double. MC, V. **Amenities:** Restaurant; mountain bike rental; tour desk; laundry service. *In room:* No phone.

3 Mountain Pine Ridge & Caracol ⟨★⟨★

69 miles (111km) W of Belize City

Few people think of pine trees as being a tropical species, but you'll see plenty of them in Belize, especially in these rugged mountains. This 3,400-foot-tall (1,020m) ridge is a natural wonderland of spectacular waterfalls, wild orchids, parrots, keel-billed toucans, and other exotic flora and fauna. **Mountain Pine Ridge Forest Reserve, Hidden Valley Falls** (also called Thousand Foot Falls), **Five Sisters Falls,** and the **Río On Pools** and **Río Frío Caves** are all located in this area.

Continuing on through the Mountain Pine Ridge, you'll eventually come to **Caracol,** which is the largest of the Belizean Mayan ruins. Caracol was a major Classic Mayan center, rivaling and frequently battling nearby Tikal. Excavation is still in its infancy here, but the site is nonetheless impressive. At nearly 140 feet (420m), the main pyramid at Caracol remains the tallest man-made structure in Belize.

In 2000 and 2001 a pine beetle infestation ravaged the forests of the Mountain Pine Ridge reserve, killing as much as 60% of the total forest and leaving broad swaths totally barren with little more than rotting trunks sticking straight up for miles. Forests are amazingly resilient, and the forests here have started to recover. Still, you will notice the effects of this insect plague.

ESSENTIALS
GETTING THERE & DEPARTING
BY PLANE   The nearest airport to this region is in San Ignacio. See section 2, earlier in this chapter, for flight schedules and details. There is a private airstrip at Blancaneaux Lodge (p. 239) for charter flights to that hotel.

BY BUS   There is no regular bus service to the Mountain Pine Ridge area.

BY CAR   If you're driving to the Mountain Pine Ridge area from Belize City along the Western Highway, the first turnoff is at Georgeville, around Mile Marker 61. This is the quickest route if you're going deep into the Mountain

Pine Ridge area and to Caracol. There's another turnoff in the town of Santa Elena that will take you through Cristo Rey and San Antonio villages, as well as to some of the lodges listed below. Whichever road you take, at Mile Marker 10, you will come to the entrance to the Mountain Pine Ridge Forest Reserve. The guard will ask you where you are going, and if you have a reservation, but there is no fee to enter the reserve.

These roads are sometimes impassable in the wet season and are pretty bad even in the dry season, so don't even think about attempting the trip in anything less than a four-wheel-drive vehicle. Even though the distances seem relatively slight in terms of mileage, the going is slow, so allow plenty of driving time if you plan on visiting this area.

Tip: The difference in time and distance between these two turnoffs is negligible, as they meet up about 9 miles (14km) in from the Western Highway (12 miles/19km if you're coming via Cristo Rey Village and San Antonio Village).

GETTING AROUND
Your best bet for getting around this area is to have your own vehicle. Short of that, you can rely on your hotel or organized tours. Taxis can be called from San Ignacio and Santa Elena. For a cab, call **Cayo Taxi Association** at ⓒ **824-2196.** A cab from San Ignacio to Five Sisters Falls costs around BZ$90 to BZ$100 (US$45–US$50), and a cab from Philip S. W. Goldson International Airport in Belize City to Five Sisters costs BZ$250 (US$125).

ORIENTATION
Once the two entrance roads join up, there is basically one "major" road leading through the Mountain Pine Forest Reserve and on out to the Caracol ruins. This rough dirt road is alternately known as the Pine Ridge Road or the Chiquibil Road. Caracol, the Río On Pools, Río Frío Cave, and Five Sister Falls, are located either right on, or just off this road. Several spurs and assorted lesser roads head off towards some of the other attractions and destinations listed below. Everything is fairly well marked and signposted.

There are no major settlements in this area. The only town of any size and note is San Antonio Village, a quaint little Mayan village,

WHAT TO SEE & DO
The easiest way to visit Mountain Pine Ridge and its many attractions is on a guided tour out of San Ignacio or one of the nearby lodges. These tours average between BZ$50 and BZ$80 (US$25–US$40) per person for a half-day tour of Mountain Pine Ridge and a visit to one of the waterfalls, and about BZ$170 to BZ$240 (US$85–US$120) for a full-day guided trip to Caracol with lunch.

HORSEBACK RIDING There's wonderful terrain out here for horseback riding. Most horseback tours will take you to one or more of the major attractions in this area, or at least to some quiet swimming hole or isolated waterfall. Most of the hotels out here offer horseback riding tours. Alternatively, you can contact the folks at **Mountain Equestrian Trails** (ⓒ **820-4041;** www.met belize.com), who have one of the better stables and horse riding operations in the Cayo District. A half-day trip including lunch costs BZ$120 (US$60) per person; a full-day trip costs BZ$160 (US$80).

MOUNTAIN BIKING This region lends itself equally well to mountain biking. The same trails and dirt roads that are used by cars and horses are especially well suited for fat tire explorations. Most of the hotels in the region have bikes for

Map of the Mountain Pine Ridge region showing locations including El Pilar, Spanish Lookout, Belize River, Teakettle, San Ignacio, Santa Elena, Georgeville, Barton Creek, Actun Tunichil Muknal, Tapir Mountain Nature Reserve, Blue Hole Nat'l Park, Sibun Forest Reserve, Vaca Forest Reserve, Mountain Pine Ridge Forest Reserve, Chiquibul National Park, Caracol, and the Maya Mountains, with Guatemala to the west.

ACCOMMODATIONS & DINING ■
Blancaneaux Lodge **10**
Crystal Paradise Resort **1**
Five Sisters Lodge **9**
Hidden Valley Inn **8**
Mountain Equestrian Trails **5**
Pine Ridge Lodge **6**

ATTRACTIONS & SHOPPING ●
Caracol **14**
Five Sisters Falls **11**
Green Hills Butterfly Ranch
  & Botanical Collection **4**
Hidden Valley Falls **7**
Magaña Zaactunich
  Art Gallery **2**
Río Frío Cave **12**
Río On Pools **13**
Tanah Mayan Art Museum **3**

rent or free for guests. If not, you'll probably have to have them arrange it for you, or contact an agency in San Ignacio (see "San Ignacio," earlier in this chapter).

WILL NATURAL WONDERS NEVER CEASE?

WATERFALLS   There is a wealth of waterfalls in this region. Perhaps my favorite are the falls found at the **Río On Pools** ✿✿. This is a series of falls and pools somewhat reminiscent of Ocho Rios in Jamaica. There's a little entrance hut and parking lot when you enter the area. From here, some concrete steps lead straight down a very steep hill to the base of the falls. While the views and swimming are fine at the bottom, it's a very strenuous hike back up, and I personally think you'll find better pools and views by hiking a few minutes upstream. Here you'll find numerous pools and rapids flowing between big rocks. Many of these rocks are perfect for sunbathing. This place can get crowded on weekends, when locals come for family picnics and getaways. The Río On Pools are located at around Mile Marker 18½ of the Pine Ridge Road. There is no entrance fee.

You can also visit the **Five Sister Falls** ✿✿, a lovely series of cascading falls, that divide into five distinct side-by-side cascades just above the riverside beach and bar area of the Five Sisters Lodge (p. 240). If you are not staying at the lodge, you may visit the falls for BZ$3 (US$1.50). For an extra charge of BZ$5 (US$2.50), a funicular will take you to and from the base of the falls, where the hotel has a little beach area and several natural swimming holes. There are some nature trails you can hike, and a small snack bar, restrooms, and changing facilities. There's even a wonderful open-air thatch palapa on the banks of the river strung with hammocks making a compelling call for an afternoon siesta.

RIO FRIO CAVE   This high vaulted cave is about 200 yards (180m) long and open at both ends, with a lazy creek flowing through it. There's a path leading through the cave, and several hiking trails through the forests surrounding it. This is a good cave for those who might normally find the thought of spelunking too claustrophobic for comfort. The views looking out from within the cave are gorgeous. Along the neighboring trails you will find other caves that you can venture into. However, be careful and be sure to have a good flashlight. To reach the Río Frío Cave, drive the Pine Ridge Road to Douglas Da Silva Village at about Mile Marker 24. Do not follow the turnoff for Caracol, but head into the little village. Here you will see signs for the turnoff to the cave. The cave is about a mile outside the village. There's a small parking area very close to the mouth of the cave and a couple of picnic tables and benches along the river. No admission is charged to visit here.

BUTTERFLIES   The **Green Hills Butterfly Ranch & Botanical Collection** is a lovely little project affording you the chance to see numerous butterfly species and a range of tropical flora. These folks raise dozens of local species of butterflies, and visitors get to see them up close and personal. This place is located at around Mile Marker 8 of the Pine Ridge Road, across from Mountain Equestrian Trails. Guided tours (BZ$8/US$4) are offered daily, between 8am and 4:30pm. Reservations are recommended.

CARACOL ★★

Caracol (www.caracol.org) is the largest known Mayan archaeological site in Belize, and one of the great Mayan city-states of the Classic era (A.D. 250–950). At one point, Caracol supported a population of over 150,000.

Caracol, which means "shell" in Spanish, gets its name from the large number of snail shells found here during early explorations. So far three main plazas with numerous structures, and two ball courts have been excavated. The largest pyramid here, **Caana** or "Sky Palace," stands some 136 feet (41m) high, and is the tallest Mayan building in Belize, and still the tallest man-made structure in the country (the Radisson Fort George in Belize City is the only modern structure that even comes close).

Caracol has revealed a wealth of informative carved glyphs that have allowed archaeologists to fill in much of the history of this once powerful city-state. Glyphs here claim Caracol defeats of rivals Tikal in A.D. 562 and Naranjo in 631. One of the earliest temples here was built in A.D. 70, and the Caracol royal family has been officially chronicled since 331. The last recorded date on a glyph is 859, and archaeologists conclude that by 1050 Caracol had been completely abandoned.

Caracol is located deep within the Chiquibil Forest Reserve. The ruins are not nearly as well cleared nor excavated as Tikal or Xunantunich. However, this is part of the site's charm. There is great bird-watching and the chance to see other wild fauna out here. Moreover, the area has been declared the **Caracol Archaeological Reserve,** and excavation and restoration are ongoing. A visit to Caracol is often combined with a stop at the Río On Pools, or one or more of the other attractions in the Mountain Pine Ridge area.

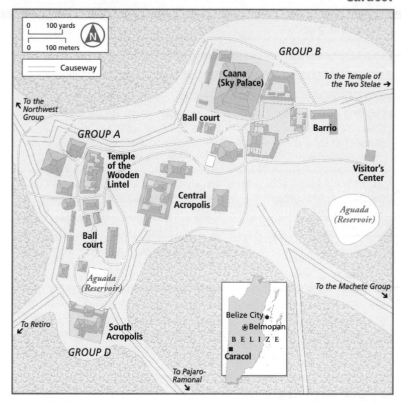

Caracol is open daily from 8am to 4pm; admission is BZ$10 (US$5). There's a small visitor center at the entrance, and a guide can sometimes be hired here, although most visitors come with their own guide as part of an organized tour. Caracol is about 50 miles (81km) along a dirt road from the Western Highway. Plan on the drive taking about 2½ hours, a little more if the road is in bad shape.

SHOPPING

If you're in the area, be sure to stop at the Tanah Mayan Art Museum ✪ (© 824-3310), run by the Garcia Sisters, some of the premier artisans working in carved slate. While it's a stretch to call their little shop and showroom a museum, you will find a nice collection of the Garcia sisters' carvings, as well as other Mayan artifacts, tools, and handicrafts. This place is located at about Mile Marker 8 of the Cristo Rey Road, about a mile before you reach the village of San Antonio. Inside the village, you should stop at the Magaña Zaactunich Art Gallery (no phone), which carries a range of local craftworks and specializes in woodcarvings.

WHERE TO STAY & DINE
VERY EXPENSIVE

Blancaneaux Lodge ✪✪✪ (Finds)   This remote nature lodge was built with style and grace, which is fitting, as the owner is director Francis Ford Coppola. The lodge is set on a steep pine-forested hillside, overlooking the Privassion

Chalillo Dam

While this is one of the most remote frontiers in Belize, all's not quite so quiet out here. A dam has been proposed on the upper reaches of the Macal River. Local and international opposition to the project, which is being undertaken by the Canadian company Fortis, is strong. Environmentalists and local business owners claim the dam would flood an area that is home to a variety of rare and endangered species, including the jaguar and a colony of 200 scarlet macaws, some of the few remaining macaws in Belize. It will also probably bury innumerable as-yet-unexcavated Mayan archaeological sites. Unfortunately, protests and legal actions have been unsuccessful so far in halting the project. In fact, large trucks now frequently rumble on the once quiet and seldom used back roads of the Mountain Pine Ridge Forest Reserve.

River and a series of gentle falls. The individual cabañas here are all comfortable and intimate, with wood floors, a private balcony or deck, and a mix of furnishings and decorations from around the world that blend together in a sort of chic world fusion. Most of these cabañas are "riverfront" units, although a couple are termed "garden view," and these are clearly the most modest rooms in the joint. The best cabañas are the "honeymoon" units, which are closest to the river and have larger decks. The seven villas are all two-bedroom, two-bathroom affairs. The best feature of the villas is their large, open-air central living area which flows into a forest and river view deck. Villa 7 is Coppola's private villa whenever he visits, and it features some of the director's photo memorabilia, as well as a painting by his daughter and fellow director Sofia Coppola. You can rent it whenever he's not around.

The restaurant serves excellent Italian and international cuisine. A wide range of tours and activities are offered. The newest addition here is a small spa, with a large horseshoe-shaped Jacuzzi, and a wooden massage room set on the banks of the river. The masseuses are allegedly being brought in from Bali. Blancaneaux has its own airstrip, and charter flights from Belize City can be arranged.

Mountain Pine Ridge Reserve (P.O. Box B, Central Farm), Cayo District. © 800/746-3743 in the U.S, or 824-3878. Fax 824-3919. www.blancaneaux.com. 17 units. BZ$450–BZ$560 (US$225–US$280) double; BZ$900–BZ$1,100 (US$450–US$550) villa. Rates include continental breakfast. Rates slightly lower in the off season, higher during peak weeks. AE, MC, V. **Amenities:** Restaurant; bar; lounge; small spa; bike rental; tour desk; laundry service. *In room:* Safe, no phone.

EXPENSIVE

Five Sisters Lodge ⚘   This hotel is located in the heart of the Mountain Pine Ridge Reserve, about 200 feet (60m) above its namesake Five Sisters Falls, a beautiful and rambling series of waterfalls and swimming holes. The individual cottages have palmetto stick walls, thatched roofs, and beds hung with mosquito netting. Some have polished wood floors, while others feature cool Mexican tiles. All have a mix of local and Guatemalan furnishings and decor as well as a screened-in veranda hung with a hammock. The luxury and junior suite units feature excellent waterfall views, king-size beds, and large tubs. There are a few economy rooms located below the main lodge that share bathrooms and showers.

A couple of these actually have private forest-view balconies, and are a very good value for budget travelers.

It's 290 steps, almost straight down, to the water and the base of the falls. Luckily, you no longer have to hoof it, unless you want to, as they've installed a little funicular. Once you're there, you'll find a snack bar, a small riverside beach, an open-air rancho strung with hammocks, and countless secluded swimming holes just a short walk up or down the river. They've even built a beautiful little open-air gazebo down on the water's edge, which has become a popular place to hold weddings. The restaurant serves good Belizean and international fare at reasonable rates.

Mountain Pine Ridge (P.O. Box 173, San Ignacio), Cayo District. © 800/447-2931 in the U.S., or 820-4005. Fax 820-4024. www.fivesisterslodge.com. 18 units (4 with shared bathroom). BZ$120–BZ$130 (US$60–US$65) double with shared bathroom; BZ$210–BZ$230 (US$105–US$115) double; BZ$270 (US$135) junior suite. Rates include continental breakfast. Rates lower in the off season. MC, V. **Amenities:** Restaurant; bar; lounge; tour desk; laundry service. *In room:* No phone.

Hidden Valley Inn ★★

This isolated mountain resort has a beautiful setting on over 7,000 acres (2,800 ha) of private land. The individual bungalows are all plenty roomy, and come with either one queen bed or two twin beds, as well as cool red tile floors, high ceilings, a couple of plush sitting chairs, and a working fireplace. The outdoor pool and Jacuzzi are surrounded by a beautiful slate deck. This is the closest hotel to the Hidden Valley, or Thousand Foot Falls, the tallest waterfall in Belize, a semi-strenuous 2-hour hike from the hotel. However, there are actually several other jungle waterfalls and swimming holes much more easily accessible, right on the property. There's an extensive network of trails, and the bird-watching is excellent. This is a great place to explore by mountain bike, and the hotel provides them free for guest use. A meal plan will run you BZ$80 (US$40) per person per day. The coffee you're served at breakfast is grown right here, as are many of the fruits and vegetables.

Mountain Pine Ridge (P.O. Box 170, Belmopan), Cayo District. © 866/443-3364 in the U.S., or 822-3320. Fax 822-3334. www.hiddenvalleyinn.com. 12 units. BZ$300 (US$150) double. Rates slightly lower in the off season. AE, MC, V. **Amenities:** Restaurant; bar; lounge; small outdoor pool; Jacuzzi; free mountain bike use; tour desk; laundry service. *In room:* No phone.

Mountain Equestrian Trails (MET) ★

This lodge is set in a very lush patch of forest, and the folks here are some of the best horse and adventure tour operators in the area. The rooms here are decidedly rustic, and a bit pricey for what you get. Housed in a series of duplex buildings, all feature high thatched roofs, cool tile floors, queen beds hung with mosquito netting, and plenty of windows for cross-ventilation. The rooms do feature colorful Guatemalan bedspreads and indigenous arts and crafts on the walls. There's no electricity in the rooms, and kerosene lanterns provide light. A much better bargain are the large safari-style tents, which feature two little single beds, a nightstand to hold your lantern, and a small throw rug, for a touch of civilization. A large open-air palapa serves as the lodge's restaurant, bar, and meeting area. A separate outdoor kitchen and dining area serves those staying at the campsite, which is about a quarter of a mile from the main lodge. While horses and horseback riding tours are the principal draw here, a whole range of tours and activities is offered. The owners at MET helped create the private Slate Creek Preserve, a 3,000-acre (1,200 ha) tract of land bordering the Mountain Pine Ridge Preserve. A meal package here costs BZ$70 (US$35) per person per day.

Pine Ridge Rd., Cayo District. ✆ **800/838-3918** in the U.S., or 820-4041. Fax 822-3361. www.metbelize.com. 10 units. BZ$60 (US$30) double tent; BZ$260 (US$130) double room. Rates lower in the off season. MC, V. **Amenities:** Restaurant; bar; tour desk; laundry service. *In room:* No phone.

MODERATE

Crystal Paradise Resort   The nicest thing about this little family-run resort is probably the Tut Family that runs it. Most of the rooms are in thatch roof duplex buildings, with tile floors, ceiling fans, and private verandas. The more expensive rooms face the Macal River Valley, with beautiful views of the surrounding forests. There's not a whole lot of difference in terms of comfort level in the various rooms, and the decor is relatively spartan throughout. Still, the most inexpensive rooms have cement floors, are definitely smaller, and lack the private veranda. A host of tours are offered, and the in-house guides—most of them family members—are excellent. The restaurant serves wonderful Belizean cuisine, and there's always a convivial vibe in the open air dining room, bar, and lounge areas.

This place is located on the road to Mountain Pine Ridge, near the tiny Cristo Rey Village.

Cristo Rey Village (P.O. Box 126), Cayo District. ✆/fax **824-2772**. www.crystalparadise.com. 20 units. BZ$150–BZ$250 (US$75–US$125) double. Rates include breakfast and dinner. MC, V. **Amenities:** Restaurant; bar; lounge; tour desk; laundry service. *In room:* No phone.

Pine Ridge Lodge   This rustic little lodge is located in the heart of the Mountain Pine Ridge area, affording excellent access to the ruins at Caracol, as well as the Río On Pools and Río Frío Cave. Most of the rooms are in duplex units, with polished concrete floors, simple wooden furniture, and local and Guatemalan crafts and textiles completing the decor. Light in the rooms is provided by kerosene lanterns, and the showers are heated by on-demand butane heaters. The grounds are loaded with a wide variety of orchids and attract an equally wide variety of bird species. The lodge is set on the banks of a small creek, and the best rooms are close to and overlooking this creek. There's also a small waterfall an easy hike from the lodge. Meals are served family-style in the small screened-in dining room and bar area.

Mountain Pine Ridge (P.O. Box 128, San Ignacio), Cayo District. ✆ **800/316-0706** in the U.S., or 606-4557. www.pineridgelodge.com. 6 units. BZ$158 (US$79) double. Rates lower in the off season. Rates include continental breakfast. **Amenities:** Restaurant; bar; tour desk; laundry service. *In room:* No phone.

9

Tikal & Guatemala's Petén

Occupying the entire northeastern section of Guatemala, the Petén is Guatemala's largest and least populated province. Most of the Petén is forest—thick tropical rainforest. It is a lush and wild landscape that contains some of Mesoamerica's richest archaeological treasures. In 1990, the government of Guatemala officially established the **Maya Biosphere Reserve,** a tract of 2.5 million acres (1 million ha) that includes most of the Petén Province. Moreover, the Maya Biosphere Reserve adjoins the neighboring **Calakmul Biosphere Reserve** in Mexico and the **Río Bravo Conservation Area** in Belize, comprising a joint protected area of over 5 million acres (2 million ha).

The Petén Province is home to perhaps the most impressive and best preserved of the ancient Mayan ceremonial cities, **Tikal.** It is also home to numerous other lesser, and less excavated, sites. In addition, the area is a rich and rewarding destination for bird-watchers and ecotourists. Given the close proximity of Tikal to the Belize border (and the terrible conditions of the roads connecting Guatemala City to the Petén), it is in many ways more convenient to visit Tikal from Belize than it is from central Guatemala. This chapter will give you all the necessary information to plan a visit to this fascinating destination, whether you want to take a quick 1-day tour of the ruins at Tikal or a multiday adventure exploring the region.

1 Tikal ✦✦✦

62 miles (100km) NW of the Belize border; 40 miles (65km) N of Flores

Tikal is the greatest of the surviving classic Mayan cities. It is estimated that Tikal once supported a population of about 100,000 people. Archaeologists have identified over 3,000 structures, and in its heyday, the city probably covered as much as 25 square miles (65 sq. km). Tikal is far more extensively excavated than any ruins in Belize, and unlike the grand cities and excavations in Mexico, Tikal rises out of dense jungle. The pyramids here are some of the most perfect examples of ceremonial architecture in the Mayan world. Standing atop Temple IV, you are high above the rainforest canopy. The peaks of several temples poke through the dense vegetation. Toucans and parrots fly about and the loudest noise you'll hear is the guttural call of howler monkeys.

Tikal is within easy reach of Belize's western border, and numerous organized tour groups and independent travelers from Belize visit the site every day. However, for the past 4 decades Guatemala has had a brutal history of political and civil violence and repression. In recent years, robberies and kidnappings of wealthy nationals, foreign businessmen and diplomats, and visiting tourists have become major industries in Guatemala. Most experts feel there is a direct connection between these activities and members of the army, police, and security forces. The Petén District, where Tikal is located, is an isolated and forgotten

Telephone Tip

Guatemala's country code is **502** (Belize's is 501). To avoid confusion between Belizean and Guatemalan telephone numbers, we have included the country code in the Guatemalan numbers, but don't forget to dial the international access code first if you're calling from abroad—otherwise, you might get someone in Kentucky.

section of eastern Guatemala. The most common attacks against tourists visiting Tikal occur on the road between the Belizean border and Flores. Taxis, local buses, and air-conditioned minivans have all been targeted. These highway robberies tend to occur in waves, and are by far the exception and not the norm. In almost all known cases, the attacks are armed but nonviolent robberies. If you plan to visit Tikal for a few days as a side trip from Belize, it is a good idea to find a hotel safe in Belize that will guard any valuables you do not need with you while in Guatemala.

ESSENTIALS
GETTING THERE & DEPARTING
BY PLANE   Maya Island Air (© 226-2435 in Belize City, or 502/926-3386 in Flores; www.mayaairways.com) has two flights daily to Flores Airport (FRS) from the Philip S. W. Goldson International Airport in Belize City at 8:30am and 2:30pm. The flights return at 9:50am and 3:50pm. Flight duration is 45 minutes, and the fare is BZ$176 (US$88) each way. *Note:* The afternoon departure from Belize and the morning departure from Flores are not offered September 1 through November 14.

Tropic Air (© 226-2012 in Belize City, or 502/926-0348 in Flores; www.tropicair.com) has two daily flights to Flores from Goldson International Airport in Belize City at 8:30am and 3pm. The flights return at 9:15am and 3:45pm. Flight duration is 45 minutes; it costs BZ$176 (US$88) each way.

Leaving Belize, you will have to pay the BZ$70 (US$35) departure tax, as well as the BZ$7.50 (US$3.75) PACT tax. Leaving Guatemala, there is a US$30 departure tax for international flights, as well as a US$2.50 Guatemalan tax on all flights to and from Flores.

The airport is on the road to Tikal, about 1½ miles (2.4km) east of Santa Elena. A taxi from the airport into Santa Elena or Flores should cost you around Q10 (US$1.25). Or you can take a local bus (usually an old yellow school bus) for around Q1.20 (US15¢). Collective taxis and minivans to Tikal are usually waiting at the airport and charge around Q32 to Q48 (US$4–US$6) per person each way. You can sometimes bargain, and you can often get a slight discount if you purchase a round-trip fare right from the start. A private taxi can be hired for the drive for Q240 to Q280 (US$30–US$35).

BY BUS   If you're traveling from Belize City by bus, there is one daily direct bus run by the **Línea Dorada/Mundo Maya** bus line (© **502/926-0070**). The bus leaves at 10am from right in front of the Marine Terminal in downtown Belize City. The fare is BZ$50 (US$25) one-way. The trip takes between 6 and 7 hours. The return bus leaves Tikal at 5am.

Alternatively, you can take one of the many buses from Belize City (or from San Ignacio) to the Guatemalan border. **Novelo's Bus Line** (© **207-2025** in Belize City, 824-3360 in San Ignacio) buses to San Ignacio leave roughly every

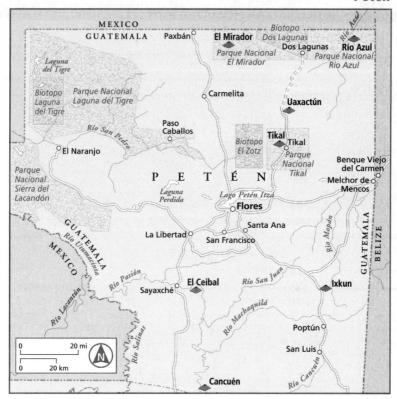

half-hour from the main bus station on West Collet Canal Street between 5am and 7pm. The fare is BZ$10 (US$5). The trip takes 2½ hours. Most of these buses continue on beyond San Ignacio to the border town of Benque Viejo del Carmen. Some of these leave you in Benque Viejo, while others go all the way to the border crossing, a little over a mile away. There are numerous taxis at the Benque Viejo bus station that will take you to the border for BZ$3 (US$1.50).

On the Belize side, you will have to fill out a departure card, have your passport stamped, and pay the departure tax of BZ$20 (US$10), plus the BZ$7.50 (US$3.75) PACT tax. Just over the bridge lies the Guatemalan border town of Melchor de Mencos. Theoretically, you will be provided with a Guatemalan tourist card for Q40 (US$5). However, border formalities in Guatemala are often open to corruption, with border officials and local touts looking to glean some extra money. Moreover, Guatemalan border formalities change from time to time and there is a running dispute between Guatemala and Belize (Guatemala claims that all of Belize is actually part of Guatemala, dating back to the mid–19th c.), so it always pays to check with the Guatemalan Embassy in your home country if you are certain you will be traveling there. The border crossing can take from 20 minutes to over an hour, depending on the crowds.

Once finished with the border formalities, it is a simple matter to find onward transportation to Tikal or Flores and Santa Elena. The least expensive means of transport is the local bus; however, none of the local buses go directly to Tikal.

Tikal

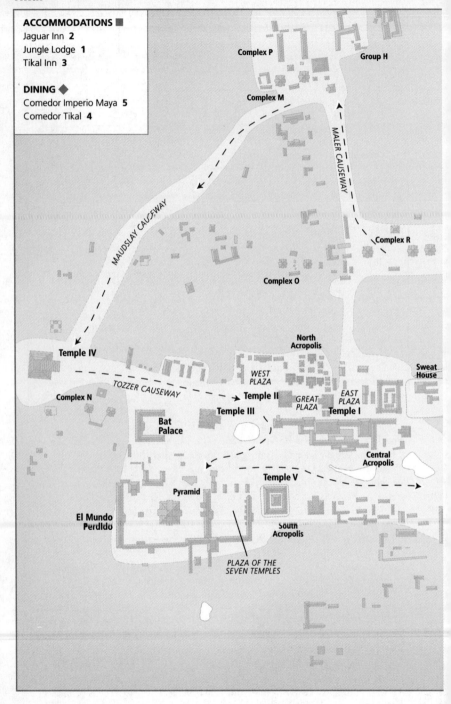

ACCOMMODATIONS ■
Jaguar Inn **2**
Jungle Lodge **1**
Tikal Inn **3**

DINING ◆
Comedor Imperio Maya **5**
Comedor Tikal **4**

Complex P

Group H

Complex M

MALER CAUSEWAY

MAUDSLAY CAUSEWAY

Complex R

Complex O

Temple IV

North
Acropolis

WEST
PLAZA

Sweat
House

TOZZER CAUSEWAY

Complex N

Temple II

GREAT
PLAZA

EAST
PLAZA

Temple III

Temple I

Bat
Palace

Central
Acropolis

Temple V

Pyramid

El Mundo
Perdido

South
Acropolis

PLAZA OF THE
SEVEN TEMPLES

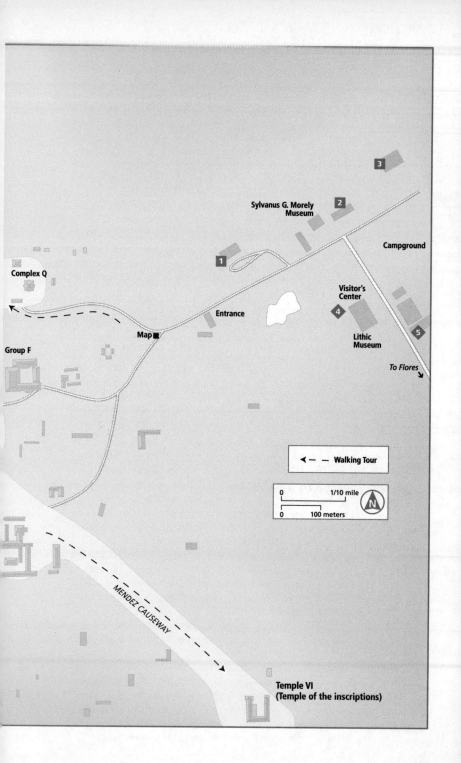

Complex Q

Group F

Map ■

Entrance

Sylvanus G. Morely
Museum

1

2

3

Campground

Visitor's
Center

4

Lithic
Museum

5

To Flores

◀ – – Walking Tour

0   1/10 mile
0   100 meters

N

MENDEZ CAUSEWAY

Temple VI
(Temple of the inscriptions)

Instead, they head to Flores and Santa Elena, but they will drop you off at Ixlú (El Cruce), where you can flag down one of the many minivans and collective taxis going from Flores and Santa Elena to the ruins (at a cost of Q32–Q48/US$4–US$6). Be forewarned that while local buses are very inexpensive (around US$1–US$2), they can be overcrowded and very slow. They stop almost constantly along the way to pick up and discharge passengers and their cargo. I recommend you take one of these buses only if you're more interested in the local color and adventure of the trip than in a speedy arrival at the ruins.

A much better bet is to take one of the collective taxis or minivans that leave right from Melchor de Mencos. Most of these wait just outside the border station and leave as soon as they fill up. Some go to Flores and Santa Elena, while others go directly to Tikal. Most charge just Q48 to Q64 (US$6–US$8) per person.

Finally, if there are no collective taxis or minivans available, you can hire a taxi that will carry up to six people for between Q320 and Q400 (US$40–US$50).

Tip: If you are only going for the day, try to arrange a round-trip fare with your taxi or minivan driver, with a specific departure time from Tikal. Usually, it's best to leave Tikal by 4pm, so as to drive during daylight and arrive at the border with plenty of time.

BY CAR   Driving from Belize City, take the Western Highway to San Ignacio, and continue on to the border town of Benque Viejo del Carmen. From Benque, follow the signs to the border at a bridge over the Mopan River, a little over a mile out of town.

Safety in Guatemala

Crime, both petty and violent, is a problem in Guatemala. The Guatemalan police and judiciary are underfunded, understaffed, and largely ineffectual. Decades of civil war, genocide, and paramilitary activity in addition to historic poverty and underdevelopment have created a dangerous climate where lawlessness is rampant. Foreign nationals—as well as everyday Guatemalans—are the targets of robberies, kidnapping, and rapes. The U.S. State Department strongly cautions visitors to Guatemala and keeps a relatively up-to-date analysis of the situation at **http://travel.state.gov/guatemala.html**.

Still, hundreds of tourists visit Tikal and Flores every day, and the vast, vast majority of them have no problems whatsoever. Be sure to take all necessary precautions. Never travel alone or at night, and stick to the most popular and populous tourist destinations and attractions. If you are driving, only stop for people holding guns; do not try to run blockades. Common wisdom cautions against using the low-fare Guatemalan buses and tour agencies; however, high-end tour groups in fancy air-conditioned microbuses do attract the attention of organized criminal gangs. Some tour groups travel with armed guards. This may or may not increase your sense of security and your actual security, to boot. (As far as I'm concerned, the jury is out on that one.) If you are confronted with any sort of criminal attempt, do not resist, as a simple mugging can easily end up turning into murder. Believe me, I am not a Chicken Little—this is a serious concern in Guatemala.

The border crossing and formalities are very similar to those described above in "By Bus." You will be corralled by touts on the Guatemalan side offering all sorts of aid and services, and demanding all sorts of fees and duties. By law you are supposed to have your tires fumigated. This should only cost a U.S. dollar or two. You should not have to pay any additional fees. Whether you are driving your own car or a rental car, be sure to have all your current registration, title, and insurance papers.

Once across the border, follow signs out of Melchor de Mencos towards Flores and Tikal. It's about a 1-hour drive to the crossroads at Ixlú, also known as El Cruce. If you are going to El Remate or Tikal, you will turn right here. If you are going to Flores or Santa Elena, you will continue on straight. From Ixlú, it's about 25 to 30 minutes either way to Santa Elena/Flores or the ruins at Tikal. The entrance to Tikal National Park is located 11 miles (18km) south of the visitor's center and true entrance to the ruins and its network of trails. Here you will have to pay the Q50 (US$6.25) entrance fee. The entrance is open daily from 6am to 6pm. If you plan to spend more than a day here staying at one of the hotels or campsites near the ruins, advise them and try to pay your entrance fee for subsequent days in advance, as sometimes they send people all the way back to the entrance gate to buy a subsequent day's ticket.

If you're traveling in a rental car, be sure that the company you rented from in Belize allows the car to cross into Guatemala. **Crystal Auto Rental** (© **0800/777-7777** in Belize; www.crystal-belize.com) does.

Beware: It is strongly advised that you do not travel at night. It is a sad fact that armed groups occasionally set up roadblocks along these isolated yet frequently trafficked roads.

BY ORGANIZED TOUR   Organized day trips leave daily for Tikal from Belize City, San Ignacio, San Pedro, Caye Caulker, and Placencia. Costs for these all-inclusive trips are approximately BZ$500 to BZ$700 (US$250–US$350) per person by air (from Belize City, or any of the other major tourist destinations in Belize), and between BZ$170 and BZ$350 (US$85–US$175) by land (from Belize City and San Ignacio), depending on group size. Budget an additional BZ$100 to BZ$300 (US$50–US$150) per person per day for multiday excursions. In Belize City, call **Discovery Expeditions** (© 223-0748; www.discoverybelize.com), **Jaguar Adventures** (© 223-6025; www.jaguarbelize.com), or **S & L Travel and Tours** (© 227-7593; www.sltravelbelize.com). In San Ignacio, you can call **Belize Eco Tours** (© 824-4290; www.belize-ecotours.com), **Cayo Adventure Tours** (© 824-3246; www.cayoadventure.com), **Mayawalk Tours** (© 824-3070; www.mayawalk.com), or **Yute Expeditions** (© 824-2076; www.inlandbelize.com), or see Bob Jones at **Eva's Restaurant** (© 804-2267).

GETTING AROUND

BY TAXI OR MINIVAN   Minivans and collective taxis leave throughout the day plying the route between Tikal and Santa Elena/Flores. Minivans and collective taxis charge between Q32 and Q48 (US$4–US$6) per person. From Santa Elena, you can catch a bus back to the border. A private cab from Tikal to Santa Elena/Flores will run around Q200 to Q280 (US$25–US$35). Between Tikal and El Remate, the fare is about Q160 to Q240 (US$20–US$30).

BY CAR   Hertz (© **800/654-3131** in the U.S., or 502/926-0415 in Flores; www.hertz.com) has an office at the Flores airport, as well as at the Camino Real Tikal (p. 258). There are also several local agencies at the airport. Of these, a good choice is **Tabarini Rent A Car** (© **502/926-0277;** www.tabarini.com).

Money

The Guatemalan monetary unit is the *quetzal*. In April 2004, the exchange rate was 8.06 quetzales to the U.S. dollar. If you're coming from Belize, your best bets for changing dollars into quetzales are at the border or at the numerous banks in Santa Elena and Flores (see "Flores & Santa Elena," later in this chapter). If you arrive by air, you will find a branch of **Banquetzal** (© **502/926-0711**) in the departure area of the small airport. It is open Monday through Friday from 9am to 1pm and 2 to 5:30pm, and on Saturday from 9am to 1pm. You will also find individuals offering to exchange money, although you're better off heading into Santa Elena or Flores if the Banquetzal branch isn't open. Most of the hotels and restaurants in Tikal, in fact, will exchange dollars for quetzales, although they may give you a slightly less favorable rate than you would get at a bank.

Most rent small jeeps and SUVs. Do get a four-wheel-drive vehicle; even though you may never need the traction or off-road ability, the extra clearance will come in handy. Rates run from Q480 to Q720 (US$60–US$90) per day.

ORIENTATION

There is no village or town inside Tikal National Park. After having paid your Q50 (US$6.25) admission at the entrance booth 11 miles (18km) south of the ruins, you will eventually come to the large central parking area and visitor center. This is where you will find the three hotels and campsite reviewed in "Where to Stay," later in this chapter, as well as the two museums and a collection of simple restaurants. The ruins themselves are about a 20-minute walk through the forest from the trail entrance here.

There is a post office and telegraph office on the left as you arrive at the parking area. You'll find a public phone in the Stelae Museum. There is no bank or ATM here in Tikal, and most of the little restaurants and gift stands only accept quetzales. Moreover, while some of the hotels here do accept credit cards, the phone connections are spotty, and they sometimes have problems getting the authorizations. It's best to bring quetzales to pay for your entire stay. Also, be sure to bring plenty of insect repellent with you—the bugs here are rapacious.

Tikal National Park is open daily from 6am to 6pm. If you'd like to stay in the park until 8pm (for sunset and nocturnal wildlife viewing), get your admission ticket stamped at the office behind the Stelae Museum. If you arrive after 3pm, your admission is good for the following day as well. If you are staying multiple days, you must pay the admission fee each day. The best times to visit the ruins are in early morning and late afternoon, which are the least crowded and coolest times of day.

FAST FACTS   There are no banks, medical facilities, laundromats, Internet cafes, or other major services available at Tikal. All of these can be found in Flores and Santa Elena, some 40 miles (65km) away; see section 3, later in this chapter.

EXPLORING TIKAL

Tikal, one of the largest Mayan cities ever uncovered and the most spectacular ruins in Guatemala, ranks with Mexico's Chichén Itzá in pre-Columbian splendor. However, unlike at Chichén Itzá, the ruins of Tikal are set in the middle of a vast jungle through which you must hike from temple to temple. The many miles of trails through the park provide numerous opportunities to spot interesting birds such as toucans and parrots and such wild animals as coatimundis, spider monkeys, howler monkeys, and deer. Together, the ruins and the abundance of wildlife make a trip to Tikal an absolute must for anyone interested in Mayan history, bird-watching, or wildlife viewing.

Tikal was a massive ceremonial metropolis. So far, archaeologists have mapped about 3,000 constructions, 10,000 earlier foundations beneath surviving structures, 250 stone monuments (stelae and altars), and thousands of art objects found in tombs and cached offerings. There is evidence of continuous construction at Tikal from 200 B.C. through the 9th century A.D., with some suggestion of occupation as early as 600 B.C. The Maya reached their zenith in art and architecture during the Classic Period, which began about A.D. 250 and ended abruptly about 900, when for some reason Tikal and all other major Mayan centers were abandoned. Most of the visible structures at Tikal date from the Late Classic Period, from 600 to 900.

No one's sure just what role Tikal played in the history of the Maya: Was it mostly a ceremonial center for priests, artisans, and the elite? Or was it a city of industry and commerce as well? In the 6 square miles (16 sq. km) of Tikal that have been mapped and excavated, only a few of the buildings were domestic structures; most were temples, palaces, ceremonial platforms, and shrines. Workers are excavating the innumerable mounds on the periphery of the mapped area and have been finding modest houses of stone and plaster with thatched roofs. Just how far these settlements extended beyond the ceremonial center and how many people lived within the domain of Tikal is still to be determined. At its height, Tikal may have covered as much as 25 square miles (65 sq. km).

MAKING THE MOST OF YOUR VISIT

Tikal is such an immense site that you really need several days to see it thoroughly. But you can visit many of the greatest temples and palaces in 1 day. To do it properly, as a first-time visitor, you should probably hire a guide. Guides are available at the visitor center and charge around Q160 (US$20) for a half-day tour of the ruins. In addition, most hotels and all tour agencies in the region offer guided tours for a similar price.

Although out of print, you might want to try to find a copy of *Tikal: Handbook of the Ancient Maya Ruins,* by William R. Coe, written under the auspices of the University Museum of the University of Pennsylvania. Archaeologists from the university, working in conjunction with Guatemalan officials, did most of the excellent excavation work at Tikal from 1956 to 1969. You can order used copies of this book in the United States, and you can also often pick up a copy in Flores or at Tikal. Two other excellent works that give a detailed historical and narrative account of this amazing site are *Tikal: An Illustrated History of the Ancient Mayan Capital,* by John Montgomery (Hippocrene Books, 2001); and *The Lords of Tikal: Rulers of an Ancient Maya City,* by Peter D. Harrison, et al. (Thames & Hudson, 2000).

A Familiar Site

Tikal provides such a stunning and unique landscape that it was chosen for an exterior shot in George Lucas's *Star Wars,* as well as the site of a famous series of Nike commercials.

A WALKING TOUR

To orient yourself, begin your tour of Tikal at the visitor center and neighboring Stelae Museum. Here you'll find some informative exhibits and relics, as well as an impressive relief map of the site. See "The Museums" below for more information on the stelae.

A full tour of Tikal will require an extensive amount of walking, as much as 6 miles (10km). The itinerary described here will take you to most of the major temples and plazas, and can be accomplished in about 3 to 4 hours. If your time is really limited, you should follow the signs and head straight to the Great Plaza. If you have a full day, consider this route:

Walking along the road that goes west from the museum toward the ruins, turn right at the first intersection to get to **Twin Complexes Q** and **R.** Seven of these twin complexes are known at Tikal, but their exact purpose is still a mystery. Each complex has two pyramids facing east and west; at the north is an unroofed enclosure entered by a vaulted doorway and containing a single stele and altar; at the south is a small palacelike structure. Of the two pyramids here, one has been restored and one has been left as it was found, and the latter will give you an idea of just how overgrown and ensconced in the jungle these structures had become.

At the end of the Twin Complexes is a wide road called the **Maler Causeway.** Turn right (north) onto this causeway to get to **Complex P,** another twin complex, a 15-minute walk. Some restoration has been done at Complex P, but the most interesting points are the replicas of a stele (no. 20) and altar (no. 8) in the north enclosure. Look for the beautiful glyphs next to the carving of a warrior on the stele, all in very good condition. The altar shows a captive bound to a carved-stone altar, his hands tied behind his back—a common scene in carvings at Tikal. Both these monuments date from about A.D. 751.

From Complex P, head south on the **Maudslay Causeway** to **Complex N,** which is the site of **Temple IV, the Temple of the Two-Headed Serpent** ★★★. Finished around A.D. 740, Temple IV is the tallest structure in Tikal and is 212 feet (64m) from the base of its platform to the top. The first glimpse you get of the temple from the Maudslay Causeway is awesome, for the temple has not been restored, and all but the temple proper (the enclosure) and its roof comb are covered in foliage. The stairway is occluded by earth and roots, but there is a system of steep stairways (actually rough hewn wooden ladders set against the steep sides of the pyramid) to the top of the temple. The view of the setting and layout of Tikal—and all of the Great Plaza—is magnificent. From the platform of the temple, you can see in all directions and get an idea of the extent of the Petén jungle, an ocean of lush greenery. **Temple III (Temple of the Great Priest)** is in the foreground to the east; **Temples I** and **II** are farther on at the Great Plaza. To the right of these are the **South Acropolis** and **Temple V.** The courageous can get even a better view by clambering up a metal ladder on the south side of the temple to the base of the roof comb. This is not for the acrophobic.

Temple IV, and all the other temples at Tikal, are built on this plan: A pyramid is built first, and on top of it is built a platform; the temple proper rests on this platform and is composed of one to three rooms, usually long and narrow and not for habitation but rather for priestly rites. Most temples had beautifully carved wooden lintels above the doorways. The one from Temple IV is now in the Völkerkunde Museum in Basel, Switzerland.

From Temple IV, walk east along the **Tozzer Causeway** to get to the **Great Plaza,** about a 10-minute walk. Along the way you'll pass the twin-pyramid

Complex N, the **Bat Palace,** and Temple III. Take a look at the altar and stele in the complex's northern enclosure—two of the finest monuments at Tikal—and also the altar in front of Temple III, showing the head of a deity resting on a plate. By the way, the crisscross pattern shown here represents a woven mat, a symbol of authority to the Mayas.

THE GREAT PLAZA ✰✰✰

Entering the Great Plaza from the Tozzer Causeway, you'll be struck by the towering stone structure that is Temple II, seen from the back. It measures 125 feet (38m) tall now, although it is thought to have been 140 feet (42m) high when the roof comb was intact. Also called the Temple of the Masks, from a large face carved in the roof comb, the temple dates from about A.D. 700. Walk around this temple to enter the plaza proper.

Directly across from Temple II you'll see Temple I (Temple of the Great Jaguar), the most striking structure in Tikal. Standing 145 feet (44m) tall, the temple proper has three narrow rooms with high corbelled vaults (the Mayan "arch") and carved wooden lintels made of zapote wood, which is rot-resistant. One of the lintels has been removed for preservation in the Guatemala National Museum of Archaeology and Ethnology in Guatemala City. The whole structure is made of limestone, as are most others at Tikal. It was within this pyramid that one of the richest tombs in Tikal was discovered. Believed to be the tomb of Tikal ruler Hasaw Chan K'awil, when archaeologists uncovered it in 1962, they found the former ruler's skeleton surrounded by some 180 pieces of jade, 90 bone artifacts carved with hieroglyphic inscriptions, numerous pearls, and objects in alabaster and shell.

The **North Acropolis** (north side of the Great Plaza) is a maze of structures from various periods covering an area of 21 acres (8 ha). Standing today 30 feet (9m) above the limestone bedrock, it contains vestiges of more than a hundred different constructions dating from 200 B.C. to A.D. 800. At the front-center of the acropolis (at the top of the stairs up from the Great Plaza) is a temple numbered **5D-33.** Although much of the 8th-century temple was destroyed during the excavations to get to the Early Classic Period temple (A.D. 300) underneath, it's still a fascinating building. Toward the rear of it is a tunnel leading to the stairway of the **Early Classic** temple, embellished with two 10-foot-high (3m) plaster polychrome masks of a god—don't miss these.

Directly across the plaza from the North Acropolis is the **Central Acropolis,** which covers about 4 acres (1.6 ha). It's a maze of courtyards and palaces on several levels, all connected by an intricate system of passageways. Some of the palaces had five floors, connected by exterior stairways, and each floor had as many as nine rooms arranged like a maze.

Before you leave the Great Plaza, be sure to examine some of the 70 beautiful stelae and altars right in the plaza. You can see the full development of Mayan art in them, for they date from the Early Classic period right through to the Late

---

(Tips Beat the Crowds

Tikal fills up with tour buses most days, with the hours between 10am and 2pm being the busiest period. I prefer visiting the Great Plaza either before or after the main crowds have left. Feel free to reverse the order of this walking tour if it will help you avoid the masses.

Moments   Sunrise, Sunset

Tikal is a magical and mystical place. Many claim that this magic and mystique is only heightened around sunrise and sunset. Sunsets tend to be easier to catch and a more dependable show. Sunrises tend to be more a case of the sun eventually burning through the morning mist than of any impressive orb emerging. However, afternoons tend to be clear, especially during the dry season, allowing for excellent sunset viewing from the tops of the main temples here. If you're staying right at the ruins, your chances are better and the logistics easier of catching either or both of these occasions. In fact, visitors staying inside the park are often admitted to Tikal as early as 5am. Still, minivans and collective taxis do leave Flores and El Remate early enough to get you to the Tikal entrance gate at 6am when it opens. This will generally enable you to get to the top of one of the main temples by 6:30am, which is usually early enough to catch the sun burning through the mist just over the rainforest canopy.

Classic period. There are three major stylistic groups: the stelae with wraparound carving on the front and sides with text on the back; those with a figure carved on the front and text in glyphs on the back; and those with a simple carved figure on the front, text in hieroglyphs on the sides, and a plain back. The oldest stele is no. 29 (now in the Tikal Museum—see "The Museums," below), dating from A.D. 292; the most recent is no. 11 in the Great Plaza, dating from A.D. 869.

If you head south from the Temple II, you will come to the area known as **El Mundo Perdido (The Lost World).** This plaza contains the **Great Pyramid,** which stands 114 feet (34m) high and is the oldest excavated building in Tikal. This pyramid is one of the most popular spots for watching the sunset. If you've timed it right, you might be able to hang out here and watch the show; otherwise, make a mental note to get your bearings and come back later, if possible. Directly east of the Great Pyramid is the **Plaza of the Seven Temples,** which dates to the Late Classic period. Bordering this plaza on the east side is an unexcavated pyramid, and behind this is Temple V. This entire area is known as the **South Acropolis.**

If you cross through the South Acropolis to the east and then turn north in the general direction of the Great Plaza, you will come to the East Plaza. From here you can walk southeast on the Mendez Causeway to **Temple VI (Temple of the Inscriptions),** which contains a nearly illegible line of hieroglyphics that are the most extensive in Tikal. It's worth coming out this way just for the chance to spot some wild animals, which seem to be fairly common in this remote corner of the park.

THE MUSEUMS

The most formal museum here has been officially christened the **Sylvanus G. Morely Museum,** but is also known as the **Tikal** or **Ceramic Museum.** This museum contains a good collection of pottery, mosaic masks, incense burners, etched bone, and stelae that are chronologically displayed—beginning with Pre-Classic objects on up to Late Classic pieces. Of note are the delicate 3- to 5-inch (7.6–13cm) mosaic masks made of jade, turquoise, shell, and stucco. There is a beautiful cylindrical jar from about A.D. 700 depicting a male and female seated in a typical Mayan pose. The drawing is of fine quality, and the slip colors are red, brown, and black. Also on exhibit are a number of jade pendants, beads, and earplugs as well as the famous **stele no. 31,** which has all four sides carved. On the two sides are spear throwers, each wearing a large feathered headdress and carrying a shield in his left hand; on the front is a complicated carving of an individual carrying a head in his left arm and a chair in his right. It is a most amazing stele from the Early Classic period, considered one of the finest. Another fine attraction here is the reconstruction of the tomb of Hasaw Chan K'awil, who was also known as Ah Cacao, or "Lord Chocolate." The museum is located between the Jungle Lodge and the Jaguar Inn, and is open daily from 9am to 5pm. Admission is Q16 (US$2).

The second museum is known as the **Lithic** or **Stelae Museum** and is in the large new visitor center, which on your left as you arrive at the parking area coming from Flores. This spacious display area contains a superb collection of stelae from around the ruins. Just outside the front door of the museum is the scaled relief map (mentioned above) that will give you an excellent perspective on the relationships between the different ruins here at Tikal. This museum is open daily from 9am to 5pm, and admission is free.

WHERE TO STAY

There are only three hotels and a campground at the little Tikal village near the entrance to the ruins. Unless you have more than 2 days to spend exploring the region, I personally highly recommend staying near the ruins, as it allows you to enter early and stay late. It also allows you to avoid the Great Plaza and North Acropolis during the peak period of the day, when they are swarmed with day-trippers.

Although the ruins are officially open from 6am to 6pm, those staying at the site can sometimes finagle their way in even earlier. Better yet, those staying at the site can have their admission ticket stamped, allowing them to stay inside the park until 8pm. When the moon is full or close to full, that's enough time to catch both the sunset and moonrise from the top of one of the temples here.

Note: Rooms are often difficult to get at the park, and making reservations is essential during the high season. However, communication with the hotels here is difficult and undependable, and many reserve all of their high-season bookings for groups and prepaid package tours. Overbooking on behalf of these hotels is also not uncommon. Demand is high, and there is a very limited number of rooms here. If you're just going for a couple of nights, go with an organized tour to save yourself some hassle; if you plan to spend more time in the area or don't mind spending a night in Flores or Santa Elena if necessary, you can probably make your arrangements in Tikal.

VERY EXPENSIVE

Jungle Lodge ✦   Also known as *Posada de la Selva,* this is the largest hotel near the entrance to the ruins, and at times there can be a cattle-car feel to the operation. Still, the rooms are probably the most comfortable right at the park. Most are in duplex bungalows, with high ceilings, tile floors, two double beds, and a ceiling fan. Each has its own little porch with a couple of chairs, so you can do some bird-watching without leaving your room. The bungalows are connected by stone paths through lush gardens. It's hot and steamy here in the jungle, but after you've spent the day traipsing up and down pyramids, you'll be thankful you can cool off in the hotel's pool, which is built on a rise and shaped like a Mayan pyramid. Meals in the large dining rooms are some of the best you can get here at Tikal. This place also rents out double rooms in a long, low unit; these are rather basic rooms, with cement floors and shared bathrooms.

Tikal village, Petén. ℂ **502/926-0519** or 502/476-8775. Fax 502/476-0294. www.junglelodge.guate.com. 46 units (34 with private bathroom). Q1,280 (US$160) bungalow (rate includes breakfast, guided tour, lunch, and park entrance fee); Q200 (US$25) double with shared bathroom. MC, V. **Amenities:** Restaurant; bar; small outdoor pool; tour desk; laundry service. *In room:* No phone.

Tikal Inn 🦅 Set back amid the trees, the Tikal Inn is the farthest hotel from the entrance to the ruins as you walk down the old airstrip, and it's my favorite option inside the park because of its intimacy and semi-isolation. The best rooms here are the individual cabins, which feature high thatch roofs, tile floors, beautiful local furniture and textiles, and rustic wood trim. The smaller rooms in the main building have cement floors but the same attention to decor. All of the rooms are airy and cool. As at the Jungle Lodge, there's a refreshing and welcome little rectangular pool here. Meals are served family-style, and the food is a definite step up from the fare served at the *comedores* near the campground.

Tikal village, Petén. ℂ **502/926-0065.** 22 units. Q1,288 (US$161) double. Rate includes breakfast and dinner. No credit cards. **Amenities:** Restaurant; bar; small outdoor pool; tour desk; laundry service. *In room:* No phone.

INEXPENSIVE

Jaguar Inn (Value) This is the most humble and economical of the hotels right at the park. Still, the rooms are all quite clean, spacious, and well-kept. Most come with two queen beds and a small veranda strung with a hammock. If you're on a tight budget, you can also camp here, or rent one of their hammocks with mosquito netting and locker for Q40 (US$5) per person. Since the folks out here run on generator power, be forewarned that the electricity is only turned on in the rooms between 5am and 11pm.

Tikal village, Petén. ℂ **502/926-0002.** Fax 502/926-2413. www.jaguartikal.com. 9 units. US$48 double. Rates lower in the off season. AE, MC, V. **Amenities:** Restaurant; tour desk; laundry service. *In room:* No phone.

CAMPING

Just off the main parking lot at the site is a nice lawn with some trees for shade, marked and designated as the camping area. You can also set up your tent on some concrete pads, under an open-air thatch palapa roof. The camping area has simple shared shower and toilet facilities, and a communal cooking area. The campground (no phone) charges Q25 (US$3.10) for the privilege of putting up a tent and using the facilities. You can also rent hammocks and pitch them under open-air palapas for an additional Q25 (US$3.10).

Tip: If you plan on sleeping in a hammock, or even taking an afternoon siesta, you should really try to get a mosquito net that fits over the hammock. Most of the places that rent and sell hammocks in this area have these nets.

WHERE TO DINE

Most folks who stay near the ruins take all their meals at their hotel. If you're looking for variety or staying at the campsite, there are several little restaurants *(comedores)* between the main camping area and parking lot and the gate at the beginning of the road to Flores. As you arrive at Tikal from Flores, you'll see them on the right side; **Comedor Imperio Maya, Comedor La Jungla,** and **Comedor Tikal** are the best of the bunch. All are rustic and pleasant, and all serve hefty plates of fairly tasty food at low prices. You can get a large serving of roast chicken, with rice, beans, and fresh tortillas, along with a drink, for around Q40 (US$5).

Within the area of the ruins there are picnic tables beneath shelters and itinerant soft-drink peddlers, but no snack stands. If you want to spend all day at the ruins without having to walk back to the parking area for lunch, take sandwiches. Most of the hotels here and in Flores, as well as the comedores, will make you a bag lunch to take into the park.

TIKAL AFTER DARK

Aside from hanging around at your hotel bar or at one of the simple comedores, or swinging in a hammock at the campsite, the best nighttime activity here is to visit the ruins by moonlight. Those staying near the entrance to the ruins can have their admission ticket validated to allow them to roam the park until 8pm, and in some cases even later. If the moon is waxing, full, or just beyond full, you're in for a real treat. *Tip:* Before venturing into the park at night, be sure to ask around as to the current level of safety inside the park after dark.

2 El Remate ★★

20 miles (32km) E of Flores; 20 miles (32km) S of Tikal; 37 miles (60km) W of Melchor de Mencos

El Remate is a tiny village on the eastern shores of Lake Petén Itzá that is rapidly becoming a preferred spot to stay while visiting Tikal. El Remate is located about midway between Flores and Tikal. Staying here cuts travel time between your hotel and the ruins. It is also much more tranquil and pristine than Flores or Santa Elena. Currently, there is a host of budget lodgings in the village, while a few more upscale options have sprung up on the shores of the lake heading north out of the village.

ESSENTIALS
GETTING THERE & DEPARTING

BY PLANE See "By Plane" under "Essentials" in section 1, earlier in this chapter.

BY MINIVAN Scheduled and independent minivans ply the route between Santa Elena/Flores and Tikal throughout the day. Any of these will drop you off in El Remate. For more information on these, see "Getting Around" in section 1 and below. Fares from Flores to El Remate run around Q32 to Q40 (US$4–US$5).

BY CAR El Remate is located about a mile (1.6km) north of Ixlú (El Cruce). The road is paved and in good shape all the way from the Belize-Guatemala border 37 miles (60km) away.

GETTING AROUND

El Remate is a tiny village, and you can easily walk anywhere in town. Some of the hotels listed below are located a mile or so north of the village, on the road that circles Lake Petén Itzá. If you're in El Remate, you'll most likely want to go to Tikal, visit Santa Elena and Flores, or explore the region.

BY TAXI Taxis charge between Q160 and Q320 (US$20–US$40) for the one-way trip between El Remate and Tikal, or between El Remate and Flores. The higher rate is for a minivan that can hold anywhere from six to eight passengers. A taxi is your best option if you decide to explore the area around the lake. There are often taxis hanging around the small village. If not, your hotel can call one for you. Be sure to have your hotel set a fair price, or be prepared to bargain, as the first price you are quoted is almost assuredly above the going rate and subject to some negotiation.

BY MINIVAN   If you don't have a car, the best way to get around is by minivan. Scheduled and unscheduled minivans ply the route between Flores and Tikal throughout the day. All of these pass through El Remate, dropping off and picking up passengers. You can get a minivan at almost any hotel in El Remate, or walk a few hundred yards out to the main road to Tikal and flag one down. The ride takes about a half-hour to either Tikal or Flores, and the one-way fare is Q32 to Q40 (US$4–US$5) per person.

WHAT TO SEE & DO

The village of El Remate itself is very small and provincial, with little of interest to tourists. Most people use El Remate as a base for explorations of the ruins at Tikal. However, as small lodges and isolated resorts start to pop up here, so do the many tour and activity options.

Just west of El Remate is the **Biotopo Cerro Cahuí,** a small nature reserve with some trails and good wildlife-viewing opportunities. I recommend you only visit this little park with a guide, as incidents of violence against tourists caused it to be closed for a period a few years ago. The reserve is open daily from 8am to 4pm, and admission is Q30 (US$3.75).

One of the most popular activities in El Remate is **renting a canoe or kayak** for paddling around on the lake. Most of the hotels in town rent either kayaks or canoes, or can arrange it for you. Rates run around Q10 to Q16 (US$1.25–US$2) per hour, or around Q80 (US$10) per day.

Similarly, most of the hotels in town either rent or provide **mountain bikes** for the guests, or can arrange for their rental. The dirt road that circles Lake Petén Itzá is excellent for a mountain bike ride. Rates are about Q120 to Q160 (US$15–US$20) per day.

Finally, the village of El Remate is gaining some local renown for its woodcarving. You'll see several roadside stands set up on the route between Ixlú and El Remate, and onwards to Tikal. If you ask around El Remate, you might even be able to visit one or more of the artisans.

WHERE TO STAY & DINE

Most folks take their meals at their hotels. There are some simple restaurants *(comedores)* in the center of the village, as well as a small market.

VERY EXPENSIVE

Camino Real Tikal ⚘   For years this was the only luxury option in the Petén, and it's still a decent choice. This is a large resort, and if a bright lobby with plenty of shiny marble and glass and rooms with all the modern amenities feel out of place for you, choose another hotel. The rooms are housed in a series of three-story thatch roof bungalows. The bungalows are set in a long line along a ridge over the lake, and all have wonderful views of the lake. Inside, the furnishings are comfortable and the decor is tasteful. Every room has a private balcony or porch, but the third-floor units are the best, with the best views. There are two restaurants and a lovely outdoor pool area, while down by the water there is a dock out into the lake, and a sandy beach area for swimming. The hotel offers a free shuttle to the park and to the airport in Flores.

3 miles (5km) west of El Remate, Petén. © 502/926-0204. Fax 502/926-0222. www.caminorealtikal.com.gt. 72 units. Q880 (US$110) double. AE, DISC, MC, V. **Amenities:** 2 restaurants; 2 bars; lounge; outdoor pool; 2 outdoor unlit tennis courts; bicycle rental; watersports equipment rental; tour desk; laundry service. *In room:* A/C, TV, minifridge, safe.

MODERATE

La Lancha Resort ★★ *Finds*   This is the latest addition to filmmaker Francis Ford Coppola's growing hotel dynasty in the Mundo Maya. The idea is that this property can be combined with stays at Coppola's Blancaneaux Lodge and Turtle Inn in Belize to provide a complete and varied visit to the area. Guests can also simply take advantage of this, or of any one of the other two resorts, a la carte. The main lodge has a commanding view of the lake and features a soaring, open-air A-frame thatch roof oriented towards the view. Below the lodge is a kidney-shaped pool. A steep trail leads down to the shore of the lake, where you'll find a swimming area. The rooms are all duplex bungalows, with plenty of room, rustic but tasteful decor, and good views of the lake. When I last visited, this place had just come under the management of the folks from Blancaneaux, and plans were in the works to add several new rooms and bungalows. These new accommodations will almost certainly be larger and more luxurious than the existing rooms, which are already nice enough as they are.

Lago Petén Itzá, Petén. © 800/746-3743 in the U.S., or ©/fax 502/928-8331 in Guatemala. www.la lanchavillage.com. 10 units. Q1,200–Q1,680 (US$150–US$210). AE, MC, V. **Amenities:** Restaurant; bar; outdoor pool; bike rental; tour desk; laundry service. *In room:* No phone.

La Mansión del Pájaro Serpiente ★ *Finds*   Set on a hillside over the lake just south of the village, this place has both budget accommodations and deluxe bungalows, beautiful gardens, and a friendly atmosphere. The bungalows feature beautiful stone and woodworking details, with local textile and crafts filling out the decor. These rooms are large and should be classified as junior suites, as they all have a comfortable sitting area just off the bedroom. The small free-form pool is set in lush gardens, and almost feels like a natural pond in the midst of the jungle. The open-air restaurant here has a great view of the water and specializes in local cuisine.

El Remate, Petén. ©/fax 502/926-4246 or 502/926-0065. 10 units. Q720 (US$90) double. MC, V. **Amenities:** Restaurant; bar; outdoor pool and Jacuzzi; tour desk; laundry service. *In room:* No phone.

INEXPENSIVE

In addition to the places listed below, there are a few very inexpensive options right in El Remate catering to the backpacker crowd. If you fit this bill, you can simply walk around and see which one best fits your fancy and budget. Or you could try perennial favorites **Casa de Doña Tonita** (no phone) and **Mirador del Duende** (© 502/926-0269).

La Casa de Don David Hotel *Value*   Rooms are located in a series of buildings arrayed around a lush garden area. All are clean and simple. The least expensive rooms here have cold-water showers. There's an open-air octagonal hammock hut for reading and resting, and you can catch a glimpse of Lake Petén from here. The hotel offers bicycles free for guest use. David Kuhn and his wife Rosita have lived in this area for almost 30 years, and are a wealth of information and advice. David was the original *gringo perdido* of the nearby nature lodge (see below), but left there to open this delightful little place.

El Remate, Petén. © 502/306-2190 or 502/928-8469. www.lacasadedondavid.com. 15 units. Q258–Q387 (US$32–US$48) double. Rates include 1 meal (breakfast, lunch, or dinner). No credit cards. **Amenities:** Restaurant; tour desk; laundry service. *In room:* No phone.

Parador Ecológico El Gringo Perdido   Two miles (3km) north of El Remate on the rough road that circles Lake Petén Itzá, you'll find one of Guatemala's oldest jungle lodges. This little offbeat paradise is arranged along the lakeshore, with shady rustic hillside gardens, a little restaurant, a quiet camping area, and rooms ranging from a rustic dormitory to some pretty plush private bungalows. You can also camp here. The whole thing seems to blend into and get swallowed up by the rainforest. El Gringo Perdido, which means "the lost American," offers good swimming in the lake, 2 miles (3km) of nature trails, and tranquillity. This little lodge borders the Biotopo Cerro Cahui.

2 miles (3km) west of El Remate, Petén. ©/fax **502/334-2305.** gringo_perdido@hotmail.com. 12 units. Q24 (US$3) per person to camp; Q80 (US$10) per person dormitory; Q224 (US$28) double room; Q400 (US$50) deluxe room. No credit cards. **Amenities:** Restaurant; tour desk; laundry service. *In room:* No phone.

EL REMATE AFTER DARK

El Remate is a quiet village. Most visitors head to the small bar at their hotel or hostal to chat with fellow travelers. One popular tour offered at night is out onto the lake to see crocodiles. This 2-hour tour involves a ride in a small motor launch with a high-powered flashlight or headlamp. The guide will scan the shore and inlets for the red reflection of the crocodiles' eyes. If you're lucky, they won't submerge as you slowly approach. All of the hotels in town can arrange this tour. The cost is between Q120 and Q160 (US$15–US$20).

3 Flores & Santa Elena ⍟

40 miles (65km) SW of Tikal; 84 miles (136km) NW of the Belizean border; 280 miles (454km) NE of Guatemala City

Accommodations in Tikal are limited and many travelers either choose to (or must) overnight in the sister cities of Flores and Santa Elena. Still, this is not necessarily such a bad thing. Flores itself is a picturesque little town built on an island in the middle of Lake Petén Itzá. A narrow causeway connects Flores to Santa Elena. There's a lot more to do and see in Flores and Santa Elena, and a far wider range of hotels and restaurants to choose from.

Seen from the air, Flores appears almost perfectly round. Buildings come right down to the water's edge. A walk around the circumference of the island presents a sort of Venetian experience. Since the lake's water level has risen over the years, the most outlying streets and alleys are flooded. Dugout canoes, kayaks, and motor launches are beached in the middle of water-logged streets, and houses rise straight up out of the water. Look around the perimeter of the island and you will find buildings that have had their first floors abandoned to the ever-deepening waters. This quiet town, with its colonial-style buildings and cobblestone streets, is one of the most fascinating in Guatemala. Though most people spend time here only en route to or from the Tikal ruins, Flores is well worth exploring for a day or two.

Santa Elena, Flores's mainland counterpart, on the other hand, is a dusty, modern boomtown with little at all to recommend it. However, Santa Elena is where you'll find the airport, the bus stations, a host of budget hotels, and a good view of Flores. Just to the west of Santa Elena is the town of San Benito, a rough and ramshackle area with little appeal to visitors. The name Flores is often used as a bucket term encompassing the island of Flores itself, along with Santa Elena and San Benito.

Flores is the unofficial capital of the Petén region of Guatemala. El Petén has always been a remote region, and it was here, on the banks of Lake Petén Itzá,

ACCOMMODATIONS ■
Casa Elena **12**
Hotel Del Patio **14**
Hotel Isla de Flores **6**
Hotel Maya Internacional **13**
Hotel Petén **3**
Hotel Petén Esplendido **11**
Hotel Villa Maya **17**
Jaguar Inn Santa Elena **16**
La Casona de la Isla **4**

DINING & NIGHTLIFE ◆
Café Luna **5**
Capitán Tortuga **2**
El Mirador Restaurant **11**
Las Puertas **9**
Maya Princess Café **7**
Restaurant El Tucán **10**

ATTRACTIONS ●
Aktun Kan **15**
CINCAP museum **8**
El Ceibal **1**
El Zotz **1**
Uaxactún **17**

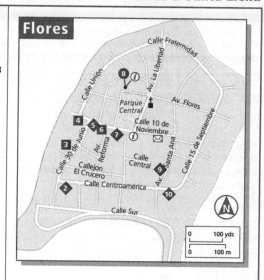

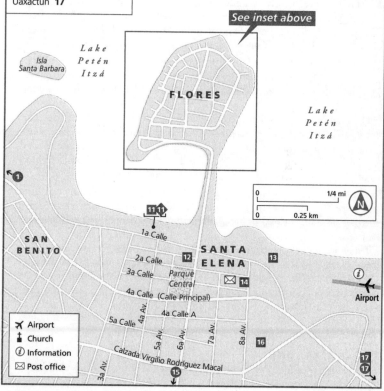

that the Itzá people, descendents of the Mayas, resisted Spanish conquest until the end of the 17th century. Hernán Cortés had visited the Itzá city of Tayasal, which once stood on the far side of the lake, in 1525 but had not tried to conquer the Itzás, who had a reputation for being fierce warriors. However, in 1697, the Spanish finally conquered the Itzás, and Tayasal became the last Indian city to fall under Spanish rule. Two years after taking Tayasal, the Spanish moved to Flores, an island that could easily be defended. They renamed this island Nuestra Señora de los Remedios y San Pablo de los Itzaes and between 1700 and 1701 built a fort here. In 1831, the island was once again renamed, this time being given the name Flores in honor of a Guatemalan patriot.

One of the most curious pieces of local history is the story of a sick horse left in Tayasal by Cortés when he passed through the area. The Itzás had never seen horses before and as soon as Cortés left, they began worshipping the horse. When the horse died, a stone statue of it was made, and the worship continued until Spanish missionaries arrived in Tayasal 100 years later. The missionaries, appalled by this idolatry, proceeded to pitch the blasphemous statue into the lake. To this day the legendary horse statue has never been discovered, though searches continue to be launched from time to time.

ESSENTIALS
GETTING THERE & DEPARTING
BY PLANE   See "By Plane" under "Essentials" in "Tikal," earlier in this chapter. The Santa Elena/Flores airport is also served by several daily flights from Guatemala City. If you choose to go on to Guatemala City from Flores, you can inquire at your hotel, with any travel agent in town, or stop by the airport yourself. A one-way fare to Guatemala City costs between Q400 and Q480 (US$50–US$60). The flight takes 50 minutes.

BY CAR   To get here from Belize, see "By Car" under "Essentials" in section 1, earlier in this chapter.

The road between Tikal and Flores is a good paved road and the trip takes around an hour by car. To get to either of the sister towns from Tikal, head south out of the ruins and turn right at Ixlú (El Cruce). Continue on past the airport. You will come to Santa Elena first. Stay on the main avenue into town and head towards the lake, where you will find the causeway over to Flores.

BY BUS   For information on getting to Flores and Santa Elena by bus from Belize, see "By Bus" under "Essentials" in "Tikal," earlier in this chapter. See "Getting Around," below, for details on getting from Santa Elena and Flores to the ruins.

There are several companies operating first-class buses to Guatemala City. **Transportes Fuentes del Norte** (© **502/926-0517**) and **Línea Dorada** (© **502/926-0070**) are both located near the corner of Calle 4 and Avenida 4 in Santa Elena. The trip to Guatemala City takes around 10 hours, and first-class fares run between Q96 and Q240 (US$12–US$30). The wide range in prices reflects the wide range in what can be considered "first class." Línea Dorada is by far the most comfortable and quickest option.

GETTING AROUND
If you're in Santa Elena or Flores, you'll most likely want to go to Tikal or explore the region around Lake Petén.

BY BUS   Very inexpensive local bus service connects Flores and Santa Elena to Tikal and several neighboring communities. However, this service is infrequent, slow, and often uncomfortably overcrowded. If you want to take this bus to Tikal, it leaves from near the corner of Avenida 4 and Calle 4 at 6am and 1pm. Return buses from Tikal leave at the same times. Ask at your hotel or around town for current schedules, as they change periodically. Duration of the trip is 2 hours; the fare is Q12 (US$1.50).

BY MINIVAN   If you don't have a car, the best way to get around this area is by minivan. Scheduled and independent minivans ply the route between Santa Elena and Flores and Tikal throughout the day. Minivans and collective taxis charge between Q32 and Q48 (US$4–US$6) per person. From Santa Elena you can catch a bus back to the border.

Minivans from Flores and Santa Elena leave roughly every hour between 5am and 10am, and less frequently thereafter. They also meet every plane arriving at the Santa Elena airport. These minivans leave from Tikal for the return trip roughly every hour from noon to 6pm. Almost every hotel in Flores and Santa Elena can arrange a minivan pickup for you. If your hotel doesn't offer one, go to the Hotel San Juan in Santa Elena. It is always best to reserve your return on a minibus back to Santa Elena when you pay for your fare out. The trip usually takes an hour and costs Q32 to Q48 (US$4–US$6) per person, each way.

BY TAXI   Taxis charge between Q200 and Q280 (US$25–US$35) for the one-way trip between Flores or Santa Elena and Tikal. Between Flores or Santa Elena and El Remate, the fare is around Q160 to Q240 (US$20–US$30). The higher rate is for a minivan that can hold anywhere from six to eight passengers. A taxi is your best option if you decide to explore the area around the lake. Be sure to bargain, as the first price you are quoted is almost certainly above the going rate and subject to some negotiation.

BY CAR   If you have your own car, the road between Santa Elena and Flores and Tikal is paved, well marked, and heavily traveled. It's about 20 miles (32km) from Flores to Ixlú (El Cruce), and another 20 miles (32km) on to the park and ruins of Tikal.

For information on renting a car, see "Getting Around" in section 1, earlier in this chapter.

ORIENTATION

The town primarily known as Flores actually consists of three smaller towns that have merged. Flores proper sits on a small island out in Lake Petén Itzá, and is connected to the mainland by a long causeway. On the mainland are Santa Elena (nearest the airport) and San Benito (closer to the bus terminal and market). Whether you arrive by air or by bus from Guatemala City or Belize, you will come into town from the east. The road in from the airport leads straight through Santa Elena to the market and bus terminal, while the causeway to Flores is a turn to the right in the middle of Santa Elena. While there are a host of budget lodgings in San Benito, especially around the bus terminal, I strongly advise most travelers to stick to Santa Elena and Flores proper.

FAST FACTS   There are numerous banks in downtown Flores and Santa Elena. Most have ATMs, and many of these will work with your debit or credit card. Check with your home bank and the PLUS or Cirrus systems in advance to confirm. Downtown banks include **Banquetzal,** Calle 4, between avenidas 4 and 5, Santa Elena (© 502/926-0711); **Banrural,** Avenida 3 and Calle 4, Santa Elena (© 502/926-1002); and **Banco Industrial,** Avenida 6, Santa Elena (© 502/926-0281). Most of the hotels and restaurants in Flores and Santa Elena will also exchange dollars for quetzales, although they may give you a slightly less favorable rate than you would get at a bank.

The **Flores post office** is on the Pasaje Progresso just off the Parque Central, or Central Park, which is in front of the church. **Santa Elena's post office** is on Calle 2 and Avenida 7. Both are open Monday through Friday from 8am to 5pm. To contact the **local police,** dial © 502/926-1365.

There is an information booth run by the Guatemalan Tourist Board, **Inguat** (© 502/926-0533) at the Flores airport, and another one in downtown Flores (© 502/926-0669). Both can help provide basic maps to the region and ruins, as well as brochures for local hotels and tour agencies. They will also usually help you find an available room if you don't have one.

WHAT TO SEE & DO

Flores is a wonderful little town to walk around. The whole island is only about 5 blocks wide in any direction. At the center is a small central park or plaza, anchored by the town's Catholic church. Be sure to take a peek inside to check out the beautiful stained glass windows. After first exploring this incipient Guatemalan Venice on foot, you should have a look at the island from the perspective of a boat. Numerous locals will approach you offering you a tour of the lake.

To learn more about the natural history and cultural traditions of Flores and El Petén, visit the **Centro de Información sobre la Naturaleza, Cultura y Artesanía de Petén (CINCAP; © 502/926-0718)**, which is located on the square in front of the church in Flores. CINCAP operates a museum with displays on the cultural and natural history of the region. Of particular interest is the exhibit on how chicle, the substance that once gave chewing gum its chewiness, is produced. There are also exhibits on the local ecology and on medicinal plants of the jungle. A gift shop here has locally made baskets, woodcarvings, and carved bone reproductions of ancient Mayan artifacts.

One of the most popular things to do in Flores is take a **tour of the lake** 🐾. You will be inundated with offers for boat tours. Ask at your hotel or one of the local tour agencies, or talk to the numerous freelancers approaching you on the street. Be sure to inspect the craft before hand, if possible, and make sure you feel comfortable with its lake-worthiness. Also, make sure your guide is bilingual. These tours last anywhere from 1 to 3 hours, and usually include stops at La Guitarra Island (Guitar Island), which features a picnic and swimming area, as well as at the mostly unexcavated ruins of Tayasal. Here, be sure to climb **El Mirador** 🐾🐾, a lakeside pyramid that offers a fabulous view of Flores. Many of these tours also stop at a small, rather desultory zoo. These tours cost between Q64 and Q160 (US$8–US$20) per person, depending on the length of the tour and the size of your group. Be sure to bargain.

You can also explore the lake on your own in a kayak or canoe. These are also rented all around Flores. Again, ask at your hotel or at one of the local tour agencies. Rates for kayaks and canoes run around Q15 (US$1.85) per hour. Be careful paddling around the lake; when the winds pick up, especially in the afternoons, it can get quite choppy and challenging.

If you're a spelunker, you might want to explore **Aktun Kan,** the Cave of the Serpent, a large cavern just outside of Santa Elena. The cave takes its name from a legend about a giant snake living there. But don't worry, it's only a legend. Yet another legend has it that this cave is connected to a cave beneath the church on Flores. To reach the cave, either walk south out of Santa Elena on the road that crosses the causeway from Flores, or ask a taxi to take you out there. The fare should be around Q12 (US$1.50). Although there are lights in the cave (admission Q15/US$1.90), be sure to bring a flashlight just in case.

EL CEIBAL & OTHER NEARBY RUINS

If your life's passion is Mayan ruins or you simply crave more adventure than you have had so far on your visit to El Petén, maybe you should visit some of the more remote ruins of this region. In addition to exploring seldom-visited Mayan ruins, you'll be traveling through uninhabited jungles where you'll likely encounter a great deal of wildlife, which might include coatimundis, howler and spider monkeys, anteaters, tapirs, and possibly even jaguars.

El Ceibal 🔆 is the most accessible of these other ruins. It is also offers one of the most scenic routes along the way. To reach El Ceibal, you must first head the 40 miles (65km) from Flores to Sayaxché, which is a good-size town for El Petén (it even has a few basic hotels). From Sayaxché, you must hire a boat to carry you 11 miles (18km) up the Río de la Pasión. El Ceibal is a Late Classic–era ruin known for having the only circular temple in all of El Petén. There are also several well-preserved stelae arranged around one small temple structure on the central plaza, as well as a ball court. Many of the designs at El Ceibal indicate that the city had extensive contact with cities in the Yucatán, but whether this contact was due to trade or to warfare is unclear. Your best bet for visiting El Ceibal is to book the excursion with one of the tour agencies in Flores or Santa Elena. Full-day trips run around Q360 to Q440 (US$45–US$55). Overnight trips can also be arranged, combining a visit to El Ceibal to even more obscure Mayan sites like Aguateca and Petexbatún. If you get to Sayaxché on your own, look for **Viajes Don Pedro** (© **502/928-6109**). These folks run regular boats to El Ceibal and charge around Q240 (US$30) per person round-trip. If you want to stay in this area, check out **Chiminos Island Lodge** 🔆 (© **502/471-0855;** www.chiminosisland.com), which has six rustic yet luxurious cabins in the rainforest on a small island in the waters of the Petexbatún Lagoon.

Uaxactún (pronounced "wah-shahk-*toon*") is another Mayan ceremonial center located 15 miles (24km) north of Tikal. Though many of the pyramids and temples here have been uncovered, they have not been restored nearly as extensively as those at Tikal have been. One of the most interesting finds at Uaxactún is what is believed to be the oldest known astrological observatory yet discovered in the Mayan world. Located in Group E, on the eastern side of these ruins, sunrise watched from the observatory temple lines up precisely with other temples on the equinoxes and solstices. Your best bet for visiting El Ceibal is to book the excursion with one of the tour agencies in Flores or Santa Elena. Full-day trips cost about Q200 to Q280 (US$25–US$35), and can be combined with a stop at Tikal, although I think that's trying to cram too much into a single day. If you have your own four-wheel-drive vehicle, you can drive here yourself. The ruins at Uaxactún are open daily from 6am to 6pm, and no admission is charged. However, you must reach it by passing through Tikal National Park, and so you must pay the Tikal entrance fee of Q50 (US$6.25). Moreover, be forewarned that the dirt road between Uaxactún is sometimes not passable during the rainy season. Be sure to ask locally about current conditions before heading off.

HOLY BATS . . . MAN!

Located some 15 miles (24km) west of Tikal is another small and relatively unexcavated Mayan site, **El Zotz** 🔆. *Zotz* means "bat" in the local Mayan dialect, and bats are what you'll find here. Each night around sunset, tens of thousands of bats exit en masse from several caves here. The sight is spectacular.

Sometimes you will see a bat falcon dive into the mass and pluck out dinner. Most of the tour agencies in Flores and Santa Elena can arrange trips to El Zotz, although these tend to be hardy overnight affairs, with a fair amount of hiking involved. Rates run between Q1,200 and Q2,000 (US$150–US$250) per person for a 3-day/2-night excursion.

STUDYING SPANISH

Eco-Maya ✯ (② 502/926-0718; www.ecomaya.com) runs two community-based language school programs in small villages and communities around the Lake Petén Itzá region. The programs cost just Q1,400 (US$175) per week, including lodging and three meals daily with a local family, as well as 4 hours of daily class time, usually one-on-one. The setting allows for intensive language instruction, as well as many chances to really interact with the local culture and natural surroundings.

WHERE TO STAY
MODERATE

Hotel Del Patio ✯ *Finds* The central courtyard with a tall fountain flowing into a clover-leaf pool is classic colonial Guatemala. The rooms are simple, but clean, modern, and comfortable. I'd opt for a second-floor unit, just so you get to admire the courtyard from above as you enter and exit your room. There's a good-size kidney-shaped pool and small gym here, as well as a good international restaurant. This place has recently been taken over by the Camino Real chain, so I expect some upgrades might be in the works.

Calle 8 and Av. 2, Santa Elena, Petén. ② 502/926-1229. Fax 502/926-3030. www.hoteldelpatio.com.gt. 21 units. Q520 (US$65) double. Rate includes breakfast. AE, MC, V. **Amenities:** Restaurant; bar; pool; small gym; tour desk; limited room service (6:30am–10pm); laundry service. *In room:* A/C, TV.

Hotel Isla de Flores ✯ This four-story hotel in downtown Flores is probably your best bet on the island of Flores itself. The decor and architecture feature a mix of modern and colonial elements. The rooms are compact, but clean and comfortable. Each comes with two double beds, a good-size television with a variety of cable channels, and a little balcony overlooking the town and lake. White wicker furniture is spread around the lobby and restaurant areas. This place has a helpful tour desk, and is run by the same folks who have the Jungle Lodge inside Tikal National Park.

Av. La Reforma, Flores, Petén. ② 502/926-0614. Fax 502/476-0294. 18 units. Q440 (US$56) double. Rate includes breakfast. AE, MC, V. **Amenities:** Restaurant; bar; tour desk; laundry service. *In room:* A/C, TV.

Hotel Maya Internacional Built on the banks of the lake over 30 years ago, this hotel has had to contend with the rising lake waters and growing competition. In fact, some of its stiffest competition comes from its sister Hotel Villa Maya (see below), which I find to be a much better option. Most of the rooms are set on a small hillside just off the lake. Despite their age, the rooms are well kept and comfortable. They have clean tile floors and plenty of space. There are beautiful lakeview balconies in most rooms. The setting is excellent, and a little bay full of water lilies has formed between the hotel's bungalows. The hotel's pool has been built with an infinity effect that makes it seem like it blends into the lake. The hotel's restaurant is in a separate, larger thatched structure at the end of a short causeway out on a little patch of land jutting into the lake. The restaurant features a beautiful dining area, with an impressive high-pitched thatch roof; however, they only serve a daily fixed menu, so if you're not interested in the nightly offering, you'll have to head into Santa Elena or Flores.

Calle 1 and Av. 8, Santa Elena, Petén. © **502/926-2083** or 502/334-1818. Fax 502/926-0087 or 502/334-8134. www.villasdeguatemala.com. 25 units. Q520 (US$65) double. AE, DC, MC, V. **Amenities:** Restaurant; outdoor pool; tour desk; laundry service. In room: No phone.

Hotel Petén Espléndido

This is probably the most upscale and modern option in town, but this is definitely not saying much. In fact, the nicest aspect of this hotel is probably the view of it from the lake or Flores causeway. The hotel is actually in Santa Elena, but it is built right on the shore, with a great view of Flores and the lake. The rooms are all clean and comfortable, with more modern amenities than you'll find anywhere around. However, the decor and furnishings are dated, and some of the rooms feel a bit small. The best rooms here are the second-floor rooms with balconies directly fronting the lake. If you don't get one of these, the hotel's waterfront restaurant has a great view and serves good international and local cuisine. There's a relaxing and refreshing pool area, with a separate Jacuzzi. This place offers a free airport shuttle, as well as free paddleboats for use on the lake, and has a helpful tour desk and concierge.

1a Calle 5-01, Zona 1, Santa Elena, Flores, Petén. © **502/926-0880** or 502/360-8140. Fax 502/926-0866. www.petenesplendido.com. 62 units. Q720–Q880 (US$90–US$110) double. AE, DC, MC, V. **Amenities:** Restaurant; outdoor pool and Jacuzzi; watersports equipment rental; concierge; tour desk; car-rental desk; limited room service (6:30am–11:30pm); laundry service. In room: A/C, TV, dataport, hair dryer, safe.

Hotel Villa Maya ⭑

This is one of the newest and most comfortable lodgings near Flores and Santa Elena. Hotel Villa Maya is located about 5 minutes from the airport, on the shores of Lake Petén Itzá, but away from the twin cities and towards Tikal. Peace and quiet, if that's what you're looking for, are an added bonus, on top of the 10 minutes of reduced travel time to the ruins. However, if you want to take advantage of the restaurants and tour options in Flores, you'll either need your own car or must take lots of taxis. Rooms are housed in a series of two-story fourplex buildings, set on the edge of the lake. Local hardwoods are used generously to trim details and furnish the place. The rooms themselves are spacious and neat; each comes with a small triangular balcony overlooking the lake. The restaurant serves respectable but uninspired Guatemalan and international fare. The hotel has an interesting and inviting trapezoidal pool with a cascading waterfall filling it, as well as a wonderful dock and deck area over the lake.

Santa Elena, Petén. © **502/926-1276** or 502/334-1818. Fax 502/926-0032 or 502/334-8134. www.villas deguatemala.com. 38 units. Q680 (US$85) double. AE, MC, V. **Amenities:** Restaurant; outdoor pool and Jacuzzi; watersports equipment rental; tour desk; car rental desk; room service; laundry service. In room: A/C, TV.

INEXPENSIVE

Casa Elena ⭑ _Value_   This is a clean, neat little hotel in downtown Santa Elena, right across from the little park and taxi stand. This would be considered a business-class hotel, if anything of the sort existed, or needed to exist in this neck of the woods. Rooms are a bit small, and don't come with a balcony, but you do get a view of either the small park in Santa Elena or the hotel's small pool and lovely interior courtyard, with shady palm trees. The pool even has a small water slide, which is a big hit with children. The hotel is kept immaculate, and there's a friendly air to the whole operation. There's a simple restaurant on the grounds, as well as an inviting rooftop terrace and bar. This place makes a good base for exploring the region.

Av. 6 and Calle 2, Santa Elena, Petén. © **502/926-2235.** Fax 502/926-0097. www.casaelena.com. 27 units. Q320–Q400 (US$40–US$50) double. AE, DC, MC, V. **Amenities:** Restaurant; outdoor pool; tour desk; limited room service (7am–10pm); laundry service. In room: A/C, TV.

Hotel Petén   From the street, this hotel looks like a very modest Caribbean town dwelling; enter the doorway, and you'll find a small courtyard with tropical plants, a tiny semi-indoor pool, and a nice brick-and-stucco building of several floors. The rooms have all been well kept and steadily improved over the years. The best rooms are those on the top floor with an excellent view of the lake. If you can't get one of these, the hotel's roof is actually a terrace that enjoys that same view. There's a popular restaurant on the ground floor. These folks have an excellent local tour company, and a couple of other nearby hotels, if this one is full.

Calle Centroamérica, Flores, Petén. ℂ/fax **502/926-0692.** www.corpetur.com. 21 units. Q280–Q520 (US$35–US$65) double. AE, DC, MC, V. **Amenities:** Restaurant; pool; Jacuzzi; tour desk; laundry service. *In room:* A/C, TV.

Jaguar Inn Santa Elena   This hotel is operated by the same people who run the Jaguar Inn at Tikal and is one of the best budget hotels in Santa Elena. Guest rooms all have high ceilings and tile floors and are decorated with Guatemalan textiles and art. Art Deco wall sconces add a touch of class here in the wilderness. There's a garden in the courtyard and an open-air restaurant and lounge where guests can chat with other adventurous explorers. To find the hotel, watch for the sign on the left as you come into town from the airport. The only drawback here is that it's a bit of a walk to Flores, which is where most of the action—whatever action there is to speak of—is.

Calzada Rodríguez Macal 8-79, Zona 1, Santa Elena, Petén. ℂ **502/926-0002.** Fax 502/926-2413. www.jaguartikal.com. 19 units. Q160 (US$20) double. AE, MC, V. **Amenities:** Restaurant; tour desk; laundry service. *In room:* TV, no phone.

La Casona de la Isla ⌖   Owned by the same family that runs the Hotel Petén, La Casona shows the same attention to quality and is, in fact, slightly nicer. The guest rooms here are all fairly small and lack much in the way of style, but they do have tile floors, ceiling fans, air-conditioning, and modern bathrooms. Most come with a private balcony, and almost all of these have good views to the lake. The hotel is built in an L-shape around a stone terrace with lush gardens and a small swimming pool featuring a sculpted stone waterfall and separate Jacuzzi. The hotel's open-air dining room and restaurant serves good Guatemalan and international fare, with an excellent view overlooking the lake.

Calle 30 de Junio, Flores, Petén. ℂ **502/926-0523.** www.corpetur.com. 30 units. Q280–Q520 (US$35–US$65) double. AE, DC, MC, V. **Amenities:** Restaurant; outdoor pool and Jacuzzi; tour desk; laundry service. *In room:* A/C, TV.

WHERE TO DINE

There are tons of places to eat around Flores and Santa Elena. Most are simple affairs serving local and Mexican cuisine, and geared towards locals and the backpacker crowd. Most of the hotels listed above have restaurants, and most of these are quite dependable. **El Mirador Restaurant** at the Hotel Petén Espléndido (p. 267), serves good but far from spectacular international fare; however, the setting is certainly the most elegant you'll find in this neck of the woods. Since my last visit, I've received good reports about a new Thai and vegetarian option in downtown Flores called **Café Luna.**

Capitán Tortuga INTERNATIONAL   Also known as the Crocodile Club, this popular restaurant has a long and wide-ranging menu. The narrow room here has walls of rough weaved reeds or cane, and the place can feel a little claustrophobic at times. However, the intimacy makes it easy to start up conversations with fellow travelers, and that's part of the charm here. You can get everything from pizzas to barbecue ribs to vegetarian shish kabobs. They also have a wide range of coffee and espresso drinks, as well as ice creams and freshly baked desserts.

Calle 30 de Junio, Flores. © **502/926-0247.** Main course Q20–Q96 (US$2.50–US$12). MC, V. Wed–Mon 7am–11pm.

Maya Princess Café INTERNATIONAL   The awning and entryway of this Flores restaurant look pretty slick, but inside you'll be quickly engulfed by the jovial, backpacker vibe that makes this place so popular. Heavy wooden tables are covered with colorful local textiles, and the walls are painted a hot pink. Local cuisine and Mexican staples are complemented by some daring (for the Petén, at least) additions like chicken teriyaki and vegetable tempura. Portions are quite filling. Semi-recent run movies are shown from a DVD projected on a large screen each night at around 9pm, making this place even more popular. Come early if you want a decent seat.

Av. Reforma at the corner of 10 de Noviembre, Flores. © **502/926-3797.** Reservations not accepted. Main courses Q24–Q64 (US$3–US$8). AE, MC, V. Daily 7am–10pm.

Restaurant El Tucán GUATEMALAN/MEXICAN   This is one of the most popular restaurants in Flores. It is built on a dock behind the hotel of the same name, and has fabulous views over the lake. The menu is primarily Mexican and portions are large, so bring a healthy appetite when you come. There are even some good vegetarian dishes on the menu, as well as fresh fish and the occasional wild game entree. Be sure to start out with guacamole. The atmosphere, with waves lapping beneath your feet and subdued lighting, is quite pleasant. The restaurant keeps a namesake toucan as well as other native bird species in their aviary here, something I'm not a big fan of.

Calle Centroamérica 45, Flores. © **502/926-0536.** Main courses Q20–Q80 (US$2.50–US$10). AE, MC, V. Daily 8am–9:30pm.

FLORES & SANTA ELENA AFTER DARK

Most folks simply frequent the bar at their hotel, or stick around after dinner at one of the local restaurants. The bar at the **Restaurant El Tucán,** Calle Centroamérica 45, is probably the most happening place in town. Grab a seat overlooking the water, grab a beer, and share your travel tales with whoever is there. However, this old standby has been getting a run for its money from **Las Puertas,** which has been playing a mix of house and chill dance tunes in a hip little space; it's located at the corner of Calle Central and Avenida Santa Ana.

Appendix A:
Belize in Depth

B elize is the youngest nation in the Western Hemisphere, having been granted independence from Britain in 1981. With a population of just 270,000, Belize is a sparsely populated country with no great cities. Tourism is currently the fastest growing segment of the economy, and the country offers a wide range of attractions for visitors, from sun 'n' fun beach vacations to active adventures and ecotourism explorations. This chapter will help you get acquainted with the history, people, and natural environment of this small yet very diverse and exciting Central American nation.

1 Belize Today

Originally a major part of the ancient Mayan empire, Belize was next settled by pirates and then colonized by the British, using slave labor. The descendants of each of these groups are woven into the historical lore and cultural fabric of modern Belize. Add to the mix the independent Garífuna people, who settled along the remote southern shore in the early part of the 19th century, and the more recent waves of Mexican, Chinese, and East Indian immigrants, and you have an idea of the cultural meld that constitutes this unique Central American country. Surprisingly, Belizeans of all cultural stripes tend to get along a lot better and with far fewer outward and untoward shows of racism than citizens of most other nations. This is a small country. The sense of community is strong and, even in the big city, people tend to know their neighbors and almost everyone is somehow related.

Belize is a developing nation, plagued with a small economy, a tiny industrial base, no oil or natural gas reserves, a huge trade deficit, and a historic dependence on foreign aid. These problems have been compounded by the British pullout and a universal reduction of international largesse. Sugar and citrus are the principal cash crops, though bananas and seafood exports also help. However, tourism is the most promising emergent source of income, and it has become an important engine in the economy. This trend is sure to continue. Increasingly, Belizeans whose fathers and grandfathers were farmers or fishermen find themselves hotel owners, tour guides, waiters, and cleaning personnel. While most have adapted gracefully and regard the industry as a source of new jobs and opportunities for economic advancement, restaurant and hotel staff can seem gruff and uninterested at times.

Belize held its first parliamentary elections in 1984. Since then, power has Ping-Ponged back and forth between the United Democratic Party (UDP) and the People's United Party (PUP). The former is a more conservative, free-market oriented party, while the latter champions a more liberal, social-democratic agenda. The most recent elections were held in August 1998. During these elections, PUP won 26 of the 29 parliamentary seats, while the UDP managed to win just three. All of the country's newspapers hold fierce party loyalties, and the strident political slant of the news stories and editorials might take some getting used to for visitors accustomed to a more passive press.

Speaking of Tongues

English is the official language of Belize, but a traveler will most likely run across a wide range of languages. Three centuries of colonization have given the Queen's English some foothold here; however, a large percentage of the local population, particularly Black Creoles, speak a Creole English that is downright unintelligible to most English-speaking visitors. In recent years there have been attempts to standardize and record the Creole dialect, and you may see it written out on billboards and in newspapers. *How fi Rite Bileez Kriol (How To Write Belize Creole),* is a widely available pamphlet sold at local bookstores and gift shops, and an excellent and entertaining reference if you want to take a stab at Creole.

Moreover, this is still Central America, and Spanish is widely spoken in Belize, especially in the northern and western regions near the borders with Mexico and Guatemala. If that's not enough, Belize has three relatively homogenous indigenous groups, the Garífunas and the Kekchi and Mopan Mayas, each of whom has a distinct language. Finally, rounding out this polyglot pastiche, you may also hear some Chinese, Arabic, Hindi, or even the archaic German used by the country's small Mennonite community.

Check out appendix B for some useful terms and phrases in Creole and Spanish.

Belize has a population of some 270,000, roughly half of whom live in one of the six major towns or cities, with the rest living in rural areas or small villages. About 45% of the population is considered mestizo, descendants of mixed Spanish, Mexican, and/or Mayan blood. Making up 30% of the population are the Creoles, predominantly black descendants of slaves and the early British colonists. Belize's three Mayan tribes—Yucatec, Mopan, and Kekchi—make up around 10% of the population. The Garífuna constitute approximately 6.5% of the population, while a mix of whites of British descent, Mennonites, Chinese, and East Indians fill out the rest.

In general, the pace of life and business is slow in Belize. You'll seldom find people rushing down the sidewalks or dirt streets. There are only four major highways in the country, and traffic is never heavy. In fact, all of these highways actually have speed bumps along their length, as they pass through the many roadside towns and villages.

2 History 101

EARLY HISTORY

Before the arrival of the first Europeans, this was the land of the ancient Mayas. Although most people think of Mexico's Mayan cities in the Yucatán and Guatemala's Tikal when they think of *El Mundo Maya,* or the Mayan World, ongoing archaeological

Dateline

- 2000 B.C.–A.D. 1000 Mayan civilization flourishes.
- 562 Caracol defeats Tikal.
- 1638 Shipwrecked English sailors establish the first European settlement.

continues

discoveries show that what is today known as Belize was once a major part of the Mayan Empire. River and coastal trade routes connected dozens of cities and small towns throughout this region to each other and to the major ceremonial and trading cities of Mexico and Guatemala. Caracol, a Mayan ruin in the Cayo District of western Belize, is a huge ceremonial city that defeated Tikal in battle in A.D. 562. Other sites, like Lamanai, Altun Ha, and Xunantunich, were thriving ceremonial and trade centers, with impressive ruins and artifacts. Moreover, ongoing excavations at sites like Pilar and La Milpa may eventually reveal other cities and ceremonial sites of equal or greater importance.

One of the earliest known Mayan cities in Mesoamerica, Cuello, is located just outside of Orange Walk Town and has been dated to B.C. 2000 or earlier. Mayan history is often divided into several distinct periods: Archaic (10,000–2000 B.C.), Pre-Classic (2000 B.C.–A.D. 250), Classic (A.D. 250–900), and Post-Classic (900–1540). Within this timeline, the Classic period itself is often divided into Early, Middle, Late, and Terminal stages. At the height of development, as many as two million Maya may have inhabited the region that is today

- 1783 English settlement rights are recognized.
- 1786 Settlements become self-governing. British superintendent takes up residence.
- 1798 The last Spanish attack is beaten off by the settlers with British support.
- 1859 The border between Guatemala and British Honduras is established.
- 1862 The area officially becomes the colony of British Honduras.
- 1926 Baron Bliss, Belize's greatest benefactor arrives, anchors, and soon dies just offshore of Belize City.
- 1931 A hurricane destroys Belize City.
- 1948 Guatemala, laying claim to British Honduras, closes the border.
- 1957 First Mennonite farmers arrive from Mexico.
- 1961 The capitol is moved from Belize City to Belmopan.
- 1964 The new constitution provides for self-government, but Guatemalan claims to the country delay independence.
- 1973 British Honduras is renamed Belize.
- 1981 Belize becomes an independent nation.
- 1984 First parliamentary election.
- 1996 Mayan medicine man Don Eligio Panti dies at an estimated 104 years of age.
- 2000 University of Belize is officially inaugurated.
- 2001 Hurricane Iris devastates southern Belize.

known as Belize. No one knows for sure what led to the decline of the Classic Maya, but somewhere around A.D. 900 their society entered a severe and rapid decline. Famine, warfare, deforestation, and religious prophecy have all been sited as possible causes. Nevertheless, Belize is somewhat unique in that it had several major ceremonial or trading cities still occupied by Maya when the first Spanish conquistadors arrived.

SPANISH ATTEMPTS AT CONQUEST

Christopher Columbus sailed past the Belize coast in 1502, and even named the Bay of Honduras, but he never anchored or set foot ashore here, and the Spanish never had much success in colonizing Belize. In fact, they met with fierce resistance from the remaining Maya. Part of their problem may have come from Gonzalo Guerrero, a Spanish sailor who was shipwrecked off the coast of Belize and the Yucatán in the early years of the 16th century. Originally pressed into slavery, Guerrero eventually married the daughter of a Mayan ruler, and became an important warrior and military adviser in the Mayan battles with the Spanish. To be sure, the Spanish led various attacks and attempts at conquest and

Mayan Sites in Belize

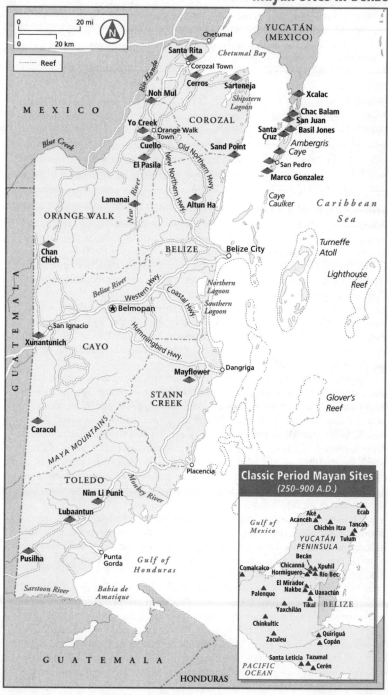

0 ———— 20 mi
0 ———— 20 km

-------- Reef

YUCATÁN
(MEXICO)

Chetumal

Santa Rita
Chetumal Bay
Corozal Town

Cerros
Sarteneja

Noh Mul
Shipstern
Lagoon

Xcalac

MEXICO

COROZAL

Chac Balam
San Juan
Basil Jones

Yo Creek
Orange Walk
Town

Santa
Cruz

Cuello
Old Northern Hwy.
Sand Point

Ambergris
Caye

El Pasila
San Pedro

Marco Gonzalez

Río Hondo

Blue Creek

New River

New Northern Hwy.

Lamanai
Altun Ha

Caye
Caulker

Caribbean
Sea

ORANGE WALK

Chan
Chich

BELIZE
Belize City

Turneffe
Atoll

Lighthouse
Reef

Belize River
Western Hwy.
Coastal Hwy.

Northern
Lagoon

Southern
Lagoon

GUATEMALA

Belmopan

San Ignacio

Xunantunich
CAYO

Hummingbird Hwy.

Mayflower
Dangriga

Glover's
Reef

STANN
CREEK

Caracol

MAYA MOUNTAINS

Placencia

TOLEDO
Monkey River

Nim Li Punit

Lubaantun

Pusilha
Punta
Gorda

Gulf of
Honduras

Sarstoon River
Bahía de
Amatique

GUATEMALA

HONDURAS

Classic Period Mayan Sites
(250–900 A.D.)

Gulf of
Mexico

Aké
Acanceh

Ecab

Chichén Itza
Tancah

YUCATÁN
PENINSULA
Tulum

Becán

Comalcalco
Chicanná
Hormiguero
Xpuhil
Río Béc

El Mirador
Palenque
Nakbe
Uaxactún

Yaxchilán
Tikal
BELIZE

Chinkultic

Quiriguá
Zaculeu
Copán

Santa Leticia
Tazumal
Cerén

PACIFIC
OCEAN

(Fun Fact By Any Other Name

There's some debate as to the origin of the name "Belize." Some claim it is the timeworn corruption of the name Wallace, one of the early buccaneer captains to set anchor here. Others claim it comes from the Mayan word *beliz*, which translates as "muddy water."

---

control of the territory that is present-day Belize. Many of these were brutal and deadly. They were also able to set up some missionary outposts, most notably those near Lamanai, where travelers today can still see the ruins of these early Spanish churches. Nevertheless, by the mid-1600s, the Spanish had been militarily forced to abandon all permanent settlements and attempts at colonialism in Belize, concentrating their efforts on more productive regions around Central and South America and the Caribbean Sea.

THE BRITISH ARE COMING

Belize likes to play up the fact that it was founded by pirates and buccaneers, and indeed, these unsavory characters were among the first to make this region their base of operations. Many of these pirates and buccaneers used the Belize coastline and its protected anchorages as hideouts and bases following their attacks on Spanish fleets transporting gold and silver treasures from their more productive colonies.

By the mid–17th century, British loggers were settling along the coast and making their way up the rivers and streams in search of mahogany for shipbuilding and other types of wood for making dyes. Proud and independent, these early settlers called themselves "Baymen" (after the Bay of Honduras). Politically, the Baymen treaded a delicate balance between being faithful British subjects and fiercely independent settlers.

Throughout this period and into the 18th century, the Spanish launched regular attacks on pirate bases and Baymen settlements in Belize. Spanish attacks devastated early settlements in Belize in 1679, 1717, 1730, and 1754, although after the dust cleared and the Spanish fleet moved on, the Baymen would always return. As the attacks increased in intensity, the Baymen sought more and more support from the British. In 1763, Spain and Britain signed the Treaty of Paris, which granted Britain official rights to log in Belize, but maintained Spanish sovereignty. Still, in 1779, Spain attacked the principal Belizean settlement on St. George's Caye, capturing 140 British and Baymen settlers and 250 slaves and shipping them off into custody on Cuba.

Diplomatic and military give and take between Spain and Britain ensued until 1798, when the Baymen won a decisive military victory over a larger Spanish fleet, again just off the shores of St. George's Caye. The Battle of St. George's Caye effectively ended all Spanish involvement and claim to Belize, and it solidified Belize's standing within the British Empire.

In 1862, with more or less the same borders it has today, Belize was formally declared the colony of British Honduras. This small colonial outpost became a major source of hardwood and dyewood for the still-expanding British Empire. The forests were exploited, and agriculture was never really encouraged. The British wanted their colony to remain dependent on the mother country, so virtually all the necessities of life were imported. Few roads were built, and the country remained unexplored and undeveloped with a tiny population, mostly clustered along the coast.

Throughout the 18th and 19th centuries, African slaves were brought to British Honduras. The slave period was marked by several revolts and uprisings. Black Caribs, today known as Garífuna, also migrated here from the Bay Islands of Honduras, although they originally hail from the Caribbean island of St. Vincent. Beginning in the early 1800s, the Garífuna established their own villages and culture along the southern coast, predominantly in the towns of Dangriga and Punta Gorda. The Abolition Act of 1833 abolished slavery throughout the British Empire, and former Belizean slaves and Garífuna villagers slowly began to integrate into the economic and cultural life of this budding colony.

During the mid–19th century, many Mexican and Guatemalan refugees of the bloody Caste Wars fled across the borders into British Honduras and founded such towns as Corozal Town and Benque Viejo. Further waves of Guatemalan, Salvadoran, and Honduran refugees, who were fleeing civil wars and right-wing death squads, immigrated to Belize during the 1970s and '80s.

FROM INDEPENDENCE TO THE PRESENT

In the early 1960s, groundwork was laid by the People's United Party (PUP) for granting British Honduras independence. In 1973, the country's name was officially changed to Belize. Although the 1964 constitution granted self-government to the British colony, it was not until September 21, 1981, that Belize finally gained its independence, making it Central America's newest nation. The delay was primarily due to Guatemala's claim on the territory. Guatemala actually sent troops into the border Petén Province several times during the 1970s. Fearful of an invasion by Guatemalan forces, the British delayed granting full independence until an agreement could be reached with Guatemala. Although to this day no final agreement has actually been inked, tensions cooled enough to allow for the granting of full sovereignty in 1981. British troops officially pulled out of the Belize in 1994. The British legacy in Belize is a relatively stable government with a parliamentary system and regular elections that are contested by two major parties and several smaller parties. The country is still a member of the Commonwealth.

3 The Natural Environment

Belize is a narrow strip of land on the Caribbean coast of Central America, located due south of Mexico's Yucatán Peninsula. It covers an area of just under 9,000 square miles (23,310 sq. km), about the same size as the state of Massachusetts, and is bordered on the west and south by Guatemala and on the east by the Caribbean Sea. Offshore from mainland Belize are hundreds of tiny islands, known as cayes (pronounced "keys"), which rise from the world's second-longest barrier reef, which extends for more than 185 miles (298km) along the Belizean coast. From the broad, flat coastal plains, Belize rises to form the **Maya Mountains,** mountain peaks of more than 3,000 feet (900m) and the source of the many rivers that wind through the country. For centuries these rivers were the principal means of transportation within Belize. Moreover, most of these mountains are limestone karst formations, which has left them coursed with caves, caverns, and underground rivers.

Despite the fact that much of Belize's primary forest and tropical hardwoods were harvested throughout the past 3 centuries, population density has always been extremely low and the forest reclaims ground quickly. Though Belize lacks much true primary tropical rainforest, it does possess large expanses of tropical moist and lowland secondary rainforest, as well as mangrove, swamp, and even highland pine forests. In fact, nearly 65% of Belize is uninhabited, while over 20% of the country and its offshore reefs are considered protected land, private reserve, or marine reserve. The combination of a low level of human population and conscious conservation efforts has been a boon for a wide range of flora and fauna. Over 550 species of migratory and resident bird species have been identified in Belize, including the massive jabiru stork, the scarlet macaw, and the keel-billed toucan. Belize is also home to the densest concentration of jaguars on the planet. Revered by the ancient Maya and feared by most jungle dwellers, the jaguar is the largest New World cat, and can reach over 6 feet in length and weigh over 250 pounds. The **Cockscomb Basin Wildlife Sanctuary** (p. 74) was created as the world's only jaguar preserve.

In addition to the jaguar, Belizean forests are home to four other wild cats, the puma, ocelot, margay, and jaguarundi, as well as such quintessential jungle dwellers as howler monkeys, green iguanas, and boa constrictors. The tapir is the country's national animal. Also called a mountain cow, the tapir is docile, curious, and entirely vegetarian. Still, these wild creatures stand nearly 5 feet tall and can weigh over 500 pounds.

Bird-watchers will have want to visit several of Belize's lowland and offshore sanctuaries, including **Crooked Tree Wildlife Sanctuary,** the **Shipstern Nature Reserve, Río Bravo Conservation Area,** and the **Half Moon Caye National Monument.**

Off Belize's coast, the barrier reef is a world all its own. Though the cayes are little more than low, flat coral and limestone outcroppings, the myriad of underwater flora and fauna here is truly astounding. Colorful angelfish, parrotfish, and triggerfish feed on the multicolored coral. Giant sponges provide homes and feeding grounds for hundreds of smaller fish and delicate coral shrimp. Under the rocks and caverns dwell lobster, moray eels, and octopus. Larger predators like sharks and barracudas cruise the reefs for their plentiful prey, while manta and spotted eagle rays glide gracefully over the sand bottoms and conch thrive in the sea grass. The **Gladden Spit** area, off the coast from Placencia, is quickly being recognized as one of the world's top spots to snorkel and dive with giant whale sharks, while Belize's three mid-ocean atolls are wonderlands for a wide range of nature-loving adventurers and travelers.

Although it might seem strange to think of it, the cayes also support a unique and endangered forest environment, the **littoral forest,** as well as rich **mangroves.** These saltwater-tolerant environments are major breeding and life-support grounds for a broad range of fauna.

See "Tips on Health, Etiquette & Safety in the Wilderness" in chapter 3 for additional tips on enjoying Belize's natural wonders, and appendix C for an illustrated wildlife guide.

4 Belizean Culture

With its tiny population and relative isolation from the outside world, Belize lacks the vibrant cultural scene found in larger, more cosmopolitan countries. Still, if you poke around, you'll find some respectable local music, literature, art, and architecture to enjoy. For current information about the arts and what might be happening while you're in Belize, contact the **Belize Arts Council** (© **227-2110**), which is housed in the Bliss Institute of the Performing Arts (p. 94) in Belize City.

There is very little in the way of a club or live music scene here. However, at the hotels in the southern Garífuna region, you are likely to be treated to a performance of traditional Garífuna drumming and dance, and at a few clubs around Belize City, San Pedro, and other popular tourist destinations you should be able to find various rock, reggae, and Punta Rock bands playing.

ARCHITECTURE

Only a few colonial buildings of any interest survive in Belize City. Most of the rest have succumbed to the ravages of time or were destroyed in the major hurricanes of 1931 and 1961. The most prominent survivors are the brick **St. John's Cathedral** and the downtown **Paslow Building,** which houses the city's main post office. **Clapboard houses** built on stilts are the most typical architectural feature, and quite a few of these buildings, often painted in the pastel colors that are so popular throughout the Caribbean, can be seen in Belize City and in small towns around the country, but most commonly along the coast and out on the cayes.

If you're looking for classic monumental architecture, however, you're in luck. Stone fares better than wood in these parts. The two tallest structures in Belize remain the Mayan pyramids at **Caracol** and **Xunantunich.** Moreover, the country is dotted with lesser sites, and one almost entirely unexcavated city, **Pilar,** which might prove to be the largest Classic-era Mayan city in the region. For those looking to see perhaps the finest example of Classic Mayan ceremonial architecture, a trip to neighboring Guatemala and the ruins at **Tikal** are a must.

ART

Belizean artists range from folk artists and artisans working in a variety of forms, materials, and traditions to modern painters, sculptors, and ceramicists producing beautiful representational and abstract works.

Out in the western Cayo district, the traditional Mayan arts are kept alive by several talented artisans working in carved slate bas-reliefs. Of these, the **García sisters,** who run a gallery and small museum in the Mountain Pine Ridge area, are the prime proponents.

Perhaps the most vibrant place to look for modern art is Dangriga, where Garífuna painters like **Benjamín Nicholas** and **Pen Cayetano** have produced wonderful bodies of work depicting local life in a simple style. **Walter Castillo** is another excellent modern painter.

Several galleries in Belize City and San Pedro carry a wide range of locally produced art; see chapters 4 and 6 respectively for more information.

LITERATURE

Belize has no strong literary tradition. However, most gift shops and bookstores around the country have a small collection of locally produced short stories, poetry, fiction, and nonfiction. In recent years, there has been a trend to resuscitate and transcribe the traditional Mayan and Garífuna tales and folklore, along with the publication of modern pieces of fiction and nonfiction either set in Belize or written by Belizeans. Perhaps the best modern Belizean author is **Zee Edgell.** See "Recommended Books, Films & Music" in chapter 2 for more details and recommendations.

MUSIC

The most distinctive and popular form of Belizean music you will come across is **Punta** and **Punta Rock.** Punta is similar to many Afro-Caribbean and Afropop music forms, blending traditional rhythms and drumming patterns with

Fun Fact

Although set in Honduras, Paul Theroux's *The Mosquito Coast* (Penguin Books, 1996) often captures the sense and feel of Belize's wild landscape. Moreover, the 1986 film of the same name was actually filmed on location in Belize.

modern electronic instruments (Punta is usually more rootsy and acoustic than Punta Rock, which features electric guitars and keyboards). Pen Cayetano is often credited as being the founder of Punta Rock; you will find his discs and cassettes for sale throughout Belize, as well as those by his successors Andy Palacio, Peter Flores (aka Titiman), and Chico Ramos. Punta music is usually sung in the Garífuna dialect, although the latest incarnations feature lyrics in English and even Spanish. Dancing to Punta and Punta Rock is sensuous and close, often settling into a firm butt-to-groin grind.

Paranda is another modern yet more traditional offshoot of Garífuna music and culture. Featuring acoustic guitars and rhythm ensembles, paranda is a lively, syncopated musical form. Paul "Nabby" Nabor is a popular paranda artist.

In northern and western Belize, near the Mexican and Guatemalan borders, the local **mestizo** musical forms reflect their Spanish roots with marimba bands and Spanish-language folk songs influenced by the mariachi and ranchero traditions.

5 Conch Fritters, Stew Fish & Belikin: Belizean Food & Drink

While it is hard to pin down any specific Belizean cuisine, what you will find in Belize is a mix of Caribbean, Mexican, African, Spanish, and Mayan culinary influences. You'll also find burgers, pizzas, Chinese food, and even Indian restaurants.

Belize's strongest suit is its **seafood.** Fresh fish, lobster, shrimp, and conch are widely available, especially in the beach and island destinations. Belize has historically been a major exporter of lobster, but over-harvesting has caused the population to decline. It is still readily available and relatively inexpensive, but there is a lobster season, usually from February 15 to July 14.

Rice and beans is a major staple, often served as an accompaniment to almost any main dish. A slight difference is to be inferred between "rice and beans," which are usually cooked (sometimes in coconut milk) and served together, and "beans and rice," which are usually cooked and served separately. Belizeans tend to use a small red bean, but black beans are sometimes used.

Aside from rice and beans, if there was such a thing as a national dish it would be **stew chicken,** and its close cousins stew beef and stew fish. These Kriol-based recipes are dark stews that get their color from a broad mix of spices, as well as red *recado,* which is made from annatto seed or achiote. A similar and related stew commonly found around Belize is **chimole,** which is sometimes called black gumbo.

Perhaps the most distinctive element of Belizean cuisine and dining is **Marie Sharp's Hot Sauce.** Almost no dining table is complete without a bottle of Marie Sharp's. The original Marie Sharp's is a very spicy sauce made from a base of habanero peppers, carrots, and onions. Currently, Marie Sharp's has a wide range of different hot sauces, jams, and chutneys. If you have a hankering for the hot stuff, you will find that your options aren't confined to Marie Sharp's. In many restaurants, you will often see a jar of habanero peppers and onions marinating in simple white vinegar.

MEALS & DINING CUSTOMS

Belizeans tend to eat three meals a day, in similar fashion and hours to North Americans. Breakfasts tend to be served between 6:30 and 9am; lunch between noon and 2pm; and dinner between 6 and 10pm. Most meals and dining experiences are quite informal. In fact, there are only a few restaurants in the entire country that could be considered semiformal, and none require a jacket or tie, although you could certainly wear them.

FOOD

BREAKFAST   The typical breakfast in Belize is quite simple, usually anchored by some scrambled eggs and refried red or black beans. However, instead of toast, you will often have a choice of tortillas, **johnnycakes,** or **fry jacks** to accompany them. Johnnycakes are a semi-dry, baked round flour biscuit, served with butter or stuffed with ham and/or cheese. Fry Jacks are a similar batter and shape, but deep-fried, and either served as is or dusted with confectioner's sugar. The most common tortillas served in Belize are corn tortillas.

APPETIZERS   **Conch fritters** are by far the country's most popular and tasty appetizer. Deep-fried balls of flour batter and chopped conch meat are on most bar and restaurant menus in the country, particularly on the cayes and along the coast. Try some.

SANDWICHES & SNACKS   Belize's light menus show a heavy Mexican and American influence. Many simple eateries and roadside carts will feature simple tacos, tamales (also called *dukunu*), or **garnaches.** The latter, a fried corn tortilla topped with beans, cheese, or shredded meat or chicken, would probably be considered a tostada by many. Popular stuffed pastries include meat pies and *panades,* small, deep-fried empanadas.

You can also get traditional sandwiches, often served on sliced white bread, as well as American-style burgers. I personally recommend looking for fish, shrimp, or conch burgers, which are available at most beach and island destinations.

MEAT, POULTRY & WILD GAME   Belizeans also eat a fair amount of meat and poultry, as well as some more interesting game. Because Belize only recently began to raise its own beef, the country relied for a long time on wild game. Some of the more interesting game items you might see on a Belizean menu include **gibnut** (paca) and **iguana.** The gibnut is actually a large rodent, which is often called "The Queen's Rat" or "The Royal Rat" because Queen Elizabeth was served gibnut during a visit here. Gibnut allegedly tastes like rabbit, a comparison I can live with, I guess. Iguana is frequently called "bamboo chicken," and it does actually taste a bit like chicken. Occasionally, you may also come across wild boar, armadillo, or some other forest-dwelling creature.

Another popular wild animal found in restaurants is the **sea turtle,** endangered all over the world, including in Belize. It's not yet illegal to sell sea turtle within Belize, but international agreements prohibit its export. Please don't order turtle steak, turtle soup, or turtle eggs. In fact, I'm a little hesitant to recommend the eating of wild game at all. So far, there's no reliable data on the impact that the hunting of wild game for restaurants has had or could have, but there is reason for concern. Belize is struggling to preserve its natural environment, and as long as people order wild game, it will continue to show up on menus. Exceptions would be any farm-raised wild animals, like iguanas. When harvested from commercial "iguana farms," this wild game actually has the potential to mix sustainable yield with modern conservation.

SEAFOOD   Seafood is the basic staple of most coastal and island destinations. It is fresh and plentiful. Shrimp, conch, lobster (in season), and a variety of fish are almost always on the menu. You're best off sticking to simple preparations, either grilled or fried. My favorite fishes are grouper, snapper, and dorado (or mahimahi). You will also come across barracuda, shark, and marlin. Rarely, you will find **snook** on the menu, and if so, you should definitely try this delicate white fish.

If you are in a Garífuna region, you should not miss the chance to try *hudut,* a fish stew or whole fish preparation served in a coconut milk broth, often accompanied by mashed fried green plantains. *Sere* is a very similar Kriol dish that seems more like a traditional fish or seafood stew, but again, based on a coconut milk broth.

Ceviche, a cold marinade of fish, conch, and/or shrimp cooked in lime juice and seasoned, is a great treat for lunch or as an appetizer.

VEGETABLES   On the whole, you'll find vegetables surprisingly lacking in the meals you're served in Belize. Fresh garden salads are rare and hard to come by. A lack of fresh ingredients makes other vegetable dishes and sides almost as uncommon. Most meals in most restaurants come accompanied by a simple slaw of grated cabbage, or a potato or beet salad.

FRUITS   Belize has a wealth of delicious tropical fruits. The most common are mangoes (the season begins in May), papayas, pineapples, melons, and bananas. Other fruits you might find include the **fruit of the cashew tree,** which has orange or yellow glossy skin, and **carambola** (star fruit), a tart fruit, whose cross-sections form perfect stars.

DESSERTS   Belize doesn't have a very extravagant or refined dessert culture. After all, the country was colonized by the British, not the French. However, you can usually find homemade coconut pie, chocolate pie, or bread pudding on most menus. Flan, an egg-and-condensed-milk custard imported from Mexico, is also popular.

DRINK

BEVERAGES   Most major brands of soft drinks are available, as are fresh lime juice (limeade) and orange juice. You're in the tropics, so expect to find fresh shakes made with papaya, pineapple, or mango.

One of the most unique drinks you're likely to sample anywhere is a **seaweed shake,** a cooling concoction made of dried seaweed, evaporated and condensed milk, cinnamon, and nutmeg, and blended with ice. Seaweed shakes are sometimes kicked up with a shot of rum or brandy.

WATER   Much of the drinking water in Belize is **rainwater.** People use the roofs of their houses to collect water in a cistern, which supplies them for the year. Tap water is generally not considered safe to drink, even in most cities and popular tourist towns. The water in Belize City and San Ignacio is relatively safe to drink, but travelers often get a touch of diarrhea whenever they hit a foreign country, so always play it safe. Ask for bottled drinking water at your hotel, and whenever you can, pick up a bottle of spring or purified water (available in most markets) to have handy.

BEER, WINE & LIQUOR   The Belize Brewing Company's **Belikin** beer is the national beer of Belize. It comes in several varieties, including a Belikin Lager, Belikin Premium, and Belikin Stout. The recipes and original brew masters all came from Germany. Both the Lager and Premium are full-bodied, hearty beers. The Belikin brewery also bottles a **locally produced Guinness Stout,** as thick and rich as its brand name demands.

As you'll find throughout the Caribbean, rum is the liquor of choice in Belize. There are several brands and distilleries producing rum in Belize. Probably the finest Belizean rum is the 5-year-aged **Prestige.** One of the most popular brands you'll come across is **1 Barrel,** which is slightly sweet for my taste.

Belize doesn't produce any traditional wines of note. The climate and soil are not very well suited for growing the right kind of grapes. On Ambergris Caye, the **Rendezvous Restaurant & Winery** (p. 279) does in fact import grape juice for the purpose of producing and bottling their own wines, although they are really more of a novelty than a delicacy.

Several different **fruit wines** are produced in Belize using native fruits, including pineapple and even banana. These wines are very sweet and are more a novelty than anything else. In remote parts of the country, you'll find home-made fruit wines that are a bit like hard cider.

Appendix B: Useful Terms & Phrases

English is the official language of Belize, but the country is one of the most polyglot places on the planet. In addition to English, many Belizeans speak Spanish, and amongst some members of the population, this is the primary language. You will find Spanish prevalent in the northern and western regions, near the borders with Mexico and Guatemala, but given Belize's long history of immigration, Spanish speakers can be found throughout the country. In fact, conversations amongst Belizeans are often a mix of English and Spanish ("Spanglish"), with a fair amount of Creole thrown in for good measure.

Creole, or *Kriol,* is the local patois, a colorful, rhythmic, and often difficult-to-understand dialect. Although based almost entirely on English, it takes some getting used to before most Westerners can grasp the pronunciations and sentence structures that distinguish Belizean Kriol. While this was originally the language of former black slaves and their descendants, today most Belizeans speak Kriol, and they will often use it amongst themselves in the presence of foreigners if they don't want to be understood.

In addition to English, Spanish, and Kriol, Belize's Garífuna (or Garinagu) people have their own distinct language, while the various Mayan tribes still speak primarily their native languages.

1 Spanish Terms

BASIC PHRASES

English	Spanish	Pronunciation
Hello	**Buenos días**	*bweh*-nohss *dee*-ahss
How are you?	**¿Cómo está usted?**	*koh*-moh ehss-*tah* oo-*stehd*
Very well	**Muy bien**	mwee byehn
Thank you	**Gracias**	*grah*-syahss
Good-bye	**Adiós**	ad-*dyohss*
Please	**Por favor**	pohr fah-*vohr*
Yes	**Sí**	see
No	**No**	noh
Excuse me (to get by someone)	**Perdóneme**	pehr-*doh*-neh-meh
Excuse me (to begin a question)	**Disculpe**	dees-*kool*-peh
Give me	**Deme**	*deh*-meh
Where is . . . ?	**¿Dónde está . . . ?**	*dohn*-deh ehss-*tah*
the station	**la estación**	la ehss-*tah*-syohn
the bus stop	**la parada**	la pah-*rah*-dah
a hotel	**un hotel**	oon oh-*tehl*
a restaurant	**un restaurante**	oon res-tow-*rahn*-teh
the toilet	**el servicio**	el ser-*vee*-syoh
To the right	**A la derecha**	ah lah deh-*reh*-chah

English	Spanish	Pronunciation
To the left	A la izquierda	ah lah ees-*kyehr*-dah
Straight ahead	Adelante	ah-deh-*lahn*-teh
I would like . . .	Quiero . . .	*kyeh*-roh
to eat	comer	ko-*mehr*
a room	una habitación	*oo*-nah ah-bee-tah-*syohn*
How much is it?	¿Cuánto?	*kwahn*-toh
The check	La cuenta	la *kwen*-tah
When?	¿Cuándo?	*kwan*-doh
What?	¿Qué?	keh
What time is it?	¿Qué hora es?	keh *oh*-rah ehss
Yesterday	Ayer	ah-*yehr*
Today	Hoy	oy
Tomorrow	Mañana	mah-*nyah*-nah
Breakfast	Desayuno	deh-sah-*yoo*-noh
Lunch	Almuerzo	ahl-*mwehr*-soh
Dinner	Cena	*seh*-nah
Do you speak English?	¿Habla usted inglés?	ah-blah oo-*stehd* een-*glehss*
Is there anyone here who speaks English?	¿Hay alguien aquí que hable inglés?	eye *ahl*-gyehn ah-*kee* keh *ah*-bleh een-*glehss*
I speak a little Spanish.	Hablo un poco de español.	*ah*-bloh oon *poh*-koh deh ehss-pah-*nyohl*
I don't understand Spanish very well.	No (lo) entiendo muy bien el español.	noh (loh) ehn-*tyehn*-do mwee byehn el ehss-pah-*nyohl*

NUMBERS

1	**uno** (*oo*-noh)		16	**dieciséis** (dyeh-see-*sayss*)
2	**dos** (dohss)		17	**diecisiete** (dyeh-see-*syeh*-teh)
3	**tres** (trehss)		18	**dieciocho** (dyeh-see-*oh*-choh)
4	**cuatro** (*kwah*-troh)		19	**diecinueve** (dyeh-see-*nweh*-beh)
5	**cinco** (*seen*-koh)		20	**veinte** (*bayn*-teh)
6	**seis** (sayss)		30	**treinta** (*trayn*-tah)
7	**siete** (*syeh*-teh)		40	**cuarenta** (kwah-*rehn*-tah)
8	**ocho** (*oh*-choh)		50	**cincuenta** (seen-*kwehn*-tah)
9	**nueve** (*nweh*-beh)		60	**sesenta** (seh-*sehn*-tah)
10	**diez** (dyehss)		70	**setenta** (seh-*tehn*-tah)
11	**once** (*ohn*-seh)		80	**ochenta** (oh-*chehn*-tah)
12	**doce** (*doh*-seh)		90	**noventa** (noh-*behn*-tah)
13	**trece** (*treh*-seh)		100	**cien** (syehn)
14	**catorce** (kah-*tohr*-seh)		1,000	**mil** (meel)
15	**quince** (*keen*-seh)			

DAYS OF THE WEEK

Monday	**lunes** (*loo*-nehss)	
Tuesday	**martes** (*mahr*-tehss)	
Wednesday	**miércoles** (*myehr*-koh-lehs)	
Thursday	**jueves** (*wheh*-behss)	
Friday	**viernes** (*byehr*-nehss)	
Saturday	**sábado** (*sah*-bah-doh)	
Sunday	**domingo** (doh-*meen*-goh)	

MENU TERMS

FISH

Atún Tuna
Calamares Squid
Camarones Shrimp
Cangrejo Crab
Ceviche Marinated seafood salad
Dorado Dolphin, or mahimahi
Langosta Lobster

Langostinos Prawns
Lenguado Sole
Mejillones Mussels
Mero Grouper
Ostras Oysters
Pargo Snapper
Pulpo Octopus
Tiburón Shark

MEATS

Bistec Beefsteak
Cerdo Pork
Chicharrones Fried pork rinds
Chuleta Cutlet
Conejo Rabbit
Cordero Lamb

Costillas Ribs
Jamón Ham
Lengua Tongue
Pato Duck
Pavo Turkey
Pollo Chicken

VEGETABLES

Aceitunas Olives
Alcachofa Artichoke
Berenjena Eggplant
Cebolla Onion
Elote Corn on the cob
Ensalada Salad
Espárragos Asparagus
Espinacas Spinach
Palmito Heart of palm

Papa Potato
Pepino Cucumber
Remolacha Beet
Repollo Cabbage
Tomate Tomato
Vainica String beans
Yuca Cassava, or manioc
Zanahoria Carrot

FRUITS

Aguacate Avocado
Carambola Star fruit
Cereza Cherry
Ciruela Plum
Fresa Strawberry
Limón Lemon or lime
Mango Mango
Manzana Apple
Melocotón Peach

Mora Raspberry
Naranja Orange
Pera Pear
Piña Pineapple
Plátano Banana
Sandía Watermelon
Toronja Grapefruit
Uvas Grapes

BASICS

Aceite Oil
Ajo Garlic
Azúcar Sugar
Frito Fried
Mantequilla Butter
Miel Honey
Mostaza Mustard

Natilla Sour cream
Pan Bread
Pimienta Pepper
Queso Cheese
Sal Salt
Tamal Filled cornmeal pastry
Tortilla Flat corn pancake

2 Creole Terms

Creole, or *Kriol,* is largely based on English, although it does incorporate words and syntax from various African languages as well. Once you get the hang of certain pronunciations and syntactical phrasings, however, it's actually quite easy to understand. Almost any Kriol speaker will understand you if you speak in English. However, they'll be really impressed if you start inserting various Kriol words and phrases into your conversations.

BASIC WORDS

Agen Again
An And
Aks To ask
Bak Back
Bwai Boy
Chinchi A very small amount
Da Is, am, are
Da At, on, in, to
Da It is
Daata Daughter
Deh/di Am, is, are (located); for instance, "Ih deh pahn di boat" means "He/she is on the boat"
Dehn Them
Doe Door
Di The

Fi To
Fo For
Ih He, she, it
Kunku Small
Nize Noise
Noh Isn't it so?
Shudda Should have
Tideh Today
Uman Woman
Unu You all
Vex/bex Angry
Waata Water
Wudda Would have
Yaiy Eye
Yaiy waata Tears, literally "eye water"
Yerriso Gossip

MENU ITEMS

Bail op Traditional dish made with cassava, cocoa, sweet potatoes, plantains, boil cake, and fish or pig's tail
Bambam Traditional dish made with cassava
Bami Cassava bread
Chimoaleh Traditional dish of blackened chicken soup and rice; *chimole* in Spanish
Dukunu Dish of mashed and steamed corn, wrapped in a leaf, similar to a *tamal*
Eskabaycheh Pickled onion soup with chicken or fish; derived from the Spanish word *escabeche* ("pickled")
Garnaaches Fried tortillas topped with beans and rice
Janny kake Traditional fried or baked bread, served at breakfast
Konks Conch
Panaades Traditional dish of finely chopped fish wrapped in a tortilla
Rekaado Red *achiote* paste
Reyeno Soup made with chicken, pork, and boiled eggs
Rise and beanz Rice and beans with coconut milk
Rompopo Alcoholic drink similar to eggnog
Strech-mi-gots Traditional taffy
Tablayta Coconut candy

WILDLIFE

Bilam   Small river fish
Chaaly prise   Large rat
Gaalin   Heron
Gibnat   Paca
Gwaana   Iguana
Hooyu   Owl
Jankro   Vulture
Janny fidla   Fiddler crab
Kwash   Coati, coatimundi

Taapong   Tarpon
Tuba   River fish
Waari   Wild pig or peccary
Waata daag   River otter
Weewi ants   Leaf-cutter ant
Wowla   Boa constrictor, also used to refer to a type of basket used for processing cassava for bread

FOLKLORE & TRADITIONAL TERMS

Anansi/Hanaasi   Popular character in local folklore, portrayed as the trickster and hero of local tales
Bram   A dance party held at Christmas; a type of dance at parties
Brokdong   Traditional folk music, from "break down"
Gombeh   Typical hand drum made with goat skin
Punta   Sensual and vigorous dance, also refers to its accompanying music
Sambai   Full-moon fertility dance
Tata Duhendeh   Mythical forest gnome, with no thumbs and backwards feet
Wine op   A lively, hip-swinging dance

Appendix C:
Belizean Wildlife

with assistance from E. Z. Weaver

For such a small country, Belize is incredibly rich in biodiversity. Whether you come to Belize to check a hundred or so species off your lifetime list, or just to check out of the rat race for a week or so, you'll be surrounded by a rich and varied collection of flora and fauna. The information below is meant to be a selective introduction.

In many instances, the prime viewing recommendations should be taken with a firm dose of reality. Most casual visitors and even many dedicated naturalists will never see a wildcat or kinkajou. However, anyone working with a good guide should be able to see a broad selection of Belize's impressive flora and fauna.

See "The Natural Environment" in appendix A for more information, as well as "Tips on Health, Safety & Etiquette in the Wilderness" in chapter 3 and "Searching for Wildlife" on p. 76 for additional tips on enjoying Belize's flora and fauna.

1 Fauna

MAMMALS

Belize has just under 150 identified species of mammals, ranging from the majestic jaguar to the rowdy howler monkey. Note that the dolphin and manatee have been included in the "Sea Life" section, later in this appendix.

Jaguar

SCIENTIFIC NAME *Panthera onca*

WORTH NOTING This cat measures from 3½ to 6 feet (1–1.8m) plus tail, and is distinguished by its tan/yellowish fur with black spots. As jaguars are protected by Belize's hunting ordinances, the country maintains one of the healthiest populations in Central America.

PRIME VIEWING Although they exist throughout mainland Belize, jaguars are extremely hard to see in the wild. The best places to spot them are in the Cockscomb Basin Wildlife Sanctuary and Río Bravo Conservation Area.

Puma

SCIENTIFIC NAME   *Puma concolor*

WORTH NOTING   Nearly 5 feet (1.5m) long when fully grown, these feline predators are the largest unspotted cats in the region. Also known as a mountain lion, the puma is brownish, reddish-brown, or tawny in color with a white throat.

PRIME VIEWING   Southeastern, western, and southern Belize in the lowland forests, and semi-open areas.

Jaguarundi

SCIENTIFIC NAME   *Herpailurus yaguarondi*

WORTH NOTING   This smallish to midsize cat, with a solid gray, brown, or reddish coat, can occasionally be spotted climbing trees.

PRIME VIEWING   Wet and dry forests throughout Belize.

Ocelot

SCIENTIFIC NAME   *Leopardus pardalis*

WORTH NOTING   The tail of the tiger cat (as it's called in Belize) is longer than its rear leg, which makes for easy identification. Ocelots are mostly nocturnal, and they sleep in trees.

PRIME VIEWING   Forests in all regions of Belize.

Margay

SCIENTIFIC NAME   *Leopardus wiedii*

WORTH NOTING   An endangered species, the margay is one of the smaller wild cats of the region, and is often found in trees like its cousin, the ocelot.

PRIME VIEWING   Forests in all regions of Belize.

Gibnut

SCIENTIFIC NAME   *Agouti paca*

WORTH NOTING   This nocturnal rodent (also called a paca) inhabits the forest floor, feeding on fallen fruit, leaves, and some tubers dug from the ground.

PRIME VIEWING   Most often found near water throughout many habitats of Belize, from river valleys to swamps to dense tropical forest. You're almost as likely to see gibnut on a restaurant menu as in the wild.

Neotropical Otter

SCIENTIFIC NAME   *Lutra longicaudis*

WORTH NOTING   The neotropical otter goes by many nicknames in Belize, including *perro de agua* (water dog) and *lobito de río* (little river wolf).

PRIME VIEWING   In rivers and streams throughout the country.

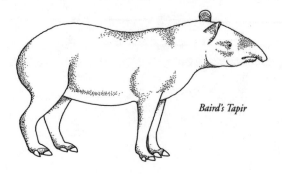

Baird's Tapir

SCIENTIFIC NAME   *Tapirus bairdii*

WORTH NOTING   Known as the "mountain cow" in Belize, the tapir is active mostly at night, foraging along riverbanks, streams, and forest clearings.

PRIME VIEWING   The Stann Creek and Toledo districts of Southern Belize and the Cayo District of Western Belize.

Coatimundi

SCIENTIFIC NAME   *Nasua narica*

WORTH NOTING   This raccoonlike mammal is one of few with the ability to adapt to habitat disturbances. During the night, they tend to hunt along open trails; during the day, they stay hidden within the deeper bush.

PRIME VIEWING   Found in a variety of habitats in Belize, from dry scrub to dense forests, on the mainland as well as the coastal islands.

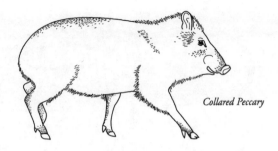

Collared Peccary

SCIENTIFIC NAME   *Tayassu tajacu*

WORTH NOTING   These black or brown piglike animals travel in small groups (larger where populations are still numerous) and have a strong musk odor.

PRIME VIEWING   Throughout most of Belize.

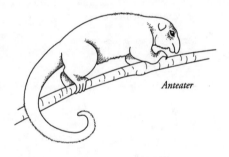

Anteater

SCIENTIFIC NAME   *Cyclopes didactylus*

WORTH NOTING   Also known as the pygmy anteater, this nocturnal creature grows up to 7 inches (18cm), not counting its thick tail (which is as long or longer than its body).

PRIME VIEWING   Wet forests in all regions of Belize.

Armadillo

SCIENTIFIC NAME *Dasypus novemcinctus*

WORTH NOTING Also known as the dilly in Belize, these prehistoric-looking animals are nocturnal and terrestrial.

PRIME VIEWING All regions.

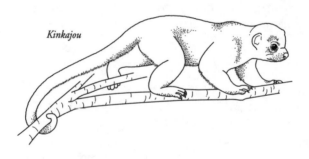

Kinkajou

SCIENTIFIC NAME *Potos flavus*

WORTH NOTING The nocturnal, tree-dwelling kinkajou is appropriately nicknamed "nightwalker" in Belize.

PRIME VIEWING Extremely hard to see, the kinkajou nevertheless is found in forests throughout Belize.

Spider Monkey

SCIENTIFIC NAME   *Ateles geoffroyi*

WORTH NOTING   A large monkey (25 in./64cm) with brown or silvery fur, this creature is often hunted for its meat and is listed as endangered in some countries.

PRIME VIEWING   The Orange Walk (northwestern), Cayo (western), and Toledo (southern) districts of Belize.

Howler Monkey

SCIENTIFIC NAME   *Alouatta pigra*

WORTH NOTING   Known locally as a baboon, this highly social creature grows to 22 inches (56cm) in size. As the species travel only from tree to tree (limiting their presence to dense jungle canopy), a community-based conservation organization protects the land along the Belize River for the howler monkey, ensuring that their food trees are not destroyed to make way for pasture.

PRIME VIEWING   In the lowland forests that encompass Belize's mainland. Sightings are pretty much guaranteed at the Community Baboon Sanctuary (see "What to See & Do" in chapter 4).

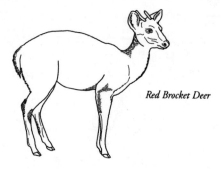

Red Brocket Deer

SCIENTIFIC NAME   *Mazama americana*

WORTH NOTING   Also known as the antelope in Belize, these small animals measure 3½ to 4½ feet (1–1.4m). Small, straight antlers distinguish the male.

PRIME VIEWING   Southern and southeastern Belize and the coastal islands.

Hairy-Legged Bat

SCIENTIFIC NAME   *Myotis keaysi*

WORTH NOTING   The hairy-legged bat grows to a whopping 2 inches (5.1cm) in length, not including the length of its tail.

PRIME VIEWING   All regions of Belize, in forests, rock crevices, gardens, and buildings.

BIRDS

Belize has over 550 identified species of resident and migrant birds. The variety of habitats and compact nature of the country make this a major bird-watching destination.

Jabiru Stork

SCIENTIFIC NAME   *Jabiru mycteria*

WORTH NOTING   One of the largest birds in the world and an endangered species, the jabiru stands 5 feet (1.5m) tall, with a wingspan of 8 feet (2.4m) and a foot-long (.3m) bill. The birds arrive in Belize from Mexico in November and fly north with the first rains in June or July.

PRIME VIEWING   The Crooked Tree Wildlife Sanctuary, located 33 miles (53km) north of Belize City, has the largest population in the country. (See "En Route North: Crooked Tree Wildlife Sanctuary" in chapter 5.)

Keel-Billed Toucan

SCIENTIFIC NAME   *Ramphastos solfurantus*

WORTH NOTING   The canoe-shape bill and brightly colored feathers make the national bird of Belize almost instantly recognizable. The toucan is about 20 inches (51cm) in length.

PRIME VIEWING   Throughout the country's lowland forests, nesting in the holes of tree trunks.

Scarlet Macaw

SCIENTIFIC NAME   *Ara macao*

WORTH NOTING   Over most of its range, the scarlet macaw is endangered. However, in 1996, a new population of over 100 birds was "discovered" south of the Cockscomb Basin Wildlife Sanctuary.

PRIME VIEWING   The wet lowland forests of the Toledo District in southern Belize.

Ocellated Turkey

SCIENTIFIC NAME   *Agriocharis ocellata*

WORTH NOTING   This colorful bird has a thin light blue head and neck with orange-yellow knoblike wattles on the top that the bird will proudly display. The wings and tail are rounded with shimmering metallic bronze primaries and metallic emerald-green shoulders; the feathers are a dark, shiny brown, barred with a metallic shimmering green that looks black in poor light.

PRIME VIEWING   Northern and western Belize.

Frigate Bird

SCIENTIFIC NAME *Fregata magnificens*

WORTH NOTING The frigate bird is a naturally agile flier and it swoops (unlike other birds, it doesn't dive or swim) to pluck food from the water's surface—or more commonly, it steals catch from the mouths of other birds.

PRIME VIEWING Corozal, Belize, Stann Creek, Toledo, and Cayes districts of Belize. Man-O-War Caye is a protected nesting site for this bird (see "Dangriga" in chapter 7).

Red-Footed Booby

SCIENTIFIC NAME *Sula sula rubripes*

WORTH NOTING This unique bird experiences many color changes during its life. Adult boobies have a blue-gray bill and eye-ring, and pink skin about the bill-base. The head and neck are washed with yellow, and the white body holds black primary and secondary feathers. The feet and legs of the aptly named species are all red.

PRIME VIEWING Half Moon Caye National Monument, Belize's first national park, is now the protected home for over 4,000 red-footed boobies. (See "The Outer Atolls" in chapter 6.)

Montezuma's Oropendola

SCIENTIFIC NAME   *Pasrocolius montezuma*

WORTH NOTING   Also called "yellowtails" in Belize, this bird has a black head and chest, a yellow-edged tail, a large black bill with an orange tip, and a blue patch under the eye.

PRIME VIEWING   All regions.

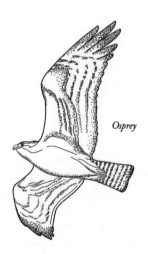

Osprey

SCIENTIFIC NAME   *Pandion haliatus*

WORTH NOTING   These large (2 ft./.6m, with a 6-ft./1.8m wingspan) brownish birds with white heads are also known as "fishing eagles." In flight, the osprey's wings "bend" backward.

PRIME VIEWING   Throughout Belize, flying or perched in trees near water.

Roseate Spoonbill

SCIENTIFIC NAME   *Ajaia ajaja*

WORTH NOTING   This large water bird is pink or light red in color, with a large spoon-shape bill. They were almost made extinct in the United States because their pink wings were sought for feather fans.

PRIME VIEWING   Along the coast and in northern Belize.

Cattle Egret

SCIENTIFIC NAME   *Bubulcus ibis*

WORTH NOTING   The cattle egret changes color during breeding: A yellowish buff color appears on the head, chest, and back, and a reddish hue emerges on the bill and legs. They are often seen following behind tractors.

PRIME VIEWING   Throughout the country. As the name implies, almost always found accompanying livestock.

Pygmy Owl

SCIENTIFIC NAME   *Glaucidium brasilianum*

WORTH NOTING   This small (about 15 in./38cm) grayish brown or reddish brown owl is also known as the *lechucita listada* ("little striped screech owl"). Unlike most owls, they are most active during the day.

PRIME VIEWING   Throughout the country.

Boat-Billed Heron

SCIENTIFIC NAME   *Cochlearius cochlearius*

WORTH NOTING   This midsize heron (about 20 in./51cm) has a large black head, a large broad bill, and a rusty brown color.

PRIME VIEWING   Throughout the country, near marshes, swamps, rivers, and mangroves.

Laughing Falcon

SCIENTIFIC NAME   *Herpetotheres cachinnans*

WORTH NOTING   This largish (22 in./56cm) bird-of-prey is also known as the *vaquero* (cowboy) in Belize. The laughing falcon's wingspan reaches an impressive 37 inches (94cm).

PRIME VIEWING   Throughout the country.

SEA LIFE

Boasting the longest continuous barrier reef in the Americas, Belize has a rich diversity of underwater flora and fauna. Any visitor to Belize's beach or island resorts should take some time to peek at the various undersea wonders of the ocean and barrier reef, whether it be by snorkeling, scuba diving, or riding in a glass-bottomed boat.

West Indian Manatee

SCIENTIFIC NAME   *Trichechus manatus*

WORTH NOTING   Manatees in Belize are Antillean manatees, a subspecies of the West Indian manatee. Belize is home to the largest known concentration of Antillean manatees in the wider Caribbean. These "sea cows" can reach lengths of 10 to 13 feet (3–4m) and weigh 1,100 to 3,500 pounds (499–1,588kg).

PRIME VIEWING   Coastal mangroves.

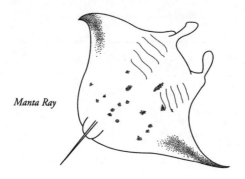

Manta Ray

SCIENTIFIC NAME   *Manta birostris*

WORTH NOTING   Manta rays are the largest type of rays, with a wingspan that can reach 20 feet (6m) and a body weight known to exceed 3,000 pounds (1,361kg). Despite their daunting appearance, manta rays are quite gentle. If you are snorkeling or diving, watch for one of these extraordinary and graceful creatures.

PRIME VIEWING   All along the barrier reef, particularly alongside steep walls and drop-offs.

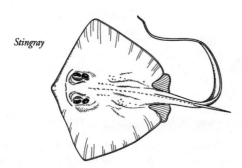

Stingray

SCIENTIFIC NAME   *Dasyatis americana*

WORTH NOTING   True to their name, these rays can give you a painful shock if you touch the venomous spine at the base of their tails. Be careful when wading in sandy areas, where they prefer to bury themselves.

PRIME VIEWING   All along the coast and barrier reef, especially in shallow sand or grassy areas.

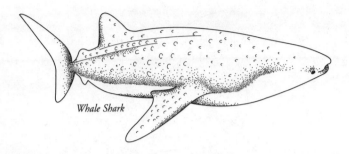

Whale Shark

SCIENTIFIC NAME   *Rhincodon typus*

WORTH NOTING   Although the whale shark grows to lengths of 45 feet (14m) or more, its gentle nature makes swimming with them a special treat for divers and snorkelers. Although 3 or 4 days before and after the full and new moons in April and May are the best times to interact with the sharks, they are often sighted in the summer months as well.

PRIME VIEWING   Gladden Spit, off Placencia (see "Placencia" in chapter 7).

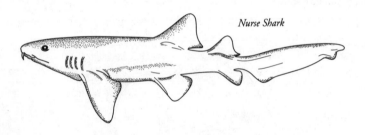

Nurse Shark

SCIENTIFIC NAME   *Ginglymostoma cirratum*

WORTH NOTING   The most frequently spotted shark in Belizean waters, this species spends most of its time resting on the ocean floor. Reaching lengths of 14 feet (4.3m), their heads are larger than those of most sharks, and they appear to be missing the bottom half of their tail.

PRIME VIEWING   All along the coast and barrier reef.

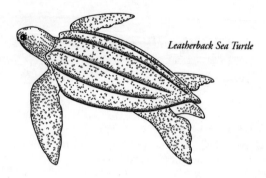

Leatherback Sea Turtle

SCIENTIFIC NAME   *Dermochelys coriacea*

WORTH NOTING   The world's largest sea turtle (reaching nearly 8 ft./2.4m in length and weighing more than 1,200 lb./544kg), it's now an endangered species.

PRIME VIEWING   Sightings are exceedingly rare, so it's highly unlikely that you'll spot them nesting on the coast of Belize, but you might get lucky and spot them in the sea.

Hawksbill Sea Turtle

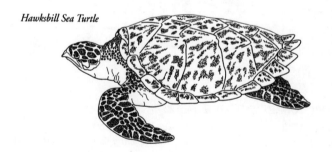

SCIENTIFIC NAME   *Eretmochelys imbricata*

WORTH NOTING   The hawksbill turtle is a shy tropical reef dwelling species that feeds primarily on sponges. Registered on the endangered species list, commercial exploitation exacerbates the species' continued decline.

PRIME VIEWING   All along the coast and barrier reef.

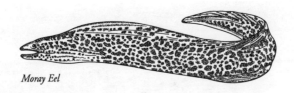

Moray Eel

SCIENTIFIC NAME   *Gymnothorax moringa*

WORTH NOTING   Distinguished by a swaying serpent-head and teeth-filled jaw that continually opens and closes, the moray eel is most commonly seen with only its head appearing from behind rocks. At night, however, it leaves its home along the reef to hunt for small fish, crustaceans, shrimp, and octopus.

PRIME VIEWING   Saltwater areas along the coast, usually near coral reefs or kelp forests.

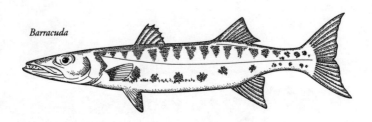

Barracuda

SCIENTIFIC NAME   *Sphyraena barracuda*

WORTH NOTING   The barracuda is a slender fish with two dorsal fins and a large mouth. Juvenile barracudas often swim near the shore, so exercise caution, as attacks on humans occasionally occur.

PRIME VIEWING   All along the coast and barrier reef.

Bottle-Nosed Dolphin

SCIENTIFIC NAME   *Tursiops truncates*

WORTH NOTING   Their wide back fin, dark gray back, and light gray sides identify bottle-nosed dolphins. Dolphins grow to lengths of 12 feet (3.7m) and weigh up to 1,400 pounds (635kg).

PRIME VIEWING   Along the coast and barrier reef.

Loggerhead Sponge

SCIENTIFIC NAME   *Spheciospongia*

WORTH NOTING   This barrel sponge is a large, stubby, purplish creature. Its large, central depression often plays host to small fish; shrimp and other sea life dwell in its canals.

PRIME VIEWING   All along the barrier reef.

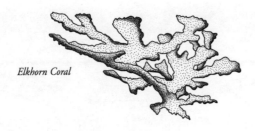

Elkhorn Coral

SCIENTIFIC NAME   *Acropora palmata*

WORTH NOTING   Elkhorn coral was formerly the dominant species in shallow water throughout the Caribbean, forming extensive thickets in areas of heavy surf. Since 1980, populations have collapsed from disease outbreaks, with losses compounded locally by hurricanes, increased predation, and bleaching.

PRIME VIEWING   Along the barrier reef.

Brain Coral

SCIENTIFIC NAME   *Diploria strigosa*

WORTH NOTING   Named for its striking physical similarity to a human brain, brain coral have been growing continuously in the waters off Belize for at least a century, though they're vulnerable to hurricanes.

PRIME VIEWING   All along the barrier reef.

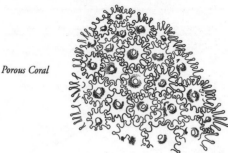

Porous Coral

SCIENTIFIC NAME   *Porites*

WORTH NOTING   The branches of this pink coral have a fuzzy appearance during the day, when their polyps are extended.

PRIME VIEWING   All along the barrier reef.

Moon Jelly

SCIENTIFIC NAME   *Aurelia*

WORTH NOTING   Like most jellies, the moon jelly is almost transparent. That four-leaf-clover-like area on its top is its reproductive organs.

PRIME VIEWING   All along the coast and barrier reef.

AMPHIBIANS

Frogs, toads, and salamanders are actually some of the most beguiling, beautiful, and easy-to-spot residents of tropical forests.

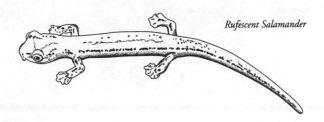

Rufescent Salamander

SCIENTIFIC NAME   *Bolitoglossa rufescens*

WORTH NOTING   This very small (1½ in./3.8cm), brown amphibian is also known as the "northern banana salamander," which is fitting since it can often be found in banana leaves.

PRIME VIEWING   In the Stann Creek, Toledo, and Cayo districts.

Red-Eyed Tree Frog

SCIENTIFIC NAME   *Agalychnis callidryas*

WORTH NOTING   This colorful 3-inch (7.6cm) frog usually has a pale or dark green back, sometimes with white or yellow spots, with blue-purple patches and vertical bars on the body, orange hands and feet, and deep red eyes.

PRIME VIEWING   Throughout Belize.

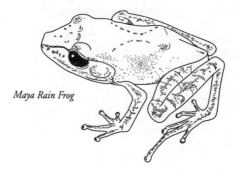

Maya Rain Frog

SCIENTIFIC NAME   *Eleutherodactyulus chac*

WORTH NOTING   This small, skinny frog is usually brown or yellowish, with webbed toes and red eyes.

PRIME VIEWING   Forests in southeastern, southern, and western Belize.

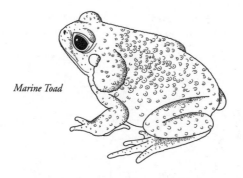

Marine Toad

SCIENTIFIC NAME   *Bufo marinus*

WORTH NOTING   This 8-inch (20cm), wart-covered toad is also known as *sapo grande,* or "giant toad." The females are mottled in color, while the males are uniformly brown.

PRIME VIEWING   In forests throughout Belize.

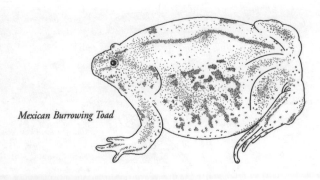

Mexican Burrowing Toad

SCIENTIFIC NAME   *Rhinophrynus dorsalis*

WORTH NOTING   This bloblike, 3-inch (7.6cm) toad will inflate like a blowfish when frightened. It often has a single red, orange, or yellow line down the center of its brown or black back.

PRIME VIEWING   Throughout the country.

REPTILES

Belize's reptile species range from the frightening and justly feared fer-de-lance pit viper and American crocodile to a wide variety of turtles and lizards.

Snapping Turtle

SCIENTIFIC NAME   *Chelydra serpentina*

WORTH NOTING   This turtle's back is brown, olive, or black, and marked with three ridges of sharp bumps—which might explain why it's also known as *tortuga lagarto* ("alligator turtle") in Belize.

PRIME VIEWING   Southern Belize.

Boa Constrictor

SCIENTIFIC NAME   *Boa constrictor*

WORTH NOTING   Adult boa constrictors average about 6 to 10 feet (1.8–3m) in length and weigh over 60 pounds (27kg). Their coloration camouflages them, but look for varying patterns of cream, brown, tan, gray, and black with ovals and diamonds.

PRIME VIEWING   Countrywide, including on some of the offshore cayes.

Fer-de-Lance

SCIENTIFIC NAME   *Bothrops asper*

WORTH NOTING   Also known as a tommygoff in Belize, this aggressive snake can grow to 8 feet (2.4m) in length. Beige, brown, or black triangles flank either side of the snake's head, while the area under the head is a vivid yellow.

PRIME VIEWING   All regions.

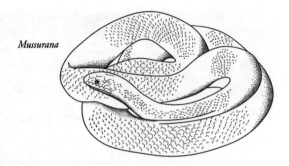

Mussurana

SCIENTIFIC NAME   *Clelia clelia*

WORTH NOTING   This bluish black, brown, or grayish snake grows to 8 feet (2.4m) in length. While slightly venomous, this snake is a rear-fanged snake and of little danger to humans. In fact, it is prized and protected by locals, since its primary prey happens to be much more venomous pit vipers, like the fer-de-lance.

PRIME VIEWING   Forests in central, southeastern, and western Belize.

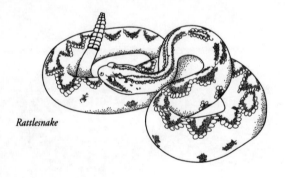

Rattlesnake

SCIENTIFIC NAME   *Crotalus durissus*

WORTH NOTING   Look out for its triangular head, 6-foot (1.8m) length, the ridge running along the middle of its back, and (of course) its rattling tail.

PRIME VIEWING   Throughout the country.

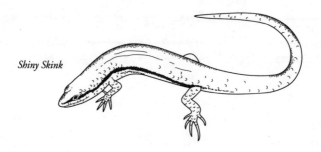

Shiny Skink

SCIENTIFIC NAME   *Mabuya brachypoda*

WORTH NOTING   This midsize (3 in./7.6cm) brown lizard with a narrow head and short legs is also known as "snake waiting boy."

PRIME VIEWING   Throughout the country.

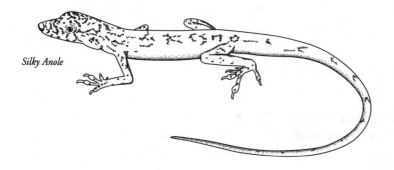

Silky Anole

SCIENTIFIC NAME   *Anolis sericeus*

WORTH NOTING   This small (2 in./5.1cm) gray lizard can be hard to spot, as it often aligns itself on a blade of grass when startled.

PRIME VIEWING   Throughout the country.

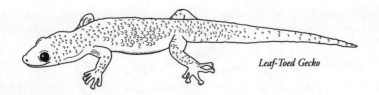

Leaf-Toed Gecko

SCIENTIFIC NAME   *Phyllodactylus tuberculosus*

WORTH NOTING   You'll have no problem spotting this 2½-inch (6.8cm) gecko on rocks and on the ground—it loves to be around buildings and other areas of human activity.

PRIME VIEWING   Central, southeastern, and western Belize.

Smooth Gecko

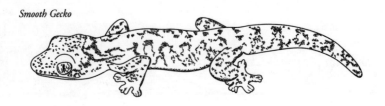

SCIENTIFIC NAME   *Thecadactylus rapicaudus*

WORTH NOTING   This gecko's autonomous tail detaches from its body and acts as a diversion to a potential predator; it grows back later in a lighter shade.

PRIME VIEWING   In northwestern, western, and southern Belize, especially where humans can be found.

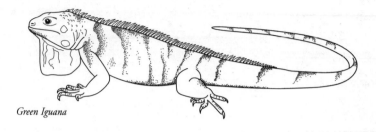

Green Iguana

SCIENTIFIC NAME   *Iguana iguana*

WORTH NOTING   Green iguanas, not surprisingly, are green in color, but vary in shades ranging from bright green to a dull grayish-green. The iguana will often perch on a branch overhanging a river and plunge into the water when threatened.

PRIME VIEWING   All regions of the country, living along the rivers and streams.

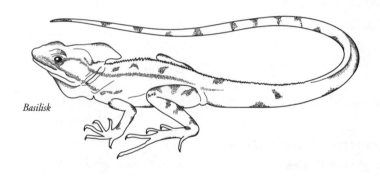

Basilisk

SCIENTIFIC NAME   *Basiliscus vittatus*

WORTH NOTING   The basilisk can run across the surface of water for short distances by using its hind legs and holding its body almost upright; thus, the reptile is also known as "the Jesus Christ lizard."

PRIME VIEWING   In trees and rocks located near water in tropical rainforests.

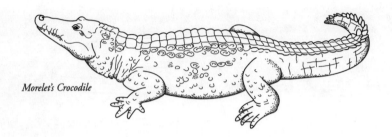

Morelet's Crocodile

SCIENTIFIC NAME   *Crocodylus moreleti*

WORTH NOTING   This reptile can grow to a length of 13 feet (4m), although the average specimen measures less than 8 feet (2.4m). Adults are brown or blackish in color, while young Morelet's crocodiles are olive or yellowish, with dark bands on their bodies and tails.

PRIME VIEWING   Northern and central coastal Belize, in most of the freshwater lowland interior rivers, lagoons, and ponds.

American Crocodile

SCIENTIFIC NAME   *Crocodylus acutus*

WORTH NOTING   This endangered species is distinguished from the Morelet's crocodile by their generally larger size and narrower snout. While they can reach lengths of 21 feet (6.4m), the majority is much smaller, usually less than 13 feet (4m).

PRIME VIEWING   Near swamps, mangrove swamps, estuaries, large rivers, coastal lowlands, and islands.

2 Flora

TREES

Despite the cliché to the contrary, it's often a good thing to be able to identify specific trees within a forest. We've included illustrations of the leaves, flowers, seeds, or fruits to get you started.

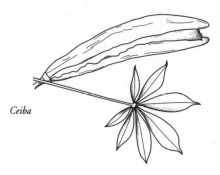

Ceiba

SCIENTIFIC NAME *Ceiba pentandra*

WORTH NOTING   Also known as the kapok tree, ceiba trees are typically emergent (their large umbrella-shape canopies emerge above the forest canopy), making the species among the tallest trees in the tropical forest. Reaching as high as 197 feet (60m), their thick columnar trunks often have large buttresses. Ceiba trees may flower as little as once every 5 years, especially in wetter forests.

PRIME VIEWING   Countrywide.

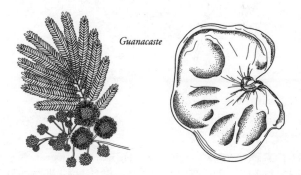

Guanacaste

SCIENTIFIC NAME   *Enterolobium cyclocarpum*

WORTH NOTING   The guanacaste, or tubroos, tree is one of the largest trees found in Central America. It can reach a total elevation of over 130 feet (39m), its straight trunk generating 30 to 40 ft. (9–12m) of the height (the trunk's diameter measures more than 6 ft./1.8m).

PRIME VIEWING   Countrywide. A particularly impressive specimen gives its name to Guanacaste National Park (see "Belmopan" in chapter 8).

Gumbo Limbo

SCIENTIFIC NAME   *Bursera simaruba*

WORTH NOTING   The bark of the gumbo limbo is perhaps its most distinguishing feature: a paper-thin outer layer is red when peeled off the tree, revealing a bright green bark underneath. The bark is reportedly used as a remedy for gum disease; and gumbo limbo bark tea allegedly alleviates high blood pressure. Another remarkable property of this tree is its ability to root from its cut branches. When a branch is cut and planted right end up, roots will develop and leaves will sprout, forming a new tree within a few year's time.

PRIME VIEWING   Primary and secondary forests, countrywide.

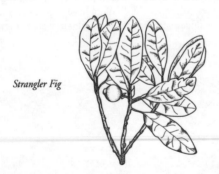

Strangler Fig

SCIENTIFIC NAME   *Ficus aurea*

WORTH NOTING   This parasitic tree gets its name from the fact that it envelops and eventually strangles its host tree. The strangler fig actually begins as an epiphyte, whose seeds are deposited high in a tree's canopy by bats, birds, or monkeys. The young strangler then sends long roots down to the earth. The sap of the strangler fig is used to relieve burns.

PRIME VIEWING   Primary and secondary forests, countrywide.

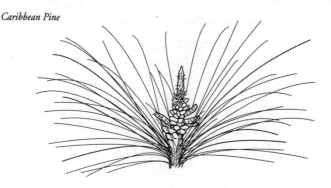

Caribbean Pine

SCIENTIFIC NAME   *Pinus caribaea*

WORTH NOTING   This fast-growing pine species is the defining tree of the Mountain Pine Ridge area of western Belize. The tree is actually fire resistant, and benefits from controlled burns. The resin is used as an adhesive and insect repellent.

PRIME VIEWING   Mountain Pine Ridge Forest Reserve (see chapter 8).

Mahogany

SCIENTIFIC NAME   *Swietenia macrophylla*

WORTH NOTING   The national tree of Belize, the mahogany tree can grow to heights of over 100 feet (30m). Mahogany wood is heavy and strong, and resists rot and termites. From its wood, artisans and carpenters craft the world's finest furniture.

PRIME VIEWING   Primary and secondary rainforests, countrywide.

Craboo

SCIENTIFIC NAME   *Byrsonima crassifolia*

WORTH NOTING   The craboo's flowers are beautiful orange and yellow racemes about 6 inches (15cm) long. The tree also bears a small orange-yellow berry, whose flavor also varies from bland to sweet, acidic, or even cheeselike. The flowers usually bloom around April, with fruits gathered around June. Hurricane Iris destroyed many Belizean craboo trees in 2001.

PRIME VIEWING   Countrywide.

FLOWERS

Belize has over 4,000 species of flowering plants, including some 250 orchid species.

Black Orchid

SCIENTIFIC NAME   *Encyclia cochleatum*

WORTH NOTING   The black orchid is the national flower of Belize. The plant's most distinguishing feature is its lip, which resembles the shape of a clamshell valve. The flower is a deep blackish color with purple veins, and its leaves are a greenish-yellow with purple spots. The black orchid is sometimes likened to an octopus because of its straggling "tentacles," and its ability to thrive in a damp environment.

PRIME VIEWING   Countrywide, particularly in moist environments.

Heliconia

SCIENTIFIC NAME   *Heliconia collinsiana*

WORTH NOTING   There are over 250 species of tropical heliconia. The flowers of this species are darkish pink in color, and the underside of the plant's large leave are coated in white wax.

PRIME VIEWING   In the Toledo and Stann Creek districts.

Hotlips

SCIENTIFIC NAME   *Psychotria poeppigiana*

WORTH NOTING   Also called "devil's ear" in Belize, its small white flowers (inside the red "lips") attract a variety of butterflies and hummingbirds.

PRIME VIEWING   In the undergrowth of dense forests, countrywide.

Index

See also Accommodations and Restaurant indexes, below.

RESTAURANTS

FROMMER'S® COMPLETE TRAVEL GUIDES

Alaska
Alaska Cruises & Ports of Call
American Southwest
Amsterdam
Argentina & Chile
Arizona
Atlanta
Australia
Austria
Bahamas
Barcelona, Madrid & Seville
Beijing
Belgium, Holland & Luxembourg
Bermuda
Boston
Brazil
British Columbia & the Canadian
  Rockies
Brussels & Bruges
Budapest & the Best of Hungary
Calgary
California
Canada
Cancún, Cozumel & the Yucatán
Cape Cod, Nantucket & Martha's
  Vineyard
Caribbean
Caribbean Ports of Call
Carolinas & Georgia
Chicago
China
Colorado
Costa Rica
Cruises & Ports of Call
Cuba
Denmark
Denver, Boulder & Colorado
  Springs
England
Europe
Europe by Rail
European Cruises & Ports of Call

Florence, Tuscany & Umbria
Florida
France
Germany
Great Britain
Greece
Greek Islands
Halifax
Hawaii
Hong Kong
Honolulu, Waikiki & Oahu
India
Ireland
Italy
Jamaica
Japan
Kauai
Las Vegas
London
Los Angeles
Maryland & Delaware
Maui
Mexico
Montana & Wyoming
Montréal & Québec City
Munich & the Bavarian Alps
Nashville & Memphis
New England
Newfoundland & Labrador
New Mexico
New Orleans
New York City
New York State
New Zealand
Northern Italy
Norway
Nova Scotia, New Brunswick &
  Prince Edward Island
Oregon
Ottawa
Paris
Peru

Philadelphia & the Amish
  Country
Portugal
Prague & the Best of the Czech
  Republic
Provence & the Riviera
Puerto Rico
Rome
San Antonio & Austin
San Diego
San Francisco
Santa Fe, Taos & Albuquerque
Scandinavia
Scotland
Seattle
Shanghai
Sicily
Singapore & Malaysia
South Africa
South America
South Florida
South Pacific
Southeast Asia
Spain
Sweden
Switzerland
Texas
Thailand
Tokyo
Toronto
Turkey
USA
Utah
Vancouver & Victoria
Vermont, New Hampshire &
  Maine
Vienna & the Danube Valley
Virgin Islands
Virginia
Walt Disney World® & Orlando
Washington, D.C.
Washington State

FROMMER'S® DOLLAR-A-DAY GUIDES

Australia from $50 a Day
California from $70 a Day
England from $75 a Day
Europe from $85 a Day
Florida from $70 a Day
Hawaii from $80 a Day

Ireland from $80 a Day
Italy from $70 a Day
London from $90 a Day
New York City from $90 a Day
Paris from $90 a Day
San Francisco from $70 a Day

Washington, D.C. from $80 a
  Day
Portable London from $90 a Day
Portable New York City from $90
  a Day
Portable Paris from $90 a Day

FROMMER'S® PORTABLE GUIDES

Acapulco, Ixtapa & Zihuatanejo
Amsterdam
Aruba
Australia's Great Barrier Reef
Bahamas
Berlin
Big Island of Hawaii
Boston
California Wine Country
Cancún
Cayman Islands
Charleston
Chicago
Disneyland®
Dominican Republic
Dublin

Florence
Frankfurt
Hong Kong
Las Vegas
Las Vegas for Non-Gamblers
London
Los Angeles
Los Cabos & Baja
Maine Coast
Maui
Miami
Nantucket & Martha's Vineyard
New Orleans
New York City
Paris

Phoenix & Scottsdale
Portland
Puerto Rico
Puerto Vallarta, Manzanillo &
  Guadalajara
Rio de Janeiro
San Diego
San Francisco
Savannah
Vancouver
Vancouver Island
Venice
Virgin Islands
Washington, D.C.
Whistler

FROMMER'S® NATIONAL PARK GUIDES

Algonquin Provincial Park
Banff & Jasper
Family Vacations in the National
    Parks

Grand Canyon
National Parks of the American
    West
Rocky Mountain

Yellowstone & Grand Teton
Yosemite & Sequoia/Kings
    Canyon
Zion & Bryce Canyon

FROMMER'S® MEMORABLE WALKS

Chicago
London

New York
Paris

San Francisco

FROMMER'S® WITH KIDS GUIDES

Chicago
Las Vegas
New York City

Ottawa
San Francisco
Toronto

Vancouver
Walt Disney World® & Orlando
Washington, D.C.

SUZY GERSHMAN'S BORN TO SHOP GUIDES

Born to Shop: France
Born to Shop: Hong Kong,
    Shanghai & Beijing

Born to Shop: Italy
Born to Shop: London

Born to Shop: New York
Born to Shop: Paris

FROMMER'S® IRREVERENT GUIDES

Amsterdam
Boston
Chicago
Las Vegas
London

Los Angeles
Manhattan
New Orleans
Paris
Rome

San Francisco
Seattle & Portland
Vancouver
Walt Disney World®
Washington, D.C.

FROMMER'S® BEST-LOVED DRIVING TOURS

Austria
Britain
California
France

Germany
Ireland
Italy
New England

Northern Italy
Scotland
Spain
Tuscany & Umbria

THE UNOFFICIAL GUIDES®

Beyond Disney
California with Kids
Central Italy
Chicago
Cruises
Disneyland®
England
Florida
Florida with Kids
Inside Disney

Hawaii
Las Vegas
London
Maui
Mexico's Best Beach Resorts
Mini Las Vegas
Mini Mickey
New Orleans
New York City
Paris

San Francisco
Skiing & Snowboarding in the
    West
South Florida including Miami &
    the Keys
Walt Disney World®
Walt Disney World® for
    Grown-ups
Walt Disney World® with Kids
Washington, D.C.

SPECIAL-INTEREST TITLES

Athens Past & Present
Cities Ranked & Rated
Frommer's Best Day Trips from London
Frommer's Best RV & Tent Campgrounds
    in the U.S.A.
Frommer's Caribbean Hideaways
Frommer's China: The 50 Most Memorable Trips
Frommer's Exploring America by RV
Frommer's Gay & Lesbian Europe
Frommer's NYC Free & Dirt Cheap

Frommer's Road Atlas Europe
Frommer's Road Atlas France
Frommer's Road Atlas Ireland
Frommer's Wonderful Weekends from
    New York City
The New York Times' Guide to Unforgettable
    Weekends
Retirement Places Rated
Rome Past & Present

Travel Tip: He who finds the best hotel deal has more to spend on facials involving knobbly vegetables.

Hello, the Roaming Gnome here. I've been nabbed from the garden and taken round the world. The people who took me are so terribly clever. They find the best offerings on Travelocity. For very little cha-ching. And that means I get to be pampered and exfoliated till I'm pink as a bunny's doodah.

*** travelocity®

1-888-TRAVELOCITY / travelocity.com / America Online Keyword: Travel

Travel Tip: Make sure there's customer service for any change of plans — involving friendly natives, for example.

One can plan and plan, but if you don't book with the right people you can't seize le moment and canoodle with the poodle named Pansy. I, for one, am all for fraternizing with the locals. Better yet, if I need to extend my stay and my gnome nappers are willing, it can all be arranged through the 800 number at, oh look, how convenient, the lovely company coat of arms.

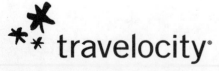

travelocity®